European Union and its Neighbours in a Globalized World

Volume 23

The series publishes monographs and edited volumes in the field of European and international law and policy. A special focus is put on the European neighbourhood policy, current problems in European and international law and policy as well as the role of the European Union as a global actor. The series supports the publishing and distribution of research results of cross-border research consortia. Besides renowned scientists the series is also open for publication projects of young academics. The series emphasizes the interplay of the European Union and its neighbouring countries as well as the important role of the European Union as a key player in the international context of law, economics and politics.

Ander Maglica

Collective Dimensions of Access to Justice

A Constitutional Study on Italian Class Actions in the European Multilevel System

Springer

Ander Maglica
Department of Italian and Supranational Public Law
University of Milan
Milan, Italy

ISSN 2524-8928 ISSN 2524-8936 (electronic)
European Union and its Neighbours in a Globalized World
ISBN 978-3-031-94521-2 ISBN 978-3-031-94522-9 (eBook)
https://doi.org/10.1007/978-3-031-94522-9

This Springer imprint is published by the registered company Springer Nature Switzerland AG
The registered company address is: Gewerbestrasse 11, 6330 Cham, Switzerland

The author has provided corrections after publication to add a Disclaimer text and a logo to the Acknowledgments section of the book's front matter. Initially, this information was not available and has now been included in the book.

Notre tâche d'homme est de trouver les quelques formules qui apaiseront l'angoisse infinie des âmes libres. Nous avons à recoudre ce qui est déchiré, à rendre la justice imaginable dans un monde si évidemment injuste, le bonheur significatif pour des peuples empoisonnés par le malheur du siècle. Naturellement, c'est une tâche surhumaine. Mais on appelle surhumaines les tâches que les hommes mettent longtemps à accomplir, voilà tout.

—Albert Camus, *Les Amandiers* (1940)

Acknowledgements

This book would not have been possible without a few, yet essential, contributions.

I am, first and foremost, deeply grateful to Prof. Barbara Randazzo, whose inspiring teaching and guidance have been foundational throughout this journey. Being able to learn from her is, every day, a true privilege.

I am also genuinely appreciative of Prof. Stefaan Voet, for generously welcoming and guiding me into his world—of collective redress, and beyond—during the doctoral cotutelle.

Special thanks are due to Prof. Maria José Azar-Baud, Prof. Adriana Ciancio, Prof. Scott L. Cummings, Prof. Jasminka Kalajdzic, Prof. Koen Lemmens, and Prof. Elisabetta Silvestri, for the meaningful exchanges and insightful advice offered along the way.

Thanks also go to Avv. Stefano Bertone, Avv. Carlo De Marchis Gómez, Avv. Michele Mennoia, and Avv. Maurizio Rizzo Striano, for sharing their time and direct professional experience, which proved essential in grounding key parts of the case study analysis. I am equally grateful to the other lawyers met along the way, and to the judges who granted access to the courtrooms and provided brief, yet valuable, exchanges.

A warm thought goes to my colleagues at the University of Milan and at the KU Leuven, where I spent sixteen wonderful months of doctoral research.

To friends and loved ones, both within and beyond academia, who accompanied me through the coming into form of this book, goes a deeply felt thank-you. They are many—too many to name here—and that makes me extremely fortunate. Those concerned will know how to find themselves, or even 'imagine' themselves, in these lines.

Last, a heartfelt thank-you goes to my parents, Carmen and Igor, to whom I owe who I am and what moves me, in the endless and collective quest for justice. To them, I dedicate this book.

Naturally, I take full responsibility for any errors or inaccuracies.

Milan, 31 March 2025 Ander Maglica

Competing Interests The author has no competing interests to declare that are relevant to the content of this manuscript.

Co-funded by
the European Union

Disclaimer: This volume was written within the framework of the EU Jean Monnet Module 'Access to Justice in a Multilevel European Constitutional System (AJ-MEUCSY - 101085204; 2022–2025)', a project coordinated by Prof. Barbara Randazzo, University of Milan, and funded by the European Union. The views and opinions expressed are those of the author only and do not necessarily reflect those of the European Union or the European Commission. Neither the European Union nor the granting authority can be held responsible for them.

Contents

Chapter 1
Premise

In the contemporary society, despite significant advancements across various scientific, political and cultural domains, the enduring prevalence of systemic injustices and deep-rooted inequalities remains an undeniable reality. Notwithstanding the extensive statutory guarantees and institutional safeguards established globally, including seminal documents like the European Convention on Human Rights or the Universal Declaration of Human Rights and similar domestic constitutional charters, an alarming surge in regressive trends has become increasingly apparent. Growing in the last decades, pushed by technological developments, it is becoming ever more dauting in the last few years.

Evident in daily media representations and palpable within our communities, these trends underscore the persistent challenges of our time, casting a shadow over the efficacy of existing legal structures in addressing the multi-faceted dimensions of societal disparities and fundamental rights enforcement. This recognition not only emphasises the critical need for a *comprehensive reassessment* of the current constitutional frameworks (national and supranational), but also stresses the urgency of identifying and fostering innovative *legal approaches* that can efficiently confront the injustices embedded within our globalised society. These are the two pillars on which the present research is based.

According to Zygmunt Bauman, justice is an 'incomplete project', 'incomplete in a radical sense, since it is the very essence of justice to be incomplete'. It is a special kind of 'sisyphusian project', due to which 'we must completely deconstruct the positive law in order to get closer to justice. In other words, we must strive to reduce the distance between the "is" and the "ought", although that distance can never be eliminated'.[1] This is probably correct, and, to some degree, gives rest to unrealistic, utopian, attempts to ensure 'world peace' or justice for everyone. Still, it does not mean that we should stop trying.

[1] Hviid Jacobsen and Poder (2008), p. 70.

A. Maglica, *Collective Dimensions of Access to Justice*, European Union and its Neighbours in a Globalized World 23,
https://doi.org/10.1007/978-3-031-94522-9_1

Ascertained that no panacea exists, nor that this research intends to be one, the goal of the present investigation is to situate itself in the scientific debate on access to justice, public interest litigation and fundamental rights enforcement.[2] Through the lens of Italian constitutional law, situated in the multilevel European system, it stems from the assumption that the traditional techniques of fundamental rights enforcement, while foundational, are not (always) efficient in today's globalised society. At least to some degree and circumstances, the implementation of new *collective* mechanisms of judicial enforcement could be beneficial in such a context.[3]

The postulation at the basis is that collective, standardised infringements require new, collective, standardised paths of enforcement. The traditional European *dualistic* mechanisms of judicial protection at times appear anachronistic.[4] As will be depicted, they must be adapted to adequately convey the contemporary complex *collective* societal patchwork, dominated by states and transnational corporations, battleground of conflicting interests, where individual stances often feel irrelevant, and the public v. private distinction fades.

Recent developments at both European and national level underscore the recognition of this limitation, evident in measures such as EU Directive 2020/1828 (hereinafter 'RAD', as per 'Representative Actions Directive'),[5] aimed at ensuring *effective* (injunctive and compensatory) representative action mechanisms for *consumers* across all Member States. Similarly, the parallel introduction, among other EU States, of Title VIII-*bis* on collective proceedings within the Italian Code of civil procedure in 2019—with a *general* scope of application—and, at CoE level, initially, the introduction in 1995 of the collective complaints procedure before the ECSR[6] and, then, since 2004, the ECtHR's development of the 'pilot judgment procedure' (Rule 61, Rules of the Court)[7] reflect the growing recognition of the need

---

[2] Without aiming for exhaustiveness, see, e.g., Randazzo (2023), Kramer et al. (2022), Amalfitano et al. (2022), Gaboardo (2022), Foddai (2021), Kramer et al. (2021), Ucín (2021), Roberge (2020), Trocker (2018), Osti (2016), Rodotà (2012), Galanter (2010), Cummings and Rhode (2009), Francioni (2007), Romboli (2006), Rhode (2004), Taruffo (2002), Anzon et al. (2000) and, especially, the seminal Cappelletti (1976, 1978, 1993, 1994).

[3] See Molavi (2021), Hodges and Voet (2018), Kalajdzic (2018), Azar-Baud (2013), pp. 6 *et seq.*, Hensler (2009), p. 7.

[4] See, foresightedly, already in 1904, Mortara, p. 30 (1904): 'the old and solid structure of legal traditions based on individualism resists pertinaciously; but this resistance must diminish the more the collective organisation of the interests of the industrial and working classes is consolidated' (translated from Italian). See also Cappelletti (1975). See also Taruffo (2001), p. 419, and Randazzo (2023), p. 78.

[5] Directive (EU) 2020/1828 of the European Parliament and of the Council of 25 November 2020 'on representative actions for the protection of the collective interests of consumers and repealing Directive 2009/22/EC', aiming 'to ensure at Union and national level at least one effective and efficient procedural mechanism for representative actions for injunctive measures and for redress measures is available to consumers in all Member States' (Article 1(2)).

[6] See, e.g., Palmisano (2022), Guiglia (2016), Lukas (2014), Cullen (2009), Churchill and Khaliq (2004).

[7] Rule 61—'pilot-judgement procedure'—of the ECtHR's Rules of the Court, relevant 'where the facts of an application reveal in the Contracting State concerned the existence of a structural or

for new *supra-individual judicial remedies* at various levels of the complex contemporary European constitutional architecture.

Specifically regarding collective actions before ordinary civil courts, a radical turn-around, from European legislative, institutional and academic actors is thence registered, considering the harsh critics the common-law *class action* model received in the Old Continent for several decades, since its innovative amendment in the US in 1966, until recent years. The much-recalled definition of 'toxic cocktail' in a 2008 EU Commission Green Paper Memo, in reference to such mechanism, is rather illustrative.[8] The changes in the European (specifically, Italian) social, cultural and legal fabric—such as to radically alter the perception of collective enforcement procedures—are worth reflecting upon.

The present study, building on these considerations, focuses exactly on the assessment of the recent Italian trans-substantive 'class action'[9] model also in light of the RAD, as a potential vehicle for driving positive social change and safeguarding fundamental rights. This is the central perimeter of analysis. Innovatively, with respect to the few European studies concerned with collective redress, which all tend to focus on consumer protection or on the procedural aspects,[10] this work aims, instead, to ponder on the use of this model for the enforcement of fundamental rights, on the one hand, and as a tool of effective access to justice, on the other hand. A similarly comprehensive *constitutional* approach on this topic is, until now, missing within the Italian, and European, academic landscape.[11]

In particular, four lines of analysis will be followed for this purpose:

(i) collective enforcement as *a fundamental right* itself;
(ii) the specific Italian penta-partite[12] class action model as a means of *enforcing fundamental rights*, advancing social change and filling contemporary adjudicatory gaps;

---

systemic problem or other similar dysfunction which has given rise or may give rise to similar applications' (Rule 61, para. 6), first used in 2004 with *Broniowski v. Poland* and finally codified in 2011. See, e.g., Lemmens and Van Drooghenbroeck (2023), Glas (2019), Kurban (2016), Sicilianos (2014), Randazzo (2012), p. 123, and Garlicki (2007).

[8] See, *infra*, Chap. 5.

[9] For a preliminary focus on the definitional aspect of 'class actions', see *infra*, Chap. 4.

[10] See, e.g., albeit with such focus, the thorough edited volumes, at European level, by Uzelac and Voet (2021) and, in Italy, by Ruffolo (2021) and Sassani (2019). See also, recently, Randazzo et al. (2025).

[11] In Italy, previous comments from a constitutional-law perspective, although brief and on different procedural models, can be found in Mezzanotte (2022), Pace (2011), Rordorf (2010). See also recently Randazzo and Maglica (2025). Already anticipatorily stressing the importance of the phenomenon, see Bognetti (1998), Trocker (1990) and Cappelletti (1975).

[12] "Penta-partite" since there are five different models, as explained in detail in Chap. 6: a compensatory and an injunctive trans-substantive regime, from 2019, under the Code of civil procedure; a compensatory and an injunctive consumer-limited regime, from 2023, under the Consumer code; a so-called 'public', or 'administrative', class action, from 2009, in front of the administrative judge.

(iii) the *effectiveness* of the class action model to provide concrete *access to justice*, both as an alternative and in coordination with other procedural tools (national and supranational);
(iv) any potential *drawbacks and abuses* related to the class action model, with special attention to fair trial guarantees, the rights of the defendants and of the class members not directly involved in the proceedings.

In doing so, the rich common-law experience of civil rights enforcement and public interest litigation is inevitably taken into account, in a multi-faceted comparative (although always constitutional, and, specifically, Italian constitutional) perspective.[13]

While the analysis anticipates the imperfections of such a procedural technique,[14] it also highlights its potential as a key instrument for societal change and for the protection of emerging meta-individual positions, as well as traditional liberties. However, this acknowledgment is not without significant caveats, which will be further explored in subsequent sections.[15]

With such objectives, after this Premise, the book is divided in four parts.

Firstly, in *Part I—Contextual Foundations. Winds of Change*, it further frames its own perimeter.

It starts by situating the contemporary European social, cultural, political and economic context, in a comparative—spatio-temporal—perspective, highlighting the significant structural changes brought by globalisation and new technologies. Drawing from socio-logical and socio-legal scholarship, it aims to highlight the concrete '*societal problem*, need or demand that prompts a legal intervention or the creation of a legal institution',[16] as well as to stress and explain the contribution of distinct social fabrics in advancing social change.

Such an approach follows Mauro Cappelletti and the access-to-justice-movement's theoretical method of a 'tri-dimensional conception' of the law and of legal scholarship: first, by reflecting on the societal problem; then, on the normative and institutional response; and, finally, on 'the results, or impact, of such a legal response on the societal need, problem or demand'.[17]

The role of constitutionalism in the contemporary times of deep social and legal transformations is, then, touched, in order to explain and justify the peculiar *constitutional* standpoint herein adopted. Such a (brief) contextualisation is instrumental in understanding the transformations of power, but also the *enforcement gaps* of

[13] See, *infra*, Chap. 6.

[14] *In primis* the fact that it is a judicial path, whereas certain problems—at least, ideally—should be solved at a political level, not in courts. See Luciani (2023), p. 178, Zanon (2021); still, see also Angiolini (2012), p. 202, Cappelletti (1994), p. 179, Calamandrei (1955), p. 572. See also Fioravanti (2016) and Zagrebelsky (1988), p. 158.

[15] See, *infra*, in particular Chap. 4.

[16] Cappelletti (1993), p. 283.

[17] Id.

today's age and, in particular, the shortcomings of the current (multi-level) architecture of fundamental rights protection.

Several, systemic and recurring, challenges emerge, on which we shall concentrate: i.e., a massification and standardisation of relationships and of infringements, a tendential failure of democratic processes, growing inequalities, new forms of 'private power' alien to traditional 'statehood', the disruption of national state barriers, an increasing trans-nationalisation of issues and incapability of current judicial processes to deliver 'effective justice'.[18]

Naturally, none of these complex matters is comprehensively addressed, for evident feasibility reasons. Rather, drawing from previous academic literature and existing jurisprudence, they are presented to clarify the current intricate framework of fundamental rights enforcement in Europe, specifically in Italy, in which the research wishes to situate itself. It thus provides the essential steppingstone for the next two Parts, respectively dedicated to legislation and case law.

Before turning to them, the Part concludes with a central focus on the *conceptual and definitional hurdles*: the necessary linguistic grasping and, especially, the evolved concept of access to justice, as well as the crucial constitutional foundations of its newfound collective dimensions in order to ensure *effective judicial protection*. This constitutes the keystone of the present research, just as 'beneath the arches of the trial [...] flows the unending torrent of human life', and, with it, the 'universal grasp for justice'.[19]

Part II—Collective Actions. Route of Change, instead, concentrates on the 'collective redress', or 'class action', models.

After a brief historical premise and contextualisation of the complex procedural mechanism's *origins in the US* and common law world—pivotal to understand the *rationale* of such a peculiar enforcement model, and how it was crafted as a '*vehicle of mobilizing capability*'[20] for *civil rights* groups (especially in the desegregation context post *Brown v. Board of Education*)[21]—, it critically describes the current European regulatory framework, both at EU level and, specifically, in Italy.

Regarding the former, the national implementation of the RAD needs to be closely followed. Fundamental rights, as is known, formally fall outside of its scope.

[18] See, *infra*, Chaps. 3 and 4.

[19] Calamandrei (1953), p. 565: 'Beneath the arches of the trial, Giuseppe Chiovenda wrote in unforgettable words, recalling Hamlet's monologue, flows the unending torrent of human fate: no one more than the processualist, looking out over those little banks can grasp, if he has an ear to hear, the voices rising from the whirlpools of this current, this universal gasp of justice, and the pain of innocence unjustly stricken and the consolation of those who realise (because this too can sometimes happen) that in the end blind force must surrender to disarmed reason' (translated from Italian). *Rectius*, rather than 'the processualist', at least for the purposes of this work, we deem it best to consider 'those who study the trial', as an instrument of effective legal protection and to ensure its fairness; thence, the *constitutional focus* on the procedural class action model herein brought, particularly urgent given its potentially disruptive effects, exponentially increased given the explosion in a collective sense of the effects of the *res judicata*.

[20] Issacharoff and Zimroth (2018), p. 110.

[21] Marcus (2011), p. 28 *et seq*. See, in detail, *infra*, Chap. 5.

Nonetheless, as will be addressed, several circumstances keep the door open for a larger application of the RAD.[22] In particular, the four lines of study abovementioned will be followed herein, too.

Subsequently, the analysis focuses on the Italian jurisdiction and on the five different 'class action' models therein available, with a special attention to the trans-substantive regime from 2019, regulated within the Code of civil procedure. Its nuances, effects and doubts on the constitutional legitimacy of certain provisions are therein addressed.

The perspective adopted in this Part is mainly *regulatory*. Each class action model, as is known, is composed of several building blocks, such as the rules for joining and forming the class (e.g., opt-in v. opt-out regime, requirements of commonality or homogeneity), scope of application, competent court and jurisdiction, rules on standing and requirements on admissibility and for joining the class, rules on funding, on adequacy of representation, on proof of causation, on liquidation of damages, remedies available, rules on settlements and executions.

A minimal change in each of the provisions regulating one of these elements can substantially shift the ability of the class action instrument to *effectively* enforce fundamental rights. A valid example, as we shall discuss, are the rules on standing: even with the best possible class action model on paper, if these provisions are excessively restrictive, the concrete implementation of the mechanisms significantly drops.

Furthermore, in the background, the need to guarantee *due process* even in a collective dimension, and hence to evaluate the possible risks inherent in this form of litigation so peculiar and distant from the continental tradition, is always firmly borne in mind.

This Part, in sum, concentrates on the array of instruments set forth by the legislators, their overlapping and coordination, under a strictly *constitutional perspective* (especially Italian, as part of the larger European integrated constitutional space).

Part III—Collective Enforcement. Exercises of Change, instead, is dedicated to *concrete judicial applications* of the class action instrument, through the aid of the case study methodology.[23] This favours a consideration of the concrete implications

[22] See, *infra*, Chaps. 6 and 7, especially in relation to the *Philips Respironics* case.

[23] The dedication of Part III of this book to case studies is to concretely evaluate the implementation, the potential and risks of the procedural device in question, since only a connection with empirical reality allows for the development of a testable, relevant and valid theory (Glaser and Strauss 1967). The case study, as is known, is a research strategy which focuses on understanding the dynamics of specific settings or procedures and which can be used to provide description, test or generate theory (Einsenhardt 1989); it is particularly helpful to answer research questions which cannot employ only, or mainly, quantitative analysis. For the purposes of this investigation, a comparative *multi-case study approach* has been selected. *Diversity* and *procedural comparativeness* have been the two guiding factors for this aim, out of the available, still-developing, case law. In relation to the methodology and benchmarks followed, instead, a mix of pattern-matching and a cross-case synthesis technique have been chosen. Contaminating differences among individual cases have been considered to highlight recurring patterns or inevitably unique findings that separate the class action cases from those with other procedural devices and which assume relevance

of using such a procedural instrument, in alternative or in coordination with the already-present mechanisms, both procedural and not. Law is, once again, seen and studied as a 'distillation of lived experience',[24] its impact being 'the centrality of the person, his dignity, understood not only in the abstract [...], but also and above all in concrete terms, that is, cast in the economic-social relations in which every man's existence is immersed'.[25]

Four enforcement scenarios are therein considered: *(i)* environmental harms and the right to health; *(ii)* workers' rights; *(iii)* prisoners' and migrants' rights; and *(iv)* cryptocurrencies, although in relation to specific access-to-court issues (class waivers, arbitration clauses and foreign defendants). Concrete Italian cases brought under the 2019 trans-substantive regime are critically presented for this purpose, always in a constitutional perspective.

Given the still-developing Italian class action case law, other EU Members States' case law and the much richer common law (mainly US and Canada) jurisprudence are also taken into account, for relevant insights for identifying potential future trends. Moreover, other non-class action paths of enforcement of the fundamental rights in question will be regarded for procedural comparative assessment, too (although always maintaining the central constitutional focus).[26]

The above-mentioned four lines of analysis are critical in this Part III, too. As will appear evident, substantial risks follow the introduction of the class action instrument, especially in relation to fair trial guarantees and potential abuses from the class representative. Furthermore, certain scenarios may require a different solution, already available in the legal order.

At the same time, nonetheless, judicial collective enforcement presents a number of features that, in specific circumstances, can overcome some of the most important barriers in the struggle for fundamental rights enforcement, social advancement and equality. The rich common law experience is unequivocal on this point. It remains to carefully understand how—in which cases, with which limitations, with which regulatory and institutional amendments—to proceed.

---

under the herein adopted constitutional lens (pursuant to the four lines of analysis explained above). While still pursuing a 'ground up' approach, a number of theoretical propositions—drawn from the analysis presented in the previous Part II, (concerned with the regulatory framework)—has been developed. The case study analysis has, thus, tested them on concrete applications, with findings further elaborated in the conclusive Part IV. For a more detailed elaboration on the methodological approach herein followed, see, also, Yin (2017) and Merriam (2002), especially pp. 29 *et seq*.

[24] Issacharoff (2021), p. 181. See also, quoted therein, Holmes (1881): 'The life of the law has not been logic: it has been experience [...] The law embodies the story of a nation's development through many centuries, and it cannot be dealt with as if it contained only the axioms and corollaries of a book of mathematics'.

[25] Donzelli (2024), p. 158, commenting on the approach of Piero Calamandrei (evidently, 'man' is to be read extensively, as referring to 'human being'). See also Rodotà (2012), p. 179, and, always topical, Cappelletti (1993), p. 282.

[26] In particular, the path of constitutional review and the application before the ECtHR; in relation to the latter, also the possible use of the pilot-judgement procedure.

The last *Part IV—Conclusive Assessment* builds on this multi-layered ('tri-dimensional')[27] analysis of the model in question, to synthetise the main findings under the proposed constitutional approach.

It does so by integrating a reflection *de iure condito* and one *de iure condendo*, to make more effective the model in question, to avoid the significant risks emerged and tackle the doubts of constitutional legitimacy. The *role of the judge*, to be rediscovered within such a new collective dimension of enforcement, stands firmly as the decisive litmus test of the reform.[28]

Finally, charts with quantitative and qualitative data on the Italian jurisprudential implementation of the trans-substantive 2019 regime are offered.

It is against this backdrop that the present research aims to contribute, bringing a novel constitutional, Italian and European, perspective.[29]

References

Amalfitano C, Violini L, Galetta DU (eds) (2022) 'Law, Justice and Sustainable Development': L'accesso alla giustizia nel quadro del SD Goal 16. Giappichelli, Torino
Angiolini V (2012) Diritti umani. Sette lezioni, Giappichelli, Torino
Anzon A, Caretti P, Grasso S (2000) Prospettive di accesso alla giustizia costituzionale. Atti del Seminario (Firenze, 28-29 maggio 1999). Giappichelli, Torino
Azar-Baud MJ (2013) Les actions collectives en droit de la consommation. Dalloz, Paris
Bognetti G (1998) Lo stato e i gruppi di interesse negli ordinamenti borghesi. Giuffrè, Milano
Calamandrei P (1953) Processo e giustizia. In: Cappelletti M (ed) Calamandrei P (1965) Opere giuridiche, I. Morano, Napoli
Calamandrei P (1954) Processo e democrazia. In: Cappelletti M (ed) Calamandrei P (1965) Opere giuridiche, I. Morano, Napoli
Calamandrei P (1955) La funzione della giurisprudenza nel tempo presente. In: Cappelletti M (ed) Calamandrei P (1965) Opere giuridiche, I. Morano, Napoli
Cappelletti M (1975) Formazioni sociali e interessi di gruppo davanti alla giustizia civile. Rivista di diritto processuale 25(3)

[27] Cappelletti (1993), p. 283.

[28] See also Randazzo and Maglica (2025). See also, with great foresightedness Cappelletti (1975), p. 394, and his mentor Calamandrei (1954), pp. 650 *et seq.*, both anticipating several of the contemporary challenges in the enforcement of rights and possible paths for solution.

[29] Despite the main focus on the Italian jurisdiction, and in particular on the judicial enforcement of fundamental rights, the decision of publishing this work in English is due to a twofold reason: on the one hand, to foster the dialogue with foreign (European and beyond) scholars and practitioners who may be investigating the same issues, which increasingly cross traditional state borders, with the hope, and the goal, of finding together better solutions; on the other hand, the growing importance of studying constitutional law not as rigidly enclosed in those very same national borders, but 'in a harmonious and complementary perspective' with the EU and the international (CoE, in particular) systems of protection, the sole perspective 'which allows one to fully grasp the integration between the guarantees enshrined in the different sources' (Italian Constitutional Court, judgement No. 181 from 2024, No. 10 of the Points on law—unofficial translation). See Pitruzzella (2024), Randazzo (2012, 2023), von Bogdandy (2022, 2023), Lenaerst and Van Nuffel (2021), Onida (2002) and Pernice (1999).

Cappelletti M (1976) Vindicating the public interest through the courts: a comparativist's contribution. Buffalo Law Rev 25(3):643
Cappelletti M (ed) (1978) Access to justice. Giuffrè, Milano
Cappelletti M (1993) Alternative dispute resolution processes within the framework of the world-wide access to-justice movement. Mod Law Rev 56(3):282–296
Cappelletti M (1994) Dimensioni della giustizia nella società contemporanea: studi di diritto giudiziario comparato. Il Mulino, Bologna
Churchill RR, Khaliq U (2004) The collective complaints system of the European Social Charter: an effective mechanism for ensuring compliance with economic and social rights? Eur J Int Law 15(3):417–456
Cullen H (2009) The collective complaints system of the European Social Charter: interpretative methods of the European Committee of Social Rights. Hum Rights Law Rev 9(1):61–93
Cummings SL, Rhode DL (2009) Public interest litigation: insights from theory and practice. Fordham Urban Law J
Donzelli G (2024) Piero Calamandrei e la genesi dei diritti sociali. In: Donzelli G (ed) Piero Calamandrei. Giustizia Diritti e Libertà. Democrazia e Diritti Sociali 1, pp 141–158
Einsenhardt KM (1989) Building theories from case study research. Acad Manag Rev 14(4):532
Fioravanti M (2016) Il legislatore e i giudici di fronte alla Corte costituzionale. Quaderni costituzionali. Rivista italiana di diritto costituzionale 1:7–20
Foddai MA (2021) Access to justice: in search of a new concept. In: Cremades J, Hermida C (eds) Encyclopedia of contemporary constitutionalism. Springer, Cham
Francioni F (ed) (2007) Access to justice as a human right. Oxford University Press, Oxford
Gaboardo M (2022) Effettività della tutela giurisdizionale e misure coercitive nel processo civile. Un'indagine di diritto comparato. Giappichelli, Torino
Galanter M (2010) Access to justice in a world of expanding social capability. Fordham Urban Law J 37:115
Garlicki L (2007) Broniowski and after: on the dual nature of 'pilot judgments'. In: Caflisch L, Callewaert J, Liddell R, Mahoney P, Villiger M (eds) Droits de l'homme – Regards de Strasbourg: Liber Amicorum Luzius Wildhaber. NP Engel, Kehl, pp 177–192
Glas LR (2019) The execution process of pilot judgements before the committee of ministers. Hum Rights Int Leg Discourse 13(2):73–97
Glaser BG, Strauss AL (1967) The discovery of grounded theory: strategies for qualitative research. Aldine Transactions, New Brunswick
Guiglia G (2016) Il ruolo del Comitato Europeo dei Diritti Sociali al tempo della crisi economica. Rivista AIC 2:1–22
Hensler D (2009) The globalization of class actions: an overview. Annals AAPSS 622:7–29
Hodges C, Voet S (2018) Delivering collective redress: new technologies. Hart Publishing, Oxford
Holmes Jr OW (1881) The common law 3. 2009 Harvard University Press, Harvard
Hviid Jacobsen M, Poder P (2008) The sociology of Zygmunt Bauman: challenges and critique. Ashgate Publishing, Farnham
Issacharoff S (2021) Rule 23 and the triumph of experience. Law Contemp Problems 84:161–182
Issacharoff S, Zimroth P (2018) An oral history of rule 23. An interview with Professor Arthur Miller. NYU Annu Surv Am Law 74:110
Kalajdzic J (2018) Class actions in Canada. The promise and reality of access to justice. UBC Press, Vancouver
Kramer X, Biard A, Hoevenaars J, Themeli E (eds) (2021) New pathways to civil justice in Europe: challenges of access to justice. Springer, Cham
Kramer X, Voet S, Ködderitzsch L, Tulibacka M, Hess B (eds) (2022) Delivering justice: a holistic and multidisciplinary approach. Liber Amicorum in honour of Christopher Hodges. Hart Publishing, Oxford
Kurban D (2016) Forsaking individual justice: the implications of the European Court of Human Rights' pilot judgment procedure for victims of gross and systematic violations. Hum Rights Law Rev 16(4):731–737

Lemmens K, Van Drooghenbroeck S (2023) How 'systematic' is the European Court of Human Rights' approach to 'systemic' violations of the Convention? German Law J 24(6)
Lenaerst, Van Nuffel (2021) EU constitutional law. Oxford University Press, Oxford
Luciani M (2023) Ogni cosa al suo posto. Giuffrè, Milano
Lukas K (2014) The collective complaint procedure of the European Social Charter: some lessons for the EU? Leg Issues Econ Integr 41(3):275–288
Marcus D (2011) Flawed but noble: desegregation litigation and its implications for the modern class action. Florida Law Rev 63
Merriam S (ed) (2002) Qualitative research in practice: examples for discussion and analysis. Jossey-Bass, Hoboken
Mezzanotte P (2022) Class action e Costituzione: dimensione metaindividuale dei diritti e ruolo della giurisdizione. Nomos: 1
Molavi M (2021) Collective access to justice: assessing the potential of class actions in England and Wales. Bristol University Press, Bristol
Mortara L (1904) Per la riforma sulla legge dei probiviri. Giurisprudenza italiana 4(5):30
Onida V (2002) 'Armonia tra diversi' e problemi aperti. La giurisprudenza costituzionale sui rapporti tra ordinamento interno e ordinamento comunitario. Quaderni costituzionali 3:549
Osti A (2016) Teoria e prassi dell'Access to Justice. Un raffronto tra ordinamento nazionale e ordinamenti esteri. Giuffré, Milano
Pace A (2011) Interrogativi sulla legittimità costituzionale della nuova 'class action'. Rivista di diritto processuale 1
Palmisano G (2022) Collective complaints as a means for protecting social rights in Europe. Anthem, London
Pernice I (1999) Multilevel constitutionalism and the Treaty of Amsterdam: European constitution-making revisited? Common Mark Law Rev 36(4)
Pitruzzella G (2024) La costruzione dello spazio costituzionale europeo nel dialogo tra Corte di giustizia e Corti costituzionali. Quaderni costituzionali 4:795–821
Randazzo B (2012) Giustizia costituzionale sovranazionale: la Corte europea dei diritti dell'uomo. Giuffrè, Milano
Randazzo B (2023) Access to justice in a multilevel constitutional system, Protecting human rights. Giappichelli, Torino
Randazzo B, Maglica A (2025) La disciplina generale delle class action italiane alla prova delle garanzie costituzionali ed europee. Federalismi.it 5:158–196
Randazzo B, Henke A, Voet S (eds) (2025) L'azione di classe italiana nel quadro europeo: profili sostanziali e processuali. Giappichelli, Torino
Rhode DL (2004) Access to justice. Oxford University Press, Oxford
Roberge JF (2020) L'accès à la justice au 21e siècle: vers une approche empirique et plurielle. Revue Juridique Themis 54:487–510
Rodotà S (2012) Il diritto di avere diritti. Laterza, Roma
Romboli (ed) (2006) L'accesso alla giustizia costituzionale caratteri, limiti, prospettive di un modello. Edizioni Scientifiche Italiane, Napoli
Rordorf R (2010) L'azione di classe nel novellato art. 140 bis cod. consumo: considerazioni (e qualche interrogativo), in Il Foro Italiano
Ruffolo (ed) (2021) Class action ed azione collettiva inibitoria. Commento sistematico alla legge 12 aprile 2019, n. 31. Giuffrè, Milano
Sassani (ed) (2019) Class action. Commento sistematico alla legge 12 aprile 2019, n. 31. Pacini Editore, Pisa
Sicilianos LA (2014) The involvement of the European Court of Human Rights in the implementation of its judgments: recent developments under Article 46 ECHR. Neth Q Hum Rights 32(3):240
Taruffo M (2001) Some remarks on group litigation in comparative perspective. Duke J Comp Int Law 11:405–421

Taruffo M (2002) Diritti fondamentali, tutela giurisdizionale e alternative. In: Mazzarese T (ed) Neocostituzionalismo e tutela (sovra)nazionale dei diritti. Giappichelli, Torino, pp 189–205

Trocker N (1990) Gli interessi diffusi e la loro tutela dinanzi al giudice civile. In: (eds) Nuove dimensioni nei diritti di libertà. Scritti in onore di Paolo Barile. CEDAM, Padova, pp 193–218

Trocker N (2018) Accesso alla giustizia e "degiurisdizionalizzazione": il tramonto del diritto al giudice e al giudizio? Diritto costituzionale 3:37–65

Ucín MC (2021) Juicio a la desigualdad. La defensa de los derechos sociales a través del proceso. Marcial Pons, Madrid

Uzelac A, Voet S (2021) Class actions in Europe. Holy Grail or Wrong Trail? Springer, Cham

von Bogdandy A (2022) Strukturwandel des öffentlichen Rechts. Entstehung und Demokratisierung der europäischen Gesellschaft. Suhrkamp Verlag, Berlin

von Bogdandy A (2023) Comparative public law for European society. MPIL Research Paper 28

Yin RK (2017) Case study research and application. Sage Publications, Los Angeles

Zagrebelsky G (1988) La giustizia costituzionale, 2nd ed. Il Mulino, Bologna

Zanon N (2021) I rapporti tra la Corte costituzionale e il legislatore alla luce di alcune recenti tendenze giurisprudenziali. Federalismi.it 3:86–98

Part I
Contextual Foundations. Winds of Change

Chapter 2
The Effects of Globalisation and New Technologies on the Social Fabric

2.1 Premise. Whispers of a New Order

In the words of Georg W.F. Hegel, to understand social phenomena, we must trace their development.[1] In the same way, to understand constitutional processes, we need to situate them in a precise historical and geographical context.

The social, cultural, scientific, economic and political framework provides fundamental elements for a better comprehension of juridical dynamics, elements and transformations. Very much alike the fact that no man is an island, no legal provision, institution or process is set in a vacuum. Rather, it takes from, gives back and adapts to the specific environment in which it is placed. Being the role of norms that of regulating human relationships, to properly analyse them, and their impact, we must preliminarily address the backdrop in which they are entangled.[2]

---

[1] See von Bogdandy (2022), p. 1.

[2] This theoretical approach follows that championed by Mauro Cappelletti and the access-to-justice-movement.

For instance, see Cappelletti (1993): 'The access-to-justice movement, as a theoretical approach, while certainly rooted in the realistic criticism of formalism and legal dogmatics, tends toward a vision more faithful to the complexity of human society. While the normative component of the law is not denied, it is seen as one element, and quite often not even the principal one of the law. The primary element is the people, with all their cultural, economic and psychological features. Moreover, the institutions and processes are prominent [...] The result of the access-to-justice approach is a 'contextual' conception of the law. Thus, instead of a uni-dimensional conception, whereby the law and legal scholarship are limited to the ascertainment of the norms, a tri-dimensional conception is affirmed. A first dimension reflects the societal problem, need or demand that prompts a legal intervention or the creation of a legal institution; the second dimension reflects the legal response or solution and, indeed, a response that includes in addition to the norms, the institutions and processes which are intended to deal with that [...]; and finally, a third dimension faces the results, or impact, of such a legal response on the societal need, problem or demand. The role of legal scholarship, and indeed the role of lawyers generally, thus becomes much more complex,

A. Maglica, *Collective Dimensions of Access to Justice*, European Union and its Neighbours in a Globalized World 23,
https://doi.org/10.1007/978-3-031-94522-9_2

Looking at the most pressing issues within our society from a merely (for now) sociological perspective, a series of underlying common trends and features can be uncovered. It is a general assumption of this work that they can all be traced back to two main phenomena, mutually dependent under a causal viewpoint: *globalisation*, on the one hand, and *technological innovation*, on the other hand. Such phenomena are, undoubtedly, the common, pervasive and entrenched traits of the current age.[3]

As summarised by Paul Hopper, *globalisation* is a 'multidimensional phenomenon'.[4] Similarly to physics' string theory[5]—according to which there are more dimensions (ten, eleven, or even twenty-six) than those that meet the eye, and they all concurrently interact, mix and overlap with each other—, globalisation, together with technological advancement, brings a kaleidoscope of effects. They can be analysed from different perspectives and, in turn, be broken down in a taxonomy of even more sub-processes and sub-layers.

Those more relevant for the purposes—studying access to justice in a constitutional perspective—and in the inevitable constraints of this research, will be pointed out in this Chapter. In particular, drawing from previous sociological scholarship, five emerging dimensions of globalisation will be considered: (i) *time*, (ii) *space*, (iii) *relationships*, (iv) *economy/finance* and (v) the relevant *players*.[6] They will be hereinafter presented to stress the main social dynamics crossing, and disrupting, the contemporary constitutional fabric.

Therewith, in close connection with globalisation, serving simultaneously as one of its effects and causal concurrents, *technological development* must be taken into account, too. As far-sightedly conveyed by Sherry Turkle, 'we have reached a cultural watershed',[7] in which scientific advancement—*in primis*, in the computer

---

but also much more fascinating and realistic. […] it does not limit itself to describing the rules, forms and procedures applying to the acts of initiating a judicial proceeding or an appeal; it must also consider the costs to be borne, the time required, the difficulties (including psychological ones) to overcome, the benefits to be obtained, etc.'. On such footsteps, the present chapter starts this work by offering a sketch of the 'first dimension': that is, the social problem(s) currently hindering effective access to justice and calling for new paths, and dimensions, again, of enforcement. To do so, it draws principally, and necessarily, from socio-legal scholarship. Always topical also Calamandrei (1953), pp. 576–578, and (1954), pp. 650 *et seq.*: in the former work, he stresses that 'the trial is essentially the study of man' and that beneath all legal schemes 'there is nothing true and alive but men, with their lights and their shadows, with their virtues and with their aberrations', and from here we can infer—he writes just after his recent experience as a member of the Constituent Assembly in Italy—'the close links that unite procedural law to constitutional law […] [since] all freedoms are empty if they cannot be enforced and defended in court', both for criminal and civil proceedings. He foresees, in fact, in the trial that place where as 'in no other field […] is it possible to meet and fathom, gathered in their anguished actuality, all the aspects, juridical, political and moral, of the central problem of human society, which is *the problem of reconciling freedom with justice*' (original emphasis, translated from Italian).

[3] See Cassese (2009).

[4] Hopper (2018), p. 359.

[5] See Rovelli (2014), Feynman (1963).

[6] See Hopper (2006).

[7] Turkle (1999), p. 336.

sector (nowadays AI), internet, digital field and in bio-engineering—is 'changing the way we think, [...] the forms of our communities, our very identities'.[8] As further developed, such innovations pose fundamental questions on the way we create and experience life itself; on what is *human*, on what is *society*.[9]

In this fluid, tottering and decentered, post-modernist age, the form of *relationships* is adjusting, the ever-more convoluted and replicable on a large, potentially non-finite, scale. Just like genetic re-engineering studies—for a purported higher goal (curing and preventing diseases)—promise to map and mutate DNA and, thereby, however, shift pieces of genetic code, and potentially risk also an alteration in the markers that determine one's personality, preferences and most intimate way of being, in a similar way the social tissue is changing so fast and so significantly to a point where it might become a completely different—virtual—fabric.[10]

The next chapter builds on these complex phenomena and processes to explain contemporary constitutional transformations, highlighting the core issues of *power* and *responsibility*, on the one hand, and of *rights* and *duties*, on the other hand, (in both cases as two sides of the same coin), which lay at the intersection between all the tangled socio-dimensions herein underscored.[11]

A reflection on the contemporary constitutional transformations, and, in particular, the consequent shortcomings in the effective legal protection of (fundamental) rights (a fundamental right itself),[12] will then assist the analysis on the implementation of class actions in such an intricate milieu, as a legal response to such a social and constitutional problem.[13]

---

[8] Id.

[9] Id. See also Harari (2024).

[10] See Rodotà (2007).

[11] See *infra*, Chap. 3. The legal and constitutional analysis will start from there, although we insist on the importance of not conducting it *in vitro*, hence the present preliminary socio-legal and socio-logical pages. See again, *supra*, Cappelletti (1993) and Calamandrei (1953).

[12] See *infra*, Chap. 4.

[13] In the following Parts II and III. Before advancing, two additional preliminary methodological clarifications seem appropriate. *Firstly*, it must be stressed that the viewpoint herein adopted is the European one: not an EU one, but rather an Italian one as part of a larger European multilevel constitutional system, integrating (at times with troubled coordination) also EU and CoE guarantees (see Randazzo 2023). As much as globalisation itself has disrupted state barriers and expanded the realms of casual interconnections, it is evident that 'European society' (see von Bogdandy 2023, referring to Article 2 TEU, but also Pizzorusso 2002 and his foresighted definition of 'European constitutional heritage') presents different characteristics than that from other continents. Even when analysing global trends and notions, hence, the standpoint from which we operate will, inevitably and even unconsciously, bias our perceptions, for instance by giving more attention to certain phenomena or expressions rather than others. As argued by Michael Ignatieff, the very concept of human rights—in theory universal and indivisible—is strictly related to the particularism of single geographical and cultural areas of the world (the Western ones, in this case). Other cultures, such as the Islamic, Hindu or Chinese one, consequently struggle with the epistemological framework based around this notion (see Ignatieff 2001). Under a *micro-comparison*, substantial differences can be found, too. This occurs within a single continent—or supranational legal order, such as the EU. For instance, declining birth rates are nowadays a critical issue in Italy

2.2 The Multiple Dimensions of Globalisation

With these premises, it seems appropriate to start by the definition of *globalisation*. According to Anthony Giddens, it can be accounted as 'the intensification of world-wide social relations which link distant localities in such a way that local happenings are shaped by events occurring many miles away and vice versa'.[14] This illustration conveys both the element of interconnection and that of capacity to overcome time and space barriers with relative ease. They are the *time*, *space* and *relationships* dimensions.

It causes, as described by Robert Roberson, a 'compression of the world and [...] concrete global interdependence',[15] achieved through technological and digital advancements. This is clearly visible in relation to the new means of communication and transportation. Diffusion does not limit itself to information, people and goods, but it also extends to ideas, news, capital, entertainment, art, culture, fashion trends, languages and—as recent experience teaches (i.e., the covid-19 pandemic)—even diseases and, to a certain degree, wars. A tendency to *homologation* and *spreading* can thus be appreciated.

---

or Spain, whereas other Member States, such as France—still witnessing a downward, but less vertical, rate—may expose other trends as more urgent. This may be, for example, the case of pension systems. Due to the current reform, which aims to increase the standard minimum age for retirement in France, the topicality of the matter is highly felt within this country, probably much more than in other EU States, such as Sweden or Norway, where the minimum age is lower. Another example is that of populist, mostly right-wing, movements recently emerging in the political scene. This tendency largely tends to regard all Europe (also since it directly affects the European Union). Evidently, nonetheless, its implications differ from State to State, where the impact of such movements, or parties, varies even significantly and presents relevant exceptions. Instead, from a strictly *juridical point of view*, these regional differences are exemplified by the doctrine of the 'margin of appreciation', granted by the ECtHR to Member States when fulfilling their Convention obligations. It is, as is known, a space of flexibility, based on their cultural and legal traditions, in delicate cases when there is no 'European consensus', while still ensuring the respect of the minimum common standard of protection (see, again, Randazzo 2023, p. 28). These intra-continental and intra-EU differences, although essential, are, in any case, less remarkable, at least for the purpose of this Chapter, which is to evidence *major global trends*, to then highlight their consequences on the concrete enforcement of rights and interests. *Secondly*, another important caveat is that sociological analysis is not the focus of the present book. Nor it aims to be the field of expertise of the present author. Various better-equipped scholars have offered, and continue to offer, precious output, from a more appropriate sociological, socio-legal and socio-political angle. Rather, this investigation draws from them, in order to put into the spotlight those '*environmental elements*' prodromal to the constitutional transformations we are currently witnessing. Without keeping them into account it would be impossible to adequately understand such constitutional changes, as well as, subsequently, even consider the possible solutions to the contemporary societal challenges. As will be highlighted, the latter transformations bring significant consequences for the *enforcement of rights* (to be conceived as a fundamental right itself), and specifically of fundamental rights, which is the central question of this work.

[14] Giddens (1991), p. 64.

[15] Robertson (1992), p. 8.

As a consequence, both social and economic relationships are radically altered. The change in the latter (*economic* dimension) is emphasised, in particular, in relation to the classic scheme of production, distribution and consumption. All these processes are exponentially sped up (*time* dimension) in an ever-connected net (*relational* dimension), where distances are annulled (*space* dimension). Global value chains are a valid example. A computer from a US brand, for instance, may be assembled in China, where labour wages are extremely lower, by using key metal pieces extracted in Africa and South America, which had been previously converted into a chip in India, on the basis of designs from Australia or Canada, and later on be sold in Europe.[16]

The effects on the economic and labour markets are substantial. Obvious advantages are a larger availability of resources and markets, as well as possible cooperation aimed at services' and goods' improvement. Nonetheless, this continuous expansion tends to push production and distribution processes to *standardisation* and, at times, even *exhaustion*. David Held and Anthony McGrew refer to this phenomenon as 'intensification, or growing magnitude of interconnections, interactions and flows across society and states'.[17]

Inequalities between top and bottom of the chain are, thus, increasingly emphasised. This pushes towards a polarisation in the distribution of richness, both from an individual and market-oriented perspective, which can be encompassed under the *economic/financial* dimension, as well as the *relational* one. According to Neo-Marxists, this favours labour exploitation and reinforces inequalities also between countries.[18] A general dissatisfaction with traditional political parties' ability (in Europe, at least) to tackle these growing cracks has given rise to populist political movements, which have, in turn, exacerbated the political context and brought (sometimes, back) anti-democratic or, in the best scenarios, nationalist stances.[19]

This layer inevitably collides with the *players'* dimension. Large, often transnational, corporations have established themselves, at times with more say and capital than single states.[20] Ever-growing gaps separate the elite of decisions-makers and the vast majority of the population, which severely struggles in achieving social mobility (*relational* dimension, too). As summarised by Yuval Noah Harari, the main struggle of the twenty-first century may very well be that against *irrelevance*.[21] This issue is only exacerbated by the 2007–2008 financial crisis and, now, the current inflation.[22] New forms of richness and commerce have established themselves, too, often relying on immaterial assets, such as data, cryptocurrencies, NFTs or,

[16] See Cassese (2009).

[17] Held and McGrew (2003), p. 67.

[18] See Ohmae (1995).

[19] See, e.g., Tushnet and Bugaric (2020), Rodrik (2018), Kessel (2015), Chieffi (2006).

[20] See, e.g., Tully et al. (2016), p. 7; Bartley (2018), p. 145.

[21] Harari (2020).

[22] See OECD (2018).

ultimately, the metaverse (*economic/financial* dimension).[23] Concomitantly, the development of AI technologies threatens the replacement of countless categories of workers in different industries (*players'* dimension).[24]

To this regard, the advent of new technologies and digital transformation finds a propulsion force in the complex processes of globalisation, which has fostered an environment conducive to the rapid advancement and dissemination of digital technologies. By forging intricate networks of international trade, communication, and interdependence, globalisation has not only accelerated the cross-border flow of information, but it has also triggered a heightened demand for new digital infrastructure and tools, essential for navigating the interconnected global landscape (*relational* and *space* dimensions). At the same time, the process moves in the opposite direction, too, as addressed in the following, with technological advancement being the motor and one of the driving factors behind globalisation itself. It is, after all, the structure on which globalisation bases its interchanges.

Consequently, the intricate interplay between these two phenomena has ushered in a *paradigm shift*, reshaping the contours of contemporary society and redefining the parameters of legal, economic, and socio-cultural discourse on a global scale. This has propelled technological research to until recently unimaginable heights and 'made it possible to overcome the barriers of space and time to an unprecedented degree'.[25]

Some authors, such as Alvin Toffler, have even described it as a 'demise of geography',[26] whereas others, like Saskia Sassen, have stressed the 'privatisation' of regulatory practices beyond state borders in favour of large corporate interests (*economic/financial*, *players'*, *relational* and *space* dimensions).

Luciano Gallino places emphasis on this *economic/financial* aspect, when defining globalisation as 'a primarily economic phenomenon' and a 'universalism of the market'.[27] What is worth stressing indeed is the traditionally '*private*' nature of the main actors (*players'* dimension) of these new markets, which evidently cannot be controlled (*relational* dimension) by states, since they go well beyond national borders (*space* dimension).

As will be further addressed, this touches the critical issue of *power* and enhances the risks of critical gaps of control and responsibility.[28] Nation-states are no longer the exclusive focal points or primary structures of governance, as authority (hence, *sovereignty*) has become increasingly dispersed among public and private entities at various levels, from local to global (*relational* and *players'* dimensions). This shift of perspective is pointed out by transformationalist socio-political scholars, such as John Ruggie or Saskia Sassen, according to whom, respectively, we are witnessing

---

[23] See Dwivedi et al. (2022).

[24] See Council of Europe Commissioner for Human Rights (2023).

[25] Läpple (2001), p. 15.

[26] Toffler (1970), p. 91.

[27] Gallino (2003), pp. 4 *et seq.*

[28] See *infra*, next Chap. 3.

an '*unbundling*' of the relationship between sovereignty, territoriality and state power, and 'sovereignty [...] partially disassembled', with an 'increasing privatization' of the executive branch of the government (no longer part of the state in the Westphalian conception),[29] whereas other 'components of the state's territorial authority, especially of the legislature, shift to other institutional homes, notably an emergent jurisdiction of global regulators'.[30]

At the same time, David Held and Anthony McGrew highlight how even local actions can have global consequences (*relational* dimension).[31] They call this feature 'impact', and a *magnification* of the events. Combined with the ability of escaping responsibility for their actions, this phenomenon allows dominant economic actors to produce *planetary damage*.

In particular, nowadays two waves of unprecedent dimensions promise to affect the whole globe concurrently. They are, on the one hand, *climate change*, with the inherent risk of ecological collapse, and, on the other hand, *AI and biotech innovations*, with the related peril of technological disruption.[32]

The former, as is well-known, increases the chances of extreme weather and climate disasters, such as floods, wildfires, hurricanes, high temperatures, droughts, decrease of biodiversity, higher sea levels or less availability of fresh water. All these phenomena inevitably carry social implications, too: for instance, they might cause climate migratory routes, if not wars, permanent health issues in more vulnerable parts of the population or, in general, impairment in the full enjoyment of one's rights in their everyday activities.[33] Migration, together with the reception and integration of immigrants, often mistreated and subjected to degrading living and working conditions, is a particularly relevant topic of the present age, exacerbated by recent wars.[34]

The latter wave—AI and biotech innovations—, instead, promises to bring numerous advantages, by reaching new frontiers in healthcare and by spearheading new commodities and automation, both in the business and personal sphere. The risks connected to these scientific and technological advancements should not be overlooked, however: from data breaches and their misuse, through influence on one's self-determination abilities, algorithmic discrimination or the spreading of misinformation, to replacement of countless categories of workers in different industries.[35]

On these shaky grounds stands the frail architecture of political governance (*players'* dimension), both at international and national level (*space* dimension). The lack of efficient cooperation (*relational* dimension) in recent global crisis, such

[29] Id.

[30] Sassen (2013), p. 21.

[31] Held and McGrew (2003), p. 68.

[32] See Harari (2020).

[33] See IPCC (2023).

[34] See European Migration Network Report (2023).

[35] See Council of Europe Commissioner for Human Rights (2023).

as the covid-19 pandemic, the Ukrainian and Israeli-Palestinian conflicts or climate change, are vivid examples. Within national borders, instead, the rise of populist parties (*players'* dimension), the struggle of democratic representation and the threats to the rule of law[36] and to judicial independence, must be accounted. Wars, religious divisions, racial hate, rises in terrorist attacks and threats contribute to this complex patchwork.

The far-reaching implications are evident, once again, across the *players'*, *economic/financial* and *relational* spheres, marked notably by the widening chasm between the leading elite and the general collectivity.[37] Consequently, this fissure amplifies discontentment with democratic representation mechanisms, as further addressed below.[38]

2.3 The Overflowing Effects of New Technologies

As anticipated, technological innovation stands as the driving force behind globalisation. Without it, 'the intensification of world-wide social relations which link distant localities in such a way that local happenings are shaped by events occurring many miles away and vice versa'[39] would simply not be possible.

Transportation, exchanges and communication through innovative technological means have contributed and keep contributing to the development of the global, interconnected market. They constitute the network on which globalisation occurs.

Concurrently, scientific progress is increasingly shaped by globalisation itself, in a cyclic causal dynamic. The exchange of ideas, knowledge, experiences, the ease in communicating and travelling has favoured and favours exponential advancements in all fields of research. In particular, as already mentioned, the sectors which are pushing to the extremes the forces behind globalisation, significantly altering the reality in which we live and its core identities, herein included the human one, are those related to the internet and computers, to artificial intelligence and to biotechnologies.[40] It is not the goal, nor the scope, of the present research that to examine the nuances of each of these fast-evolving fields. Rather, from a constitutional perspective, two grounds of concern, further elaborated in the next Chapter, emerge as specifically notable.

On the one side, the ramifications of new technologies on the *democratic process* and structures need to be underscored.[41] As the means of communication and acquisition of knowledge evolve, the mechanisms through which auto-determination and

[36] See European Commission (2022).

[37] Guterres (2023), p. 2.

[38] See *infra*, next paragraph, but also next Chap. 3.

[39] Giddens (1991), p. 64.

[40] See Rodotà (2007).

[41] See Winner (1992).

propaganda occur change.[42] The difference between truth and fake news becomes a thin line. The actors driving information and the public debate are no longer physical Parliaments or (to some degree) in-person manifestations, but mainly virtual fora and personae, like social networks or influencers, and related hashtags. In this ever-connected web, every detail ('data') about one's preferences, movements, actions and even body is collectable and collected, both by private and public entities, often invisible to the human eye. Against this backdrop, the balancing between the 'personal sphere' and the collective interaction, in Orwellian fashion, is the evermore blurred.

On the other side, *inequalities* are vastly enhanced. As science progresses, most of the new advancements are not immediately available to the general public. Furthermore, as the global market enhances investment opportunities and gains, the differential margin widens dramatically between all corners of the globe and societal groups. Those that can afford to play with the new tools exponentially bolster their economic and personal, now even physical and mental,[43] abilities; whilst, for the others, trailing behind, social elevation becomes utopia rather than a concrete possibility. Such a reasoning is valid both at state-level and from an individual viewpoint. The ramifications at the level of *critical constitutional concern* (in Italy, with particular reference to Article 3, second paragraph, of the Constitution), for a constitution that is programmatic and founded on *substantive equality*, are obvious and will be better detailed in the following.

In sum, the 'cultural watershed' portrayed by Shelly Turkle in 1999 appears nowadays overcome by the incessant and overwhelming flow of unregulated and, to various degrees, unregulatable flow of technological innovation.

2.4 Concluding Remarks. The Rise of New 'Global Classes'

Numerous discussion points emerge from the picture just painted (certainly a piece of abstract art, if any) which could be further in depth explored. The goal of this Chapter, however, is not that of portraying a thorough socio-logical analysis of the current age. Rather, it is that of highlighting the multi-faceted, convoluted and multi-dimensional—globalised and highly technological—reality in which we live.

Time and *space* are contemporarily shrunk and 'exploded'[44] in a tangled multi-directional *relational* network primarily guided by *economic and financial* interests, in which new *players* arise and distances between all players, under *new power-balances*, accumulate. The repercussions on the enforcement of fundamental rights

[42] See Pinelli and Ruffolo (2023).

[43] See e.g. Neuralink's implant: 'Our brain-computer interface is fully implantable, cosmetically invisible, and designed to let you control a computer or mobile device anywhere you go', at: <https://neuralink.com>.

[44] See Harvey (1989), pp. 260 *et seq.*, and his well-known elaboration of the 'time-compression' concept.

are both substantial and pressing, under the constitutional perspective herein of interest, as addressed in the next Chapter.

The main lesson to be taken here, against this backdrop, draws from the considerations advanced by Saskia Sassen in her ground-breaking work 'A Sociology of Globalization'.[45] Given how the current globalised dynamics 'partially disaggregate the national from within' and the previously-established social groups—that is the 'intermediate bodies' or 'social formations' further developed *infra*, [46] namely political parties or workers' unions—new *'global classes'* emerge.[47]

As Manuel Castells further elaborates, in the rise of the 'network society', as traditional structures change, also social groups—*classes*—change, transcending state boundaries. Yet, they remain 'partially denationalized classes' (rather than fully 'global'), as their 'particular features [...], especially their ambiguous position between the global and the national, point to the ongoing, even if partial, embeddedness in the national domains', too.[48]

While Sassen thoroughly addresses the subjective and objective features[49] of these new global, or partially denationalised, classes, their significance for the present analysis resides on at least *three axes*.

First, the emerging classes in the globalised and highly-technological context are not necessarily *new* social forms as such. To this regard, Sassen offers the examples of 'transnational immigrant households' or 'international class of powerful elites'. Another valid illustration can be that of workers in the various industry sectors. All these social groups are *not per se new*. Still, due to the multi-dimensional dynamics of globalisation described earlier, they assume new *meaning* and carry novel *implications*. New classes 'arise from a subjective, self-reflexive repositioning of an old social practice or condition in a transnational framing'. It is, in particular, the process of '*incipient denationalization*'—'a changed attachment to the national as historically constructed'[50]—to give propulsion to such transformations.[51]

Second, the issue of power is central to the development of, and any reflection on, these new '*global classes*'. Such denationalising dynamics of globalisation engender *radical power shifts*: from national states to supranational public and transnational private entities, eluding traditional categories, representation processes and oversight mechanisms; from Enlightenment-derived one-on-one perspectives to collective and diffuse, supra-individual, dimensions; from being (tendentially)

---

[45] Sassen (2007).

[46] Id., pp. 164 *et seq*. See, *infra*, Chaps. 3 and 4.

[47] In relation to political parties, see Ciancio (2016), on their features, role and challenges in the process of European integration, and their problematic dependence from national parties.

[48] Sassen (2007), pp. 164 *et seq*. See also Castells (1999).

[49] Sassen (2007), pp. 166–168.

[50] Id., p. 173.

[51] Here, Pierre Bourdieu's notion of *habitus* can be insightful in reflecting on how these global classes develop new practices and structures of understanding, that navigate both the global and the national spheres. See Bourdieu (1977), pp. 77 *et seq*.

regulated to chasing innovations and the risks associated with them, as well as the irresponsibility of increasingly multi-layered and elusive actors.

The outcome manifests itself as a progressively deepening schism and disparity among different social cohorts. Accordingly, the global classes at the bottom of the societal hierarchy (which Sassen, again, refers to as 'the new global classes of the disadvantaged', but which, in essence, echo significant similarities with their pre-globalisation counterparts, as outlined earlier)[52] face increasing marginalisation, compounded by the deficiencies and inadequacies of *non*-global(ised) *representation* mechanisms.[53]

Third, following Pierre Bourdieu's extensive reflections on the concepts of '*habitus*', of classes and of social fields as spaces of potential agency and struggle,[54] it is possible to conceive these new (but still not really new) 'global classes' as the 'strategic context for *collective action*'.[55] As subsequently addressed, this strategic context can become the fertile ground for *class actions*[56] which, through their collective nature, serve as instruments for these groups to assert their rights and influence *social change*.

Collective actions become a mechanism to advance social change by *addressing the imbalances* created by the global dynamics that the traditional forms of representation and state-based governance may struggle to contend with. Against this backdrop, in its virtuous use, collective action is not a mere tactical maneuver, but becomes a form of what Anthony Giddens refers to as 'structuration', where agents and structures are mutually constitutive.[57] These classes, operating within the globally influenced but nationally embedded spaces, use their collective capacity to redefine the parameters of their agency, negotiating new forms of 'social contracts'[58] that transcend traditional state and enforcement borders. This way, as argued below, individuals find a path, however circumstantial, to regain possession of their relinquished and '*sconfinata*' (i.e., borderless) sovereignty.[59]

Additionally, this potential for collective action reflects the lessons that David Harvey's analysis of the condition of postmodernity suggests about the space for counter-movements within the dynamics of capital flow and the reconfiguration of spatial dimensions.[60] As classes mobilise, they also re-territorialise the global space, asserting place-based claims that are simultaneously global in scope. Illustrative examples are those of climate change, global value chains or immigrant suits. By doing so, they challenge the fluidity and seeming omnipotence of global capital

---

[52] Sassen (2007), pp. 164 *et seq.*

[53] See *infra*, next Chap. 3.

[54] Bourdieu (1977), specifically at p. 82.

[55] Sassen (2007), p. 167.

[56] For a precise definition of such a procedural mechanism, see, *infra*, Chap. 4.

[57] Giddens (1991), pp. 17 *et seq.*

[58] See Rousseau (1795).

[59] See Ferrarese (2006).

[60] Harvey (1989), pp. 338 *et seq.*

with a grounded, often resistant, power of collective human action. This dialectical process echoes Bauman's view of globalisation as a 'state of interregnum'—a gap between an old order dying and a new one yet to be born,[61] where these new 'global classes' both respond to and shape the emerging contours of global society.

In essence, 'strategic'[62] collective, namely *representative*, lawsuits can redefine the nature of *agency* within a global context, presenting both a challenge and an opportunity for the enforcement of fundamental rights. The transformations are not just economic or political, but carry also deep legal and constitutional implications, demanding attention in the next two Chapters where the repercussions for constitutionalism and fundamental rights, within this globalised and high-tech reconfiguration, will be critically examined. In particular, the issue of *fair trial guarantees*, as a primary consideration, and that of *judicial activism*, as an ever-present background theme, should be accounted.

The 'new' global classes, therefore, become critical actors in the reconfiguration of new governance structures and the recalibration of justice systems in light of societal and technological most profound developments. As depicted by both Sassen and Bourdieu, collective suits *can* become the means through which groups or individuals enforce their positions against the new higher—otherwise unsurmountable—powers, as well as a means for marginalised groups to redefine—circles in a circle[63]—the new—otherwise (too) unbalanced—rules of the field.

References

Bartley T (2018) Transnational corporations and global governance. Annu Rev Sociol 44:145

Bauman Z (2012) Times of interregnum. Ethics Global Polit 5(1):49

Bourdieu P (1977) Outline of a theory of practice. Cambridge University Press, Cambridge (first published in French in 1972 by Librairie Droz)

Calamandrei P (1953) Processo e giustizia. In: Cappelletti M (ed) Calamandrei P (1965) Opere giuridiche, I. Morano, Napoli

Calamandrei P (1954) Processo e democrazia. In: Cappelletti M (ed) Calamandrei P (1965) Opere giuridiche, I. Morano, Napoli

Cappelletti M (1993) Alternative dispute resolution processes within the framework of the world-wide access to-justice movement. Mod Law Rev 56(3):282–296

Cassese S (2009) Il diritto globale. Giustizia e democrazia oltre lo Stato. Einaudi, Torino

[61] Bauman (2012), p. 49.

[62] Sassen (2007), p. 167: 'they define a strategic context for collective action'.

[63] 'Circles in a Circle', by Kandinsky (1923). The same Vasily Kandinsky later wrote that such a form, to be intended as a symbol of both individuality and connection, of dynamic interconnection, of both renewal and regeneration, 'points more clearly to the fourth dimension'—a dimension (or *dimensions*) which we like to conceive here as (a) *collective* (one) (see Zander Rudenstine 1976, p. 310, quoting Kandinsky's letter to Will Grohmann, from 12 October 1930).

Castells M (1999) The information age: economy, society and culture, vol I. The rise of the network society. Blackwell, Oxford
Chieffi L (ed) (2006) Rappresentanza politica, gruppi di pressione, élites al potere. Giappichelli, Torino
Ciancio A (2016) European parties and the process of political integration in Europe. Dirittifondamentali.it 2:1
Council of Europe Commissioner for Human Rights (2023) Human rights by design. Future-proofing human rights protection in the era of AI, follow-up Recommendation to Unboxing AI (2019), May 2023
Dwivedi YK et al (2022) Metaverse beyond the hype: multidisciplinary perspectives on emerging challenges, opportunities, and agenda for research, practice and policy. Int J Inf Manag 66:102542
European Commission (2022) Rule of Law Report, July 2022
European Migration Network Report (2023)
Ferrarese MR (2006) Il diritto sconfinato. Laterza, Roma
Feynman RP (1963) Six easy pieces. California Institute of Technology. Translated in Italian in: Feynman RP (2000), Sei pezzi facili. Adelphi, Milano
Gallino L (2003) Globalizzazione e diseguaglianze. Laterza, Roma
Giddens A (1991) The consequences of modernity. John Wiley and Sons Ltd, Hoboken
Guterres A (2023). Foreword. In: United Nations' Sustainable Development Goals Report 2023: Special Edition: 5
Harari YN (2020) How to Survive the 21st Century, open transcript from the presentation at the World Economic Forum Annual Meeting 2020, Betazone from 23 January 2020
Harari YN (2024) Nexus. A brief history of information networks from the Stone Age to AI. Random House, New York
Harvey D (1989) The condition of postmodernity. Blackwell, Oxford
Held D, McGrew A (2003) Global transformations reader. Polity, Cambridge
Hopper P (2006) Living with globalization. Berg, Oxford and New York
Hopper P (2018) Understanding development, 2nd edn. Polity, New York, e-book
Ignatieff M (2001) Human rights as politics and idolatry. Princeton University Press, Princeton
IPCC (2023) AR6 Synthesis Report Climate Change 2023
Kessel S (2015) Populist parties in Europe. Agents of discontent? Palgrave Macmilann, London
Läpple D (2001) City and region in an age of globalisation and digitization. German J Urban Stud 40(2):15
OECD (2018) A broken social elevator? How to Promote Social Mobility, June 2018
Ohmae K (1995) The end of the nation state: the rise of regional economies. Free Press, New York
Pinelli C, Ruffolo U (2023) I diritti nelle piattaforme. Giappichelli, Torino
Pizzorusso A (2002) Il patrimonio costituzionale europeo. Il Mulino, Bologna
Randazzo B (2023) Access to justice in a multilevel constitutional system, protecting human rights. Giappichelli, Torino
Robertson R (1992) Globalization: social theory and global culture. Sage Publications, New York
Rodotà S (2007) Dal soggetto alla persona. Editoriale Scientifica, Napoli
Rodrik D (2018) Populism and the economics of globalization. J Int Bus Policy
Rousseau JJ (1795) Du Contrat social ou principles de droit politique. Paris
Rovelli C (2014) Sette breve lezioni di fisica. Adelphi, Milano
Sassen S (2007) A sociology of globalization. WW Norton, New York
Sassen S (2013) When territory deborders territoriality. Territ Polit Gov 1(1):21
Toffler A (1970) Future Schock. Random House, New York
Tully J, Dunoff JL, Lange AF Jr, Kumm M, Wiener A (2016) Introducing global integral constitutionalism. Global Const 5(1):1–15
Turkle S (1999) Identity in the age of internet. In: Mackay H, O'Sullivan T (eds) The media reader. Continuity and transformation. Sage Publications, New York, p 302

Tushnet M, Bugaric B (2020) Populism and constitutionalism: an essay on definitions and their implications. Harvard Public Law Working Paper 20(17)
von Bogdandy A (2022) Strukturwandel des öffentlichen Rechts. Entstehung und Demokratisierung der europäischen Gesellschaft, Suhrkamp Verlag, Berlin, 11
von Bogdandy A (2023) Comparative public law for European society. MPIL Res Pap 28:1–46
Winner L (1992) Democracy in a technological society. Springer, Cham
Zander Rudenstine A (1976) The Guggenheim Museum: Paintings 1880–1945, vol 1. Solomon R. Guggenheim Foundation, New York

Chapter 3
A Multilevel Constitutional Context

3.1 Premise. A Shifting Landscape

The constitutional landscape provides the bedrock upon which the edifice of fundamental rights enforcement is built. In the same way, the social, cultural and historical context provides a pivotal element of constitutional change. Moving in Aristotlic fashion, syllogistically, the social cultural and historical context, addressed in the previous Chapter, intrinsically touches the issue of fundamental rights enforcement, too.

Bruce Ackerman, in his ponderous 'We the People. Volume 2: Transformations' outlines the crucial role played in (American) constitutional history by social and political upheaval, especially (but not only) in times of great crisis.[1] Similar reflections can be applied to the current Italian, European and global dynamics. As described until now, globalisation, together with technological revolution, is a complex process which continuously affects societal and individual life in very different ways. Time, space, relationships, economy and relevant players are only some of the dimensions through which society and, consequently, constitutional equilibria are touched by this phenomenon.[2]

The present Chapter, building on established legal scholarship and case law, aims to underscore the main *constitutional transformations* characterising our time. Such a dissection will pinpoint a series of *systemic* dysfunctions,[3] or *adjudicatory gaps*, burrowed by the contemporary unrelenting forces that severely change the social and constitutional landscape, thus hampering the enforcement of fundamental rights

[1] See Ackerman (2000).

[2] See *supra*, the previous Chap. 2.

[3] The word systemic is borrowed by the ECtHR case law with specific regard to its pilot-judgement procedure. On the lack of a clear definition given by the Strasbourg Court, as well as for critical view on such procedure, see Lemmens and Van Drooghenbroeck (2023).

A. Maglica, *Collective Dimensions of Access to Justice*, European Union and its Neighbours in a Globalized World 23,
https://doi.org/10.1007/978-3-031-94522-9_3

in given, and increasing, sets of circumstances. Against such a backdrop, the class action device will be assessed in the next Parts.

As will be herein argued, a point of convergence between all the layers of constitutional consideration is the issue of *power*.

On the one hand, *new gravitational centres* of power have emerged. The discontent of old actors counter-surfaces, as conflictual tensions play out in the tangled-up multilevel and multidimensional global structure, simultaneously propelled by both centrifugal and centripetal forces. In the middle, powerless, stands an overwhelmed *citoyen*.[4]

On the other hand, it is becoming alarmingly difficult to keep these new transnational, borderless and a-institutional entities *accountable* for the exercise of such power. A lack of effective control and an increasing, general irresponsibility of those *in concreto* holding power favours substantial *serial* and *structural* violations to both individual and collective spheres.

To present these arguments, the Chapter will start from the *role of constitutionalism*, since the two pillars of constitutionalism are precisely the legitimacy (and limitation) of power and the respect of rights.[5] In particular, it shall be addressed how the social changes of the current globalised age are questioning the notion itself of *constitutionalism*, as well as the special lens that adopting such a perspective entails.

Furthermore, the puzzled and blurred *multilayered nature* of the current *constitutional system* shall be briefly recalled, to explain the peculiar stage on which new and old actors are called to perform (all 'merely players').[6] Last, the mutations of the traditional concept of *sovereignty* will be accounted, with their favouring the emergence of new gravitational centres of power, beyond the national Westphalian conception, with their questioning the traditional public v. private paradigm, as well as the very concept of statehood, and with their deep capsizing of legislative, executive and judicial functions.

As anticipated, such a brief and instrumental—thus without any claim to exhaustiveness—analysis will help situate the present research and justify the choice of focusing with a constitutional lens on the class action procedural device in the European context, as a possible, partial, solution; but, also, as a potential element of further turmoil.

---

[4] See *Déclaration des droits de l'Homme et du citoyen de 1789*.

[5] Id., Article 16.

[6] Always on point, Shakespeare (1623), Act II, Scene VII, line 146.

3.2 Constitutionalism's Role in the Transforming Context

It has been stated that 'what 'human justice' can do is solve, or attempt to solve, concrete problems of individual and societal life: to enact and enforce norms, to create institutions, to design processes, all with that one goal in mind—to solve actual problems'.[7]

If justice is to be conceived—following the thought, *inter alia*, of Henri Bergson[8] or Noam Chomsky[9]—as the most (possible) complete realisation of the personality, and, consequently, of the 'humanity', of each person, the respect of human—or fundamental[10]—rights is its benchmark.[11]

In a postmodern society shaped by severe inequalities, tensions, depletions of traditional centres of gravity and an overall, pervading, feeling of discontent and insecurity,[12] the *effective* enforcement of fundamental rights is becoming increasingly daunting.[13] Obstacles appear both under the procedural perspective of the guarantees and remedies available and under the more substantive standpoint of rights' concrete enjoyment.[14] Ironically, this occurs in an historical period characterised by the vastest, ever, array of written *substantive* guarantees, both at national and supranational level.[15]

Several issues concerning rights' enforcement and implementation, power structures and strands, procedural and institutional (in)efficacy stand out on the horizon. Wars, environmental damage, pandemics, new risks posed by technological and AI developments, fake news, growing inequalities, discriminatory and exploitation practices, populism and anti-democratic backsliding are only some of the most evident challenges, already discussed *above*.[16] Other more subtle issues affect people's everyday lives: inflation and the rising price of basic needs, poor working conditions, difficulties in buying or renting houses, waiting lines for public medical

---

[7] Cappelletti (1986), p. 2.

[8] See Bergson (1937). Bergson's philosophical work, as is known, was a large influence in the drafting of the UN Declaration of Human Rights (see Curle 2010).

[9] See Chomsky and Foucault (2011).

[10] Under a substantive conception, a close connection between the similar notions of human and fundamental rights emerges. To this regard, it should be noted that the former concept is more employed in international law and 'aspire[s] to universal validity'. They are a moral theory of what is owed to every human (see Palombella 2006). Fundamental rights, on the other hand, constitute a transposition of human rights into the positive law of a specific legal order, to which they are strictly connected. Through their recognition and guarantee into the constitution, a specific democratic State sets them as one of its building blocks (see Olivetti 2020). See also Alexy (2006).

[11] See Angiolini (2012), especially pp. 4 *et seq.*

[12] See Zolo (2010).

[13] See EU-FRA, Fundamental Rights Report (2023).

[14] See Gentile (2023).

[15] Aside from national constitutions, at supranational level the CFREU, binding since 2009, the ECHR and the ESC can be accounted, for example.

[16] See *supra*, Chap. 2.

assistance, struggles in achieving social mobility, inadequate public education, lower and deferred pension systems. Clearly, deeper *systemic* wounds run through the social tissue. They mostly concern an *insufficient* implementation of social rights (but not only), depicting, in Cannettian jargon, the contemporary power-*less* nature of crowds, in an intricate, multi-dimensional, grid where traditional democratic wires (in particular, political parties)[17] appear exposed and worn out.

Concurrently, also the issue of the *cost* of rights is raised, in general (even traditional liberties), and of social rights, in particular.[18] Faced with limited financial resources, as well as with national (the so-called '*equilibrio di bilancio*', or balanced-budget rule, under Article 81, Italian Constitution) and supranational (mainly EU) constraints, states inevitably cannot accommodate all rights.[19] At the same time, financial resources have become a key piece of governance within the multilevel constitutional system, even in defence of the rule of law, through the development of new instruments such as *conditionality*, based on the so-called 'power of the pursue', capable of exercising public authority without normative regulation or pure coertion.[20]

Even when costs are not the major obstacle, legislative and executive national authorities may *deliberately* choose not to proceed. As accounted in the last Council of Europe's report on the *Supervision of the execution of judgments and decisions of the European Court of Human Rights*, 'there has been an increase in the total number of judgments currently pending full execution (6,081 compared to 5,533 in December 2021)'.[21] The 2022 findings of the European Committee of Social Rights on the *Follow-up to decisions on the merits of collective complaints*, paint an even bleaker picture, with the Committee almost in every case considering that 'the situation has not yet been brought into conformity with the 1961 Charter at this point'.[22] As stated by the Steering Committee for Human Rights in its *Report on the longer-term future of the European Convention on Human Rights* from 2016, the functioning of the ECHR system is contingent on 'the quality, cogency and coherence of the Court's judgments and the ensuing acceptance thereof of all actors of the system, including governments, parliaments, national courts, applicants and the public at

[17] See Chieffi (2006a).

[18] See, e.g., Holmes and Sunstein (1999), Wouters et al. (2020), Bin (2018), Luciani (2016), Morrone (2013).

[19] Id. This has a direct impact also on judges: 'fundamental rights cannot be protected without considering the politico-financial objectives of the State. The balanced budget is not indeed only an economic- accounting rule: it relates to values and rights that can enter the balancing process and thus limit the subjective claims brought before the Constitutional Court' (translated from Italian), Morrone (2015), p. 575.

[20] See, e.g., Baraggia (2023), Baraggia and Bonelli (2022), Pinelli (2019).

[21] See Supervision of the execution of judgments and decisions of the European Court of Human Rights (2023), p. 12.

[22] Id.

large'.[23] Also the role of the *judiciary*, as a subsidiary power, hence, is put into question. On this crucial point we shall return.[24]

Intimately connected to such a matter, is the question of *who* (and *how*) should be tasked with determining which rights should be satisfied over others: which values should prevail over others in case of *balancing* or whether some should always prevail, and, if so, to which degree.[25] The underlying question of *democratic legitimacy*—and how to safeguard it—is closely linked, both at political and judicial level. As further addressed, it is also intimately connected to that of *authority*.[26]

Such developments concern the European context, in which this research is framed, but also—with different intensity—the whole globe, gradually shattered by the new challenges. In the words of Antonio Guterres, Secretary-General of the United Nations, in the recent *Sustainable Development Goals Report 2023: Special Edition*, 'we are leaving more than half the world behind. Progress on more than 50 per cent of targets of the SDGs is weak and insufficient; on 30 per cent, it has stalled or gone into reverse. These include key targets on poverty, hunger and climate'.[27] According to the report, 'structural injustices, inequalities and emerging human rights challenges are putting peaceful and inclusive societies further out of reach'.[28]

Again, following Guterres, 'inequalities will continue to deepen, increasing the risk of a fragmented, two-speed world. [...] Unless we act now, the 2030 Agenda could become an epitaph for a world that might have been'.[29]

[23] Id., Overview of major developments by the Director General, p. 43, recalling 13. CDDH, Report on the longer-term future of the European Convention on Human Rights (2016), p. 96.

[24] See, *infra*, Chaps. 4 and 11.

[25] See Angiolini (2016), p. 37, criticising the traditional conception of balancing, 'rather than as a search for equilibrium, as an exercise of discretionary power through which the democratic political authority, the Court or the judge, or the administration, could determine what should take precedence—whether in a specific case or even for a broader category of cases' (translated from Italian).

[26] See von Bogdandy (2023), pp. 234 *et seq.*

[27] See United Nations' Sustainable Development Goals Report (2023), p. 5. As is known, 'the SDGs are the universally-agreed road map to bridge economic and geopolitical divides, restore trust and rebuild solidarity' (Id.).

[28] Id., on Goal 16 'Peace, justice and strong institutions', p. 44, which reports: '*(i)* Ongoing and new violent conflicts around the world are derailing the global path to peace and achievement of Goal 16. Alarmingly, the year 2022 witnessed a more than 50 per cent increase in conflict-related civilian deaths, largely due to the war in Ukraine; *(ii)* As of the end of 2022, 108.4 million people were forcibly displaced worldwide – an increase of 19 million compared with the end of 2021 and two and a half times the number of a decade ago; *(iii)* In 2021, the world experienced the highest number of intentional homicides in the past two decades; *(iv)* Structural injustices, inequalities and emerging human rights challenges are putting peaceful and inclusive societies further out of reach. To meet Goal 16 by 2030, action is needed to restore trust and to strengthen the capacity of institutions to secure justice for all and facilitate peaceful transitions to sustainable development'.

[29] Guterres (2023), p. 2.

3.2.1 From Traditional Conceptions…

Under a legal perspective, in such a challenging scenario it can be argued that it is the role—or, at least, the objective—of constitutionalism to search for answers.[30] After all, the protection of fundamental rights against the arbitrary exercise of power falls within its realm of consideration.[31]

Aimed at ensuring the best political order, constitutionalism has, indeed, been defined as 'the juridical technique of freedoms'.[32] It is, historically, the legal technique through which *citizens* are ensured the enjoyment of their rights (and interests) and, at the same time, the state is placed in a position where it cannot violate them.[33]

From a definitional standpoint, as further addressed, modern transformations bring terminological adjustments: in an extensive view, 'citizens' should now be substituted by 'individuals' (in the sense of all human beings) and, more controversially, 'state' by 'power'. The emergence of supranational, inter-state organisations, on the one hand, and the establishment of private hyper-centres of power, on the other hand, calls for the latter amendment.[34] As further addressed, the disruption of traditional statehood is an essential feature of the current constitutional landscape, with pervasive and, at times, perturbing consequences on fundamental rights' enforcement.

Whilst the global chart of power-balances is changing—not just from a geopolitical standpoint, but also from that of its protagonists—,[35] the concept itself of constitutionalism has indeed evolved, and must evolve, too.[36] From Thomas Hobbes', John Locke's and Benjamin's Constant's classic foundational theories on constitutionalism as a means of limitation of political power (and, consequently, of ensuring respect of fundamental rights), the notion has now developed into different directions. *Inter alia*, neo or transformative constitutionalism, multilevel, global, European, liberal or illiberal, cosmopolitan, pluralist, punctiform, popular, democratic, political, financial, digital, future, societal and, even, irenic v. polemic

---

[30] Zagrebelsky et al. (2023), p. 193. See also Fioravanti (2009).

[31] Rosenfeld (1992), p. 497: 'There appears to be no accepted definition of constitutionalism but, in the broadest terms, modern constitutionalism requires imposing limits on the powers of government, adherence to the rule of law, and the protection of fundamental rights. Moreover, although not all constitutions conform to the demands of constitutionalism, and although constitutionalism is not dependent on the existence of a written constitution, the realization of the spirit of constitutionalism generally goes hand in hand with the implementation of a written constitution'.

[32] Matteucci (2008), p. 202.

[33] Id.

[34] Yet it is also increasingly clear that constitutionalism is a meaningful concept beyond the state context, that it 'is relevant to, indeed constitutive of, all polities—state or non-state, mature or emergent', Walker (2001), p. 32.

[35] Ferrarese (2018), p. 2.

[36] See von Bogdandy (2023).

constitutionalism can be accounted.[37] They all depict societal and doctrinal evolutions, as well as a general confusion and an overall lack of clear direction within the ranks of academic scholarship. Some authors have even gone as far as arguing the 'decline of constitutionalism',[38] insisting on its distortion and anachronism; whereas, in any case, many question its role and ability to still serve in the defying contemporary age.

Some authors, such as Massimo Luciani in Italy, advocate for the restoration of an ancient (national, constitutional) order, based on written regulation and devoid from any kind of judicial law-making.[39] He has long argued 'the modest democratic yield of decision-making procedures in 'network' or 'multilevel' systems'.[40] Other academics, such as Armin von Bogdandy, push for a new European (comparative) constitutionalism, guided by courts in light of European society's core values, set forth under Article 2 TUE: 'respect for human dignity, freedom, democracy, equality, the rule of law and respect for human rights, including the rights of persons belonging to minorities[,] [...] pluralism, non-discrimination, tolerance, justice, solidarity and equality between women and men prevail'. Moreover, in relation with EU integration, many fear the consequences of a possible—currently debated—enlargement of the EU towards new, less liberal, members, as well as the rise of anti-democratic regimes, most notably the Polish and Hungarian ones.[41]

Another point on which the large majority of scholars seems to converge is that we are living in a defining moment of radical change, probably on the crest of a one-direction wave.[42] Current institutions appear anachronistic and unable to offer the answers that the complex challenges of our time pose. A reform on the systems of representation, representativeness and participation to the democratic processes (at all levels) is imperative.[43] A reform of public—national, European and global—governance is urgent.[44] A reform in the way of ensuring justice, but also in the way of *conceiving* justice is necessary.[45]

In the words of Alessandro Pace, 'the real, great task facing constitutionalism today is that of rediscovering and reaffirming its original identity as a legal theory'.[46] He questions the role of constitutionalism as a movement called upon to scrutinise any issue of general—and, as such, political—interest, as serious as it may be. At

---

[37] See, e.g., in order, Mazzarese (2008), von Bogdandy et al. (2017), Pernice (1999), Tuoori (2015), Rosenfeld (2025), Galtson (2011), Kumm (2013), Somek (2020), Ferrarese (2018), Pinelli (2016), Pollicino (2006), Luciani (2006).

[38] Wilkinson (2021).

[39] See Luciani (2023), especially pp. 176 *et seq*. See also Zanon (2021), p. 89.

[40] Luciani (1996), p. 1643. See also Bin (2018).

[41] See Bonini (2021).

[42] Antonini (2019), p. 319.

[43] See, e.g., Ciancio (2021), on the current challenges of political representation. See also Chieffi (2006a).

[44] Cassese (2016), p. 17.

[45] See Kavanagh (2023) and Angiolini (2016), pp. 126 *et seq*.

[46] Pace (2003), p. 5.

the same time, still, the same author stresses how, aside from its five core elements (written constitution, constituent power, enshrinement of rights, separation of power and judicial constitutional review of laws), modern constitutionalism 'always keeps seeking to draw out the *limitations of power* in order to avoid its arbitrariness, whichever the issue under discussion'. This is its essential trait.

At the same time, still, constitutionalism should not be regarded in a mere negative sense, as a form of 'resistance', in the words of Maurizio Fioravanti, but also in a positive sense, as a '*participatory movement*' that claims to contribute to the formation of the structured political will, tasked with *defending* the distinct spaces of autonomy of the individuals that make up the whole, but also in *representing* their stances, while pursuing the common interest and building political unity.[47]

The other side of the coin is, then, following long-standing doctrinal consensus, the *guarantee of fundamental rights*. Together with the separation of powers, it is enshrined as the cornerstone of any constitution since the French *Déclaration des droits de l'homme et du citoyen*, from 1789, and its Article 16.

The main test of our time is ensuring such a fundamental rights' guarantee *in spite* of the transforming sovereign power, as declined in the complex fringes of the new millennium. As stated by Vittorio Angiolini, there is 'the *need* for a rethinking of the proposals advanced with regard to fundamental rights, by which people's identity and cultural choices, their interests and values, both collective and individual, should remain subject to the conditioning of force or sovereign power, which is also, or can be, a constant threat to the manifestation of differences with equal opportunities'.[48]

It stands as an ontological basis of this research that such a feature of constitutionalism cannot remain indifferent in the contemporary, primarily social, context, where the traditional concept of sovereignty—and, thus, power—has been revolutionised.[49] Quite the opposite, it is enhanced by the transformations of the modern world, as new—individual and societal—challenges continuously appear on the horizon, requiring a statutory, institutional and procedural re-thinking of our systems for delivering justice, if not of society (or Society)[50] itself.[51]

[47] See Fioravanti (2009), especially pp. 70 *et seq.*

[48] Translated from Italian, Angiolini (2016), back cover; see also Id., especially footnote No. 2, at pp. 41 *et seq.* See also Tosato (1957) and Berti (2007), pp. 1080 *et seq.*

[49] See, e.g., Morrone (2018).

[50] von Bogdandy (2023), p. 217.

[51] See, e.g., Olivetti (1952) and Olivetti (1945).

3.2.2 … to New Challenges

Taking a step back—for the moment—it is worth considering that the changes, and challenges, within the contemporary society are carried by the streams of scientific, digital and technological innovation, as well as by significant socio-political shakings.[52] Evidently, they are not the result of an abrupt shift, but, rather, of decades-long dynamics involving the core of democratic institutions, economic and financial markets with their players, and the general system of international relationships, with relevant effects both on a macro and micro-scale. In short, as previously argued, of globalisation and technological innovation.[53]

As sustained, these phenomena radically alter the multi-level constitutional framework,[54] requiring the scouting of new routes for ensuring fundamental rights' enforcement.

Globalisation is a term often overused, also by the media, to easily encompass under a general label the way of living of the third millennium. This carries the risk of oversimplification, by emptying the concept of its true meaning.[55] As explained *supra*,[56] under a broad, critical and in-depth examination, it represents the (extremely) complex motor of a series of very specific processes that range through different fields of science. As noted by Ian Clark, these transformations 'need[s] also to be understood as a number of changes *within* the state, and not simply as a range of external forces set *against* it'.[57] They touch deeply the economy, international relations, communications, transportation, military operations, work distribution, the environment and the law. These processes are often interconnected, present common features and underlying trends that have concrete repercussions on people's everyday life.[58]

[52] See *supra*, previous Chap. 2.

[53] Id. See also Cassese (2009) and Zolo (2010).

[54] Among the firsts to employ this term, see Pernice (1999). Cassese (2009), instead, does not agree with the definition of 'multi-level system': 'The global legal order does not, therefore, overlap with the state as another layer. These are not two layers, because inequalities and fragmentation are strong, because states are not the only subjects, they mix with other subjects and lose their unity, because no 'level of government' manages to maintain a monopoly of relations with its constituent parts'.

[55] Zolo (2010).

[56] See *supra*, Chap. 2.

[57] Clark (1997), p. 52 (emphasis added).

[58] Naturally, attributing to globalisation every political matter of any relevance, shared or echoing in different parts of the world, would be blatant naiveté. It could be simplistic, for instance, to state that climate change is caused by globalisation. In particular, issues regarding the enforcement of fundamental rights are the consequence of various phenomena: i.e., *inter alia*, from private infringements to the limited amount of state budgets, or, primarily, the executive and legislative powers' inability to properly regulate pressing or complex issues. Returning to the same example, climate change is caused by a multiplicity of concurring factors: *inter alia*, greenhouse gas emissions from private citizens and companies, as well as the absence of the political vision, unity and economic resources necessary to draft an appropriate plan of action. Still, at closer look, globalisa-

As already explained, the analysis of the globalised society's features is not the focus of the present research. Nonetheless, it is a necessary steppingstone, that contributes to justify and to explain it. The process of globalisation, together with technological innovation, has substantial consequences on the limitation (as well as on the individuation) of powers and on the respect of fundamental rights, the two cornerstones, among the above-depicted ones, of constitutionalism. It is, in sum, as stressed by Gustavo Zagrebelsky, an issue which, given its possible 'tragic effects', cannot be ignored by constitutionalism, 'if its minimum essential core and its *raison d'être* are—according to John Rawls' synthesis—the protection of everyone's right to equal respect'.[59]

From a legal perspective, the globalised dimension erodes the three conventional pillars of *statehood*: territory, citizens and authority.[60] As observed by Maria Rosa Ferrarese,[61] the disruption of traditional state barriers, loss of territoriality, mixture of national identities and the emergence of new centres of power—often transnational, private and barely responsible—are a few of its most evident effects.

Collectivisation, massification, standardisation of relationships,[62] on the one hand, and the decline of the traditional systems of democratic representation, on the other hand, substantially enhance these issues. As maintained, the notion of constitution in a material sense[63]—elaborated by Italian academic scholarship and strictly connected in a finalistic way, through the key role of political parties, to that in a formal sense—is now weakened and may not be fully compensated by that of

tion (in the above-depicted broad sense) is, by all means, the differentiating element between the contemporary age and the previous ones. It is the turning point of a series of economic, scientific and sociological propulsions that have revolutionised the way of living. Again, under the case of climate change, one could argue that all its concurring factors stem from this complex process of growing connection and interdependence between the world's economies, cultures and population, often labelled as 'globalisation'. Greenhouse gas emissions could, therefore, be understood as—at least—exacerbated by the constant travelling of people and goods, by the population growth, by mass production and consumption, with a consequent radical exploitation of natural resources and an increase in industrial pollution in order to meet market demands. With an extensive reading, then, the origins of climate change could indeed be traced back to such phenomenon, at least partially and under a socio-logical and casual mathematical model. See, e.g., Shahbaz et al. (2018), p. 141: 'The empirical results reveal that globalisation increases carbon emissions, and thus, the globalisation-driven carbon emission hypothesis is valid. This empirical analysis suggests insightful policy guidelines for policy makers using 'globalisation' as an economic tool for better long-run environmental policy'.

[59] Zagrebelsky (2013), p. 19.

[60] See von Bogdandy (2022), *supra*.

[61] Ferrarese (2018), pp. 5 *et seq*., stressing how the global power structure, and its distribution, has radically evolved, mainly in two directions: towards international organisations, on the one hand, and in favour of new private economic authorities, on the other hand.

[62] See, once again, Cappelletti (1976), p. 643.

[63] See, e.g., Mortati (1998) and Mortati (1971), p. 75, a notion elaborated, as is known, with special regard to the role of political parties in the mass society. See also Ridola (2023).

constitution as a living instrument, advanced by supranational multi-level courts, but also questioned (in its efficacy) by a not irrelevant number of commentators.[64]

In particular, as subsequently argued, the inability of traditional *intermediate*—namely political, but also trade unions—*bodies* to adapt, represent and communicate with the different fringes of society creates a growing disconnection (and dissatisfaction) between the rulers and the ruled.[65] The increasing inequalities between the large parts of the population and the financial-ruling elite is testing the capacity of the democratic process throughout the world and, in general, the communities' essence.[66]

Inevitably, all these elements put into question the very concept of *sovereignty* and the ability of state authorities to *effectively* grant fundamental rights, as declined in modern constitutions. In particular, two elements of transformation demand special emphasis, on which we shall return in several sections of the following.

The increasingly *collective*—or supra-individual—nature of fundamental rights' violations in the contemporary society must be preliminarily stressed. The way in which the society and economy are structured tends to create *standardised* relationships, usually between large numbers of individuals and a much more powerful opponent (public entities or private companies, often transnational). These situations can be either contractual (i.e., work, consumer, service-related) or extra-contractual (i.e. mass harms). They can relate to both traditional civil and political rights (i.e., the basic right to life, to private life, to freedom of speech), but also to more programmatic rights (i.e. the right to social welfare or that to health care). They can also encompass individual subjective positions, as well as even diffuse interests, for instance in relation to climate change. They are characterised by an *unbalanced power-relationship* between the common opponent and each individual, and a similar, or homogeneous,[67] subjective position between all the individuals concerned.

An essential matter for consideration, as mentioned, is the emergence of *new rights* and substantive positions, some of which are not even individual.[68] The technological, digital and, in general, scientific developments have contributed to new situations, in which new claims and duties can be presented, and new types of violations and omissions can occur, at times not even predicted, or predictable, by the drafters of the various constitutional catalogues. Other relevant examples touch, among others, the fields of biotechnologies, neuro-rights or artificial intelligence; they have revolutionised, or are promising to revolutionise, intimately and radically the way of living of the third millennium, putting into question the very essence of being human and what, until not so long ago, were conceived as insurmountable

[64] As argued by Lancaster (2018).

[65] Already in 1992, Elia (1992), pp. 552–553, arguing for an increased pluralism through 'social formations', *à la de Toqueville* (see *infra*, Chap. 4).

[66] See Tönnies (2011), p. 61.

[67] See, *infra*, Chap. 4.

[68] See, e.g., Bobbio (2014).

barriers to that essence.[69] As anticipated, they promise outstanding advancements, from the point of view of better, faster care; still, in such a quest, they risk impinging the roots of self-determination and human dignity, as well as enhancing already expanding inequalities.

The two trends do not run separate rails.[70] Sometimes they interact, generating situations encompassable under both. This is, for instance, the case once again of climate change: a new situation, until a few decades ago unpredicted (to this degree, at least), which unites all humankind. At the same time, the two tracks (*standardisation* of the infringements, on the one hand, and emergence of new subjective, *meta-individual*, positions, on the other hand) share a common ground: that of a simmering multi-faceted and *transforming sovereign power*, where private, economically-driven, forces feast in the tension and discretionary gaps left by national and supranational courts and legislators.

Against such a backdrop, a last bulwark for single individuals, to even *claim* their interests, appears that bearing the *judicial* pennant.[71] A similar *ultima facie* resort, however, is not devoid of questionable and perilous scenarios, all involving a blurring of the separations of powers principle, concerns on fair trial guarantees (*in primis*, independence and impartiality), and executability of judgements.

3.3 A Multidimensional, Multifaceted and Multilevel Constitutional Framework

It has already been discussed how globalisation and technological innovation affect *time*, in the sense that they speed up numerous processes and activities, through technological advancement (industrial and digital) and a much wider network to tap into, e.g. for resources, workforce, markets or information. Transportation,

---

[69] E.g., see, *supra*, Chap. 2, Neuralink.

[70] For further elaboration on both trends, under a more nuanced and specific Italian constitutional perspective, see *infra*, the next Chap. 4.

[71] See, e.g., Bognetti (1998), pp. 118–119, emphasising 'the contribution that the judge must bring by his work, within the limits allowed by the techniques of interpretation, to the development of the law. This in itself directs the judge's attention to the problems of weighing values and interests, and thus to the identification of the "general interests" that must preside over the development of law, through knowledge and evaluation of the "particular interests" that underlie and are at stake. Under different names, in different ways, the jurisprudence of all the legal systems of our time has ended up by becoming to some extent "sociological". Judges are invited—and have adhered to the invitation—to take into account the large group interests on which their sentences fall, with regulatory effects'. He then foresightedly underscores, how 'Procedural law has made more room for interventions in court, in defence of group interests, by their exponential organisations' and how 'the recognition variously expressed in western countries to the procedural protection of "diffuse interests" and the expansion given in certain jurisdictions to "*class actions*" remain facts of no little significance', stressing a new structuring of the articulations of the state-apparatus and a new set of principles for their action (emphasis added, translated from Italian).

communication, production and distribution are highly favoured. From a constitutional standpoint, this creates two different types of consequences.

In the present, it makes it harder for public authorities to *keep up* with the fast-paced developments and practices. A clear example is brought nowadays by AI, with legislators from all levels—national, supranational and international—unable to effectively regulate, if not anticipate, all the potential risks. The scientific complexity of most developments makes it even harder for *policy-makers* to address them in a timely and exhaustive manner. As further addressed, this difficulty is shared by the *judiciary*, which often—and understandably—lacks the *technical expertise* to appreciate new technological advancements.[72] Hence, the necessity to seek a *synergy with scientific advisors*. Their role, however, would need to be framed under the impartiality and independence requirements set for the judiciary, too. Mechanisms for selecting and keeping them accountable would also be advisable.

For the future, it must be noted how numerous effects of globalisation's processes are *not immediately* visible, but may appear even after years. Climate change is a visible example of this, with consequences of polluting conducts starting to be perceived, according to research, only after five to ten years. Some authors have, consequently, tried to theorise the concept of '*intra-generational rights*'—in this case of future generations—, to be respected by current ones, too.

As suggested by Gustavo Zagrebelsky,[73] however, this is an improper expression: a subjective right implies an already living (or, at minimum, conceived) person, with the ability to bring legal action to defend their position. The protection of future—not living, not conceived, merely abstractly considered—generations is, therefore, conceptually incompatible with this legal category. Rather, as pointed out by the same scholar, the category of 'duties'—to be considered autonomously and not just as the other side of the rights' coin—appears more suited.[74]

The German Federal Constitutional Court in 2021 embraced this interpretation in relation to national climate change legislation:

> The fundamental right to the protection of life and health enshrined [...] obliges the state to afford protection against the risks of climate change. [...] The state's duty of protection [...] does not take effect only after violations have already occurred. It is also oriented towards the future [...]. The duty to afford protection against risks to life and health can also establish a *duty to protect future generations* [...]. This is all the more applicable where irreversible processes are at stake. However, this duty to afford intergenerational protection has a solely objective dimension because future generations – either as a whole or as the sum of individuals not yet born – do not yet carry any fundamental rights in the present.[75]

Similar attention to 'intergenerational burden sharing' has been recently stressed by the ECtHR, too, in the case *Verein Klimaseniorinnen and Others v. Switzerland,* in

[72] See, in particular, *infra*, Part III, with the case studies, and the subsequent conclusive reflections from Chap. 11.

[73] Zagrebelsky (2013), p. 19.

[74] Id.

[75] German Constitutional Court, Order from 24 March 2021, 1 BvR 2656/18, §§ 144–146.

which it declared a violation of Articles 6 and 8 of the Convention in relation to Switzerland's climate change policy:[76]

> In this connection, the Court notes that, in the specific context of climate change, intergenerational burden-sharing assumes particular importance both in regard to the different generations of those currently living and in regard to future generations. While the legal obligations arising for States under the Convention extend to those individuals currently alive who, at a given time, fall within the jurisdiction of a given Contracting Party, it is clear that future generations are likely to bear an increasingly severe burden of the consequences of present failures and omissions to combat climate change (see paragraph 119 above) and that, at the same time, they have no possibility of participating in the relevant current decision-making processes. By their commitment to the UNFCCC, the States Parties have undertaken the *obligation* to protect the climate system for the benefit of *present and future generations* of humankind (see paragraph 133 above; Article 3 of the UNFCCC). This obligation must be viewed in the light of the already existing harmful impacts of climate change, as well as the urgency of the situation and the risk of irreversible harm posed by climate change. In the present context, having regard to the prospect of aggravating consequences arising for future generations, the *intergenerational perspective* underscores the risk inherent in the relevant political decision-making processes, namely that short-term interests and concerns may come to prevail over, and at the expense of, pressing needs for sustainable policy-making, rendering that risk particularly serious and adding justification for the possibility of judicial review.[77]

Globalisation affects *space*, too. Distances are shortened, and the whole world is now fairly rapidly reachable. People, goods and news travel around constantly in a deeply interconnected net. An establishment of personal and, mainly, business relationships outside national borders is favoured. Traditional *national borders*, as a consequence, tend to fade, leaving room for both international and transnational contamination, pushed by centrifugal forces. This process has implications also from the point of view of the *players*' dimension, as new actors appear on the global scene. At the same time, as subsequently developed, emerging nationalist centripetal forces push back, as a consequence and refuge from the globalised dimension.

The international push is conveyed by the process of integration within the European Union, started with the European Coal and Steel Community in 1951, as well as by the progressive consolidation of *international organisations*, such as the Council of Europe or the United Nations.

The key aspect of internationalisation is that national States voluntarily limit and give up portions of their sovereignty in order to be part of these international organisations (new *players*), operating on a larger, border-less scale. Extremely positive results have been achieved in terms of cooperation and integration. Nonetheless, from a constitutional standpoint, critical aspects must be highlighted, too.

One issue with international organisations, as highlighted by Maria Rosa Ferrarese, is that they tend to cause *fragmentation* and *decentralisation* of *power*.[78]

---

[76] ECtHR, *Verein KlimaSeniorinnen Schweiz and Others v. Switzerland* [GC], No. 53600/20, 2024. See also ECtHR, *Duarte Agostinho and Others v. Portugal and 32 Others* (dec.) [GC], No. 39371/20, 2024.

[77] Id., § 420.

[78] Ferrarese (2019), pp. 17 *et seq.*

The multiplication of provisions, courts and mechanisms of enforcement, on the one side, enhances the overall level of protection, but, on the other side, also causes confusion, differences and potential coordination problems. As further observed by Massimo Luciani, the 'dilution of decision-making centres and procedures prevents a precise allocation of *responsibilities*'.[79] This is especially relevant considering the lack of *direct* democratic legitimacy presented by most international organisations (and courts).[80] It also 'allows for an infinite referral of political responsibility: if all levels are equally responsible, then no one is, per se, responsible'.[81]

Another challenging element worth stressing with regard to the decision-making process of international organisations is the large majorities often required for significant action, or in certain cases—such as the United Nations and its Security Council—even veto rights granted to specific States. These mechanisms, albeit designed to reach uniform and shared decisions, have in different stances stalled votes on critical matters. The overall institutional public power, fragmented and at times even paralysed, is thus decreased.[82]

The decentration tendencies operate on a transnational and private level, too, which emphasises once again the *players'* dimension, but also the *economic/financial* one. New centres of private power have emerged in the global landscape, now dominated by the economic interests of large corporations which operate across different jurisdictions, if not the whole world. Symptomatically, in the words of Giovanni Pitruzzella, 'the State must, therefore, be given a '*double trust*': the loyalty of its citizens and the trust of the financial markets'.[83] Naturally, this second type of 'trust' is not formalised in the constitutional process,[84] but it is still extremely relevant in practice and can, at times, contribute to significant political choices from the public authorities.

As noted by Luca Antonini, the traditional principle of responsibility of governments towards their voters is certainly affected, as a *new responsibility* towards the markets is introduced.[85] Rather ironically, it was the States themselves that caused this overturn of roles, by pushing for a liberal and *transnational market* immediately after the Second World War. The sensation, according to several authors, however, is that nowadays States cannot retrieve back the sovereignty left in favour of the

[79] See Luciani (2023), p. 179 (translated from Italian).

[80] On the delicate issue of judicial review—specifically in relation to the Italian Constitutional Court—and democratic legitimacy, instead, see, e.g., Crisafulli (1978), p. 73, Elia (1982), p. 515, Rodotà (1982), p. 489, Mezzanotte (1984), Zagrebelsky (1988), p. 158, Cappelletti (1994), p. 157, Cheli (1996), Fioravanti (1999), Mezzetti (2007, 2010) and Morrone (2019); more generally, see Angiolini (2012), pp. 202–205.

[81] Id. See also von Bogdandy and Venzke (2012), p. 20: 'A functionally fragmented international judiciary threatens to weaken democratic generality in the further development of the legal order'.

[82] Ferrarese (2019), *supra*.

[83] Pitruzzella (2013), p. 4, translated from Italian.

[84] Antonini (2019), p. 319.

[85] Id.

newly formed *private, economic and financial, authorities*.[86] Two trends must be highlighted to this regard.

On the one hand, authors such as Gunther Teubner have argued 'the emergence of a multiplicity of civil constitutions beyond the nation state. [...] Increasingly, global private regimes are creating their *own substantive law*. They make use of their own sources of law, which lie outside the spheres of national law-making and international treaties'.[87] The fast-paced economy and scientific advancements bring a pressing demand for regulation, which cannot be timely and properly satisfied by states and international organisations. The adopted solution is, hence, *self-regulation*, with prominent examples being the so-called *lex mercatoria* for international commercial practices and *lex digitalis* for the internet.[88] Other blatant cases include those of rating agencies, private actors which, quite paradoxically, rate even public states now.[89]

A recent trend in *investment arbitration*, instead, regards compensation due by states to fossil fuel companies in light of multilateral trade agreements: due to specific clauses, increasingly often states' decisions to withdraw from such agreements in relation to the climate change emergency have obliged to pay hundreds of millions to the private oil and gas companies. In 2022, for instance, Italy was ordered to pay more than 190 million euros, plus interests, to Rockhopper Explorations in the context of the Energy Charter Treaty. Rather interestingly, this sum is considerably higher than Rockhopper's initial investment of merely 29 million euros.[90] It is also worth noting that such a decision, binding a *public* national authority towards a *private* transnational corporation, was handed out in the form of an *arbitral award* by an arbitral tribunal. The economic and relational dimensions of globalisation put into the spotlight *new players*, who are given extremely relevant *power*, capable of binding even state authorities and completely overturning the traditional power *balances*. These circumstances fundamentally question the traditional *public v. private* paradigm.[91]

On the other hand, the issue of *responsibility* must be raised once again. The transnational nature of most large corporations brings them to operate under several jurisdictions, with different regulations. They are, thus, induced to set their seat under the most favourable one, in order to escape stricter control or fiscal responsibility, in a defendant-oriented *forum-shopping*.[92] Unregulated legislative competition between states, even inside the EU, for instance for fiscal matters, drives private corporations towards venues with slacker rules and, in general, *reduces* the minimum standard of protection for the collectivity. It is not a coincidence, for example,

[86] See Pinelli (2016).

[87] Gunther (2010), p. 327.

[88] Id.

[89] See Pinelli (2016).

[90] See Sole 24 Ore, 24 August 2022.

[91] On the conflicts between arbitral tribunals' and state courts' *potestas iudicandi*, see Henke (2022).

[92] See Bell (2003).

that all the major global digital firms—such as Google, Meta, Apple, LinkedIn—have set their headquarters in Ireland, where the corporate tax rate is set at 12,5% and *regulation* is highly corporate-friendly.

A similar trend is predictable for *passive litigation strategies*, with both potential defendants and claimants aiming at conducting proceedings in and basing their substantive merits on provisions from favourable jurisdictions. This is illustratively conveyed by Shell's decision to move its headquarters to London from The Hague after a major blow in the 2021 Dutch injunctive class action brought by Milieudefensie.[93] Unharmonised substantive and procedural frameworks are fertile soil for such *forum-shopping* incentives within the EU.[94]

The fiscal forum-shopping phenomenon has significant consequences on the general population, as conveyed by the above-mentioned Saskia Sassen's research:[95] a lower tax revenue, in fact, substantially decreases the *state budget* for social welfare and increases the *inequality gap* between powerful transnational corporations and single individuals who, deliberately or not, are put in contact with their products, services or activities, thus being subject to possible violations to their rights. The *relational* dimension of globalisation—in the form of an extremely intricated net of casual connections, where one action from a major player can substantially and simultaneously affect the positions of several thousands, or even hundreds of thousands, of unprotected people throughout the whole word—becomes relevant once again. The *economic* dimension, true motor driving and ruling the unregulated wilderness of global exchange practices, transpires, too.

At the same time, it must be noted how these large transnational players often operate through a complex *global value chain*, with branches and sub-branches all over the world (*relational* dimension). The question of which subject should be responsible for violations at the bottom of the supply chain has been raised now in a vast number of circumstances. Major scandals were that of the Nike sweatshops in 1991 in Indonesia—where children were found out to be employed as workers in extreme conditions by Nike's suppliers[96]—or the still-ongoing cocoa one in Africa, where global chocolate firms, such as Nestlé, Mars or Hershey constantly buy cocoa harvested by children.[97] A lack of effectiveness is commonly perceived in holding transnational corporations to account for their suppliers' misconducts in a far-away (host) country due to another (home) country's legislation.[98] This has paved the way to transnational exploitation and modern slavery, especially in the labour market

[93] See BBC News, 15 November 2021.

[94] For a concrete example, and major risk, in relation to class actions in Italy, see, *infra*, the *Binance* case, analysed in Chap. 10.

[95] See, *supra*, Chap. 2.

[96] See The Guardian, 20 May 2001.

[97] See The Washington Post, 5 June 2019.

[98] Nolan and Bott (2018), p. 44.

(*e.g.*, the garment industry),[99] with new forms of hardly-liftable corporate veils. This circumstance will be further developed in the next paragraph, too.

Before doing so, another final constitutional challenge brought by the *economic* dimension of globalisation should be considered: the *cost of rights* in general and of social ones, in particular.[100] In a massified society with growing inequalities, with a stark increase in the world population, but, at the same time, also a decrease in natality (at least in Europe), it is becoming alarmingly more complex for public authorities to grant everyone an *effective* enjoyment of all the rights enshrined in the constitutions, especially *programmatic* ones, but also basic *civil liberties*. Examples can vary from the inhuman conditions of numerous detention or immigrant centres to the lack of health treatments, of proper education, of freedom of speech platforms or of social housing support, but also of adequate pension systems and a control over decent working conditions.

Naturally, also *political choices* brought by the governing *majorities* can be a cause. *Minorities* could even be *economically discriminated*, beyond their sex, ethnicity or orientations, but rather simply because of a less-favoured social background.

The ability of both national political parties and election systems to effectively filter and represent the interests of all the collectivity in the new global asset of powers and necessities should therefore be questioned (*relational* dimension). The gap between the powerful, decision-making elite of transnational economically-driven corporations and the rest of the population seems indeed to be widening everyday.

The emerging populist reaction towards which a growing part of the population is turning in several countries conveys the general discontent. Such a tension towards nationalist stances, paradoxically, moves *centripetal forces*.

At the same time, Constitutional Courts, such as the Italian one, have affirmed the notion of '*constitutionally necessary expenses*'[101] in order to ensure the effectivity of a *minimum level* of respect of core fundamental rights, such as that to health or to legal defence. Inevitably, as will be further addressed, a delicate balance between the *legislator*'s discretional authority and its *inertia* needs to be struck, while considering the *judiciary*'s role and the principle of the *separation of powers* in a power dynamic increasingly stretched by *centrifugal forces*.[102]

[99] See, e.g., Cummings (2021), and, specifically, therein Chapter 2—'Garment Workers: Fighting to End Sweatshops'.

[100] See, e.g., Holmes and Sunstein (1999), Wouters et al. (2020), Bin (2018), Luciani (2016), Morrone (2013).

[101] See, e.g., Italian Constitutional Court, Judgements No. 169 from 2017, No. 10 from 2022, No. 161 from 2022.

[102] See, e.g., von Bogdandy and Venzke (2012), Kavanagh (2023), Zanon (2021), p. 3, and Luciani (2023), *supra*.

3.4 Sovereignty and Its Discontents

In his seminal 'Civilization and its Discontents', from 1930, Sigmund Freud theorised civilisation as a phenomenon simultaneously in conflict and necessary for man's happiness.[103] Civilisation ensures comfort, cultural advancement and protection from an otherwise too chaotic world; still, this very set of stabilising social relationships is one of the main sources of distress and suffering for single individuals. In sum, according to the father of psychoanalysis, to be happy one must renounce their full freedom; in doing so, however, one loses the possibility of being fully happy.

Interestingly, following Freud, the first step of civilisation is the regulation of *social relationships*. From a raw world, decided by brute force and the rule of the strongest, 'the substitution of the *power* of a united number for the power of a single man'[104] becomes the turning point of civilised life.[105]

These considerations to several degrees recall the 'social contract' idea first developed by Hobbes, Locke and Rousseau.[106] Their relevance for the current analysis stands in the aggregation of individuals within *communities*, where they limit their freedom and happiness under the rule of law. Everyone relinquishes a portion of their absolute individual self-determination and 'natural' advantage for the collective justice and well-being, here included the security of their own.

All these psychoanalytical and, most importantly, political theories, nonetheless, stem from an *anachronistic* societal vision. They are based on the idea of a single, well-*structured* State (the 'community'), holding all the *power*. The contemporary world's multidimensional, multifaceted and multilevel *a-structured* nature, intertwined and constantly shifting, as demonstrated, is quite the opposite. The sovereign community, conceived by John Locke as an impartial and responsible (towards its members), *super partes*, 'commonwealth' no longer exists. Against the current backdrop, the law—either national, supranational or international—often fails to catch '*predatory individual*[s]' towards the collectivity. This occurs in reason of the fast-paced rhythm at which possible predatory (harmful) conducts are even created

---

[103] See Freud (1961).

[104] Id.

[105] Id., pp. 59–60: 'Human life in communities only becomes possible when a number of men unite together in strength superior to any single individual and remain united against all single individuals. The strength of this united body is then opposed as 'Right' against the strength of any individual, which is condemned as 'brute force'. [...] The essence of it lies in the circumstance that the members of the community have restricted their possibilities of gratification, whereas the individual recognized no such restrictions. The first requisite of culture, therefore, is justice – that is, the assurance that a law once made will not be broken in favour of any individual. [...] This implies nothing about the ethical value of any such law. The further course of cultural development seems to tend towards ensuring that the law shall no longer represent the will of any small body – caste, tribe, section of the population – which may behave like a predatory individual towards other such groups perhaps containing large numbers. The end-result would be a state of law which all – that is, all who are capable of uniting – have contributed by making some sacrifice of their own desires, and which leaves none – again with the same exception – at the mercy of brute force'.

[106] Rousseau (1795).

by technological innovation, as well as their complexity, which makes it harder to adequately regulate. It also accrues from the very nature of sovereign power: no longer 'public', rigid, solid, under a Westphalian conception of the state, but often 'private', transnational, flexible, fluid and highly elusive.[107]

The crisis of the traditional monistic State poses two fundamental sets of problems.

From a *structural* point of view, it resonates with the stark decline of the traditional means of *representation*. In particular, their deficiencies in the political arena have long been identified as one of the factors of the traditional states' failure to provide substantial democracy.[108] Political parties and labour unions, for instance, are characterised by a general loss of trust from their members and an inability to effectively represent their needs. It is the crisis of the '*intermediate bodies*', discussed *infra.*[109] It must be stressed again that constitutionalism does not have a mere 'defensive' approach, but, rather, it is to be conceived as a movement aiming at concrete participation and representation of the single individuals' interests.[110] The pluralist principle under Article 2 of the Italian Constitution has exactly this aim.[111]

These crucial failures are consequently transposed to institutional representatives from the legislative (the Parliament) and executive power (the Government). The abovementioned shifting, fragmented and decentred constitutional framework restricts the room for freedom of decision and space of (effective) action of such institutional bodies.[112] At the same time, the classic Montesquieuian division of powers into three separate branches appears superseded today, with an ever more frequent tendency from the executive power to displace the legislative one, becoming *in concreto* the main, if not the only, decision maker.[113]

Visible consequences of these critical tensions are insurgent nationalist trends and populist movements, often seen as an escape alternative from the 'fake' self-oriented political elites. At the same time, such gaps in representativeness also favour—when possible, in their limited freedom for action—the exacerbation of *inequalities* and abuse, often through passive conducts, from the political under-represented majorities. The positions of *minorities* and less-advantaged fringes of the population, as a consequence, are increasingly hampered, especially in relation to social and, in general, to rights that require *budget allocation.*[114]

---

[107] Horwitz (1982), p. 1423; Hartmann and Kjaer (2018), p. 3.

[108] See Höffe (2007).

[109] See *infra*, next paragraph and Chap. 4.

[110] Fioravanti (2009), *supra*.

[111] See *infra*, Chap. 4. See also the beautiful pages written by Fioravanti (2017), according to whom this Article 'contains the entire Constitution in a condensed form' (p. 1).

[112] Morrone (2021), p. 192. See also Calamandrei (1954), pp. 645–650, cited more extensively in Chap. 4.

[113] Id.

[114] See, e.g., Italian Constitutional Court, Judgements Nos. 10 and 275 from 2016 and Nos. 62 and 152 from 2020, clarifying that 'It is the guarantee of incompressible rights that affects the budget, and not the balancing of the budget that conditions its due distribution' (Italian Constitutional

A different haven, especially against the latter abuse, is sought in the *judicial system*. A growing trend is that of picturing it as a last resort against the other two (or simply one, now) institutional powers' inertia or mistreatments. An essential difference from these (or this) latter power(s), as underscored by Piero Calamandrei, in relation to the Italian Constitutional Court, is that they are free to act 'under the impetus of political opportunity alone'.[115] The judicial power, on the contrary, must act, 'as commanded by the Constitution'. In the case of the Constitutional Court, Calamandrei went so far as to ascribe to it the *necessary* 'power to legislate'.[116]

Such a lack of freedom, as recently advanced by Andrea Morrone, derives from two paradigms: on the one hand, the subordination of the judge to the law and, on the other hand, the prohibition of *non liquet*, even in absence of law. Precisely the absence of a stable constitutional framework of reference, however, increases the intrinsic value of their function. Their expertise, professionalism and purported impartiality and independence may enhance their legitimacy in the eyes of the population. Concurrently, the abovementioned paradigms justify a growing discretion, to the point where the same author, Morrone, argues that in practice 'there is no more actual principle of subordination'.[117]

The latter view could appear, at least to a certain degree, especially if generalised, as categorical. Nonetheless, it conveys a risk and growing critique towards the role of the judge, according to several commentators—and sometimes also courts, when handing over decisions—too discretionary and political.[118] This appears particularly relevant for cases in which, although in the presence of a blatant violation of fundamental rights, even on a large scale, there is a lack of a 'constitutionally necessary filling-criterion'.[119]

Furthermore, *judicial review*, apart from political deviations without an elective and direct legitimacy, presents a series of other problems. Among the most notable, growing questions on *impartiality* and *independence* need to be addressed, but also on the *authority* of certain, especially first degree, fora. Establishing jurisdiction and executing judgements against transnational entities may prove at times hardly feasible. As mentioned above, States may even give up their own jurisdiction in favour of purportedly impartial arbitral tribunals, in business investment engagements with

Court, Judgement 275 from 2016, point No. 11 of the Points of law, translated from Italian). In particular, while recognising the constitutional value of balanced budgets, the Court has repeatedly emphasised that 'the budget allocation choices proposed by the Government and made by Parliament, while having a highly discretionary nature within the limits of balanced budgets, are naturally reduced by the guarantee of constitutionally necessary expenditure, inherent in the provision of incompressible social benefits' (Italian Constitutional Court, Judgement No. 152 from 2020, point No. 6 of the Points of law, translated from Italian).

[115] Cited in Morrone (2021), p. 192.

[116] Id.

[117] Id.

[118] See Fioravanti (2016), pp. 7 *et seq*.

[119] In Italian '*criterio di riempimento costituzionalmente necessario*'. See, e.g., Italian Constitutional Court, Judgement No. 242 from 2019, point No. 4 of the Points of law. See also Italian Constitutional Court, Judgements No. 236 from 2016, Nos. 222 and 233 from 2018 and No. 40 from 2019.

large corporate entities.[120] Moreover, as examined in following, other fair trial guarantees must be ensured: for instance, a timely decision and concrete participation of all the stakeholders concerned with the merits of the trail. This proves to be particularly challenging in the highly interconnected global societal system.

From an *individual* standpoint, an overall, deep discontent emerges. Depression and anxiety are widely registered as the most prevalent psychiatric disorders of the new century, in a consumption-oriented civilisation increasingly perceived as too grand and elusive for single individuals.[121] Dissatisfaction stems from the lack of being part of well-structured and solid communities, counterbalanced by a general loose web of (ir)responsibility of elusive actors, exponentially more powerful than any single individual.

From *citizens*, entitled to rights from the State, there has been a gradual yet fundamental shift to *consumers*, whose vulnerability is exploited by irresponsible markets. New forms of *effective* participation and representation in the global market need to be found. Ways to keep accountable those concretely holding power bound only by economic and financial rules must be put into place, too. On a larger scale, conditionality, as mentioned *supra*, may be one of them, also in relation to the rule of law, as shown recently with Hungary.[122]

Finally, tools to counterbalance the extraordinary *power asymmetries* of the contemporary age are much needed.

3.5 The Fall of 'Intermediate Bodies' in Italy

The key role played by intermediate bodies in Europe, in Italy especially, in the first decades after World War II, while implementing and enforcing constitutional provisions, has long been underscored by academic scholarship.[123] The centrality of the community dimension as the core of political society is, after all, an ancient and well-established idea, since the Greek *πόλεις*, through the Middle Ages, until modern times.[124]

Rather ironically, however, it is precisely with modern statism that the constitutional value of intermediate communities starts being lost. In the Enlightenment-Jacobin conception, the sovereign, strongly centralised nation-State, with its bureaucratic and administrative apparatus, gradually becomes the sole protagonist of public life, aspiring to regulate the various aspects of social life without any mediation. The individual is 'naked', sole before the State, relevant 'mainly as *homo*

[120] See, *supra*, in relation to Rockhopper Explorations and the Energy Charter Treaty.

[121] See, e.g., Bandelow and Michaelis (2015), p. 327.

[122] See, e.g., Commission press release, 13 December 2023.

[123] See, e.g., most notably Tosato (1965), Rescigno (1966), Mortati (1971), Cappelletti (1975), Mortati (1978), Pizzorusso (1979), Tosato (1982), Elia (1992). See also, more recently, Clarich (2016) and, essential, Maritain (1936), on pluralism and its different conceptions.

[124] Rosboh (2017), pp. 11–12.

oeconomicus, interested above all in defending and increasing personal property and wealth, which find protection and guarantees in the new instruments of legislation'.[125]

With the advent of the Italian Republican Constitution, there is a nuanced recovery of the value of intermediate communities, with an express affirmation of protection in Article 2 of the Constitution under the formula of 'social formations' (see *infra*, Chap. 4). However, the new forms of manifestation and conformations of power often render inadequate the responses of traditional intermediate communities, which were established and developed, with fair success, in response to a nation-state constitutional construct. The sighs of globalisation and new technologies have opened up a new constitutional order, constantly expanding, in ferment, which has overturned, and emptied, all previous centres of gravity. How can national political parties maintain their representative function in an increasingly global, meta-state world? How can trade unions continue to advance their demands in the face of elusive, foreign employers, often hidden by multiple corporate veils? How can family, religious and educational associations hold their own in an increasingly liquid, changing world, subject to multiple and constant, all-pervasive stimuli?

Traditional domestic (but also EU) instruments of political representation have proven largely inadequate for decades now, at least in Italy.[126] The 'progressive deterioration of the typical vehicles of representation', and in particular of political parties, 'burdened, in recent years, by rampant corruption', has caused their failure to perform their 'fundamental function as an interlocutor (a sort of "transmission belt") between representatives and the represented'.[127] In other words, voters no longer have, nor feel they have, the capacity to rely on political parties 'as a trait d'union with elected assemblies',[128] once they have cast their vote, being thus prevented from an *effective participation*, through such a mediation, in the determination of their own interests. This has caused well-known challenges in terms of electoral dissatisfaction, trends towards a personalisation of the party system and populist stances, turning to 'the progressive erosion of the democratic method itself'.[129]

A possible (but alone certainly insufficient) response, we argue, is a *renewed form of pluralism*—global, digital, technological—, that same pluralism which has disaggregated the traditional configurations of community-power, and is now charged with mediating with a state-subject that no longer exists or at least is no longer the same, single and principal, interlocutor.[130]

[125] Id. (translated from Italian). See also Ciancio (2016).

[126] See, particularly valuable, Chieffi (2006a) and Zanon and Biondi (2001).

[127] Translated from Italian, Chieffi (2006b), pp. 11 *et seq.*

[128] Id. See also Zanon and Biondi (2001).

[129] Id. See also Tushnet and Bugaric (2020).

[130] See Maritain (1936).

3.6 Concluding Remarks. Regaining Paradigms Lost

As argued in the following, a consideration at the basis of this work is exactly that pluralism needs to enter also the field of judicial enforcement, in order to grant its necessary effectiveness.[131]

For a while the one v. one model of adjudication, typical of civil law jurisdictions, backed by constitutional (domestic and supranational) courts, has partially worked. Today, nevertheless, the inevitable and increasing, as already emphasised, complexity of social life exposes the shortcomings of such a model of (judicial) *responsibility*, just as those of the traditional systems of *representation* and *participation* in the political arena.

The result is an arisen calling for a new form of 'social contract', one that starts from the bottom and sets on a renewed 'pluralism revolution' of rights enforcement. In the intricacies of modernity, to face elusive and transient, invisible, powers, single individuals must learn again to work together. In such a sense, the democratic benefit of *associationism*—in this context, a judicial, or procedural, one—can already be found in Alexis de Tocqueville's reflections from the seminal 'Democracy in America'.[132] In this work, the XIX century's French thinker underscored the centrality of the foreign country's 'spirit of association', as 'the universal and, so to speak, unique means that men can use to attain the various ends that they propose'.[133]

'In democratic countries the science of association', according to de Tocqueville, 'is the mother science; the progress of all the others depends on the progress of that one [...] Among the laws that rule human societies there is one that seems more precise and clearer than all the others. In order that men remain civilized or become so, the art of associating must be developed and perfected among them in the same ratio as equality of conditions increases'. Social articulations, in sum, carry an inestimable value for substantial democracy, since they are able to ensure widespread political and effective *participation* by individuals.[134]

It is this very spirit of associationism, and private entrepreneurialism, that led to the development and success of class action litigation in North America since the 1960s. It is also this exact spirit of associationism, considered as a union of forces for a common good, that must now be reproduced, under new forms, new channels and towards new challenges. Only this way, as held by Robert Dahl, democratic 'polyarchy' can be reached, that is a virtuous state in which 'multiple institutions and people share power'.[135]

---

[131] See, e.g., *infra*, Chap. 11.

[132] de Tocqueville (1999).

[133] Id., p. 114, translated from Italian.

[134] Id., p. 526, translated from Italian.

[135] Dahl (1971), p. 221. See also Angiolini (2016), *supra*, footnote No. 2, at pp. 41 *et seq.*

As already underscored in the 1960s by Egidio Tosato, 'it is precisely freedom of association that implements the principle of social and political pluralism, which, incidentally, calls for the greatest possible freedom of association'.[136]

Building upon these reflections, this work argues for the necessary connection—particularly in light of the transformations already extensively discussed—not only between freedom of association and social and political pluralism but also with *judicial* pluralism, in which the plurality relates to the paths of judicial enforcement. The latter, in fact, constitutes—or can (and should) constitute—a means of limiting power (which is increasingly private and elusive), thereby serving as a counterbalance, if not an actual remedy, to power imbalances and asymmetries (ultimately, to sovereignty itself). This becomes especially relevant given the structural shortcomings of public bodies (both social and political, in line with Tosato's reading of pluralism) that would otherwise be entrusted, in (traditional constitutional) theory, with those functions.

Moreover, this connection must be understood in coordination with the fundamental principle of effectiveness of judicial protection, which, as will be argued in the following sections, requires a concrete and practical approach.

Judicial pluralism—encompassing all the components of the right to a *fair trial* (the other side of access to justice) and, primarily, for the purposes of this discussion, the principles of *equality of arms*, *impartiality* and *publicity* (see *infra*)—entails, in its physiological evolution, two significant advantages. First, it enhances the *legitimacy* of judges, also in a democratic sense, fostering a bottom-up approach that, in line with the principle of *vertical subsidiarity*, can help bridge *sovereignty* (understood, in this context, as the power to decide) and the *people* (to whom it belongs, as per Article 1 of the Italian Constitution). Second, it favours the overcoming of both *legal barriers* (the recognition of new legal positions) and *practical obstacles* (power asymmetries) that would otherwise be insurmountable for the individual alone (see *infra*).

In other words, declined innovatively (in its physiological evolution—the pathological downside being the forfeit of critical fair trial and separation of powers guarantees), this would be a fair state in which there is no '*tyrant power*'—just like there is no 'tyrant right' over others, as famously stated in 2013 by the Italian Constitutional Court—; no tyrant power as in freedom against standardised, repetitive, systemic and structural abuses from both public and private entities; no tyrant power as in a constitutional framework in which fundamental rights are granted not merely on paper but also in practice, both civil and social ones; no tyrant power in which neither practical nor legal obstacles stand in the way of seeking justice when necessary; no tyrant power as in a sort of power that cannot be contrasted, due to unrecoverable inequalities.[137]

---

[136] See Tosato (1957, 1965). The citation, however, is from Tosato (1982), p. 229.

[137] See Chilton and Versteeg (2020), p. 20, quoting Fukuyama (1995): 'Francis Fukuyama described associations and organizations as crucial to the creation of social capital, the 'ability of people to work together for common purposes in groups and organizations'.

It is a state of disruption, in which individuals, *lost*, unnamed and 'unseen',[138] learn again to collaborate together, finding, and, *regaining*, purpose under the pennant of solidarity and true equality.

As analysed in the next Chapter, fundamental constitutional (and supranational) principles, such as that to *solidarity*, to *effective protection* and to *juridical pluralism*, all enshrined under Article 2 of the Italian Constitution,[139] not only legitimise but, rather, call—with *necessary caveats*, to search—for a pursuit of *collective dimensions* of adjudication.

References

Ackerman B (2000) We the People. Volume 2: Transformations. Harvard University Press, Cambridge

Alexy R (2006) Discourse theory and fundamental rights. In: Menéndez A, Eriksen EO (eds) Arguing fundamental rights. Springer, Cham

Angiolini V (2012) Diritti umani. Sette lezioni. Giappichelli, Torino

Angiolini V (2016) Sulla rotta dei diritti: diritti, sovranità, culture. Giappichelli, Torino

Antonini L (2019) Globalizzazione e nuove sfide del costituzionalismo. Diritto pubblico 25(2):319

Bandelow B, Michaelis S (2015) Epidemiology of anxiety disorders in the 21st century. Dialogues Clin Neurosci 17(3):327

Baraggia A (2023) La condizionalità come strumento di governo negli Stati compositi. Una comparazione tra Stati Uniti, Canada e Unione Europea. Giappichelli, Torino

Baraggia A, Bonelli M (2022) Linking money to values: the new rule of law conditionality regulation and its constitutional challenges. German Law J 23(2)

Bell A (2003) Forum shopping and venue in transnational litigation. Oxford University Press, Oxford

Bergson H (1937) Les deux sources de la morale et de la religion. Paris Libraire Felix Alcan, Paris

Berti G (2007) Sovranità. In: Enciclopedia del diritto. Annali, I. Giuffrè, Milano

Bin R (2018) Critica della teoria dei diritti. FrancoAngeli, Milano

Bobbio N (2014) L'età dei diritti. Einaudi, Torino

Bognetti G (1998) Lo stato e i gruppi di interesse negli ordinamenti borghesi. Giuffrè, Milano

Bonini M (2021) Revolution and populism in Italy: the path from constitutional resentment to constitutional renaissance. In: Belov M (ed) Populist constitutionalism and illiberal democracies. Intersentia, Cambridge, pp 253–273

Calamandrei P (1954) Processo e democrazia. In: Cappelletti M (ed) Calamandrei P (1965) Opere giuridiche, I. Morano, Napoli

Cappelletti M (1975) Formazioni sociali e interessi di gruppo davanti alla giustizia civile. Rivista di diritto processuale:361–402

Cappelletti M (1976) Vindicating the public interest through the courts: a comparativist's contribution. Buffalo Law Rev 25(3):643–690

Cappelletti M (1986) Repudiating Montesquieu? The expansion and legitimacy of 'constitutional justice'. Catholic Univ Law Rev 35(1):1

Cappelletti M (1994) Dimensioni della giustizia nelle società contemporanee. Il Mulino, Bologna

Cassese S (2009) Il diritto globale. Giustizia e democrazia oltre lo Stato. Einaudi, Torino

[138] 'Millions of spiritual Creatures walk the Earth / *Unseen*, both when we wake, and when we sleep', Milton (1667), Book IV, lines 677–678.

[139] See Fioravanti (2017), *supra*.

Cassese S (2016) Sugli usi di governance. Parolechiave 2:17

Cheli E (1996) Il giudice delle leggi. Il Mulino, Bologna

Chieffi L (ed) (2006a) Rappresentanza politica, gruppi di pressione, élites al potere. Giappichelli, Torino

Chieffi L (2006b) I paradossi del costituzionalismo contemporaneo e le 'promesse non mantenute' dalle democrazie occidentali. In: Chieffi L (ed) Rappresentanza politica, gruppi di pressione, élites al potere. Giappichelli, Torino, pp 11–46

Chilton A, Versteeg M (2020) How constitutional rights matter. Oxford Scholarship, Oxford, e-book

Chomsky N, Foucault M (2011) Human nature: justice versus power: The Chomsky-Foucault Debate. Souvenir Press Limited

Ciancio A (2016) European parties and the process of political integration in Europe. Dirittifondamentali.it 2

Ciancio A (2021) Le sfide della rappresentanza politica nell'epoca di internet. Brevi note a mo' di introduzione. Federalismi.it 15

Clarich M (2016) Stato, gruppi intermedi e individuo. Diritto pubblico 3:133–150

Clark I (1997) Globalization and fragmentation. Oxford University Press, Oxford

Crisafulli V (1978) La Corte costituzionale tra Magistratura e Parlamento. In: Scritti giuridici in memoria di Piero Calamandrei, IV. Cedam, Padova

Cummings SL (2021) An equal place. Oxford University Press, Oxford

Curle C (2010) International Human Rights and the Intuition of Justice: Bergson v. Kant. ISSRN

Dahl R (1971) Polyarchy: participation and opposition. Yale University Press, New Haven

de Tocqueville A (1999) La Democrazia in America. In: Candeloro G (ed) BUR, Milano (first published in French between 1835 and 1840)

Elia L (1982) La Corte nel quadro dei poteri costituzionali. In: Barile P, Cheli E, Grassi S (eds) Corte costituzionale e sviluppo della forma di governo in Italia. Il Mulino, Bologna, p 489

Elia L (1992) Le norme sulle formazioni sociali nella Costituzione repubblicana. In: Studi in onore di G. Vignocchi. Mucchi, Modena, pp 545–553

Ferrarese MR (2018) Il costituzionalismo puntiforme e l'invisibilità dei poteri globali. Nomos. Le attualità nel diritto 2

Ferrarese MR (2019) Percorsi della sovranità. Aggirandosi tra varie definizioni e sfaccettature. Nomos. Le attualità nel diritto 2

Fioravanti M (1999) Costituzione. Il Mulino, Bologna

Fioravanti M (2009) Costituzionalismo. Percorsi della storia e tendenze attuali. Laterza, Roma

Fioravanti M (2016) Il legislatore e i giudici di fronte alla Corte costituzionale. Quaderni costituzionali. Rivista italiana di diritto costituzionale 1:7–20

Fioravanti M (2017) Costituzione italiana: articolo 2. Carocci Editore, Roma

Freud S (1961) Civilization and its discontents. WW Norton, New York (first published in German in 1930)

Fukuyama F (1995) Trust: the social virtues and the creation of prosperity. Free Press, New York

Galtson WA (2011) Pluralist constitutionalism. Soc Philos Policy 28(1):228–241

Gentile G (2023) Effective judicial protection: enforcement, judicial federalism and the politics of EU law. Eur Law Open 2(1):128

Gunther G (2010) Fragmented foundations societal constitutionalism beyond the nation state. In: Dobner P, Loughlin M (eds) The twilight of constitutionalism? Oxford University Press, Oxford, p 327

Guterres A (2023) Foreword. In: United Nations' Sustainable Development Goals Report 2023: Special Edition

Hartmann E, Kjaer PF (2018) The status of authority in the globalizing economy: beyond the public/private distinction. Indiana J Global Leg 25

Henke A (2022) I conflitti di potestas iudicandi tra arbitro e giudice statale nel diritto italiano e comparato. Giappichelli, Torino

Höffe O (2007) La democrazia nell'era della globalizzazione. Il Mulino, Bologna

Holmes S, Sunstein CR (1999) The cost of rights. Why liberty depends on taxes. WW Norton, New York
Horwitz MJ (1982) History of the public/private distinction. Univ Pa Law Rev 130:1423
Kavanagh A (2023) The collaborative constitution. Cambridge University Press, Cambridge
Kumm M (2013) The cosmopolitan turn in constitutionalism: an integrated conception of public law. Indiana J Global Leg Stud 20(2):605–628
Lancaster F (2018) La stella polare del costituzionalismo. Nomos. Le attualità nel diritto, 1
Lemmens K, Van Drooghenbroeck S (2023) How "systematic" is the European Court of Human Rights' approach to "systemic" violations of the convention? German Law J 24(6)
Luciani M (1996) Costituzionalismo irenico e costituzionalismo polemico. Giurisprudenza costituzionale: 1643
Luciani M (2006) Costituzionalismo irenico e costituzionalismo polemico. Giurisprudenza costituzionale: 1643
Luciani M (2016) Diritti sociali e livelli essenziali delle prestazioni pubbliche nei sessant'anni della corte costituzionale. Rivista AIC 3:1–18
Luciani M (2023) Ogni cosa al suo posto. Giuffrè, Milano
Maritain J (1936) Humanisme integrale. Cerf, Paris
Matteucci N (2008) Costituzionalismo. In: Bobbio N, Matteucci N, Pasquino G (eds) Il Dizionario di Politica. UTET, Torino, p 202
Mazzarese T (2008) Towards a positivist reading of neo-constitutionalism. Jura Gentium 18:345–364
Mezzanotte C (1984) Corte costituzionale e legittimazione politica. Tipografia veneziana, Roma
Mezzetti L (2007) La giustizia costituzionale: storia, modelli, teoria. In: Mezzetti L, Ferioli E, Belletti M, D'Orlando E (eds) La giustizia costituzionale. Cedam, Padova
Mezzetti L (2010) Legittimazione democratica e tecniche interpretative della Corte Costituzionale italiana. Pensamiento Constitucional 14:70–139
Milton J (1667) Paradise lost, London
Morrone A (2013) Pareggio di bilancio e Stato costituzionale. Lavoro e diritto 3:357
Morrone A (2015) Le conseguenze finanziarie della giustizia costituzionale. Quaderni costituzionali 3:575
Morrone A (2018) Sovranità. Rivista AIC 3
Morrone A (2019) Suprematismo giudiziario. Su sconfinamenti e legittimazione politica della Corte costituzionale. Quaderni costituzionali 2:251–290
Morrone A (2021) Suprematismo giudiziario II. Sul pangiuridicismo costituzionale e sul lato politico della Costituzione. Federalismi.it 12:192
Mortati C (1971) La persona, lo Stato e le comunità intermedie. ERI, Torino
Mortati C (1978) Note introduttive ad uno studio sulle garanzie costituzionali dei diritti dei singoli nelle formazioni sociali. In: Studi in onore di Salvatore Pugliatti, III. Giuffrè, Milano
Mortati C (1998) La costituzione in senso materiale. In: Zagrebelsky G (ed) Giuffrè, Milano
Nolan J, Bott G (2018) Global supply chains and human rights: spotlight on forced labour and modern slavery practices. Aust J Hum Rights 24(1):44
Olivetti A (1945) L'ordine politico delle comunità. Nuove edizioni Ivrea, Svizzera
Olivetti A (1952) Società, stato, comunità: per una economia e politica comunitaria. Edizioni di Comunità, Milano
Olivetti M (2020) Diritti fondamentali, 2nd edn. Giappichelli, Torino
Pace A (2003) Le sfide del costituzionalismo del XXI secolo. Diritto pubblico 3:887–906
Palombella G (2006) From human rights to fundamental rights: consequences of a conceptual distinction. European University Institute Law Working Paper 34
Pernice I (1999) Multilevel constitutionalism and the Treaty of Amsterdam: European constitution-making revisited?. Common Mark Law Rev 36(4):703–750
Pinelli C (2016) Oligarchie finanziarie mondiali, democrazie nazionali e la dicotomia pubblico/privato. Qualche riflessione per i giuristi, Costituzionalismo.it 1

Pinelli C (2019) Conditionality and economic constitutionalism in the eurozone. Ital J Public Law 1:22
Pitruzzella G (2013) Crisi economica e decisioni di governo. Relazione al XXVIII convegno annuale dell'AIC. Rivista AIC
Pizzorusso A (1979) Stato, cittadino, formazioni sociali. Zanichelli, Bologna
Pollicino O (2006) Di cosa parliamo quando parliamo di costituzionalismo digitale?. Quaderni costituzionali, Rivista italiana di diritto costituzionale 3:569–594
Rescigno P (1966) Le società intermedie. In: Rescigno P (ed) Persona e comunità. Il Mulino, Bologna
Ridola P (2023) Costantino Mortati, la "Costituzione in senso materiale", la Costituzione repubblicana. Spunti di riflessione. Nomos. Le attualità del diritto 3:1–10
Rodotà S (1982) La Corte, la politica, l'organizzazione sociale. In: Barile P, Cheli E, Grassi S (eds) Corte costituzionale e sviluppo della forma di governo in Italia. Il Mulino, Bologna, p 515
Rosboh M (2017) Le comunità intermedie tra storia e istituzioni. In: Rosboh M (ed) Le comunità intermedie e l'avventura costituzionale. Heritage Club, pp 11–12
Rosenfeld M (1992) Modern constitutionalism as interplay between identity and diversity: an introduction. Cardozo Law Rev 14(3–4):497
Rosenfeld M (2025) Illiberal constitutionalism: viable alternative or nemesis of the modern constitutional ideal? In: Jacobson G, Schor M (eds) Comparative constitutional theory, 2nd edn. Edward Elgar, Cheltenham
Rousseau JJ (1795) Du Contrat social ou principles de droit politique. Paris
Shahbaz M et al (2018) Does globalisation worsen environmental quality in developed economies? Environ Model Assess 23:141
Shakespeare W (1623) As You Like It
Somek A (2020) Cosmopolitan constitutionalism: the case of the European Convention. Global Const 9(3):467–489
Tönnies F (2011) Comunità e società. Laterza, Roma
Tosato E (1957) Sovranità del popolo e sovranità dello Stato. In: Tosato E (ed) (1989) Persona, società intermedie e Stato. Giuffrè, Milano, p 26
Tosato E (1965) Persona e bene comune nello stato contemporaneo. In: Tosato E (ed) (1989) Persona, società intermedie e Stato. Giuffrè, Milano, p 138
Tosato E (1982) I diritti umani. Dottrina e prassi. In: Tosato E (ed) (1989) Persona, società intermedie e Stato. Giuffrè, Milano, p 224
Tuoori K (2015) European constitutionalism. Cambridge University Press, Cambridge
Tushnet M, Bugaric B (2020) Populism and constitutionalism: an essay on definitions and their implications. Harvard Public Law Working Paper 20(17)
von Bogdandy A (2022) Strukturwandel des öffentlichen Rechts. Entstehung und Demokratisierung der europäischen Gesellschaft. Suhrkamp Verlag, Berlin
von Bogdandy A (2023) Comparative public law for European society. MPIL Research Paper 28
von Bogdandy A, Venzke I (2012) In whose name? An investigation of International Courts' public authority and its democratic justification. Eur J Int Law 23(1)
von Bogdandy A, Ferrer Mac-Gregor E, Morales Antoniazzi M, Piovesan F, Soley X (eds) (2017) Transformative constitutionalism in Latin America. The emergence of a new Ius Commune. Oxford University Press, Oxford
Walker N (2001) The EU and the WTO: constitutionalism in a new key. In: de Búrca G, Scott J (eds) The EU and the WTO: legal and constitutional, 32
Wilkinson M (2021) The rise and fall of world constitutionalism. VerfBlog
Wouters J, Lemmens K, Van Poecke T, Bourguignon M (2020) Can we still afford human rights? Critical reflections on universality, proliferation and costs. Edward Elgar Publishing, Cheltenham
Zagrebelsky G (1988) La giustizia costituzionale, 2nd edn. Il Mulino, Bologna
Zagrebelsky G (2013) Constitucionalismo. Derechos y Libertades 29(2):19
Zagrebelsky G, Marcenò V, Pallante F (2023) Lineamenti di diritto costituzionale, 4th edn. Mondadori, Milano

Zanon N (2021) I rapporti tra la Corte costituzionale e il legislatore alla luce di alcune recenti tendenze giurisprudenziali. Federalismi.it 3:86–98

Zanon N, Biondi F (2001) Percorsi e vicende attuali della rappresentanza e della responsabilità politica. Giuffrè, Milano

Zolo D (2010) Il tramonto della democrazia nell'era della globalizzazione. Jura Gentium 28 December 2010

Chapter 4
Constitutional Foundations of (Collective) Access to Justice in Italy and Concepts

4.1 Premise. Linguistic and Conceptual Nuances

To lay a solid foundation for the present research, a thorough examination of the fundamental terminologies hereinafter adopted is imperative.

This preliminary step seeks to create a precise and comprehensive understanding of the key concepts employed in this study, namely 'access to justice' and the collective connotations it takes on to address contemporary constitutional challenges. A brief clarification of expressions such as 'class actions', 'representative actions', 'collective redress', 'collective enforcement', 'injunctive' or 'compensatory' relief, as well as between the different enforceable positions, appears useful, too.

Such an examination, for obvious focus-concerns, is limited to the purposes of the current analysis. Drawing upon established legal scholarship and case law, although brief, it proposes to elucidate the exact perimeter of the investigation.

Furthermore, it looks to serve as a necessary basis for the subsequent in-depth evaluation of the effectiveness and implications of the class action model in judicially enforcing fundamental rights in Italy, as well as in addressing contemporary societal challenges within the transforming and multi-faceted European constitutional landscape.

A. Maglica, *Collective Dimensions of Access to Justice*, European Union and its Neighbours in a Globalized World 23,
https://doi.org/10.1007/978-3-031-94522-9_4

4.2 Sources of Law and Access to Justice in the Multilevel Constitutional Architecture

Access to justice, it is known, is now a widely employed expression which can simultaneously encompass a scientific strand of research, a fundamental right and a social movement.[1]

The *trait d'union* between the three appears to be unmistakably its 'unfinished', or incomplete, nature, as highlighted in the Premise.[2] In other words, it is a *servient concept* which aims at allowing the enforcement of rights, traditionally within a judicial setting. For this reason, despite its ancillarity, it constitutes the basis for the enjoyment of all fundamental rights and one of the most essential cornerstones of any constitutional architecture wearing democratic colours.[3]

Specifically as a fundamental right itself, its *evolving development* through the decades deserves attention, in order both to enrich the number and quality of individuals' guarantees and to adapt them to new challenges.

In particular, its close connection to the principle of *effective* judicial protection emerges, whereby, as it shall be addressed, 'effective' is to be conceived in a 'practical' and concrete manner, under a case by case and goal-oriented approach.[4] In this light, the Italian constitutional lens herein adopted—just like that from other EU domestic jurisdictions—cannot disregard in its analysis the key role played by the ECHR in feeding this concept with an until-then atypical approach, at least for civil law systems.[5]

Such an approach, as is well known, has directly entered and completely permeates the Italian Constitution through Articles 11 and 117, first paragraph, of the Italian Constitution.[6]

Similarly, the guarantees set under EU law integrate the 'European constitutional space'[7] under the principles of loyal cooperation, direct effect and 'primacy of EU

[1] For literature on the matter, see *supra*, Chap. 1.

[2] See *supra*, Chap. 1, fn. 1, Hviid Jacobsen and Poder (2008), p. 70.

[3] See Randazzo (2023), p. 75.

[4] See, for instance, in relation to the right to a fair trial (Article 6 ECHR) and to the right to an effective remedy (Article 13 ECHR), ECtHR, *Scordino v. Italy (no. 1)* [GC], No. 36813/97, 2006, § 192; ECtHR, *Prince Hans-Adam II of Liechtenstein v. Germany* [GC], No. 42527/98, ECHR 2001-VIII, § 45, both clarifying that 'The Convention is intended to guarantee not theoretical or illusory rights, but rights that are practical and effective […] This is particularly true for the guarantees enshrined in Article 6, in view of the prominent place held in a democratic society by the right to a fair trial with all the guarantees under Article 6'. For the ECHR relevance on the national constitutional level, see *infra*, No. 6.

[5] Randazzo (2012), pp. 239–242.

[6] On the relationships between the different levels, and, specifically, the impact of supranational (EU and CoE) sources and case law on the national constitutional order, see, e.g., Bin and Pitruzzella (2024), pp. 341–354; Pitruzzella (2024); Randazzo (2023), pp. 21–74; Adam and Tizzano (2022), pp. 192–214.

[7] See Pitruzzella (2024).

law', which, together with Articles 2, 'Article 4(2) and (3) TEU [...] constitute the lintel on which the community of national courts, held together by converging rights and obligations, rests'.[8]

Together with national constitutional ones—*in primis*, in Italy, the centralised review of constitutionality pursuant to Article 134 of the Italian Constitution—they cooperate 'in the construction of increasingly integrated safeguards'.[9] Such a 'concurrence of remedies' should be intended to 'enrich the means of protection of fundamental rights',[10] as part of a context 'in which both the ordinary courts and [the Constitutional] Court are committed to implementing European Union law in the Italian legal order, each with its own instruments and each within the scope of its respective competences'.[11]

The main challenge, to this regard, evidently is that of navigating possible tensions between apex courts, on the one hand, and for the common judge that of individuating the preferrable sources of law or paths of enforcement,[12] on the other hand. As stressed recently by the Italian Constitutional Court, it falls on the ordinary judge 'to choose the most appropriate remedy, weighing the particularities of the case before him'.[13]

This specifically relates to *legislative acts* violating fundamental rights, enshrined, often simultaneously, under different levels of protection. It does not seem far-fetched, still, to extend such a reasoning also to *other types of violations* characterised by a meta-individual nature: for instance, large-scale infringements of similar subjective positions or conducts against collective or diffuse goods.

In these cases, the same tensions and coordinative urges emerge, placing the ordinary judge in a key yet tangled position of moving among the different levels, as well as via diverging procedural paths of enforcement, but also, and even more, of walking along the evermore blurring line of the separation of powers.[14]

---

[8] Italian Constitutional Court, Judgement No. 67 from 2022, point No. 11 of the Points of law.

[9] Italian Constitutional Court, Judgement No. 1 from 2025, point No. 3.1 of the Points of law; see also Judgment No. 15 from 2024, point No. 7.3.3 of the Points of law; Judgement No. 269 from 2017, point No. 5.2 and 5.3 of the Points of law; Judgement No. 117 from 2019, point No. 2 of the Points of law.

[10] Italian Constitutional Court, Judgment No. 20 from 2019, point No. 2.3 of the Points of law.

[11] Italian Constitutional Court, Judgment No. 149 from 2022, point No. 2.2.2 of the Points of law, cited in the recent Judgment No. 181 from 2024.

[12] E.g. the so-called 'double prejudiciality'. See Randazzo (2023), p. 63.

[13] Italian Constitutional Court, Judgment No. 181 from 2024, point No. 6.1 of the Points of law.

[14] See, e.g., *ex plurimis*, Ruggeri (2024), Cassese (2023), and all contributions therein included, Silvestri (2023), Bognetti (2001), and authors therein recalled, Elia (1982), pp. 515–521, Matteucci (1976) and McIlwain (1947) for the well-known distinction between '*gubernaculum*' and '*iurisdictio*'.

4.2.1 *Emerging Substantial Power Asymmetries. Practical Enforcement Gaps*

The issue of power, a classic one in constitutional history,[15] introduces the first milestone at the basis of this book.

Its shifting nature towards new forms of sovereignty should be stressed, often times towards forms of private rather than public sovereignty, moved both by centripetal (with a tendency to centralise power and, thus, increase inequalities) and centrifugal (outside national state borders and beyond the physical dimension) forces. Such trends have been more accurately developed in the above.[16]

For now, it suffices to underscore the consequences of such general constitutional transformations—which aggregate power in the hands of a few, often private, actors—on the specific enforcement of subjective rights and interests.

A series of '*enforcement gaps*' that hinder *in concreto* the judicial protection of the rights and principles enshrined in the rich European constitutional catalogues, of both national and supranational nature, can be identified to this regard.[17]

These 'practical' elements are manifold and regard all rights, not just fundamental ones. They are *economic*, understood as the lack of financial resources to face the high costs of a trial; *informational*, understood as unawareness of being entitled to act in protection of ones' infringed subjective position; *temporal*, understood as the

---

[15] Fioravanti (2009), p. 82.

[16] See, *supra*, Chaps. 2 and 3.

[17] The linguistic choice of the word 'gap' specifically aims to convey the lack of power precluding *effective* judicial enforcement, either economical, informational, organisational or time-related. It also seeks to underscore the substantial difference between the 'law in the books'—that is, the rights guaranteed *on paper*—and the 'law in practice'—that is, the way in which *in practice* those very rights are enforced in courts, or not. See Cappelletti (1993); see also Luciani (2014). Methodologically, identifying such gaps is not an easy task. Certainly, it suffices to browse any media outlet or simply walk on the streets to perceive the stark difference between the inspiring provisions written in the several catalogues and regulations and their everyday enactment. For a juridical analysis, still, this is far from satisfactory. The institutional and non-institutional reports, safe for relevant but not too recent examples (i.e., the 'Handbook on European law relating to access to justice', from the European Union Agency for Fundamental Rights and Council of Europe, 2016), appear often more focused on purported implementation strategies rather than on the identification of the concrete systemic and recurring gaps. Academic scholarship, on the other hand, offers precious guidance for understanding the wider constitutional and socio-legal trends underlying the current structures or, quite the opposite, very thorough sectorial analysis. However, for a fully comprehensive, truly global, and yet micro-oriented—that is, focused on the concrete delivery of justice to single individuals—one needs to go back to the landmark Florence Access-to-Justice Project from the 1970s, led by Mauro Cappelletti and Bryant Garth (see Cappelletti (1978)): policy-oriented, counting on the surveys and multi-disciplinary expertise of scholars from all over the world, the research identified common 'barriers to access to justice', investigating promising solutions from various countries to overcome them. The present work builds on the findings of the four-volume book resulted from that Project [that is, Cappelletti (1978)], as well as on more sector-oriented scientific contributions on its wake, also from more recent years, to highlight the main enforcement gaps of the current multilevel European system of fundamental rights protection (see, e.g., also Hodges and Voet (2018)).

difficulty in waiting the excessively long times of judicial proceedings; *organisational*, understood as the incapacity to navigate through the complexities of the legal and procedural system against economically and informationally stronger subjects, as well as habitual litigators, and thus, far more accustomed to that type of dispute (such as large multinationals or even state entities); *psychological*, understood as a feeling of intimidation towards the far more powerful procedural opponent.[18]

These concrete obstacles are hardly surmountable through individual action, and occur even more frequently in *marginalised social groups*, whose members, precisely because of this, already start from a position of disadvantage, in what soon becomes a dangerous vicious cycle.[19]

Furthermore, even if an individual—despite all rational calculation and managing to overcome the aforementioned barriers—acted successfully against the much more powerful counterpart, their personal procedural victory would entail nothing but a mere 'insignificant fragment' of the damage actually caused within society by the defendant found guilty. The latter, in fact, would not be obliged to compensate the additional hundreds or thousands, or hundreds of thousands, of subjects affected by their illicit activity for the damage suffered or to be suffered, nor, even less, obliged to stop or concretely discouraged from it. There would be, in sum, no *deterrent effect*, nor, in theory, *judicial efficiency*, if one was to expect that individual actions were concretely viable.[20]

All these elements conjunctively determine several substantial practical disincentives for private individuals to even start proceedings.

Therefore, from a purely economic analysis of law perspective, barring extraordinary incentives, very few rational *individuals* undertake litigation *alone* against such players, but rather expect the governmental authorities to tackle the problem or free ride behind the rare idealistic plaintiffs, if any.[21]

4.2.2 Emerging Substantive Positions. Rights and Interests 'Without a Holder'

The second trend to highlight, is the emergence—or, rather now, the consolidation—of new substantive positions which shatter the traditional conception of litigation as a mere 'two-party affair'.[22]

Without delving into an excessively detailed taxonomy, for the purposes of this examination it is useful to distinguish between *individual rights*, on the one hand,

---

[18] See Cappelletti (1993), pp. 283 *et seq.*

[19] See Issacharoff (2012), pp. 374 *et seq.*

[20] See Hodges (2021).

[21] Visscher and Faure (2021), p. 455. See also Homburger (1974).

[22] See Randazzo and Maglica (2025). On the emergence of new rights, see, e.g., Zolo (2010) and Bobbio (1990).

and what we shall call '*meta-individual*' *positions*,[23] on the other hand. This follows, both on the terminological and the conceptual side, Cappelletti's approach since the 1970s.

The former are characterised by being subjective legal situations, active and full, pertaining to an individual holder and enforceable in the courts by the same individual holder.[24] The latter, on the other hand, also include the category of collective rights, collective interests and diffuse interests.[25] They constitute the emerging subjective positions stressed here.

Differences, albeit significant, occur between these last three categories, so-called 'meta-individual', on which we shall not dwell here. The element to underscore is, rather, that of consonance between them: that is, the fact that—in contrast to individual rights—none of these positions can generally be exercised or protected in the courts by the single individual, according to the traditional categories of civil procedural law. At most, as is well known, they attribute active standing to the *exponential body*, but not to the individuals, albeit interested.[26]

The role of intermediate bodies has been paramount to this regard, as recognised in multiple constitutional texts of the twentieth century. This is, for instance, the case of Article 2 of the Italian Constitution,[27] whereby '*formazioni sociali*' ('social formations') constitute 'a series of societies which bridge the otherwise suffocating gap between the individual and the state',[28] and, thereby, as intermediate bodies, 'give life to the [constitutional] order in general'.[29]

For these reasons, the expression 'meta-individual' is used, to indicate how we are dealing with situations that touch the sphere of the individual, but which at the same time go *beyond* (in ancient Greek, '*μετά*').[30] They affect him, or her, as a member of a group, a community or society as a whole. Illustrative examples include the environment, the climate or social policies.

As anticipated, in front of the administrative judge the protection of such positions has been traditionally demanded to the so-called exponential entities, whose role has been 'decisive and meritorious, since it has allowed these interests to take on a juridical dimension and have a subjective centre of reference'.[31] This orientation has been reaffirmed recently by the Plenary Assembly of the Italian Council of State,[32] which has clarified how the 'diffuse interest [...] is a substantial interest that

---

[23] See Cappelletti (1976), p. 646, already using such an expression.

[24] See, e.g., Gentile (2023).

[25] See Clarich (2024), Cudia (2012), Iudica (2004), Alpa (1993), Trocker (1990) and Cappelletti (1976).

[26] Id.

[27] See Fioravanti (2017), cited also, *supra*, in Chap. 3.

[28] Tosato (1982), p. 229.

[29] Mortati (1999), p. 999, cited in Pisani (2022).

[30] Cappelletti (1976), *supra*.

[31] Italian Council of State, Section VI, Judgement No. 3303 from 2016. See also Cudia (2012).

[32] Italian Council of State, Plenary Assembly, Judgement No. 6 from 2020.

goes beyond the sphere of individuals to assume a shared and non-exclusive connotation, as an interest of 'all' in relation to a good from the enjoyment of which no one can be excluded, and the enjoyment of which does not exclude that of all others'.[33]

This creates an *enforcement gap* inasmuch as the substantial interest of the individual, as an individual component of the broader diffuse interest, is not offered, autonomously, legal protection. It is, in fact, 'only as a synthesis and not a sum of the interest of all those belonging to the community or the category' that such a meta-individual position 'becomes susceptible of protection'.[34]

Traditionally, as explained, such a need for the interest to be 'projected into the collective dimension'[35] in order to access the court, seeking enforcement, has been resolved in the *administrative field* through actions brought by representative associations and other exponential entities.[36]

Still, as recognised by the same Plenary Assembly of the Italian Council of State, a 'process of expansion of legal positions towards a collective dimension in the *civil law context*'[37] can be identified, too. This regards the need to address the practical gaps depicted in the previous paragraph (i.e., disparity of contractual strength and/or information asymmetry) in cases of standardised infringements or mass harms to individual subjective rights, but also to protect positions which cannot be tagged to an individual holder (that is, meta-individual ones).

A classic example is the right to live in a healthy environment. Other rights, even traditional liberties or programmatic rights, can be concerned, too, however. This is the case when their violations are systemic or structural, hence in such a way that it is not possible for the individual holder of the right to obtain through ordinary binary litigation a reform with effects over all those similarly affected. Cases of overcrowded prisons, of migrants' degrading conditions, concerning forms of social assistance, but also freedom of expression or the right to vote are valid examples.[38]

4.2.3 *...and Their Immediate Rebounding on the Remedial Field*

The recognition of positions 'in search of an author' ('*in cerca di autore*', borrowing the Pirandellian formula)[39] has repercussions, at a procedural level, not only on the issue of standing to sue, but also on the types of actions that can be brought. As

---

[33] Id. See also Randazzo and Maglica (2025).

[34] Id.

[35] Id.

[36] For further elaboration, see also *infra*, Chap. 4.

[37] Italian Council of State, Plenary Assembly, Judgement No. 6 from 2020.

[38] For illustrative cases, see, in particular with regard to prisoners and migrants, *infra*, Chap. 9.

[39] First used, again, by Cappelletti (1976), p. 648, quoting the classic Italian play by Pirandello (1921).

it shall be addressed, class actions are, in fact, one of the means developed to tackle these issues in front of the civil judge.[40]

Preliminarily, however, it seems relevant to linger briefly on the different types of relief that can be brought to enforce such positions. The Italian class action regime from 2019, herein analysed, just like the EU Directive 2020/1828 on representative actions (hereinafter 'RAD'), proposes two types of redress: on the one hand, the compensatory one and, on the other hand, the injunctive one.

These models, as analysed in detail in the following,[41] are radically different. Whereas the former is centred on providing economic redress as compensation for a harm already suffered, the latter aims to stop or prevent a conduct, even omissive, which may be even just potentially harmful.

At the same time, they also cover different objective perimeters of application. While the former is set to enforce individual subjective positions, with a degree of commonality, and thus requires the explicit (in Italy) adhesion to the lawsuit, the latter can protect also meta-individual positions.

In a sense, the *compensatory* collective action appears designed for positions which are '*accidentally collective*',[42] in the sense that their aggregation stems from the defendant's conduct, against whom damages are sought. Without it, and without the class proceedings, they maintain an individuality of their own; thus, they could be, in theory, enforced autonomously by the single individual holder. Still, for the reasons depicted above—often practical enforcement gaps, led by power asymmetries—it is in most circumstances inconvenient, and therefore rare, to do so.

Injunctions, instead, intrinsically carry a collective nature whenever the conduct, commissive or omissive, that they aim to cease or prevent is directed towards more than one person. In this sense, they are evidently '*essentially collective*' and can, consequently, be used to enforce also (but not only) meta-individual positions, which, otherwise, could not be litigated individually (since they have no exclusive individual holder).[43] A key aspect of the 2019 Italian reform, to this regard, is that standing to sue is not attributed just to exponential entities, but also to individuals, as will be discussed further.[44]

There appear to be two common elements linking these two types of remedies.

The first aspect is a certain *commonality*—defined as 'homogeneity' by the Italian legislator[45]—among the different rights and interests (even material ones, in the case of diffuse interests) enforced. In other words, as explained in the following,[46] they share factual or legal elements—such as a common origin—at the basis of the individual claim for protection.

[40] Not certainly the only one: see, e.g., the various alternatives presented in Hodges and Voet (2018).

[41] See, in particular, *infra*, next Part II.

[42] Expression first used in Barbosa Moreira (1985), p. 195.

[43] See Ruffolo (2021), pp. 7 *et seq.*

[44] See, in particular, *infra*, Chap. 6.

[45] Id.

[46] Id.

The second feature brings us back to the very core of the concept of access to justice: that of a fair trial, which requires, inherently, in order to be such, *equality of arms*. Such a concept, as is known, is to be conceived in the sense of a 'fair balance [...] between the parties'[47] and implies that 'each party must be afforded a reasonable opportunity to present his case – including his evidence – under conditions that do not place him at a *substantial disadvantage vis-à-vis* his opponent'.[48]

4.3 Collective Dimensions of Access to Justice. Defining the Tools

The introduction of class actions meets the increasing need for new procedural paths of effective judicial protection, until now illustrated.

Of course, this is not the only possible response that can be given on the procedural level to the requirements of effectiveness illustrated so far, and further discussed below. *Legal aid*, for instance, has already been mentioned as a possible solution. Reducing the costs and time of justice, also through *ADR* instruments, is another way.[49]

The procedural scheme of class actions, however, seems to be one of the main ones. The introduction into the Italian legal system, with law No. 31 of 2019, of a dual trans-substantive class action governed by the Code of civil procedure, coupled with the already-mentioned RAD and other novelties,[50] makes the analysis even more pressing also from a constitutional law perspective, which has been lacking until now, at least in a comprehensive manner.[51]

Before continuing with the analysis, it seems appropriate to briefly address the term 'class actions' and its synonyms, given the possible confusion between them and their importance for the constitutional reflections of the present work.

'Class actions', first of all, is a term often avoided at EU level (with some national exceptions, such as the Italian one), but forever nestled in the common law experience of private enforcement and public interest litigation. 'Representative actions' or 'collective redress' are, instead, synonym expressions preferred within the EU, as per the abovementioned RAD or the previous 2013/396 'collective redress' Recommendation.[52] They are mainly used at EU level since the early 2000s to

---

[47] ECtHR, *Feldbrugge v. the Netherlands*, No. 8562/79, 1986, § 44.

[48] ECtHR, *Dombo Beheer B.V. v. the Netherlands*, No. 14448/881993, § 33. See Randazzo (2023), p. 104, Angiolini (2012), pp. 197–198.

[49] See, e.g., Hodges and Voet (2018) and Cappelletti (1993).

[50] See, *infra*, Part II.

[51] See *supra*, Chap. 1. See also, recently, Randazzo and Maglica (2025).

[52] Recommendation 'on common principles for injunctive and compensatory collective redress mechanisms in the Member States concerning violations of rights granted under Union Law.

underscore a (formal) distance from the common law mechanism, until then harshly criticised in the continent.[53]

It is worth briefly anticipating here, for now, that the class action mechanism is a complex procedural device that derives its success from the 1966 amendments to Rule 23 of the Federal Rules of Civil Procedure in the US.[54] Since then, it became a key component of the common law legal panorama, proving particularly effective for enforcing rights of both constitutional and statutory nature; at first, to fight racial desegregation and advance civil rights, subsequently, for public interest litigation in general; concurrently, in consumer and securities field, too.[55]

Judicial economy, maximisation of access to justice and deterrence of potential wrongdoers have been accounted, in particular, among the benefits of class actions.[56] By following the old adage that 'there is strength in numbers', power imbalances against large corporations or state entities have indeed been re-equilibrated in a significant number of cases. Notable examples, after the first civil rights cases from the 1960s in the US, vary from consumer and competition law, securities, employment discrimination to prisoners' rights, foster care, education or social housing cases, through environmental, tobacco, asbestos, LGBT+ and police brutality litigation.[57]

On the other hand, however, the common law class action model was often criticised for being exploited by greedy lawyers fishing for cases in search of large contingency fees. Its inability, at times, to offer sufficient safeguards to class members not participating in the proceedings also raised several doubts.[58] This contributed to regional legislative and judicial backlash,[59] as well as severe critiques from European shores.[60]

---

[53] It is often underscored how the same EU institutions infamously defined the 'US-style class action' as a 'toxic cocktail' in a 2008 official European Commission Memo, on a Green Paper on consumer collective redress (Memo No. 08/741). For precision, it must also be pointed out that 'collective redress', at least in the scholarly world (see, e.g., Hodges and Voet (2018)) has been deemed to encompass a larger number of situations. Moreover, it displays its focus on the objectives of the policy ('redress') rather than on the mechanisms ('action'), under the realisation that techniques other than ordinary litigation may attain the proposed goal of compensation, too. Until now, nonetheless, the EU legislator uses both 'collective redress' and 'representative actions' as synonims of the 'class action' model originated from the common law tradition, as clearly visible in the recent 1828/2020 EU Directive. To this regard, it can further be noted how national legislators from the EU, even when implementing the EU Directive, adopt other terms: e.g., group actions (i.e. France), collective actions (i.e. the Netherlands), popular actions (i.e. Portugal) or even class actions (i.e. Italy).

[54] See, *infra*, Chap. 6.

[55] Id.

[56] See, *infra*, Part II. See also, for instance, Piché (2021), Hodges (2021), Voet (2017) and Hensler (2016).

[57] See, e.g., Marcus (2015) and Greenberg (1997). See also, *infra*, Chap. 6.

[58] See Mullenix (2014). See also, *infra*, Chaps. 6 and 10.

[59] Id.

[60] See also, *infra*, Chap. 6.

Nonetheless, after numerous—mainly consumeristic—scandals, the Old continent, with a significant turn-around, has recently opened the door to a 'legal transplant' of such a complex procedural tool.[61] The abovementioned RAD on 'representative actions' for consumers' 'collective redress', now to be implemented in all Member States,[62] is the result of such a lengthy process, begun in the early 2000s.

At thorough analysis, it is evident that, despite the name and some minor (variable) differences—on which we shall return in detail[63]—, the 'representative action' model proposed by the EU legislator is the same as the US 'class action' technique. For this reason, for the purposes of the present research, adopting the traditional 'class action' terminology seems appropriate. It is, after all, a choice of *continuity* with the main academic literature on the matter, mostly from common law jurisdictions.[64] This approach is also coherent with that of single *national* legislators from the EU, among which the Italian one (see Article 840-*bis*, titled 'compensatory class action').[65]

Under a definitional-functional standpoint, class actions should be conceived as a judicial action brought by a representative on *behalf* of a number of people who are confronted with the same or similar factual or legal issues, and who are no party to the proceedings, but are still bound by the *res iudicata* effects of the final decision (unless, for compensatory suits, they do not opt in or they opt out).[66]

The suit can aim either for a compensatory or injunctive remedy (see *supra*). This extensive reading follows the inclusion of both types of action under the RAD, as well as under the recent Title VIII-*bis* of the Italian c.p.c.[67]

Examples of 'classes' range from pre-formed social groups (i.e., in discriminatory suits), voluntarily-formed groups (i.e., in employment or consumer issues) and

---

[61] Expression first employed by Hensler (2016).

[62] Id.

[63] Id.

[64] In the wake of Uzelac and Voet (2021), with a comprehensive evaluation of the current state of the field in Europe.

[65] Moreover, this option will also hopefully foster a dialogue with extra-continental scholars, in line with the decision of producing the research output in English language. As elaborated, most challenges of the contemporary society have a transnational, if not global, dimension, a feature which indeed demands inter-jurisdictional coordination. Consequently, for reasons of uniformity, the term 'class action' will be hereinafter used to encompass also European mechanisms of 'collective redress' or 'representative actions', notwithstanding the different name tag.

[66] See Homburger (1974), p. 343.

[67] Additionally, in Italy also another (third) mechanism, the so-called '*public class action*' (d.lgs.198/2009), in front of the administrative judge, is thus encompassed, as well as the newly-introduced—and quite unnecessary (see *infra*)—dual 'consumer representative action' in implementation of the RAD (both injunctive and compensatory). Hence, the penta-partite nature of class actions in Italy. Such a large definition is not devoid from necessary fundamental distinctions, *in primis* historical, in light of the civil law long-standing experience with the '*actio popularis*' (since Ancient Rome), on which we shall return in the relevant section of this work. See, *infra*, more in detail, Chap. 6.

involuntarily-formed social groups (i.e., mass harms) to the whole collectivity, either local or national (i.e., lack of sufficient health care measures) or even global (i.e., climate change).

The (self-chosen) *representative* function of the claimant(s) and the extension of the *res judicata* effects of the decision to individuals who are not, formally, parties to the proceedings are central elements of this type of litigation, as further analysed.[68] Its affirmative *regulatory* objective is also a key feature, as shown by the rich litigative experience from common law countries.[69]

Finally, the potentially *private* nature of the enforcement must be stressed, in the sense that, despite having collective—sometimes public—effects, it can be initiated *also* by private non-institutional actors, as opposed to public and institutional ones (i.e. public administrations or public prosecutors, for instance in criminal matters).[70]

All these components, evidently, contribute to the potential, but also to the risks of the technique at hand, on which we shall return in the relevant sections,[71] together with the recent *ouverture* of EU institutions towards it.

4.4 The Constitutional Relevance in Italy of 'Classes' as Intermediate Bodies ('*Formazioni Sociali*')

The reference in Article 2 of the Italian Constitution to the '*formazioni sociali*' ('social formations', that is intermediate bodies)[72] in which the individual's personality develops, and in which their inviolable rights are guaranteed is paramount to this regard. As is known, their constitutional recognition stems from catholic solidarism and the so-called doctrine of '*juridical pluralism*', referred to by Giorgio La Pira during the Constituent Assembly's discussions as that doctrine 'which recognises the rights of the individual and the rights of communities and thereby gives a truly integral view of the imprescriptible rights of man, [...] lead[ing] to a type of state that corresponds to the social needs of our time, as much as to the organic structure of the social body.'[73] Among such communities, the family, above all, should be counted, well-rooted in the catholic Italian cultural tradition, but also, among others, political parties, labour unions, schools, and, in general, associations.[74]

---

[68] See, *infra*, Part II.

[69] See Taruffo (2001), p. 408.

[70] See Homburger (1974).

[71] See, *infra*, Chap. 5.

[72] Article 2 of the Italian Constitution: 'The Republic recognises and guarantees the inviolable rights of the person, both as an individual and in the *social formations* where human personality is expressed'. See Fioravanti (2017).

[73] Translated from Italian, discussion from 9 September 1946.

[74] See Cappelletti and Gordley (1975), Tosato (1982) and Elia (1992). See also *supra*, previous Chap. 3.

The words of Aldo Moro in relation to these 'social formations' *ex* Article 2 of the Italian Constitution, during a subsequent session of the Italian Constitutional Assembly, are particularly enlightening:

> And we identify and specify them in this way, presenting them as those in which man's dignity and freedom is expressed and unfolds. By referring to man as the holder of a right that finds his expression in a social formation, we can clearly clarify the humanistic character that essentially pertains to the social formations that we want to see guaranteed in this article of the Constitution. And from another point of view, speaking in this case of the rights of man,[75] both as an individual and in social formations, makes it clear that the protection accorded to these formations is nothing more than a further explication, a development of the rights of autonomy, dignity and freedom that have been recognised and guaranteed in this constitutional article to man as such. That is, the source of the dignity, autonomy and freedom of these social formations is emphasised, which are expressions of human freedom, expressions of the essential rights of man, and as such must be valued and recognised. In this way, we establish a coherent democratic development; for the state truly ensures its democratic nature by basing its order on respect for man seen in the multiplicity of his expressions, man who is not just single, who is not just an individual, but who is society in its various forms, a society that is not exhausted in the state. Man's freedom is fully guaranteed if man is free to form social aggregates and develop within them. The truly democratic state recognises and guarantees not only the rights of the isolated man, which would actually be an abstraction, but the rights of the man associated according to a free social vocation.[76]

These words take on significant relevance in a coordinated reading with Article 24 of the Italian Constitution, enshrining the right to action. If one interprets the 'social formations' referred to in Article 2, in fact, as illustrated by Moro, as vehicles for the *full guarantee* of the inviolable rights of individuals, it is evident how, in the current unbalanced social and constitutional context, the free possibility of *forming social aggregations*—that is 'social formations'—must be recognised in order to re-equilibrate the growing inequalities, imbalances of power and the very distortions of the democratic-representative process.[77]

It does not appear accidental that Moro emphasises how man (or woman) is not just a single individual, but he (or she) is society in its various forms, 'a society that

[75] Moro (1947), discussion from 24 March 1947 (translated from Italian). Evidently, to be intended generally as 'human being'.

[76] Id. He follows: 'With these clarifications and these corrections of form, which may not be perfect (we are not absolutely satisfied with the wording either), but which are the best we have been able to find to express this essential concept, it seems to me that this article of the constitution takes on a more stringent and proper form, a more juridical form, and that consequently the objections raised by various colleagues, tending to exclude this article, as a whole, from the constitutional charter, must be considered less well-founded. In this way, it has a clear legal significance and contributes to defining an essential aspect of the characteristic purposes, of the historical face of the Italian state. And I hope that the formula we have drafted will receive the sympathy of most of my colleagues, so much so that this article—which expresses a fundamental position in the construction of the new Italian state—will receive almost unanimous consensus, so that it, also through this large vote, will be manifested as a fundamental stone of the new political constitutional edifice that we are raising'. Moreover, it has been reported by several authors that at one point it was discussed whether this article should be the first of the Italian Constitution.

[77] See Mortati (1999).

does not end in the state'. Well, today, in view of the evident inefficiencies and already-addressed dysfunctions of the *democratic* state, *in primis* in reason of *representative* and *participatory* gaps,[78] those words are enriched with meaning, with a new teleological and interpretative value.

At the same time, such an interpretation also carries considerable practical effects, intimately tying in with the Chiovendian atypical conception of the right of action.[79]

Not only the legal obstacles (i.e. the meta-individuality of otherwise unenforceable positions), but also the practical gaps (e.g. power asymmetries) that concretely, systematically, hinder individual access to justice must be overcome in practice.[80] In sum, in the current shattered de-structured framework, which 'is not exhausted in the state',[81] but rather goes beyond, and behind, it, intermediate bodies stand as the ultimate device capable of bridging otherwise unsurmountable gaps for the single individual.[82]

In a world with such unbalanced economic and social relations, on the other hand, only a union of forces of individuals seems to be able to rebalance their positions in the face of massified and standardised violations of their rights and interests. It is, in other words, a direct realisation of the *principle of social solidarity*, expressed in the remainder of Article 2 of the Italian Constitution, as underscored by the Italian Constitutional Court in different stances.[83] The 'original connotation of man *uti socius*', using the latter's words, is 'the basis of social coexistence as normatively prefigured by the Constituent Assembly'.[84]

In relation to volunteering—understood as 'a fundamental model of the positive and responsible action of the individual who spontaneously and gratuitously performs personal services in favour of other individuals or of *collective interests* worthy of protection by the community'—, the '*Consulta*' has long expressed the need for the national legislator to 'establish the necessary conditions to ensure that it is carried out as uniformly as possible' throughout the country.[85] According to the Court, volunteering should be considered as an expression of the solidaristic principle at hand, through the means of social formations, as a general scheme of action in societal life to contribute to the guarantee of everyone's inviolable rights.

Equally, all '*formazioni sociali*' are to be conceived as a way to overcome the 'atomistic limit of individual freedom [...] beyond the constraints deriving from public duties or commands of authority'[86]—in short, beyond the constraints deriv-

[78] See *supra*, previous Chap. 3.

[79] See Chiovenda (1903). See also Proto Pisani (2012), p. 125.

[80] Italian Constitutional Court, Judgement No. 75 from 1992.

[81] See Moro (1947), *supra*.

[82] See Tosato (1982) and Elia (1992). See also *supra*, previous Chap. 3.

[83] See Fioravanti (2017), *supra*.

[84] Italian Constitutional Court, Judgement No. 75 from 1992. See also Moro (1947), *supra*.

[85] Id.

[86] Id.

ing from *sovereignty* and the concrete manifestations of power, whether it be public, private or hybrid in nature.[87]

Among them, on the side of the effective protection of rights, and the correlated personalist principle, also recognised by Article 2 of the Constitution, one cannot forego the intuition, even *in fieri*, of a series of (atypical) social formations—such as the 'classes' in the class action, herein examined—which would come into existence with this fundamental purpose. They dovetail seamlessly, after all, in the Constitutional Court's above-mentioned definition in relation to volunteering, as 'a fundamental model of the positive and responsible action of the individual', that is the name plaintiff of the class, 'who spontaneously and gratuitously performs personal services in favour of other individuals or of *collective interests* worthy of protection'.[88]

Furthermore, one can find in this type of intermediate bodies a key expression of the principle of *social pluralism*, precisely the cardinal junction—rather than a balancing point—between the other two principles expressed by Article 2 of the Italian Constitution, the *personalist* one, on the one hand, and the *solidaristic* one, on the other hand.[89]

Just as the legal public/private dichotomy has become blurred,[90] so too the evanescent role of political parties—themselves '*formazioni sociali*' in which the personality of the individual is expressed—, which today are in deep crisis, as are other 'social formations' such as trade unions (but also family itself, under different respects), appears replaced by new intermediate bodies capable of more *effectively representing* their demands for the enforcement of rights, otherwise unfulfilled.[91] 'Social formations', manifested through collective and representative judicial actions, become the means through which old paradigms lost are regained.

These groups therefore allow the individual to 'overcome the limits of isolation and integrate into a series of groups each characterised by common goals, which the individual alone, increasingly aware of his inadequacy, could not satisfy':[92] in this case precisely the goal, or, rather, the need, for justice, for the aforementioned reasons, both legal and practical.

Indeed, it appears not so radical, also in the light of the aforementioned constituent debate, to identify in the 'classes' of class actions a *new (procedural) type of social formation*, pursuant to Article 2 of the Constitution, that implement, albeit in an *atypical* manner,[93] the right of action set forth in Article 24, first paragraph, of the Constitution. The '*public character*' of the latter provision thus vigorously emerges,

---

[87] See, e.g., Pinelli (2016) and Angiolini (2016): for both, see, more in detail, *supra*, Chap. 3.

[88] Italian Constitutional Court, Judgement No. 75 from 1992.

[89] See Fioravanti (2017) and Elia (1992).

[90] See, more in detail, *supra*, Chap. 3.

[91] See Ridola (1987), p. 37.

[92] See, e.g., Taruffo (2001), Tosato (1982), p. 230, Bognetti (1977), Cappelletti (1976), Rescigno (1966). See also Bognetti (1998), p. 109, quoting specifically the use of class actions.

[93] See *supra*, Proto Pisani (2012), p. 125.

too, just like traditional public enforcers are flanked, if not replaced, by new 'private' enforcers.[94]

This reading, based on the emergency valve of Article 2 of the Constitution, which chisels a collective dimension in the guarantee of rights, hereincluded that to a judge, finds correspondence in Article 3 of the Italian Constitution. The latter norm, as is known, has long been considered in the Italian constitutional framework as a general *reasonableness* clause, that is a limitation for the legislative discretion, an 'all-pervasive criterion for measuring the legality and appropriateness of the political choice',[95] prohibiting provisions incompatible with the overall logic of the constitutional system. In relation to the right to action, *ex* Article 24 It. Const., such a provision has been described as 'a directive of rationality', i.e. a principle pursuant to which the *structure* of the judicial proceedings must not be to the detriment of the *concrete substantive* position of the plaintiff who is in the right.[96]

In the—reasonable—balancing of the different interests at stake—that of an *effective* protection of rights, on the one hand, and those opposing collective procedural instruments, on the other hand—, one cannot account a purported upholding of the individuality of the right of action or an undefined (current) structural deficiency of the judicial system to sustain collective treatment.[97]

The effective protection of rights must always prevail in such cases.[98] This stands a *fortiori*, according to the solidaristic principle recalled above and to the principle of substantive equality *ex* Article 3 of the Italian Constitution, when confronting deep-rooted, systemic or standardised, mass inequalities, involving entire communities and, especially, those vulnerable parties to whom the Italian Constitution—in the same Articles 2, 3 and 24, but in general throughout the text—refers for a preference of protection, as individuals whose patrimony of rights is 'more subjected, due to their human condition, to influences and compressions'.[99] As argued by common law scholarship (see *infra*),[100] class actions can become a fundamental tool of counter-majoritarian force.[101]

It is possible, moreover, to refer to the principle of horizontal subsidiarity, introduced in the Italian Constitution in 2001 with the reform of its Title V, in Article 118, fourth paragraph.[102] Such a principle, as is well known, favours the autonomous initiative of citizens, also in associated form, promoting the realisation of

---

[94] See Cappelletti (1975b) and Homburger (1974).

[95] See Zagrebelsky (1977), pp. 27 *et seq.*, then further elaborated in more detail in Zagrebelsky (1988), pp. 147 *et seq.* See also Morrone (2001 and 2015).

[96] Proto Pisani (2012), p. 125.

[97] *Trenord* case. Italian Court of Cassation, Section III, 31 May 2019, No. 14886. See *infra*, Chap. 6.

[98] On the delicate issue of balancing, see Angiolini (2016), pp. 17–21.

[99] See Martines and Silvestri (2011).

[100] See, *infra*, Chap. 5.

[101] Issacharoff (2012), pp. 374–375, and Elia (1992); see also, not completely in favour of the 'counter-majoritarian' perspective, Angiolini (2012), p. 205.

[102] See, e.g., *ex plurimis*, Mulazzani (2023), Frosini (2008), Violini (2004), Berti (2002) and Poggi (2001).

activities of general interest by the subjects, in concrete terms, *best placed* to give protection, or implementation, to the rights and interests of citizenship.[103] This reading in terms of effectiveness is even more pronounced under Article 117, first paragraph, of the Italian Constitution, in relation to Articles 6 and 13 ECHR and 47 CFREU. The public function and '[the] activity of general interest' *ex* Article 118, fourth paragraph, of the Italian Constitution carried out by the organisation would, in this case, correspond precisely to the exercise of the right of action (for the protection of collective or diffuse positions), whose 'content [is] protected by Articles 24 and 113 of the Constitution and to be counted among those inviolable and characterising the democratic state of law'.[104]

4.5 Constitutional Foundations of Access to Justice in Italy

The right to judicial protection, as is well-known, has long been recognised by the Italian Constitutional Court as 'among those inviolable of man, which the Constitution guarantees in Article 2'.[105] This right should, in fact, be accounted 'among the supreme principles of our constitutional order, in which it is intimately connected with the same principle of democracy to ensure to all and always, for any dispute, a judge and a judgment'.[106]

The close link to such a principle has been reiterated on numerous instances also by the ECtHR, as well, according to which access to justice and the right to a fair trial constitute 'one of the fundamental principles of any democratic society',[107] as 'one of the consequences of the rule of law, [...] inherent in all the Articles of the Convention'.[108]

Also the CJEU has clarified how 'the very existence of effective judicial review' is 'of the essence of the rule of law',[109] to be conceived as a 'general principle of EU law', enshrined under Article 19(1) TEU as 'stemming from the constitutional traditions common to the Member States [...] now reaffirmed by Article 47 of the

[103] See Italian Constitutional Court, Judgements No. 235 from 2009, point No. 9 of the Points of law, and No. 179 from 2019, point No. 12.3 of the Points of law.

[104] Italian Constitutional Court, Judgements No. 120 from 2014 (translated from Italian), No. 386 from 2004, No. 29 from 2003 and No. 26 from 1999.

[105] Again, 'man' is to be read in a large conception, in the sense of 'human being'. See Fioravanti (2017). See Italian Constitutional Court, Judgements No. 98 from 1965, point No. 2 of the Points of law, and No. 70 from 1961. See also Randazzo and Maglica (2025), where the reflections of this paragraph have also been proposed. See also Randazzo (2022, 2023).

[106] Italian Constitutional Court, Judgements No. 18 from 1982 and No. 82 from 1996 (translated from Italian).

[107] See ECtHR, *Pretto and Others v. Italy*, No. 7984/77, 1983, § 21.

[108] See ECtHR, *Čonka V. Belgium*, No. 51564/99, 2002, § 83, and ECtHR, *Iatridis v. Greece* [GC], No. 31107/96, 1999, § 58.

[109] CJEU, Judgment of 27 February 2018, *Associação Sindical dos Juízes Portugueses*, C-64/16, § 35.

Charter',[110] to be guaranteed in the 'fields covered by Union law', irrespective of whether the Member States are implementing Union law within the meaning of Article 51(1) of the Charter'.[111] In particular, in more general terms, it has emphasised that 'it is […] for the national courts to ensure that individuals enjoy the judicial protection deriving from the rules of Community law and to guarantee its full effectiveness'.[112]

Furthermore, the Italian Constitutional Court has underscored how 'the judicial action to defend one's rights [...] is itself the content of a right, protected by Articles 24 and 113 of the Constitution and to be counted among those inviolable and characterising the democratic rule of law'.[113] That of judicial enforcement of rights is an 'absolute, inviolable and universal'[114] principle, pursuant to which, in a perspective of effectiveness of the protection, 'there can[not] be legal positions under substantive law without there being a jurisdiction before which they can be enforced'.[115]

This is seamlessly in line, once again, with the consolidated jurisprudence from the European Courts, in particular the Strasbourg one, which, starting from the landmark Golder v. UK case from 1975, expressed how 'the "right to a court", of which the right of access, that is the right to institute proceedings before courts in civil matters',[116] constitutes the first aspect, directly inherent, of the wider right to a fair hearing, as 'one of the universally "recognised" fundamental principles of law'.[117] In fact, all other guarantees (such as 'the fair, public and expeditious characteristics of judicial proceedings') are 'of no value at all if there are no judicial proceedings'.[118]

Precisely in these terms of effectiveness, the Italian constitutional jurisprudence on legal aid appears highly relevant.[119] Even recently, the Italian Constitutional Court has reaffirmed that, in harmony with Article 3, second paragraph, of the Constitution, this institution is aimed at removing 'the economic difficulties that may oppose the concrete exercise of the right of defence [...] ensuring the

[110] CJEU, Grand Chamber, Judgement of 24 June 2019, *European Commission v Republic of Poland*, C-619/18, § 49–50.

[111] Id.

[112] CJEU, Grand Chamber, Judgement of 5 October 2004, *Pfeiffer and Others*, C-397/01, § 111, clarifying that this applies 'all the more so when the dispute submitted to the national court concerns the application of internal rules which, as in the present case, were introduced precisely for the purpose of transposing a directive intended to confer rights on individuals'.

[113] Italian Constitutional Court, Judgements No. 120 from 2014 (translated from Italian), No. 386 from 2004, No. 29 from 2003 and No. 26 from 1999.

[114] Italian Constitutional Court, Judgements No. 26 from 1999, point No. 3.1 of the Points of law (translated from Italian) and No. 212 from 1997, point No. 2 of the Points of law.

[115] Italian Constitutional Court, Judgement No. 212 from 1997 (translated from Italian).

[116] ECtHR, *Golder v. United Kingdom*, No. 4451/70, 1975, §§ 35–36.

[117] Id.

[118] Id.

[119] On the topic of legal aid, see, e.g., Trocker (2018) and Cappelletti and Gordley (1975).

effectiveness of the right to act and defend oneself in court'.[120] The ECtHR, too, despite not finding a general right to legal aid for every dispute on civil rights, has stressed how there needs to be a concrete assessment 'on the particular circumstances' of each case, in order to evaluate whether there is a 'safeguard [of] the individual in a real and practical way', also in light of 'implications of a social or economic nature'.[121] Such a reference to practical obstacles pivots on the enforcement gaps created by contemporary and increasing power asymmetries, as highlighted above.[122]

These judgements clearly demonstrate how the right of access to a judge, as one of 'the great principles of legal civilisation in any democratic system of our time',[123] needs to be considered in a 'pratical and effective'[124] manner.

A similar approach has been envisaged also by the Italian Court of Cassation, according to which Article 24 of the Italian Constitution is to be understood not 'only as access to the judgment and the exercise in it of a certain procedural power, but [...] also, under a content perspective, as the right to the appropriate measure to satisfy the need for protection of that specific, unique, sometimes unrepeatable substantial situation of legally protected interest'.[125]

In particular, coming back to the consolidated approach of the Italian Constitutional Court, the 'power to take legal action to protect one's rights finds concrete expression in the discipline of the trial, with a multiplicity of institutions intended to make this guarantee effective'.[126]

These positions dovetail, logically and historically, with the teachings from the most prominent Italian academic scholarship on the right to action, since the beginning of last century.

Giuseppe Chiovenda's reflections, in particular, appear extremely topical and valuable. On them, it can be maintained, is based much of the structure of the current Italian Code of civil procedure from 1940, as well as, inevitably, the Constituent Assembly's reflections in relation to Article 24 of the Italian Constitution, dedicated to the same right.[127]

This provision, as is known, has been notably defined by another great civil proceduralist (and judge of the Italian Constitutional Court), Virgilio Andrioli, as 'the keystone of the [Italian] system of judicial protection'.[128]

---

[120] Italian Constitutional Court, Judgment No. 46 from 1957, subsequently cited in Italian Constitutional Court, Judgment No. 149 from 1983 (translated from Italian); in a similar sense, see Italian Constitutional Court, Judgments No. 35 from 2019, No. 175 from 1996 and No. 127 from 1979; see also the recent Judgement No. 121 from 2024.

[121] ECtHR, *Airey v. Ireland*, No. 6289/73, 1979, §26.

[122] See, *supra*, para. 4.2.1 of this Chapter.

[123] Italian Constitutional Court, Judgement No. 238 from 2014 (translated from Italian).

[124] See, *supra*, fn. 4.

[125] Italian Court of Cassation, Section III, Judgement No. 21255 from 2013 (translated from Italian).

[126] Italian Constitutional Court, Judgement No. 388 from 1999 (translated from Italian).

[127] See Fioravanti (2017), *supra*.

[128] Andrioli (1954), p. 6.

Pursuant to Article 24, first paragraph, of the Italian Constitution, '[e]veryone can take legal action to protect their rights and legitimate interests'. The legislator is thus prevented from surreptitiously depriving individuals from the substantive rights recognised. It enshrines, in short, the key principle, summarised by Chiovenda, according to which 'every concrete will of law whose formation according to a substantive law is possible, must find *suitable means* of implementation in procedural law'.[129] It is exactly in the words of the great Italian civil-proceduralist that one can find two illuminating principles in relation to such a 'right to action': that is, its '*atypicality*' ('*atipicità*') and its *public character*.

The former, in particular, emphasises, with foresight, the need for *effectiveness* of judicial protection, to be construed as absolutely *instrumental* to substantive provisions.[130] The consequence, of great practical significance, is that 'the process must, as far as concretely possible, give those holding a right everything and precisely what they are entitled to. [...] To sum up: *every way* of enforcing the law (and *every means* of enforcement) that is *practically* possible and not contrary to any general or special legal norm must be deemed admissible'.[131]

These considerations, therefore, reveal a fundamental obligation on the part of the legislature to provide the most appropriate procedural instruments for the *concrete* protection of the substantive subjective rights guaranteed in the abstract. At the same time, still, one cannot forego to consider the 'social' nature of such types of proceedings,[132] and the consequent necessity to adapt the notion, as well as the structure, of fair trial to such a new found and multi-faceted dimension, as discussed in the following.

The same considerations can—indeed, must—be proposed with regard to any interpretative effort of the right of access to justice itself, which is under consideration here in its collective dimension.

This tension, as desirable as is necessary, becomes even more pressing in the light of the entry into force of the 1948 Italian Republican Constitution, which makes the cardinal principles of procedural law its own by bathing them in the supreme values with which it is imbued.

It is true that, notwithstanding the principle of *atypicality* of the action, the aforementioned Article 24 of the Italian Constitution, at least on a historical-literal level, posits a *subjectivist* concept of protection.[133]

Nevertheless, it is still possible—indeed, necessary—in view of the key values of Articles 2 and 3 of the Italian Constitution, as well as of a conception of the national constitution as a 'living instrument' on par with the ECHR, to argue in favour of an *ouverture* to collective procedural techniques for the judicial enforcement of rights

[129] Proto Pisani (2012), p. 125.

[130] See Caponi (2012); Trocker (1990), p. 193; Barile (1984).

[131] Proto Pisani (2012), p. 125.

[132] Denti (1976), p. 20, mentioning 'society' as 'the real protagonist of these proceedings'. See also Rodotà (1976).

[133] See Donzelli (2012).

(group litigation techniques which, it should be recalled, were far beyond the imagination of the Italian constitutional drafters from 1948, the decisive reform in the US, discussed *infra*, dating back to 1966).[134]

Were this not sufficient, the developments at EU level—which, as is well-known, assume significance domestically through the windows of Articles 11 and 117, first paragraph, of the Italian Constitution—call for an opening, a necessary one, to the implementation of collective judicial actions. This is, in fact, required, as will be treated further,[135] by the RAD Directive, which requires 'that a representative action mechanism for the protection of the collective interests of consumers is available in all Member States, while providing appropriate safeguards to avoid abusive litigation', also aiming '[t]o this end [...] to improve [...] access to justice'.[136] A direct solution, hence, to the fact that '[g]lobalisation and digitalisation have increased the risk of a large number of [individuals] being harmed by the same unlawful practice'.[137]

These last considerations match with the abovementioned findings from 2020 from the Plenary Assembly of the Italian Council of State, exactly in relation to the previous, consumer-limited Italian class action regime (see *infra*, Chap. 6), pursuant to which '[t]he circumstance that the legislator intervened expressly to regulate, in the field of civil procedure, a case of extraordinary standing to sue for the protection of collective interests certainly [...] represents the definitive recognition of the legal relevance of interests in their collective dimension, even in a sphere, the civil law one, in which [...] the issues of disparity of contractual force, information asymmetry and abuse of dominant position gather relevance'.[138] That is, since such a 'process of expansion of legal positions towards a collective dimension in the civil law sphere makes it possible to shift the threshold of protection, freeing it from the individual contractual bond',[139] and, thereby, re-equilibrating power imbalances or synthetising under a common, collective, procedural vehicle fragmented situations (meta-individual ones) which solely would have no concrete chance of enforcement.[140]

It should be noted how both the EU Directive and the Plenary Assembly of the Italian Council of State refer to the rights and interests of *consumers*. This is due to the specific sector-oriented approach that both the Directive and the Italian class action regime (at the time) carried, as will be explained in the following.[141]

---

[134] Pagni (2012), pp. 1144–1145, Trocker (2011), p. 128, Taruffo (2001).

[135] See *infra*, Chap. 5.

[136] Article 1 of said Directive.

[137] Recital 1 of said Directive. Instead of individuals, the Directive cites 'consumers', as it is focused on mere consumer protection. See *infra*, Chap. 5.

[138] Italian Council of State, Plenary Assembly, Judgement No. 6 from 2020, point No. 7.2. of the Points of law.

[139] Id.

[140] Cappelletti (1975b) and Taruffo (2001).

[141] See *infra*, Chap. 5.

Still, the *principle of equality* set under Article 3 of the Italian Constitution, pursuant to which homogeneous situations should not be regulated in an unjustifiably different manner,[142] coupled with the key novelty of the 2019 reform—that is the adoption now of a *trans-substantive* class action model, regulated under the general Code of civil procedure (rather than the mere Consumer code)—clearly support the extension of such a reasoning also to a class action regime allowing the enforcement of rights pertaining to *all* individuals and in all areas of law, not only consumers. This occurs in light, once again, of the right to an effective judicial protection, enshrined under Article 24 of the Italian Constitution (and Articles 6 and 13 ECHR, as well as 19 TEU and 47 CFREU) and to be conceived 'among those inviolable of man, which the [Italian] Constitution guarantees in Article 2'.[143]

4.6 Adapting the Right to a Fair Trial to the Collective Sphere

Among the possible risks within proceedings characterised by a 'poly-centric'[144] and 'social'[145] nature, those concerning the respect of fair trial guarantees emerge as paramount. These guarantees, as is well known, are enshrined under Article 111 of the Italian Constitution and Articles 6 ECHR and 47 CFREU. The collective nature of the proceedings requires, in fact, their adaptation to the new peculiar dimension of judicial enforcement.

In particular, two directions appear critical.

First, the protection of *defendants*, potential and not, with respect to possible unfounded suits aiming for settlement or against competitors is to be ensured. This closely concerns the element of *publicity*, as a procedural requirement of the fair trial, as clearly conveyed under Article 6 ECHR and the Strasbourg case law. Such publicity necessarily regards the initial phases of proceedings, the hearings, but also the delivery of the judgement. It also entails a special attention during the administration of evidence.

The position of defendants, however, is also delicate in relation to the principle of the *equality of arms*, to be encompassed as an aspect of fairness, the other procedural requirement together with the reasonable length of proceedings. In fact, it

[142] See e.g., Italian Constitutional Court, Judgement No. 40 from 2024, No. 108 from 2023, No. 270 from 2022 and No. 172 from 2021. Exactly in relation this principle, albeit in another context, the Italian Constitutional Court recently underscored how 'the principle of equality (Article 3 of the [Italian] Constitution) and the requirements of EU law converge to make equal treatment effective, in a harmonious and complementary perspective, which allows the integration of the guarantees enshrined in the different sources to be fully grasped' (Italian Constitutional Court, Judgment No. 181 from 2024).

[143] Italian Constitutional Court, Judgement No. 98 from 1965, point No. 2 of the Points of law.

[144] See Fuller (1978), stressing the '*polycentric texture*' of political issues.

[145] See *supra*, Denti (1976), p. 20.

needs to be verified whether, while pursuing a re-equilibration of power positions, the scales are not moved too much in favour of the class plaintiffs. This could occur, for instance, by providing special one-sided provisions in relation to the bearing of costs, the production of evidence or the extension of the *res judicata* effects (i.e., by allowing the class members to renounce or adhere to the proceedings also at a particularly late phase.[146]

Second, as discussed more in detail in the following,[147] the most critical position appears, in any case, that of all the *members of the class* who are represented, and whose positions are enforced, but who do not formally participate to the proceedings. Here again, the elements of *publicity* (through appropriate notice and explanation of the judicial action and possible consequences), but also of *fairness*—in the sense of *equality of arms* and the *adversarial principle*, *intra-class*, rather than simply towards the defendant—stand out as most relevant.

Adversarial proceedings, especially, mean in principle 'the opportunity for the parties to a criminal or civil trial to have knowledge of and comment on all evidence adduced or observations filed [...] with a view to influencing the court's decision'.[148] It is evident that in such complex proceedings, with potentially competing substantive, or merely substantial, positions at stake even within the class, the respect of such a principle must be guaranteed differently than in individual one-to-one litigation. *Adequacy of the representation* will, thus, need to be properly assessed at all times.[149]

The role of the judge, as an independent and impartial actor, in ensuring these guarantees becomes hence crucial, in order to allow a necessary flexible and case-by-case approach.[150] It must not be forgotten, in fact, that while the right of access to a court constitutes the first, instrumental, fundamental aspect of the wider right to a fair hearing (as notably underscored in the landmark *Golder v. UK* case, before the ECtHR), the latter cannot be sacrificed in the pursuit of a mere *access* to a court, by allowing potential abuse.

Access to justice, and with it effective judicial enforcement, is a much richer concept, even (and especially) in its collective dimension.[151]

---

[146] See *infra*, Chap. 6.

[147] See *infra*, Chaps. 6 and 11. For a concrete verification through case studies see also *infra*, Part III in general.

[148] See, *ex plurimis*, ECtHR, *Ruiz-Mateos v. Spain*, 12952/87, 1993, § 63; ECtHR, *Kress v. France* [GC], 39594/98, 2001, § 74.

[149] See Cappelletti (1975a). See also *infra*, Chaps. 6 and 11.

[150] Randazzo (2023), pp. 10 *et seq.*

[151] See Hodges (2021), p. 20, stressing the importance of focusing on the *delivery* aspect, too.

4.7 Concluding Remarks. Modern *Commenda* and Water Drops

As a final note, it is the very concept of fair trial 'that must be transformed into a solidaristic perspective, overcoming its original merely individualistic conception, 'since this is the only possible way to assure judicial vindication of the new rights''.[152]

Clearly, as just discussed, fair trial guarantees are fundamental, too, to be strenuously defended in any democratic order. There would be no effective protection, no justice accessed or delivered, if not through due process; for all the parties involved: plaintiffs, but also defendants and possible third parties. Their guarantee is crucial.

However, it would be incorrect to argue that these important interests are in *direct* conflict with that of effective protection, including through representative collective procedural instruments. The latter do not in themselves constitute a violation of the former, nor does one exclude the other.[153]

On the contrary, there are numerous arguments already raised in doctrine, for several decades, to the effect that they can facilitate better *participation* in the process and a concretisation of the principle of *equality of arms*.[154] It is simply necessary to rethink judicial forms and structures to support such a litigation more effectively, while also guaranteeing the interests outlined above. Just as there are obvious examples of procedural distortions and violations of these interests within class actions (but, it is worth remembering, also within binary, one-on-one litigation), there are also numerous practical examples—mostly from overseas, returned by comparative analysis—of virtuous use of the same, with total respect for the due process.[155]

The alternative, after all, is very simple: in radical contrast with the key *solidaristic* spirit of the Constitution, to not even allow the vulnerable members of society to have access to a trial for the protection of their substantive rights—which, consequently, would become mere abstract words, erasing any concrete possibility of ever testing, in accordance with the principle of the rule of law, the democratic nature of the system itself.[156]

In this sense, as anticipated so far and illustrated in more detail in the following,[157] albeit with the necessary caveats, the vehicle of class actions appears particularly well-suited to advance demands that would otherwise remain only vain words on

[152] See Randazzo and Maglica (2025), p. 160, quoting Cappelletti (1976), p. 686.

[153] On the issue of balancing and sovereignty, see Angiolini (2016), especially his footnote No. 2, at pp. 41 *et seq.*

[154] See, e.g., Ucín (2021). See also Cappelletti (1994) and Denti (1976). See also *infra*, Chaps. 6 and 11.

[155] Id. See also *infra*, Chap. 5.

[156] See, e.g., *ex plurimis*, recalled above, Italian Constitutional Court, Judgement No. 238 from 2014.

[157] See *infra*, Chaps. 6 and 11. For a concrete verification through case studies see also *infra*, Part III in general.

paper. It is reminiscent, in some ways, as academic scholarship has already represented, of another 'fictious vehicle', this time commercial, of medieval Venice: namely the *commenda*.[158] The latter, as is known, was a form of temporary society that lasted the time of a single commercial voyage, often of navigation. The aggregation of capital, the flexibility and the fact that only one or a few, more competent or motivated partners, possibly with the contribution of third parties, carried on the enterprise for the benefit of all, is largely reminiscent of the instrument of class actions.[159]

Similarly, in order to navigate the complexities of the contemporary seas, all these elements appear necessary today, developing a kind of 'society'—an intermediate one, precisely—that can mediate as a new centre of power, of representative nature (in some respects, especially for the injunctive remedy, self-imposed) to the shifts in terms of sovereignty, to the growing inequalities of power, to the development of new meta-individual positions worthy of protection and to the loss of statehood.[160]

The circumstance that such an intermediate body is a procedural one is simply owing to the fact that—in a sentence attributed to Calamandrei—'the process reflects the structure of the state [...] as a drop of water refracts the sky'.[161] In other words, the solidity of the constitutional system is verified (also) by its ability to guarantee effective access to justice to everyone, thereby adapting its ways to legal and social changes, even—especially)—under 'new dimensions'.[162]

References

Acemoglu D, Robinson JA (2012) Why nations fail: the origins of power, prosperity, and poverty. Random House, New York

Adam R, Tizzano A (2022) Lineamenti di diritto dell'Unione Europea, 5th edn. Giappichelli, Torino

Alpa G (1993) Interessi diffusi. In: Digesto delle discipline privatistiche. Sezione civile, 9th edn. UTET, Torino, p 609

Andrioli V (1954) La tutela giurisdizionale dei diritti nella Costituzione della Repubblica italiana. In: Andrioli V (ed) (2007) Scritti giuridici, I. Giuffrè, Milano

Angiolini V (2012) Diritti umani. Sette lezioni. Giappichelli, Torino

Angiolini V (2016) Sulla rotta dei diritti. diritti, sovranità, culture. Giappichelli, Torino

---

[158] Issacharoff (2012).

[159] Acemoglu and Robinson (2012), first cited in Issacharoff (2012), p. 385.

[160] Issacharoff (2012), pp. 385 *et seq*. See *infra*, Part II.

[161] It is a quote attributed to Calamandrei by Xin (2024). See also Italian Constitutional Court, Judgement No. 388 from 1999, cited above, according to which 'the power to take legal action to protect one's rights finds concrete expression in the discipline of the trial, with a multiplicity of institutions intended to make this guarantee effective'.

[162] We wish to recall here especially two contributions, foresightedly highlighting the need for '*new dimensions*' in the protection of fundamental rights and civil liberties: Various authors (1990) and Cappelletti (1994).

Barbosa Moreira JC (1985) Tutela jurisdicional dos intereses coletivos ou difusos. Temas de Direito Procesal 3:195 ss
Barile P (1984) Diritti dell'uomo e libertà fondamentali. Il Mulino, Bologna
Berti G (2002) Principi del diritto e sussidiarietà. Quaderni fiorentini per la storia del pensiero giuridico moderno 31:381
Bin R, Pitruzzella G (2024) Diritto costituzionale. Giappichelli, Torino
Bobbio N (1990) L'età dei diritti. Einaudi, Torino
Bognetti G (1977) Pluralismo nella società civile, in Atti del convegno di studi del comitato cattolico docenti universitari. Civiltà cattolica 4:314
Bognetti G (1998) Lo stato e i gruppi di interesse negli ordinamenti borghesi. Giuffrè, Milano
Bognetti G (2001) La divisione dei poteri, 2nd edn. Giuffrè, Milano
Caponi R (2012) Azione di classe: il punto, la linea, la discontinuità. Il Foro Italiano:151
Cappelletti M (1975a) Appunti sulla tutela giurisdizionale di interessi collettivi e diffusi. Giurisprudenza italiana 127:49–63
Cappelletti M (1975b) Governmental and private advocates for the public interest in civil litigation: a comparative study. Mich Law Rev 73(5):793–884
Cappelletti M (1976) Vindicating the public interest through the courts: a Comparativist's contribution. Buffalo Law Rev 25(3):643–690
Cappelletti M (ed) (1978) Access to justice. Giuffrè, Milano
Cappelletti M (1993) Alternative dispute resolution processes within the framework of the worldwide access to-justice movement. The Modern Law Review 56(3):282–296
Cappelletti M (1994) Dimensioni della giustizia nella società contemporanea: studi di diritto giudiziario comparato. Il Mulino, Bologna
Cappelletti M, Gordley J, Johnson E Jr, Varano V (1975) Toward equal justice: a comparative study of legal aid in modern societies. Giuffrè, Milano
Cassese S (ed) (2023) La separazione dei poteri. Rivista trimestrale di diritto pubblico. Giuffre, Milano
Chiovenda (1903) L'azione nel sistema dei diritti. Zanichelli, Bologna
Clarich M (2024) Manuale di diritto amministrativo, 6th edn. Giappichelli, Milano
Cudia C (2012) Gli interessi plurisoggettivi tra diritto e processo amministrativo. Maggioli, Rimini
Denti (1976) Relazione introduttiva. In: Le azioni a tutela di interessi collettivi. Atti del convegno di studio. Cedam, Padova, p 3
Donzelli R (2012) Azione collettiva inibitoria. Treccani.it, Roma
Elia L (1982) La Corte nel quadro dei poteri costituzionali. In: Barile P, Cheli E, Grassi S (eds) Corte costituzionale e sviluppo della forma di governo in Italia. Il Mulino, Bologna, p 489
Elia L (1992) Le norme sulle formazioni sociali nella Costituzione repubblicana. In: Various Authors (ed) Studi in onore di G. Vignocchi. Mucchi, Modena, pp 545–553
Fioravanti M (2009) Costituzionalismo. Percorsi della storia e tendenze attuali. Laterza, Roma
Fioravanti M (2017) Costituzione italiana: articolo 2. Carocci Editore, Roma
Frosini TE (2008) Sussidiarietà (dir. cost.). Enciclopedia del diritto, II. Giuffrè, Milano
Fuller LL (1978) The forms and limits of adjudication. Harv Law Rev 92(2):353–409
Gentile G (2023) Effective judicial protection: enforcement, judicial federalism and the politics of EU law. Eur Law Open 2(1):128
Greenberg J (1997) Civil rights class actions. Procedural means of obtaining substance. Ariz Law Rev 39:575–586
Hensler D (2016) The global landscape of collective litigation. In: Hensler D, Hodges C, Tzankova IN (eds) Class actions in context. How culture, economics economics and politics shape collective litigation. Edward Elgar Publishing Limited, Cheltenham
Hodges H (2021) Evaluating collective redress: models, evidence, outcomes and policy. In: Uzelac A, Voet S (eds) Class actions in Europe. Holy grail or wrong trail? Springer, Cham, pp 20–42
Hodges C, Voet S (2018) Delivering collective redress: new technologies. Hart Publishing, Oxford
Homburger A (1974) Private suits in the public interest in The United States of America. Buffalo Law Rev 23:343

Hviid Jacobsen M, Poder P (2008) The sociology of Zygmunt Bauman: challenges and critique. Ashgate Publishing, Farnham
Issacharoff S (2012) Class actions and state authority. Loyola Univ Chicago Law J 44:369–390
Iudica G (2004) Diritti diffusi. Enciclopedia del Novecento, III Supplemento. Treccani.it, Roma
Luciani M (2014) Garanzie ed efficienza nella tutela giurisdizionale. Rivista AIC (4):1–54
Marcus D (2015) The public interest class action. Georgetown Law J 104:777
Martines T, Silvestri G (2011) Diritto costituzionale. Giuffrè, Milano
Matteucci N (1976) Organizzazione del potere e libertà. Storia del costituzionalismo moderno. Società editrice, Torino
McIlwain CH (1947) Constitutionalism. Ancient and modern. Cornell University Press, Ithaca
Moro A (1947) Italian Constitutional Assembly, Report of the discussion from 24 March 1947
Morrone A (2001) Il Custode della ragionevolezza. Giuffrè, Milano
Morrone A (2015) Ragionevolezza a rovescio. L'ingiustizia della sentenza n. 70/2015 della Corte costituzionale. Federalismi 10
Mortati (1999) Lettera a Pietro Rescigno. In: Rescigno P (ed) Persona e comunità. Saggi di diritto privato, III. Cedam, Padova
Mulazzani G (2023) L'attualità del principio di sussidiarietà da mero principio statico a modello dinamico alla luce della legislazione e della giurisprudenza. Federalismiit 28:120
Mullenix LS (2014) Ending class actions as we know them: rethinking the American class action. Emory Law J 64:399–449
Pagni I (2012) Linee e percorsi della tutela giurisdizionale dei diritti dall'unificazione ad oggi. Riv Trimest Dirit Proced Civ 66(4):1137–1151
Piché C (2021) Class actions in Quebec: highlights of a unique procedure. Revista Eletrônica de Direito Procesual 5:170
Pinelli C (2016) Oligarchie finanziarie mondiali, democrazie nazionali e la dicotomia pubblico/privato. Qualche riflessione per i giuristi, Costituzionalismo.it 1
Pirandello (1921) Sei personaggi in cerca di autore
Pisani G (2022) Da Costantino Mortati al principio di sussidiarietà orizzontale. Rivista di filosofia del diritto 2:391–414
Pitruzzella G (2024) La costruzione dello spazio costituzionale europeo nel dialogo tra Corte di giustizia e Corti costituzionali. Quaderni costituzionali 4:795–821
Poggi A (2001) Le autonomie funzionali 'tra' sussidiarietà verticale e sussidiarietà orizzontale. Giuffré, Milano
Proto Pisani A (2012) Introduzione sulla atipicità dell'azione e la strumentalità del processo. Il Foro italiano
Randazzo B (2012) Giustizia costituzionale sovranazionale: la Corte europea dei diritti dell'uomo. Giuffrè, Milano
Randazzo (2022) Accesso alla giustizia e diritti fondamentali nella dimensione costituzionale nazionale e sovranazionale. In: Amalfitano C, Violini L, Galetta DU (eds) 'Law, Justice and Sustainable Development': L'Accesso alla giustizia nel quadro del SD Goal 16. Giappichelli, Torino
Randazzo B (2023) Access to justice in a multilevel constitutional system, protecting human rights. Giappichelli, Torino
Randazzo B, Maglica A (2025) La disciplina generale delle class action italiane alla prova delle garanzie costituzionali ed europee. Federalismi.it 5:158–196
Rescigno P (1966) Le società intermedie. In: Rescigno P (ed) Persona e comunità. Il Mulino, Bologna
Ridola (1987) Democrazia pluralistica e libertà associative. Giuffrè, Milano
Rodotà (1976) Le azioni civilistiche. In: Le azioni a tutela di interessi collettivi. Atti del convegno di studio. Cedam, Padova, p 81
Ruffolo U (2021) Interessi collettivi (e diffusi), azione inibitoria collettiva e "misure idonee" correttive. In: Ruffolo U (ed) Class action ed azione collettiva inibitoria. Commento sistematico alla legge 12 aprile 2019, n. 31. Giuffrè, Milano, p 7
Ruggeri A (2024) Separazione dei poteri e dinamiche della normazione. Consulta online 1:381

Silvestri G (2023) Separazione dei poteri e indirizzo politico, in Enciclopedia del diritto. Giuffrè, Milano, p 1122
Taruffo M (2001) Some remarks on group litigation in comparative perspective. Duke J Comp Int Law 11:405–421
Tosato E (1982) I diritti umani. Dottrina e prassi. In: Tosato E (ed) (1989) Persona, società intermedie e Stato. Giuffrè, Milano, p 224
Trocker N (1990) Gli interessi diffusi e la loro tutela dinanzi al giudice civile. In: Various Authors (ed) Nuove dimensioni nei diritti di libertà. Scritti in onore di Paolo Barile, Cedam, Padova, pp 193–218
Trocker (2011) La formazione del diritto processuale europeo. Giappichelli, Torino
Trocker N (2018) Accesso alla giustizia e "degiurisdizionalizzazione": il tramonto del diritto al giudice e al giudizio? Diritto costituzionale 3:37–65
Ucín MC (2021) Juicio a la desigualdad. La defensa de los derechos sociales a través del proceso. Marcial Pons, Madrid
Uzelac A, Voet S (eds) (2021) Class actions in Europe. Holy grail or wrong trail? Springer, Cham
Various authors (1990) Nuove dimensioni nei diritti di libertà. Scritti in onore di Paolo Barile. CEDAM, Padua, pp 193–218
Violini L (2004) Attuazione della sussidiarietà orizzontale in Lombardia. Giuffrè, Milano
Visscher L, Faure M (2021) A law and economics perspective on the EU directive on representative actions. J Consum Policy 44:455
Voet S (2017) Where the wild things are. Reflections on the state and future of European collective redress. In: Keirse A, Loos MBM (eds) Ius Commune Europaeum. Intersentia, Cambridge, p 138
Xin X (2024) La natura del processo. Una recensione di 'Processo e democrazia' di Calamandrei. In: Donzelli G (ed) Piero Calamandrei. Giustizia Diritti e Libertà. Democrazia e Diritti Sociali 1. Edizioni Università di Cassino, Cassino, p 247
Zagrebelsky G (1977) La giustizia costituzionale, 1st ed. Il Mulino, Bologna
Zagrebelsky G (1988) La giustizia costituzionale, 2nd ed. Il Mulino, Bologna
Zolo D (2010) Il tramonto della democrazia nell'era della globalizzazione. Jura Gentium 28 December 2010

Part II
Collective Actions. Route of Change

Chapter 5
Class Actions: Origins, US Development and Current EU Context

5.1 Premise. Disrupting Old Ways

The previous Part aimed at delineating the socio-constitutional transformations that have fundamentally altered power dynamics across broad and narrow scopes. This foundational context paves the way to delve into the pivotal inquiry of this study: discerning if, and in which manner, the class action framework can facilitate the enforcement of fundamental rights and foster societal progress. The analysis will focus on the Italian class action model instituted by Law No. 31 from 12 April 2019, into force since 19 May 2021. This dual procedural instrument, crafted to 'bolster access to justice',[1] has been cast—partially unexpectedly[2]—into the Italian regulatory landscape, with a general scope of application and, on paper, a disruptive potential. While further jurisprudential implementation is still necessary for a comprehensive evaluation of the instrument, it is clear that its introduction has substantially shuffled the cards, altering the established paradigms of fundamental rights enforcement. Its injunctive and compensatory mechanisms could empower marginalised and politically under-represented groups, challenging inequities and reducing power asymmetries. On the contrary, there is also a risk of class representatives' systematic abuses against the class interest or of strategic engagement in litigation to undermine business rivals. A spectrum of different scenarios looms on the horizon, including the potential ineffectiveness of the mechanism due to minor

[1] See, *infra*, Chap. 6.

[2] Id. The populist nature of the two majority parties at the Government at the time (MoVimento 5 Stelle, especially, and Lega) has certainly played a key role, as therein explained.

A. Maglica, *Collective Dimensions of Access to Justice*, European Union and its Neighbours in a Globalized World 23,
https://doi.org/10.1007/978-3-031-94522-9_5

yet key legislative and interpretative decisions,[3] each with significant constitutional implications.

Investigating these prospective outcomes necessitates a detailed review of the Italian regulatory framework, declined, also comparatively (horizontally and vertically), in the multilevel European constitutional context (to which is dedicated the present Part), as well as an evaluation of its concrete jurisprudential enactment via case studies (to which is dedicated the next Part).

Still, this necessitates *additional groundwork*. It is essential to first reflect on the *origins and objectives* of the class action model that emerged especially in the United States since 1966. Furthermore, the *European Union milieu*, within which the Italian model is embedded, requires scrutiny for potential intersections and overlaps. The already much-mentioned RAD (Directive 2020/1828) is particularly pertinent in this regard, as well as European society's[4] fundamental shift from perceiving class actions as a 'toxic cocktail'[5] to recognising them as a 'necessary mechanism',[6] driven by the crisis in representative governance and the amplification of inequalities through multi-dimensional relational imbalances.[7] To this additional contextualisation will be dedicated the present Chapter. The subsequent Chapter, instead, will draw the constitutional focus on the Italian jurisdiction.

Finally, while conducting these reflections, it is critical to consider the multifaceted and multilevel landscape of judicial enforcement within which the Italian class action mechanism is called to operate in Europe. Various enforcement avenues exist, both national and supranational, individual and collective. Throughout this analysis, while still maintaining the focal point on Italian class actions, a *comparative* lens should be kept towards the most notable among them.[8]

Considering traditional techniques' main adjudicatory gaps and strengths allows for a proper backdrop against which class actions' effectiveness can be benchmarked. Among the former, for instance, certain apex courts' requirements

---

[3] Id., i.e., regarding standing, competence or the meaning of 'homogeneous rights'.

[4] On the notion of European society, and its constitutional implications, see von Bogdandy (2022).

[5] See Questions and Answers to the Green Paper on Consumer Collective Redress, European Commission, 27 November 2008, Question No. 9.

[6] Directive (EU) 2020/1828 of the European Parliament and of the Council of 25 November 2020 on representative actions for the protection of the collective interests of consumers and repealing Directive 2009/22/EC (hereinafter 'RAD'), Recital No. 5.

[7] See *supra*, Part I.

[8] On the increasing importance of comparative analysis, in all fields of legal study, see von Bogdandy (2023).

for a previous exhaustion of domestic remedies or a previous establishment of ordinary proceedings where the specific legal question becomes relevant come into play.[9] Other collective enforcement routes, at national and supranational level, but also individual claims—i.e. for injunctive redress—should be accounted, too.[10]

These other pathways of enforcement, nonetheless, are not only *alternatives*, but can also function in a *complementary* fashion with the class action technique. The remedial processes before the European Higher Courts (ECtHR and CJEU) and the Constitutional Court are, once again, illustrative examples. Therefore, the mechanisms of *coordination* and collaboration among the different levels and routes of enforcement are also an integral part of this discussion.[11] No specific chapter will be dedicated to them, but rather they will be the *evaluative backdrop* against which the class action mechanism will be presented and discussed, throughout this Part and the next. At the same time, as will be expanded, the *other powers*, aside from the judicial one, i.e. the legislative one, should not be seen in an antagonistic fashion, but in a similarly—if not cooperative, at least—coordinated perspective.[12]

5.2 United States and Common Law Origins

Any reflection upon group representative litigation must start in the common law world and, more specifically, in the United States in 1966.

[9] I.e., respectively the ECtHR, under Article 35, para. 1 ECHR, and the Italian Constitutional Court, under Article 1, Constitutional Law No. 1 from 9 February 1948.

[10] Among the alternative collective enforcement routes, a distinction should be kept between national and supranational ones. Among the former, the other 'class action' mechanisms available in the Italian jurisdiction should be considered: the so-called (dual) 'consumer class action', (unnecessarily, as subsequently argued) introduced in 2023 in implementation of the 'RAD' Directive, and the so-called 'public class action' in front of the administrative judge. Among the latter, the pilot-judgement procedure in front of the ECtHR, under Rule 61 of the Rules of the ECHR Court, holds special comparative relevance. Individual actions, instead, should always be considered in alternative to injunctive class actions, considering why (if) a collective claim, rather than an individual one, should be more effective. The next Part III, focused on case studies, will address this question.

[11] See Randazzo (2023), especially pp. 21 *et seq.*

[12] See Kavanagh (2023).

It is true that multi-party suits originated way, even centuries, before in the United Kingdom.[13] It is also correct that 'public interest' actions have long been present in the civil law tradition (see, e.g., the Roman *actio popularis*).[14]

---

[13] Historical records show that the roots of this complex procedural model date back to the Middle Ages, with some examples as far as in the twelfth century and most forerunners amid the seventeenth and eighteenth century. See Yeazell (1987), Sternlight (2000) and Andreotti (2017).

The very first cases, which took place in the English countryside on the eve of the agricultural revolution, portrayed a rather different concept of group litigation, mostly regarding cohesive social groups of tenants already formed before the 'suit', who *specifically* consented to being represented in their manorial disputes for reasons of status rather than economy and sparing of time. A very good example is *Brown v. Howard*, from 1701, where tenants were fighting with the lord of the manor over the sum he could exact for permitting succession to a tenancy—described in Yeazell (1980), p. 514. See also Hazard et al. (1998), p. 1423. In contrast, see Chafee (1950), according to whom: 'In such situations, each member of the multitude had the same interests at stake as every other member, so that it was an obvious waste of time to try the common question of law and fact over and over in separate actions [...] It was much more economical to get everybody into a single chancery suit and settle the common questions once and for all.' In Yeazell's, Hazard et al's and Andreotti's opinion, instead, these cases had an all-or-nothing character and more of a regulatory function, where 'the judicial system would perform a legislative function with the judgement serving as a basis for a change in the substantive law governing the relationship between the parties' (Id.). The reason for this was the social structure itself: the groups were small, cohesive and had exactly identical rights to one another, since their relationship with the manorial lord or parishioner was the same. In a way, they were already institutionally and almost politically organised against their direct administrative unit/social superior (the manorial lord or parishioner). It was only in the middle of the nineteenth century that a new form of group litigation started to emerge, with substantial differences with regards to the members of the group and, thus, more similar to the modern one. Cases from the epoque show a noteworthy transmutation: the 'multitude' seeking litigative recognition were no longer a pre-existing social group (tenants fighting the same lord of the manor for the same tenancy issues, i.e. in *Brown v. Howard* in 1701 in England, but now had no apparent connection with one another, except the unlawful event giving rise to their damage and consequent claim. Aggregating their suit was now indeed a question of economic and time-saving efficiency. An example would be that of shareholders defrauded by the same company while buying stock or creditors entitled to be paid out of the same transaction or fund. Hence, together with the shift from an agricultural, customary and rural society to an entrepreneurial-capitalist, individualistic and urban world, 'group litigation began its transformation into class litigation' (Id.). The more the opportunities for working together and connecting with each other in everyday life increased, the more the demand for new procedural instruments capable of aggregating similar claims from similar plaintiffs against common defendants for common questions of fact and law increased as well. It was, therefore, the evolution of society itself to foster legal practitioners and scholars' creativity in order to devise the necessary new legal technologies.

[14] The so called *actiones populares* from Ancient Rome, that could be brought to protect the *res publica*, which literally translates as the 'public thing', or 'good'. They are accounted in *De popularibus actionibus*, Title XXIII, Book XLVII of the Digesto. See, also, Fadda (1984), Casavola (1958) or, more recently, Caielli (2015). Among the examples from these Authors, actions aimed at removing an object which may dangerously fall from a building (*actio de posito et suspenso*), actions for the good mainteinance of aqueducts (*lex Quinctia de aquaeductibus*, from year 745) or actions against those violating a grave (*actio sepulchri violati*) can be reported. Rather interest-

The class action model, as herein intended and analysed, however, dates back to a precise historical context and legislative amendment: that, from 1966, to the well-known Rule 23 of the US Federal Rules on Civil Procedure, first adopted in 1938.[15]

Since then, until modern times, it has collected vibrant praise for its access-to-justice and deterrent functions, as well as harsh critiques for its favouring of abusive litigation and fair trial guarantees' infringements.[16] An undisputed point, still, by all

---

ingly, all these actions could be brought by anyone from the community having the right to vote (hence, not women or children), and in most of them damages could be retrieved in favour of public funds. In general, they were conceived as actions in which 'the plaintiff, by defending the interest of the people, defends also his own interest' (Di Porto 2013, translated from Italian). This was certainly encouraged by the identity between private interests and those of the whole community, in Ancient Republican Rome, as opposed to the distinction between the public and private sphere of the modern State from the nineteenth and twentieth centuries (Caielli 2015), which, nonetheless, lately seems to be increasingly merging.

[15] In the US, three initial legislative steps were taken—in the years 1848, 1921 and 1938—in order to regulate aggregate litigation, but none of them managed to explicitly and in a clear-cut way answer the question. The result were a series of contrasting decisions, with some courts clearly pushing for bindingness on all the potential members of the group while others kept preserving the absentees' rights in the due process' name. It was only in 1966, with the amendment of Rule 23 of the Federal Rules of Civil Procedure, that the issue was definitively tackled and that the class action model was brought to its current design.

In 1848, Federal Equity Rule 48 was introduced, according to which 'where the parties on either side are very numerous, and cannot, without manifest inconvenience and oppressive delays in the suit, all be brought before it, the court in its discretion may dispense with making all of them parties, and may proceed with the suit, having sufficient parties before it to represent all the adverse interests of the plaintiffs and defendants in the suit properly before it. But in such cases the decree shall be *without prejudice* to the rights and claims of all the *absent* parties' (emphasis added, in Bassett 2006, p. 1415). In 1912, the Federal Equity Rules were revised and aggregate litigation became governed by Equity Rule 38, which did not explicitly state that class actions could be binding on absent class members but neither denied such a possibility; in 1938, instead, with the promulgation of the Federal Rules of Civil Procedure, Rule 23 was issued, allowing class actions, although raising different problems, among which 'the proper labelling of a class action, the effects arising from it, the extent of the judgements in class actions and the lack of binding effect of a 'spurious' class action on non-party class members' (Andreotti 2017; see also Ford 1966, p. 254): 'spurious' was in theory the main of the three categories of class actions envisaged by the Federal Procedural Rules, although in practice it was very difficult to identify the proper cases where it could be used.

See also *Smith v. Swormstedt*, from 1853, and *Supreme Tribe of Ben-Hur v. Cauble*, from 1921, where the Supreme Court found that 'if the federal courts are to have the jurisdiction in class suits to which they are obviously entitled, the decree when rendered must bind all of the class properly represented'. These decisions were read by different federal courts as an establishment of the possibility of binding effects of collective actions on absent members. Still, other federal courts (i.e. in *Hansberyy v. Lee*, from 1940), 'holding that the doctrine of res judicata does not apply to absent class members whose interest were not represented by the parties to the original suit', kept ruling in favour of the absentees' right to sue, 'thus creating legal uncertainty' (see Hazard et al. 1998; Andreotti 2017).

[16] Mullenix (2014), p. 399.

means, is its central role in the common law—US, especially[17]—legal system, built over the last six decades. In such a length of time, an enormous, almost incalculable, amount of class actions has been filed over all the concerned jurisdictions. The results, from a socio-legal point of view, have been various: at times extremely positive, in other stances neutral and in a not-indifferent percentage even negative. The guiding parametres for these assessments can be, also inter-changeably: *judicial economy*; concrete and fair *redress* for the injured—or at risk of injury—parties; effective *deterrence* from otherwise repetitive harmful activities; respect of *fair trial* guarantees; *systemic* consequences (beneficial or detrimental) for specific societal groups or for the society at large.[18]

The societal fields concerned are numerous, too. Examples of this *trans-substantive nature* are offered, *inter alia*, with regard to the enforcement of civil rights, in consumer law, product liability, anti-trust, securities frauds, discriminatory practices, employment law, police brutality, foster care, mass torts, environmental and data protection.[19] This large variety of cases is in line with the fundamental goals of the US legislator when amending Rule 23.[20]

5.2.1 *Objectives: Advancing Social Change*

Before further delving into the main features of the 'US-style' class action suits, it seems relevant to briefly dwell on such goals. Drawing from local scholarship's insights, two main reasons, partially merging into one, can be attributed behind the bold amendment-choice from 1966. They both respond to the precise historical socio-economic context and to the peculiarities of the US (and common law) constitutional framework and ways of adjudication. Somehow, as will be discussed in the following, similar *liaisions* undergo the most recent process of introducing collective redress within EU-civil law jurisdictions; safe for the crucial distinction of an antonymic legal fabric and tradition, which affects the tolerability of the 'legal transplant' at hand.

The first reason was already highlighted with farsightedness by Holmes Jr (1897), when he underscored the *shifting nature of tort-law*, based on the then-establishing new industrial, social and economic structures:

> Our law of torts comes from the old days of isolated, ungeneralized wrongs, assaults, slanders, and the like, where the damages might be taken to lie where they fell by legal judgment. But the torts with which our courts are kept busy to-day are mainly the incidents of certain well known businesses. They are injuries to person or property by railroads, factories, and the like. The liability for them is estimated, and sooner or later goes into the price

[17] But also Canada and Australia. To a lesser degree the United Kingdom, although there seems to be a growing trend in recent years.

[18] See Uzelac and Voet (2021).

[19] See, *inter alia*, Greenberg (1997) and Marcus (2011, 2013, 2015).

[20] Id., and, in particular, Marcus (2011), p. 657.

> paid by the public. The public really pays the damages, and the question of liability, if pressed far enough, is really the question how far it is desirable that the public should insure the safety of those whose work it uses.[21]

Such a view was subsequently, with reason, emphasised by several other scholars, as it is nowadays in the European continent as well.

Some argued, from an economic analysis of law perspective, 'the economic justification of the class action',[22] stressing the importance of assigning the correct market value to injury-causing activities, however small,[23] and of offering sufficient economic incentives for pursuing interests shared by however large groups.[24] Similar reasoning has been offered in relation to the recent EU Directive on collective redress (the above-mentioned RAD),[25] underscoring how, in theory, 'collective actions can potentially provide a solution for the problem that individual litigation will not take place due to rational apathy, information problems, free-riding, etcetera'.[26]

Others have focused on the changing role of the judiciary and of the nature of civil litigation, to explain how the class action model answered the growing 'proliferation of more or less well-organized groups in our society and the tendency to perceive interests as group interests, at least in very important aspects'.[27]

Others again expanded the vision to the society at large, to demonstrate how, from the initially binary, *one v. one*, common sets of relationships, the society had (is) progressively and exponentially evolved (evolving) towards a *one v. multitudes* typical connection in every-day life.[28] It is, in short, the process of *standardisation* and *massification* of human relationships brought by technological innovation and globalisation.[29] As argued, from a judicial standpoint, this created (creates) a series of *adjudicatory gaps* which can't be addressed by the single individual alone, with the traditional one v. one paths of enforcement.[30]

The second reason—which partially falls back into the first—pertains to the specific rise of *racial desegregation* and, in general, *civil rights movements* in the United States starting from the late 1938 and culminating in the 1960s, at the time of the Rule 23 amendment.[31] The class action model emerged as an ideal mechanism for bringing the political instances of such upcoming groups into the judicial arena, and, in general, in subsequent years, as a valuable instrument of the liberal

---

[21] Wendell Holmes (1897), p. 457. Extract first cited in Issacharoff (2013), p. 699.

[22] Adler (1972), p. 533.

[23] See Calabresi (1970).

[24] See Olson (1965).

[25] See, *infra*, paras. 3 *et seq.* of this Chapter.

[26] Visscher and Faure (2021), p. 455.

[27] Chayes (1976), p. 1281; see also Taruffo (2001).

[28] Cappelletti (1976), p. 643.

[29] See *supra*, Chap. 2.

[30] See *supra*, Chap. 4.

[31] Marcus (2013), p. 587.

'left' wing of the political spectrum.[32] It was a technique capable of posing '*counter-majoritarian force*'[33] against the governmental and legislative inertia, if not intentional stalling, and advancing social change through the courts. It was also, and most importantly, in the minds of the amendment drafters, a mechanism capable of litigation-driven *systemic integration*. Its design was specifically aimed at overcoming segregationist judges' delaying tactics through repetitive individual (and burdensome) litigation.[34]

Rule 23(b)(2), regulating the injunctive class action, in particular, was designed with this aim, as shown by the notes of the Advisory Committee to the 1966 Amendments: '[i]llustrative [...] various actions in the *civil-rights* field where a party is charged with *discriminating unlawfully* against a class'. On this noble altar, certain due process procedural guarantees were sacrificed, especially for the injunctive remedy, to favour wider substantive justice.[35]

The class action model, in sum, established itself as a form of *private enforcement*, as opposed to the public one, through which *private individuals*, self-appointed champions of the (or a) community, brought issues which concerned not just themselves, but a large part of the *public interest*.[36] Under this viewpoint, it shattered the traditional divide between private and public law, still largely followed in the contemporary civil law experience.[37]

On the one hand, it entrusted, if not outsourced, the enforcement of public goals to private individuals; this is particularly evident in the litigation for the civil rights movement. Its counterbalance is the significantly lower number of public 'administrative agencies', if not 'public enforcers', in the common law world, as opposed to the civil law tradition.[38] On the other hand, returning to Wendell's premonitory evaluations of tort law from the end of the nineteenth century, as well as to the already-discussed social and constitutional shifts of the recent decades (see *supra*), it fundamentally questioned the legal paradigms of 'public' and 'private' interests.[39]

---

[32] Cummings (2020), p. 184.

[33] Issacharoff (2012), p. 44.

[34] Marcus (2011), p. 657. See also Elia (1982), p. 519, referring to the Warren court's role of 'deep social reform'.

[35] Marcus (2011), p. 657.

[36] See Homburger (1974).

[37] See *supra*, Chap. 3.

[38] Miller (2010), p. 6, quoted also in Issacharoff (2012), p. 390: Miller 'powerfully makes the point about the deregulatory impulse behind the private attorney general model: 'Even though private lawsuits might be viewed as an inefficient ex post method of enforcing public policies, they have dispersed regulatory authority; achieved greater transparency; provided a source of compensation, deterrence, and institutional governance; and led to leaner government involvement. Without this private-attorneys-general concept, the substitution of an alternative methodology would be necessary. This probably would mean the establishment of the type of continental-style, centralized bureaucracies and administrative enforcement that many think are inconsistent with our culture and heritage".

[39] Chayes (1976), p. 1281.

Social change was no longer sought just in the Parliament (or, rather, in Congress), but also, with larger impact, in the courts.

5.2.2 *Class Actions and the Civil Rights Movement*

The historical reconstruction from US scholarship clarifies the central role played by the objective of creating an effective tool for desegregation suits in the drafting of the 1966 class action model, especially for its injunctive remedy.[40] After the first successes in desegregation litigation through the new tool, by the NAACP Legal Defense Fund and similar associations, their attention turned to other ventures of progressive/liberal stance.[41]

It is not a coincidence, therefore, that in 1983 'civil rights class actions' represented 38,6% of all registered class action suits filed under Rule 23, the largest percentage of any category in front of federal courts.[42] A non-exhaustive list of cases touches: discrimination in employment or education settings, the education of children with disabilities, the safety and health of children in foster care, the right to public housing and other facilities, promotion of welfare reforms, police brutality, immigrants' and prisoners' rights.[43]

The main justification behind the use of a collective action, instead of an individual suit, was twofold: firstly, ensuring extensive effects of the *res judicata* (almost *erga omnes*, at least in respect to the whole class); secondly, obtaining *systemic* 'diffuse' effects, often quasi-regulatory, to overcome legislative or executive inertia.

The former goal (*trans-individual* effects) was repeatedly mentioned by the Advisory Committee to the 1966 US Federal Amendments in its working papers and exchanges.[44] Unsuccessful cases from the previous class action regime, from 1938, and from individual injunctive suits, which had failed to obtain a wide application, were specifically taken into account. Illustrative examples are those allowing on otherwise all-white means of transportation or schools only the named plaintiffs,

---

[40] Marcus (2011), p. 657.

[41] Marcus (2013), p. 587.

[42] Ancheta (1985), p. 283

[43] See, e.g., Greenberg (1997), p. 575: 'Class actions have been used to challenge discrimination in employment, education, the use of public facilities and housing, to assert prisoners' rights, and to promote welfare reform, to name just a few areas that conventionally are put in the civil rights category. In one case, a district court granted a stay of execution in a class action habeas corpus proceeding on behalf of a class consisting of all Florida inmates on death row'. See also Carroll (2021), p. 25: 'Injunction-only class actions, however, continue to be certified, and they continue to play an important role in civil rights litigation. For example, federal courts have recently certified injunction-only class actions in cases involving family separation at the border, the education of children with disabilities, the health and safety of children in foster care, medical care for incarcerated persons, and the reproductive rights of immigrant detainees, to name just a few'.

[44] Marcus (2011), p. 657.

or individual claimants, rather than the whole concerned group.[45] This significantly raised the litigation costs and time, obliging to litigate one by one and making even successful suits quite unattractive for potential plaintiffs, since they would have been the only ones allowed from the concerned group (black bus-riders or students, in this case).[46] Furthermore, information asymmetries and possible fear of retaliation in appearing as plaintiffs were considered, too. Class actions, brought by (self-) elected champions for the whole community, solved this apparently minor yet crucial issue.[47]

The latter justification, that is the possibility of reaching systemic and structural effects became the evermore evident after the 1966 amendments. Other cases, too, such as those concerning prisoners' rights, clearly demonstrate the problem. An overcrowded prison system, for instance, could not be tackled systemically by an individual suit.[48] Through it, an individual could merely receive modest economic redress for the suffered treatment. Certainly, individuals could not file a complaint regarding the widespread and structural violations resulting from systemic overcrowding. Moreover, being it about just one person—further compounded by the ordinary economic, organisational, informational, and psychological disincentives dictated by their circumstances—, the economic incentive for state authorities to pursue structural change would be none.

Another key issue raised by US commentators is the fact that prisoners there lack(ed) voting rights.[49] This fundamentally hindered(s) their possibility to participate to the political process through elected representatives, thus making it even harder for them to have their stances advanced in *fora* other than the judicial one. To this regard, further comparative assessments emerge in relation to other mechanisms available in the EU multilevel constitutional system—*in primis*, the pilot-judgement procedure before the ECtHR.[50]

For now, it suffices to underscore the ability—and goal—of class actions, at least in the initial US experience, to transcend the individual rights and interests of the parties involved in the proceedings.[51] Evidently, not only individual, but also collective rights and diffuse supra-individual interests can thus be enforced, as discussed *supra*.[52] The general right to breath clean air or to live in a healthy environment, not affected by climate change's adverse effects, is an extremely relevant example today. Despite the most recent drawbacks and backlash,[53] class actions in the US, as its case law demonstrates, have been an invaluable tool for landmark systemic and

---

[45] Id.

[46] Id.

[47] See Issacharoff (2012), p. 44, commenting *Brown v. Board of Education*.

[48] Id.

[49] Id.

[50] See, *infra*, Chap. 9.

[51] Cappelletti (1976), p. 643.

[52] See *supra* Chap. 4.

[53] Mullenix (2014), p. 399.

structural reforms, in light of otherwise-dormant civil rights and constitutional substantive regulations.[54]

The defendants in such cases are both private (in particular, discriminating employers or polluting companies, recently even 'private detention centres')[55] and public, in the sense of governmental agencies if not the State itself. The latter option, is, as we shall see, not always guaranteed under the EU-model class suits. This evidently significantly curtails the concrete perimeter of application of the collective procedural device.

---

[54] In sum, they assume a public-almost regulatory role. In this perspective, it has long been stated that litigation can serve as a powerful 'governance tool' in any attempt to ensure compliance and enforceability of substantive laws and prevent or discourage dangerous activities causing loss or injury to others (Hensler 2001, p. 211; Murphy and Cameron 2006, p. 399; Rosenberg 1987). To this regard, it should be stressed that such a need for concrete justice flows in most cases not from a lack of substantive rights, but simply because there is no adequate and effective procedural remedy to enforce them. After all, as it has often been stated (i.e., Uzelac 2014), substantive and procedural rights are nothing but two sides of the same coin and, as advanced and innovative some rights recognised by the legal system may be, no real value would come from them to society and to the individuals who compose it, unless there is a proper and solid structure to hold them and, at the same time, grant, not only to each citizen, but to each human being and to each legal entity their true and concrete recognition and enforcement. In this case, it has been noted (Rosenberg 1987), the class representatives and legal counsels bringing the class action would assume the function of a sort of 'private attorney general'.

The premise is that the government administration and 'captured or resource-strapped public agencies cannot [always] adequately enforce the substantive law' (Marcus 2013, p. 587), but rather, quite often, find themselves unable to control and offer appropriate deterrence to large businesses' improper activity. If, in addition to this, we count the abovementioned notoriously high costs of individual justice and unbalanced, almost prohibitively, power relationships between weak parties and corporate defendant 'repeat players', it is evident that, without an alternative tool like class actions, 'a great deal of substantive law would go under-enforced' (Id.) as no one would sue or act to vindicate those claims and impede the unlawful activity.

On the other hand, economies of scale rising from a class action's joinder of claims enable an independent, well-financed and specifically-prepared 'cadre of private attorney generals' to compensate for the inadequacies of government regulators and individual litigants, thus helping 'implement a positive program[me] of social or economic reform' and making Rule 23 'an evolutionary response to the existence of [otherwise] unremedied injuries' (Id.). It must be noted, in any case, to this regard, that the critics to this 'regulatory conception' (in favour of the so called 'adjectival conception', which stresses the importance of the substantive law over the procedural and the necessity to strictly abide by formal procedural rules) claim it 'prioritizes regulatory efficacy as a primary rule' (Id.), while leaving individual remediation as a secondary goal, if that (Moore 1977, pp. 837–42: arguing that 'the primary function of the class action is the deterrence of harmful conduct' and 'judicial efficiency and compensation of small claimants are merely desirable by-products').

[55] See the case known as the *Kids for cash scandal*, which regarded hundreds of children sent to a private detention center by two judges from Pennsylvania in exchange for large amounts of money from the developers of the detention center (Mericle Properties). Several of the children were sent for minor issues (such as, literally, stealing candy) or none at all, and suffered traumatic stress from this experience, leading some of them even to suicide. After the criminal trial, a settlement was reached with Mericle Properties for around 20 million dollars, which were put in a specifically set foundation. In August 2022, moreover, a 206 million-dollar verdict was handed down in a civil law class action against the two judges who had been sentencing them there.

As depicted by the above-mentioned percentages, in any case, other types of claims were brought through class actions, too. Largely concerned fields of law were *consumer*, defective products and securities disputes, on the one hand, and *mass harm* cases, on the other hand.[56] As subsequently argued, it is merely this kind of class-litigation (with partial doubts on mass harms) that has been subject of the EU legislator's most recent initiatives on collective redress.

Consumer, defective products and securities class actions respond to the *rationale*—first proposed by economic-analysists of law, such as Guido Calabresi[57] or Richard Posner,[58] followed by several other commentators[59]—pursuant to which also *small claims* deserve to be litigated for the economic well-functioning of the societal markets. As notably argued by the same Posner, acting as a judge (after having been an academic), 'only a lunatic or a fanatic sues for $30'.[60]

In today's society, it is indeed rather common that in different areas of law and everyday life potential claims arise,[61] but they are so small that it wouldn't be worth pursuing them for a single individual. Especially in consumer law, several examples can be found of claims of few hundred dollars which cannot be pursued singularly.[62]

Hence, even though *substantively* one party may have the right to ask for a refund or have its damage repaid, *procedurally* and practically it is impossible for them to have legal satisfaction, because their 'claims may be so small and unmanageable [...] that the cost of enforcing them outruns any promise of benefit'[63] and, also, since the power and resource advantages 'repeat litigation players' enjoy over 'one-shooters' create a fundamental power imbalance.[64] Additionally, some authors have noted that in some cases, 'single players', apart from the resources, may even lack

[56] See Greenberg (1997).

[57] See Calabresi (1970).

[58] See Posner (1973).

[59] E.g., Visscher and Faure (2021), p. 455.

[60] *Carnegie v. Household International, Inc*, 376 F3d 656, 660–62 (7th Cir 2004). See also Lester (2016), pp. 208–215.

[61] The availability of such a mechanism is of increasing importance in a global economy in which civil wrongs are often committed on a mass scale by large and powerful entities (see Murphy and Cameron 2006).

[62] See, e.g., Yan (2011), p. 551; Sternlight (2000). See also *Eisen v. Carlisle & Jacquelin*, 417 U.S. 156 (1974): 'A critical fact in this litigation is that petitioner's individual stake in the damages award he seeks is only $70. No competent attorney would undertake this complex antitrust action to recover so inconsequential an amount. Economic reality dictates that petitioner's suit proceed as a class action or not at all'; *Phillips Petroleum Co. V. Shutts*, 472 U.S. 797 (1985): 'class actions [...] may permit the plaintiffs to pull claims which would be uneconomical to litigate individually. For example, this lawsuit involves claims averaging about $100 per plaintiff; most of the plaintiffs would have no realistic day in court if a class action were not available'.

[63] Galanter (1974), p. 95.

[64] Id.; See Cappelletti (1993).

the legal knowledge to realise that they have been harmed and are entitled to raise a claim.[65]

Furthermore, from an economic analysis of law standpoint,[66] this entails a major incentive for large corporations to pursue illicit activities or fraud schemes, knowing that they will be shielded by the lack of procedural protection for injured people and that the few hundred dollars saved for every single one of them, if multiplied by hundreds or even thousands, represent significant sums.[67] The consequent risk is the start of a vicious circle, where strong parties get away with their business, despite repeatedly harming large groups of people, and thus become stronger, bolster their presence on the market, enhance their lobbying network and, possibly, even gain a dangerous monopoly position, while weak and single individuals are left alone, in rational apathy, with their empty substantial rights and worthless claims.[68]

This applies to consumer law and small claims, but it can be easily transposed to torts law, securities and other fields as well,[69] where, despite having suffered major

---

[65] See Resnik (2011).

[66] See Posner (1973).

[67] See Cappalli and Consolo (1992).

[68] A fundamental critique, to this regard, is that potential defendants would just raise the prices of their product, or services, to cover the risk of class litigation.

[69] In torts law, for example product liability, oil spills or asbestos exposition. The securities field has probably seen the largest class action settlement awards. In fact, the early 2000s were characterised by several shareholder suits against large corporations for faulty accounting, price fixing, falsification of financial statements to investors, schemes to conceal the internal losses and similar scandals which unexpectedly had led the companies to bankruptcy, leaving the shareholders overnight with nothing but complete loss of their savings and pensions. The result, thanks to the class action mechanism, were the awards of literally billions of dollars in damages. Some examples are *Enron* from 2006, with 7.2 billion dollars (688 millions of which were destined to the law firm who led the class action during 6 years) awarded in settlement to approximately 1.5 million individuals and entities, *WorldCom*, with 6.1 billion dollars awarded in settlement in 2005 to approximately 830.000 investors, and several other settlements, like *AOL Time Warner* (2005), with 2.5 billion dollars, *Cedant* (2000) with 2.5 billion dollars and *Tyco International* (2007), with 3.2 billion dollars. To this regard, it's interesting to note, on the one side, that, after certification, all the defendants were interested in a settlement rather than risking a jury trial and, on the other side, that after this short period of time not so many big cases have come up in this field, making it believable that companies have learned the lesson the hard way and, therefore, that, at least to some extent, the deterrence objective has been attained. Second, although less advertised because of the considerably lower sums and number of members involved, consumer class actions are certainly worth a mention as a typical example of collective lawsuit, where individuals obtain redress for small damages which, solely, they would have never been able to vindicate. A ground-breaking case to this regard was *Vasquez v. Superior Court* from the California Supreme Court in 1971, where the class sued a frozen food and freezers company to rescind their instalment contract, claiming that the company's door-to-door salesmen had employed fraudulent sale's talk. The key for certification of the class action was managing to prove that all the buyers/class members had been subject to a common 'sales pitch', based on a monologue contained in a training book and sales manual that all salesmen of the company were employing, thus creating on all buyers common reliance for common reasons. The Court reasoned that the '[p]rotection of unwary consumers from being duped by unscrupulous sellers is an exigency of the utmost priority in contemporary society' and that 'class action by consumers produces several salutary by-products, including a therapeutic effect upon

injuries and losses, individual claimants are incapable of dealing equally or even dealing at all with governments, corporations and other powerful, 'deep-pocketed and well-informed' defendants,[70] who manage to swamp and bury any single claimant's rightful claim under endless discovery, appeals and unsustainable legal fees.[71]

Against such a backdrop, the class action model set itself up, in several stances, safe for most recent backlash and still relevant causes for concern, subsequently analysed, as the appropriate tool to level the juridical field between weak single parties and otherwise dominant players. Suddenly, by aggregating the common interests of a certain group of individuals, weak parties were able to enforce their rights in a single suit and reduce the power imbalances.[72]

In sum, proving correct the old adage that 'there is strength in numbers', class actions offered a 'way of enforcing rights which exist on the books but are meaningless because there is no practical way to protect them',[73] in a (worldwide) trend[74] to *effectively* make the law work.

5.2.3 *Procedural Hallmarks and Constitutional Nuances*

As already expressed, the modern model of class action, largely portrayed as a 'uniquely American procedural device',[75] came to life in 1966, after the revision of Rule 23 of the US Federal Rules of Civil Procedure.[76] These Rules, adopted in 1938 and subject to different amendments since, govern civil proceedings in the United

those sellers who indulge in fraudulent practices, aid to legitimate business enterprises by curtailing illegitimate competition, and avoidance to the judicial process of the burden of multiple litigation involving identical claims' (*Vasquez v. Superior Court*, 1971 Cal., accounted by Cappalli and Consolo (1992)).

70 *Fostif Pty Ltd. v. Campbells Cash & Carry Pty Ltd*, 63 NSWLR 203, 226 (2005), on the issue of litigation funders.

71 Rosenberg (1987), p. 563: 'In mass tort cases involving claims for personal injury, which pose daunting problems of causation and remedy, the price of individual justice is notoriously high. Because they typically involve complex factual and legal questions, mass tort claims are exceedingly, if not prohibitively, expensive to litigate. The questions of whether the defendant's conduct failed to satisfy the governing standard of liability frequently entail interrelated technological and policy issues that require extensive discovery, expertise, and preparation to present and resolve adequately. Equally demanding are the causation issues in mass tort cases, such as whether the plaintiff's condition was caused by exposure to the substance in question or to some other source of the same disease risk'.

72 See Galanter (1974).

73 Homburger (1974), pp. 346–347.

74 See Cappelletti (1993).

75 Sherman (2002), p. 401; Born and Salas (2012), p. 3.

76 In particular with the introduction of Rule 23(b)(3) and of the opt-out approach, which will be further on analysed.

States district courts with the purpose 'to secure the just, speedy, and inexpensive determination of every action and proceeding.'[77]

The modern Rule 23, titled 'class actions' and still nowadays rather similar to the 1966 version, is structured in a way as to present: *(i)* the four prerequisites necessary in order to form a class action; *(ii)* the three different kinds of class actions available, characterised by a trans-substantive nature; *(iii)* the certification, notice and judgement phases; *(iv)* the orders the court may make in the conduct of actions; *(v)* the eventuality of settlement (rather common in practice, once certification is obtained), voluntary dismissal or compromise; *(vi)* the possibility of appeals; *(vii)* the appointment of the class counsel; *(viii)* the award of attorney fees.

All these issues will be hereinafter briefly presented and synthetised (without mentioning more specific and related rules), highlighting the relevant features for the purposes of this work. Procedural and constitutional nuances will then be brought on the comparative table against the backdrop of the current EU and, in particular, Italian regime of representative litigation.

The very first preliminary question pertaining any class action regime should be *who* brings the claim before a court, given that the class is all but formed at this stage. The one to take this task under the US Rule 23 is a *member of the class* (or more than one), who will assume the role of named plaintiff. Despite this peculiarity, it is important to stress that, in the future, his or her position will not be in any way different from that of the other class members; in fact, this individual is not rarely recognised as a 'mere figurehead' used by the class lawyer as a 'pawn needed to gain entry to court.'[78] As will be discussed, the 2019 Italian class action presents, formally, a similar figure, who bears the same name ('class representative'), but has a substantially different function.[79]

Retaining focus on the US regime, the peculiarity distinguishing this first named plaintiff from *general* society is the fact that he or she, like the rest of the class, has suffered a *specific* wrong. In particular, what puts them into motion is an act or omission from the defendant, 'radiating outwards and harming different people', at which point they 'step[s] forward to champion the rights of all those affected.'[80]

The latter, that is the future class, may form in different backgrounds, depending on the setting where the act or omission of the defendant was perpetrated. Its members could come from a pre-existing group, such as a school's students, a factory's workers, a company's shareholders, a small town's residents; alternatively, they could be united only by the act or omission suffered, such as being the consumers

---

[77] Rule 1, US Federal Rules of Civil Procedure. It must be noted that, for matters governed by State and not Federal law, these Rules do not apply, although some States have adopted the very same or at least extremely similar provisions with regards to class actions. Hence, as most authors have done in the past, for reasons of simplicity and clarity, only Rule 23 will be herein considered.

[78] Cappalli and Consolo (1992), p. 235, fn. 88. See also Cappelletti (1976). Some authors even argue that such a figure causes confusion and should hence be eliminated: see, e.g., Burns (1990), p. 165.

[79] See *infra*, Chap. 6.

[80] Cappalli and Consolo (1992), p. 224.

of the same defective product or harmful service. What, under any circumstance, connects them is a common complaint against a common defendant for 'common questions of law or fact.'[81] An example could be a company which sells defective products to its customers. In this case, the initial plaintiff would be one of the customers, who previously bought the company's defective product and now suffered damage from it. Other examples could be the depositors from the same bank suing the bank directors for breach of trust,[82] or the inhabitants of a small region fighting the same corporation that has been dumping its wastes in the local water and thus contaminating it.[83]

A key feature of this regime is, hence, the existence of a *class* of people. It cannot be the general society; however large, it still needs to be a *confined* group or category of individuals. As argued by Samuel Issacharoff, this key trait sets the procedural technique at hand as a specific mechanism of *counter-majoritarian* stances.[84] Looser rules, instead, seem to have been set for the Italian class action, especially for the injunctive one, as subsequently discussed in the following.[85]

The *representative* nature of this type of suit is central. Per Rule 23(a), 'One or more members of a class may sue or be sued as representative parties *on behalf* of all members'. This entails the *non-participation* (at least directly) to the judicial proceedings of all the other members of the class (potentially even millions of people), who will be bound by the *res judicata* effects of the decision. In favour of judicial economy, effectiveness of justice and injury-deterrence, the right to 'a day in court' is therefore sacrificed. Constitutional concerns for the respect of fair trial guarantees arise, only partially tempered by the prominent guarantor role of the judge and by notice and opt-out possibilities—the opt-out option evidently not for injunctive actions *ex* Rule 23(b)(2), though.

Another characteristic is that the class—conceptually at least—*preexists* the filing of the action. This is strictly connected to the opt-out regime established in 1996, presented in the following.

Ordinarily, the individual willing to 'champion' both his or her own harmed rights and those of the other people (members) similarly situated contacts a lawyer or is contacted by one already aware of the issue at stake. It is not unusual for the latter circumstance to occur, given the *entrepreneurial* nature of this type of litigation for class attorneys. In this regard, it is important to note that the lawyer should be ready to take the risk as well, since litigation costs, and, in particular, the heavy costs of notice to all class members, are borne by them.[86] Hence, the importance of

[81] Rule 23 of the US Federal Procedural Rules 'One or more members of a class may sue or be sued as representative parties on behalf of all only if [...] there are questions of law or fact common to the class'.

[82] *Perry v. Mea*k, Oklahoma (1980).

[83] *Sterling v. Velsicol Chemical Corp*, sixth Circuit (1988).

[84] See Issacharoff (2012), pp. 374 *et seq.*

[85] See, *infra*, Chap. 6.

[86] Although third-party funders are increasingly gaining importance in this field as well. See Voet (2016).

'*adequacy*' and '*representativeness*', as prerequisites for all class actions under Rule 23. The benefits class lawyers can gain from this 'legal bet' are usually well worth the gamble. In case of successful outcome, in fact, all costs will be either recovered from the losing party or from the fund set for the compensation of the class and, most importantly, the *contingency fees* they work on could grant them a massive payoff, especially in case of settlement.

Statistics often show that most of the certified class actions end with a *settlement*, without further continuing the proceedings. As a consequence, attorneys have often been criticised for their tendency to 'create' class actions in order to pursue their own interests (i.e., the contingency fees), rather than those of the class. In fact, one of the main and most condemned (especially on European shores) issues regarding class actions is this: on the one hand, class lawyers have at times been found to push for a settlement adverse to the interests of the class, sometimes leaving its members with just 'coupons' or very modest paybacks, in order to close deals—very beneficial to their own pockets—with the corporate defendants (not so rarely in *collusive* agreements); on the other hand, they have in other circumstances tried to ride the mediatic wave of certain disputes against corporate businesses by creating an '*in terrorem* regime' and pushing for settlement, once the suit is certified.[87]

Once these preliminary issues are settled and the class named plaintiff and legal counsel are found, the suit is brought before the court, where a judge will hear the parties and decide on the question of class certification, which represents a fundamental step, since it's aimed at granting class action status to the lawsuit. After that, it is not rare at all to start negotiations for settlement.[88] On this matter, most of class actions' critics emphasise how corporate defendants, despite not being guilty, might often be pushed to settle in order to avoid all the bad publicity arising from the trial or the risk of a potentially financially-destructive judgement for their business, also in light of the juries' notorious unpredictability and, in particular, because of the high costs of discovery. The issue of *equality of arms* and, in general, of *fair process* regarding defendants needs to be considered, too.[89] In particular, the role (and boundaries) of the media and the possibility of class actions filed by competitors should be accounted.

In this context, in order to grant certification, Rule 23 sets four prerequisites to be assessed by the court. They are the following: '*numerosity*', meaning that joinder of all class members in ordinary litigation is otherwise impracticable[90]; '*commonal-*

---

[87] Mullenix (2014), p. 399.

[88] See Note (1978).

[89] See, *supra*, Chap. 4 and, *infra*, Chap. 11.

[90] There has been a lot of discussion on which is the exact number to render a class 'numerous' and whether such a number really exists. Some courts argue that a class is numerous if it counts at least forty members (*Marcus v. BMW of N. Am.*, LLC, 687 F.3d 583, 591–92 (third Cir. 2012)), while others insist that no fixed number is sufficient and that such a prerequisite must be addressed case by case on the basis of the members' geographical dispersion, the ease with which they can be identified, the size of the claims and the nature of the action (*TWL Corp.*, 712 F.3d 886, 894 (fifth Cir. 2013)).

ity' of the questions of fact and law, meaning that the harmful event from the defendant is the same and that the decision can resolve 'in one shot' all the claims of the class[91]; '*typicality*', meaning that the representative's claims or defences must have equal characteristics to those of the rest of the class[92]; '*adequacy*' or '*representativeness*', that is, worthiness[93] of the class representative to protect the class interests in a 'fair and adequate' way and of the class counsel's competence and financial capability to sustain the considerable expected expenses.[94]

For certification, in addition to meeting all the four prerequisites under Rule 23(a), the class action must be of one of the three types presented under Rule 23(b). As a matter of fact, one of 1966's main amendments to Rule 23 regarded this classification and the introduction of the following, not mutually exclusive, three categories.[95]

---

[91] A very important decision to this regard was *Wal-Mart Stores, Inc. v. Dukes*, 564 U.S. Supreme Court, 131, 2541 (2011), where it was clarified that merely reciting a list of common questions is not sufficient. Instead, '[w]hat matters [...is] the capacity of a classwide proceeding to generate common answers apt to drive the resolution of the litigation' [emphasis added]. The class members' claims 'must [therefore] depend upon a common contention [...] of such a nature that it is capable of classwide resolution—which means that determination of its truth or falsity will resolve an issue that is central to the validity of each one of the claims in one stroke'.

[92] It is usually sufficient to show that the claims of the named plaintiff and class members 'arise from the same event or pattern or practice and are based on the same legal theory' (*Ault v. Walt Disney World Co.*, 692 F.3d 1212, 1216 (11th Cir. 2012)). Moreover, although not significantly, some variations between the claims are permissible. What matters is that the named plaintiff's claim is not subject to a unique defence which will likely become a major focus of the litigation (*Marcus v. BMW of N. Am.*, LLC, 687 F.3d 583, 591–92 (third Cir. 2012)).

[93] Also defined as '*seriousness*' by Cappelletti (1976), p. 687.

[94] Rule 23 specifically demands that 'the representative parties will fairly and adequately protect the interests of the class'. In particular, potential conflicts of interests, between the named plaintiff and the defendant, intra-class and with the class counsel are analysed by the court. The suit is deemed not to be in the interests of the class when plaintiffs seek relief 'that duplicates a remedy that most buyers already have received and that remains available' to class members (*Aqua Dots Prods. Liability Litig.*, 654 F.3d 748, 752 (seventh Cir. 2011)). Additionally, other courts view these requirements as 'unrealistic' given the 'nominal' role of the named plaintiff in a lawsuit that 'is in fact entirely managed by the class counsel' (*Phillips v. Asset Acceptance, LLC*, Case No. 13–2251, 2013 U.S. App. 23,984, 8–10 (seventh Cir. Dec. 2, 2013)). This last consideration about the class counsel is shared by Cappalli and Consolo (1992), p. 235, fn. 89, who argue that 'the class lawyer represents three often conflicting sets of interests: his own financial stake; his named client; and the class', although noting that 'yet no special set of rules has been devised to manage conflicts between class lawyer and plaintiff, apart from the court's duty to supervise class action settlements'.

[95] Until then, in the 1938 original version, the categories were defined in terms of the theoretical nature of the rights involved and each one of them was associated with an applicable scope or extent of the possible judgment, so as to determine the res judicata effect and who was it to be considered binding upon. The 'true' category involved 'joint, common or secondary rights', the 'hybrid' category involved 'several' rights related to 'specific property', while the 'spurious' category concerned 'several' rights associated with a common question and common relief. This classification, however, generated vast confusion, contrasting decisions and a scarce use, thus proving an ineffective resource to address collective concerns regarding access to justice (see Andreotti 2017). See also Issacharoff and Zimreth (2018).

First, Rule 23(b)(1) starts by addressing circumstances where separate individual actions would create uncertainties or prejudice to individual rights either for the defendant or for other individual parties not participating in the case. Two kinds are presented.

Rule 23(b)(1)(a), the so-called '*incompatible standards*' class, is specifically designed for defendants seeking insulation from repeated similar individual actions and inconsistent judgements, 'establish[ing] incompatible standards of conduct'. An example could be a trustee facing the challenge of more and more cases springing up from different beneficiaries, with each of these cases potentially decided in a different way with incompatible standards concerning the distribution.[96]

Rule 23(b)(1)(b), the so-called '*impeding of interest*' class action, instead, is devised for absent potential class members in a common property or right, whose interests 'could be impaired if issues are resolved by individual actions'. A classic example is that of the 'limited fund', where the claims of the class members exceed the defendant's assets and separate suits could leave nothing for other potential class members to satisfy their claims.

Both these types, that is the first category in general, have seen a very limited use.[97]

The second category is presented under Rule 23(b)(2) and is also called the '*injunctive*' or 'declaratory relief' class action. As the name says, its aim, rather than pursuing monetary damages (which can still be pursued by this means incidentally, although with some limitations),[98] is to alter the common defendant's conduct, to prohibit or require it to act in a certain way, on the basis of a court order issued on grounds applicable to the entire class. The most paradigmatic case is that of the 'civil rights suits' of the 1960s–1980s, by which several constitutional and important civil rights were enforced.[99] Some notable examples are those which brought an end to racial segregation, or those that ensured a wide range of statutory standards in prison or mental institutions.[100]

The main constitutional concerns, to this regard, appear to be the extension of the *res judicata* effects on the whole class, without a concrete (formally, at least) participation of all its members to the proceedings. A similar issue appears relevant today in the injunctive class action filed against ILVA and Acciaierie d'Italia by

---

[96] See Sherman (2002), p. 401.

[97] Id.

[98] The express wording of Rule 23 is 'where the *primarily* relief sought is injunctive or declaratory, not monetary' (emphasis added). Although some courts have held a restrictive reading, the main perception is that monetary damages may be recovered under this class suit if they are incidental to the injunctive relief (Sherman 2002). An interesting example is that of class members who were exposed to hazardous substances or took allegedly dangerous medical drugs, hence significantly increasing the risk of contracting a serious disease, for which 'medical monitoring' is deemed necessary (i.e. periodic examination for early detection and treatment) (see *Abuan v. Generally Electric Co.*, ninth Circ. (1993)).

[99] Id.

[100] Shlanger (2006), p. 550.

some residents of the province of Taranto, under the 2019 Italian regime, further analysed in the subsequent Part.[101]

Last, the third category under Rule 23(b)(3), also known as the '*common questions*' class action, is a 'catch-all' device,[102] which, in the words of the Supreme Court in 1997, has the purpose to allow 'vindication of 'the rights of groups of people who individually would be without effective strength to bring their opponents into court at all".[103] In the same decision, the Court continued by quoting a seventh Circuit opinion, which reminded how 'the policy at the very core of the class action mechanism is to overcome the problem that *small recoveries* do not provide the incentive for any individual to bring a solo action prosecuting his or her rights. A class action solves this problem by aggregating the relatively paltry potential recoveries into something worth someone's (usually an attorney's) labor'.[104] The class action's fundamental goal to provide an effective instrument of *access to court* to weak, individual parties harmed in their *everyday life* by powerful players emerges once again.

In addition to Rule 23(a)'s previously enunciated four prerequisites, these class suits present two additional requirements to be met: *predominance* and *superiority*. On the one side, the court must verify whether the 'questions of law or fact common to the members of the class predominate over any questions affecting only individual members'[105] and, on the other side, whether 'the class action is superior to other available methods for the fair and efficient adjudication of the controversy'.[106]

In order to make these determinations, the court should consider the following factors: 'the interest of class members to individually control separate actions'; 'whether and to what extent any litigation concerning the controversy has already been undertaken' by or against class members; 'the advantages or disadvantages of litigating the claims in the particular form'; 'any likely difficulties in managing the class action'.[107] In particular, class certification has been denied on numerous occasions, especially in mass torts cases, for lack of the last element, 'manageability', for instance because of the large number of potential class members, inability to properly locate and identify them, conflicts of law or difficulties in the determination of damages.

Despite most recent backlash, the number of successful lawsuits (and, consequently, effective redress) by means of this mechanism is massive. Most of American

---

[101] See *infra*, Chap. 7.

[102] Sherman (2002), p. 406.

[103] In *Amchem Products, Inc. v. Windsor*, 521 U.S. 591 (1997), quoting the Advisory Committee to the Rule's revision.

[104] *Mace* v. *Van Ru Credit Corp.*, 109 F.3d 338, 344 (1997).

[105] A recent example of denial of certification for lack of 'predominance' was in an anti-trust class action from 2013, where it was found that the damages where too individualized to be calculated on a classwide basis and, hence, common class questions didn't predominate over the individual damages questions (*Comcast v. Behrend*, 133 S. Ct. 1426 (2013)).

[106] Rule 23(b)(3).

[107] Id.

class actions are under Rule 23(b)(3)[108] and most authors agree that, since its introduction in 1966, it was this very provision to exponentially boost the success of the US model,[109] becoming the vehicle for *damage* class action suits and, consequently, concrete economic redress for millions of otherwise weak parties across a broad spectrum of legal matters.[110]

In particular, the key element which, since 1966, managed to boost this mechanism's power-force was the *'opt-out'* approach adopted with said revision of the Rule.[111]

As is known, a crucial distinction between different types of collective redress is the one between the 'opt-out' and the 'opt-in' procedure. The former approach stands on the idea that, at the start of any class action, *everyone* who would theoretically be entitled to be part of it (by falling within the defined class)—that is everyone who is in a similar position to that of the plaintiff/now class representative, having suffered from the same defendant's act or omission and having, therefore, the same rights—is, very simply, part of it.

Consequently, unless the potential class members decide to *exclude* themselves from the suit by a certain date (that is to 'opt out'), they will be automatically included in it, with no explicit consent needed. The judgement (and so the *res judicata* effects), whichever the outcome, will be binding for all of them unless they leave the class themselves. The class members might, thus, receive compensation without ever appearing in court with a totally passive conduct. Still, they will be precluded in the future to litigate the whole claim or any particular issue relating to it, even if they were absent to all the proceedings.

The introduction of this approach in 1966 and the abandoning of the 'opt-in' one, where, instead, all potential class members are required to *sign-in* in order to become part of the suit, set a revolutionary thrust.[112] It was no longer necessary to hold open 'absurdly lengthy opt-in periods to encourage as many [potential] class members as possible',[113] who perhaps were not even aware of their legal entitlements,[114] or who were too lazy or doubtful to actually opt-in. It simply sufficed to raise the claim in order to immediately count with the large numbers of the class and its consequently higher *negotiating-power*. Any initial and structural power unbalance with corporate defendants was immediately removed.

Two major concerns, are commonly raised with regards to this approach. On the one hand, as already mentioned, the risk is that the *attorney gambles* with the class numbers and, thus, creates class actions without class awareness or real necessity or,

---

[108] Sherman (2002).

[109] Cappalli and Consolo (1992).

[110] Sherman (2002).

[111] This approach, however, regarded only the third type of class actions, while Rule 23(b)(1) and 23(b)(2) were deemed mandatory and did not require even individual notice.

[112] See Cappalli and Consolo (1992).

[113] Marcus (2013), p. 601.

[114] See Cappelletti (1993).

even worse, in shady attempts to conclude settlements favourable only to their pockets.[115] The issue, in short, is that no real control on the decision-making is held by the class itself. Furthermore, European scholars, who have been the most sceptical to this approach, find difficulties in 'conceptually framing' the merely formal role of the named plaintiff/class representative (in favour of the class attorney).[116] On the other hand, major *due process* concerns are raised in relation to the awareness of absent class members of a dispute which will be binding on them, as well as their loss of the right to 'a day in court'.[117]

In light of these considerations, a proper *notice* to all the potential members appears of the outmost importance.[118] *First*, for questions of justice and to answer their right to be informed on a dispute whose effects will be binding on them. *Second*, for logistics and consistency reasons, in order to avoid future challenges on the basis that some members were not properly made aware of the proceedings. To this regard, Rule 23(c)(2)(b), referring to the 23(b)(3) 'damages' class action, requires 'the best notice that is *practicable* under the circumstances, including individual notice to *all* members who can be identified through *reasonable effort*'.[119]

In different consumer and product liability cases, where there are insufficient records of purchase and therefore it is not possible to identify all the class members, notice through public media, such as newspapers, radio and television, or through posting in calculated locations frequented by potential class members has been deemed acceptable.[120] Recent cases have even seen publicity through very modern means: e.g., podcasts, TV spots, or even subways posters with QR codes. The issue of notice is still a delicate one and always in the limelight, especially after the quite recent amendments from 2019, which, in the extensive commentary to the Rule, declared that the notice was to be not only 'practicable' but also '*appropriate*',[121]

---

[115] See Sternlight (2000). Apart from the absentees' rights and lack of involvement in any decision regarding the case, the most delicate issue here is that class counsels may easily use the class' numbers to their complete advantage. With class actions that can involve literally millions of people and without the need to concretely seek their approval, the negotiating power class counsels have is as immense as their liberty in taking relevant decisions, without any control, expect that from the judge, over their sensitive choices.

[116] See Cappalli and Consolo (1992).

[117] See Marcus (2013).

[118] See Sternlight (2000), and the *Mullane Case* (1950), the *Eisen Case* (1974), the *Phillips Petroelum Case* (1985) therein recalled, cases in ehich it was held that notice of class action, sent by first-class mail to the home address of all the known potential members and including notification of the 'opt-out' right, satisfied due process. Despite traditional mail still being the standard, some concerns have been raised: first, standard mail notice programs for millions of people can be extremely expensive and deter low-value class actions from even being brought in the first place; second, individuals may move and change the address, so there could be inaccurateness.

[119] See in particular the *Eisen Case* (1974), accounted in Id., where it was held that the costs of adequate notice to all class members must be paid by the representative plaintiff, even when such costs are so high as to make litigation infeasible.

[120] See Sherman (2002).

[121] Advisory Committee, from Rule 23, as reported in Marcus (2013).

based on the unique circumstances of each case,[122] in what is seen as a general trend towards enabling the class to make more informed decisions.

Subsequently, once the notice phase is concluded, all opt-out members are tabulated and the final number of class members can be assessed.[123] Provided the number is still sufficiently high and, thus, satisfies the requirement of 'numerosity' of the class suit, pre-trial activities can start; discovery for the purpose of gathering evidence on the disputed issues and pre-trial conferences follow. Finally, should no settlement agreement be found between the parties (a rare circumstance), the trial takes place.[124] The judgement will precisely identify all class members, in order to provide certainty regarding *res judicata* in any future dispute. In practice, almost every certified class action case is settled before reaching the judgement phase.[125]

Important comparative reflections with the EU, especially Italian, opt-in regime will be presented in the following.

5.2.4 Lessons from the Common Law Experience

Different authors agree that American class actions with the beginning of the new century are facing an evolving dysfunction, caused by a large variety of factors.[126]

The 'romantic narrative'[127] of the white-knight-in-shining-armour attorney who comes to save the day and rescue multitudes of weak parties harmed by large, dark and greedy corporations is not always true. There is also another (dark) side of the coin: for instance, the numerous concerns regarding the capacity of legal counsels to duly represent the interests of the whole class, not to fall prey to easy and tempting collusions with defendants or, perhaps worse, not to push for '*in terrorem*' settlements or actions, conducting what have been defined as 'fishing expeditions'.[128] At the same time, relevant questions on bindingness of the decisions on totally unaware absent class members with absolutely no decision-making status emerge, too, as well as the possible counter-effects of the aimed deterrence: with large corporations starting to view class judgements and settlements as a '*cost of doing*

[122] I.e., for the elderly using electronic means of communication may not be sufficient.

[123] See Hanotiau (2004).

[124] Instead, should a settlement be found, class members would still have the option to opt-out.

[125] See Mullenix (2014).

[126] Id., see also Marcus (2013).

[127] Mullenix (2014), pp. 406 *et seq.*

[128] This expression refers to an attempt to collect incriminating information against large corporations without having real proofs of their wrongdoings, usually by means of extensive discovery (i.e., by having access to the company's business records). Such a threat is often used by ruthless attorneys in order to leverage settlements.

business'[129] and, consequently, simply raising and passing along the costs to the very same consumers.[130]

On the other side, 'doctrinal complexity and disarray in class action jurisprudence'[131] has all but helped, with the increasing risk of 'endless rounds of reactive pleading'[132] frustrating litigants' ability to reach the merits of the dispute or Rule 23's initial purposes.

Moreover, after many years of growth in the use of the class action device, the current trend sees both the US Supreme Court and the Congress acting in order to limit them, in particular by providing courts with a greater power in the scrutiny of settlements and by *raising the threshold* for certification of the class.

Furthermore, the recent additions of conservative Justices to the Supreme Court's composition are casting concerns on further limitations in the years to come. An alarming example is the one regarding arbitration clauses and class waivers, by means of which, in certain circumstances and business fields,[133] companies can now prevent class litigation in general[134] simply by requiring that consumers (or workers) agree to *individual arbitration* of any future claims.

In sum, all these elements show how the US class action mechanism—once-envisaged as the perfect sling in David's hands in order to defend himself from Goliath's abuses—may still provide collective redress to weak parties, but, at the same time, is all but flawless and requires a substantial restructuring or even rethinking,[135] in order to deliver effective justice to everyone in the most efficient way.

5.3 Collective Redress in the European Union

For several years, decades even, the US class action model was a dazzling comet flying through the legal universe of substantive rights and procedural mechanisms. Internationally speaking, it was a thunderous exception, often admired at distance, always with great care and, not seldom, wary suspicion. While in some countries

[129] See Drahozal (2001) and Joyce (2014).

[130] See Sternlight (2000).

[131] See Mullenix (2014), p. 424, who notes how the Wright, Miller & Kane standard treatise on federal practice and procedure dedicates four entire volumes to the class action practice.

[132] Id.

[133] Mostly in consumer law and product liability cases, although also in employment cases (for example, see *Lamp Plus v. Varela*, from 2019). See, *infra*, Chap. 10 for recent developments in Italy under this sense, too.

[134] Thus, both ordinary class actions and class arbitration.

[135] See Mullenix (2014).

traditionally close to the US culture and influence, such as Australia[136] and Canada,[137] similar models were shortly after adopted and still seem to thrive well,[138] the European reaction was much more complex.

First, the continental civil law tradition was deeply marked by an *individual approach* to judicial protection, 'constructed around individual rights and individual access to justice rather than collective interests and collective litigation.'[139] This deep-rooted, *dualistic mindset*, 'one against one, incident by incident',[140] made it extremely difficult for European jurists to accept a different kind of litigation from the one 'conducted by and on behalf of the individual *named parties only*'.[141]

Second, the 'rough justice' and *potentially abusive* incentives set by the US model, which often 'slighted or even trampled [...] venerable rights and ethics',[142] frightened and repelled European commentators, to the point that even the EU Commission itself described it as a '*toxic cocktail*', to avoid at all costs.[143] As subsequently addressed, the political upheaval caused by the so-called *Dieselgate scandal* was crucial in shifting the perspective.

Still, it was undeniable that globalisation and economic transformation of the society (see *supra*, Part I)—in which production, distribution and consumption had now become 'mass phenomena'—had created a new 'organisational obstacle' to

[136] The first Australian class action regime was enacted in 1992, with the amendment of Part IV-A of the Federal Court Act from 1976. For further analysis see, e.g., Murphy and Cameron (2006).

[137] Class actions were first introduced in Quebec in 1976, then in Ontario in 1992 and in British Columbia in 1996, whereas in other provinces subsequently. For further analysis see, e.g., Winkler et al. (2014).

[138] See Voet (2017).

[139] See Gaboardi (2019), p. 4, according to whom there 'is a traditional approach in civil law countries to emphasizing an inherent link between individual rights and their claims of protection'.

[140] Cappalli and Consolo (1992), p. 220, noting how this bipolar model is 'a subtly powerful suppressant of substantive legal development' in the European Continent, being 'so protective of violators and blind to individual justice'.

[141] *Wal-Mart Stores, Inc. v. Dukes*, 564 U.S. 338, 348 (2011), quoting *Califano v. Yamasaki*, 442 U.S. 682, 700–701 (1979).

[142] Cappalli and Consolo (1992), p. 219, referring to venerable rights such as 'notice of proceedings, to choosing your counsel, to being free from ad hoc courts, to suffering juridical harm only after having been heard' or venerable ethics such as 'lawyers [...] 'buying into' lawsuits, clients [being] puppets not puppeteers, and meritless lawsuits [...] brought for the mere in terrorem settlement value' and, thus, comparing the class action model to the American Wild West.

[143] As discussed above, the expression 'toxic cocktail' was first used in 2008 in the questions and answers to a Green Paper from the EU Commission: 'US style class action is not envisaged. EU legal systems are very different from the US legal system, which is the result of a 'toxic cocktail'—a combination of several elements (punitive damages, contingency fees, opt-out, pre-trial discovery procedures. [...] This combination of elements—'toxic cocktail'—should not be introduced in Europe. Various effective safeguards, including the loser pays' principles, the judges's discretion to exclude unmeritorious claims and the accreditation of associations which are authorised to take cases on behalf of consumers, are built into existing national collective interest schemes in Europe'. See Questions and Answers to the Green Paper on Consumer Collective Redress, European Commission, 27 November 2008, Question No. 9.

effective justice.[144] In the farsighted words of Mauro Cappelletti, in this new, fast-paced, fully-connected society 'social rights have emerged as most important', in the need to protect 'broad categories of [otherwise] discriminated or weak persons: children, women, old people, racial or linguistic minorities, those affected by a handicap, *etc*', with significant examples being those of an 'isolated consumer of a good produced *à la chaine* and distributed in large quantities' or 'the case of the individual damaged by mass pollution'.[145] In these cases, even the harshest European critics had to agree that 'the individual alone is usually incapable of vindicating effectively the rights involved; since these are collective or 'diffuse' rights, the only really effective protection is one which reflects the 'collective' or 'class' character of the rights'.[146]

In sum, new economically and socially complex situations required new substantive rights, which, in turn, required new procedural mechanisms, in order to enforce them and grant *de facto* what otherwise would remain as vain and empty liberties for the weakest members of our society. With this premise, the US model of class actions could certainly be criticised or feared because of its potential abusive backfire power; nonetheless, although flawed, it was an answer to the cultural, economic and social growth of our world. In Europe, on the contrary, 'nothing worth mention [was] being done to offer procedural justice in cases of mass victimization'.[147] Once assimilated this, it appeared clear that a solution had to be found in the Old Continent as well, keeping in mind the EU's strong desire to set itself up in the international landscape as a champion of human rights, democracy, justice and equality. Serious discussions, therefore, began at both academical and institutional level on which was the most appropriate tool, and are still ongoing in what has been called a 'never ending story'.[148]

In this vast, lingering and uncoordinated debate, the first step was a *radical break* from the US class action model; a distancing which started even with the use of a *different name*. In fact, in the beginning, until the late 1990s, the European discussion on the protection of weak parties was all about the viability of 'class actions', with the US mechanism being perceived as the only alternative. Later on, instead, the discussion moved on to the concept of 'collective actions', in an attempt to distinguish the European approach from the US mechanism, depicted overseas as a 'toxic cocktail' or a 'Rube Goldberg artefact—a strange-looking melange of pushes and pulls and bells and baubles'[149] because of its complexity and potentially abusive incentives. Finally, the current terminological stage of '*collective redress*' (and 'representative actions—'see infra) was reached, under the notable consideration that

---

[144] Cappelletti (1993), p. 282.

[145] Id.

[146] Id.

[147] Cappalli and Consolo (1992), p. 220.

[148] See Hess (2014).

[149] Cappalli and Consolo (1992), p. 219.

terminology should encompass the ultimate goal, that is the compensation of harmed individuals.

In particular, this last shift reflects the intention to substantially cover wider situations and focus on the *objectives* of the policy rather than on the mechanisms,[150] under the realisation that private litigation is not always the only nor the most appropriate device to deliver mass redress, as other techniques, such as public regulatory redress, constitutional review, consumer ombudsmen, ODR, ADR mechanisms or civil '*piggy-backing*'[151] on criminal prosecutions, may be cheaper, simpler and quicker.[152] Moreover, these terminological changes show the intensity of the debate and the *struggle* Europe has faced in taking a clear position and establishing a *coherent legal framework*.

The historical evolution of this piecemeal and totally uncoordinated legislation, both at the EU level and in relation to national models, will be analysed in the following, with a focus on the *consumer-oriented goals*. The *procedural hallmarks* and *constitutional nuances*, together with the main questions left in the current regulatory context will be subsequently detailed.

5.3.1 Objectives: Avoiding Consumer Scandals

The debate on collective redress reached European shores around the 1980s, increasing between the late 1990s and the early 2000s, first at national level,[153] then at EU level, with a complete eruption around 2005 and the so-called Dieselgate scandal (see *infra*).[154] Before the RAD on consumer representative actions, particularly significant was the Commission's Recommendation from 2013, aiming at harmonising and delivering a clear common legal framework; although with very poor results.

The reasons for the arise of this intense and evolving discussion were only partially overlapping those that had originally brought the US to develop the class action model. The goal of providing effective access to justice and protecting weak parties was present. The enforcement of *small claims*, seldom brought because of cost-effectiveness and rational apathy, was indeed a central point of the European debate. Ensuring *fair competition* and deterrence of illicit activities from large

[150] See Hodges and Voet (2018).

[151] Id. The term '*piggybacking*', which literally intends the act of 'rid[ing] on someone's back with your arms around the person's neck and your legs round their waist' (Cambridge Dictionary, 2020), has been employed by different scholars, such as Hodges and Voet (2018), in order to refer to civil claims brought as '*partie civile*' by one of the victims in already-pending criminal prosecutions.

[152] Id.

[153] For example, in Italy, in Cappalli and Consolo (1992), regarding the introduction of class actions in Italy. See also, in Italy, apart from Cappelletti (1975), Rodotà (1976), Pizzorusso (1976), Trocker (1990), Bognetti (1998) and Taruffo (2001).

[154] Hodges (2010).

business corporations were principles closely linked to the EU's traditional attention to the common market.[155] Nonetheless, the other goal of the 1966 US amendment drafters, that is providing an effective procedural tool for fighting racial discrimination (and civil rights in general) in courts, was lacking in the EU political agenda for collective redress.

This is portrayed by the historical evolution of collective redress in Europe, which took place around the continent at different paces in a highly confused and (still) unharmonised way.[156] To this regard, three phases can be identified.

First, a few single countries, in the wake of the common law-class action experience, were frontrunners in developing—*autonomously*—their own national models of collective litigation. In particular, Spain, Greece, Portugal, and Hungary introduced collective litigation mechanisms respectively in 1984, 1994, 1995, and 1996.[157] The results in these four countries, safe for Portugal in recent years, nonetheless, are still rather unsatisfying, (mainly consumer and competition) sector-based, with extremely rare cases and no significant change brought by the new procedure.[158] Around the same years, discussions on collective redress were starting in the Scandinavian countries as well, which led to the adoption of group procedures in Sweden for the first time in 2003 and, subsequently, between 2007 and 2008, in Demark, Finland and Norway, too.[159] The remarkable feature of these four Nordic countries—which makes them stand out in relation to the other initial European models of collective redress—is the fact that they all give standing and great importance to *public regulatory bodies*, in particular to Consumer Ombudsmen. The

---

[155] Some authors insist it is more appropriate to talk about 'affecting future behaviour' rather than 'deterrence', since both behavioural psychology and empirical evidence show that 'supportive, responsive and often no-fault regulatory policies' appear to be more effective than 'legal systems [simply] based on principles of fault and deterrence' (see Hodges and Voet (2018)).

[156] See Voet (2017).

[157] According to Article 20(1), from the Spanish 'Ley General para la Defensa de los Consumidores y Usuarios' from 1984, now Article 24 of the Royal Legislative Decree 1/2007 of 16 November ('*Texto refundido de la Ley General para la Defensa de los Consumidores y Usuarios y otras leyes complementarias*'), Spanish associations of consumers and users were entitled to file lawsuits to defend their members and the general interests of consumers and users. In Greece, instead, in 1994, with the adoption of law 2251/1994 on 'Consumers' Protection', consumer organizations were allowed standing to claim damages on behalf of groups of injured consumers. In Portugal, the so- called 'Popular Action Law' was introduced by means of Portuguese Law 83/95, of August 31st, 1995, combined with Art. 52(3) of the Portuguese Constitution. In Hungary, finally, an opt-out mechanism was introduced in 1996 for cases relating consumer and competition law.

[158] See, for an updated comparative evaluation, Azar-Baud et al. (2024).

[159] The so-called 'Swedish Group Proceedings Act' (SFS 2002:599 '*Lagen Om Grupprättegång*') from 2002; the 'Danish Administration of Justice Act' (AJA), chapter 23a, section 254(a-k) from 2008; the 'Finnish Class Action Act' (444/2007); the Norway 'Civil Procedure Act', Section 35–1(2). In Sweden, the first among the four, a governmental reporting team lead by Professor Lindblom was first issued in 1995, expressing itself in favour of the introduction of an efficient procedural system aimed at granting effective justice to certain types of smaller claims. Initially, the implementation of an opt-out system was proposed, similarly to the US class action's model. However, the political debate continued and it was only in 2003 that the new law for group actions entered into force, with a more lenient approach and favouring an opt-in procedure, among others.

Scandinavian model shows a way to deal with mass victimisation and group proceedings under certain aspects innovative—alternative too, in the sense depicted by Mauro Cappelletti when talking about the 'procedural obstacles', which must be overcome by 'alternatives to the ordinary courts and the usual litigation procedures'[160]—and certainly not afraid to look past the beaten track of the US class action. Other notable examples of this kind include the Netherlands' WCAM model and the German KapMuG (Capital Markets Model Case Act), both from 2005 and both inspired by concrete cases demonstrating the inefficiency of the judicial system to provide effective and tangible justice. Last, by the end of the first decade of the twenty-first century, discussions were progressing both at EU level and, autonomously, in other national States. Following their footsteps, both Italy and Poland, for example, adopted an opt-in consumer-limited mechanism in 2010, although with mediocre results.[161] The main element to underscore hereby is the generally scarce use of these mechanisms and their limited scope of application, mainly to consumer, securities and competition law issues.

The *second phase*, instead, saw a protagonist role from the EU institutions, in order to contrast the otherwise hazy, poor and uncoordinated collective redress panorama, described, not coincidentally, in an-early 2000s study as 'one of astonishing diversity and total underdevelopment'.[162] To this regard, alongside the autonomous national developments from the first phase, discussions had indeed been ongoing in EU political chambers and institutions for decades already. However, fundamental difficulties arose in balancing the opposite interests of consumer groups and of the lobbying industry, that is between the needs for easily accessible, flexible instruments, and the necessity of protecting corporate defendants from abusive litigation. The EU Directive from 1998 'on injunctions for the protection of consumers' rights' was the first step of this process of harmonisation. Its goal was to facilitate *cross-border* injunctive relief against infringements harmful to large groups of consumers. Said Directive, subsequently amended several times, aimed at 'terminating in good time' infringements harming a cumulation of interests of individuals. Actions could

[160] Cappelletti (1993), p. 287, in what has been defined as the 'third wave' of the access to justice movement. Cappelletti, it must be said for completeness, referred mostly to conciliation, mediation and arbitration. However, the rationale behind his considerations, that is the idea that 'in certain areas or kinds of controversies, the normal solution—the traditional contentious litigation in court—might not be the best possible way to provide effective vindication of rights', still applies today to other forms of redress. This analysis, as will be presented in the last chapter, is strongly supported by Hodges and Voet (2018), who argue that ordinary litigation should be avoided and effective justice should be pursued by means of public regulatory figures and coordinated ADR. Nonetheless, it must also be noted that in other circumstances Cappelletti himself (1993), p. 285, despite acknowledging the 'special expertise' Ombudsmen could bring, was sceptic about the fact that said solution could 'burden the state with more bureaucratic machinery and regulations. Also, […] there might be a decline of the agency's zeal and activism; and the agency might tend to be 'captured' by the very interests it was expected to control. Moreover we should keep in mind that the interests involved are primarily private, not public in nature, even though they belong to groups or classes of people'.

[161] For Italy, see, *infra*, next Chap. 6.

[162] Waelbroeck et al. (2004), p. 1, often cited as 'Ashurst Study'.

be brought by 'qualified entities', such as independent public bodies or organisations with coinciding statutory purposes. A list of the 'qualified entities' was provided by each Member State, in order to allow intra-community infringements and foreign qualified entities to apply other Member States' courts. Moreover, orders requiring the cessation or prohibition of any unlawful activity, as well as penalty fees to be paid in case of delay, were among the possible measures. Currently repealed by the RAD, its application was limited.

With regards to compensatory claims, instead, different commentators criticised the complete lack of coordination and coherence in the European legal framework in relation to competition law. The debate became even more intense, just like the need for a harmonised and consistent response was even more evident. Numerous soft-law initiatives took place, such as a Green and White Paper respectively from 2005 and 2008, another Green Paper from 2008, a public consultation from 2011 and a Resolution of the European Parliament in 2012. Yet, it was only in 2013, that the EU Commission took a fundamental step, by issuing the aforementioned Recommendation 'on common principles for injunctive and compensatory collective redress mechanisms in the Member States concerning violations of rights granted under Union Law'.[163] At least provisionally, despite the choice of another non-binding instrument, the debate at EU level was thus paused.[164]

As delineated in its first operative paragraph, the aim of the Recommendation was to 'facilitate *access to justice*, stop illegal practices and enable injured parties to obtain compensation in mass harm situations caused by violations of rights granted under Union Law, while ensuring appropriate procedural safeguards to avoid abusive litigation'. For that purpose, 'Member States should ensure that the collective redress procedures are fair, equitable, timely and not prohibitively expensive', on the assumption that 'the possibility of joining claims and pursuing them collectively may constitute a better means of access to justice, in particular when the cost of individual actions would deter the harmed individuals from going to court.'[165]

The main feature of the Recommendation was its *horizontal*—also called 'trans-substantive'—approach. The Commission, in fact, aimed at a general and common framework of collective redress in *all* areas of EU law, rather than a sectorial one, relating, for example, only to consumer or competition law. The reason for this was to avoid 'inconsistencies between the different Commission initiatives on collective redress, a fact which points to the need for a more coherent system'.[166] As will be discussed *infra*, the RAD from 2020 represented a partial *step back* from this decision, since it narrowed down again the scope of application to mere consumer and competition issues. At the same time, however, this Recommendation served as a guiding compass for a number of countries, among which, for instance, Italy or the

---

[163] Commission Recommendation of 11 June 2013 on common principles for injunctive and compensatory collective redress mechanisms in the Member States concerning violations of rights granted under Union Law

[164] Hess (2014).

[165] Para. 1 of the same Recommendation.

[166] EU Commission's Communication regarding the same Recommendation, para. 1.3.

Netherlands, which adjusted their group litigation tools *before* the publication of the RAD.[167] These national implementations, hence, present horizontal scopes of application, notwithstanding the latter's narrower model.

The instrument chosen—a Recommendation—, still, was *non-binding*. Member States were not bound to introduce new legislation, but simply provided with a series of, suggested, rules.[168] Despite the good intentions and some 'revolutionary' elements,[169] the Recommendation received from the beginning numerous criticisms. One author, for example, described it as 'a squeaking mouse hurrying over the floor of the EU Commission, frightening no one'.[170] Several others wondered whether it was 'a breakthrough or a damp squib'[171] and, in general, doubted if efficiency and concrete access to justice could really be attained thanks to the (or, simply, a) new Recommendation. In particular, the fact that it was a *non-binding* instrument was stressed as a major disincentive for Member States to follow the EU Commission's presented guidelines, as further proved.[172]

In fact—and this leads to the current *third phase*—, following the 2013 EU Recommendation, Member States were expected by the Commission itself to implement efficient collective regimes by July 2015, with a reassessment on the collective redress landscape in the EU by July 2017. Nonetheless, the impact of said Recommendation on different national systems was indeed—quoting an emblematic comment from a Study commissioned by the EU Parliament in 2018—'*small*'.[173]

---

[167] See, *infra*, next Chap. 6.

[168] Those guidelines advocated for a model which—on paper—was purposely different from the U.S model of class actions, only a few years before described, as abovementioned, as an abusive 'toxic cocktail'. In particular, it proposed that any European approach follows a series of standards and adopts several safeguards in order to avoid the risk of abusive litigation and economic incentives to bring speculative claims, like the experience across the Atlantic had showed. Accordingly, the list of suggested safeguards were: first, collective actions should be brought only at the fulfilment of certain admissibility conditions; second, the class representative should be subject to scrutiny of its both financial and personal adequacy to act in the best interests of the represented group; third, the opt-in model should be preferred, although the opt-out procedure (which some Member States already had) could be 'justified by reasons of sound administration of justice'; fourth, effective information on pending collective actions should be provided to all potential claimants; fifth, effective cross-border enforcement should be ensured; sixth, alternative dispute resolution methods (such as mediation) should be available as well; seventh, the 'loser pays' principle should generally be followed with regards to litigation costs; eighth, contingency fees and punitive damages should under all circumstances be avoided, considering the dangerous incentives they set for 'fishing expeditions', collusions between corporate defendants and class counsels or '*in terrorem* actions' pushing for settlements; last, third-party funding should be allowed only within certain terms.

[169] Hodges (2013), p. 87.

[170] Goldsmith (2013).

[171] Hodges (2013).

[172] Id.

[173] State of Collective Redress in the EU In The Context of the Implementation of the Commission Recommendation (2018) p. 66. This report, prepared by the British Institute of International and Comparative Law for the European Commission, together with a few similar ones and some major scandals (such as the Dieselgate), brought the EU Commission to propose the 'RAD'.

On its Report on the implementation of the 2013 Recommendation, the Commission later on acknowledged that only '9 Member States [out of 28, at the time] 'still ha[d] no compensatory relief mechanism in place and only 7 Member States ha[d] reformed their respective laws on collective redress after its adoption'. Moreover, said reforms had not always followed the Recommendation's guidelines, 'neither regarding the broad scope suggested for the collective redress vehicle, nor the opt-in principle.' Not only *inequality* in the *availability* of the collective redress instruments, but also the 'implementation of *safeguards* against the potential abuse of such mechanisms [wa]s very unevenly distributed across the EU.'[174] In sum, such a non-binding attempt of harmonisation had been a failure.

Another key element to take into account, at this point, was the series of *consumer scandals* which vexed hundreds of thousands of individuals all over Europe, gaining major relevance on the media. Among them, the *Volkswagen 'Dieselgate'* is probably the most notable example. The strikingly different compensation experiences between US and EU consumers in this case—see *infra*—pushed even further the debate for collective redress. In similar fashion to how the *historical context*—that of racial segregation, and its fight against it—had ended up fundamentally shaping the class action model in the US in 1966, and consequently in the common law world, these scandals became the propulsion engine behind the launch of the currently-in force RAD.[175]

In particular, following the EU 2016 Inquiry into emission measurements in the automotive sector due to said scandal,[176] in 2017 the EU Parliament called on the Commission to 'propose legislation on a harmonised system of collective redress for EU *consumers*, based on practices within and outside the EU', in order to 'end the current situation where consumers lack protection in many Member States which do not allow them to enforce their rights collectively.'[177] In April 2018, with the so called '*New Deal for Consumers*', the European Commission launched a series of initiatives, among which a Proposal for a Directive on representative actions for the protection of the collective interests of *consumers* (which later became the RAD). As stated in the related 'Explanatory Memorandum', the aim of such a proposal was to 'modernise and replace Directive 2009/22/EC ('the Injunctions Directive')',[178] addressing its shortcomings,[179] broadening the scope

[174] Id.

[175] See, *infra*, New Deal for Consumers.

[176] 2016/2908 EU (RSP).

[177] Para. 1, 'Explanatory Memorandum', EU Commission Proposal 'on representative actions for the protection of the collective interests of consumers, and repealing Directive 2009/22/EC', from 11 April 2018.

[178] Id.

[179] As mentioned in the 'Explanatory Memorandum', 'the 2008 and 2012 Commission reports on the application of the Injunctions Directive and the 2016–2017 Fitness Check confirmed the Directive's importance. However, the Fitness Check concluded that it had considerable shortcomings, which, if left unaddressed, would continue to hinder its full effectiveness and lead to suboptimal use. Even in Member States where injunctions are considered effective and are widely

also to compensatory relief and harmonising the otherwise uncoordinated and unbalanced European legal framework for *consumer* redress.

5.3.2 *From 'Toxic Cocktail' to 'Necessary' Consumer Representative Actions*

Aside from the goals and concrete historical events (consumer scandals) that brought its entry into force, the 2020 RAD represented an extraordinary and unprecedented step for the civil law word. For the first time, a *binding* instrument was issued by EU institutions accepting that 'Globalisation and digitalisation have increased the risk of a large number of [individuals][180] being harmed by the same unlawful practice'. 'The lack of *effective* means for the enforcement' of such hampered positions was also acknowledged by EU institutions, together with the crucial realisation that 'it is *necessary* to strengthen procedural mechanisms for the protection of the collective interests of [individuals][181] to cover *injunctive* measures as well as *redress* measures'.[182]

With this step, therefore, the EU definitively abandoned the long-defended civil law tradition of binary litigation, one v. one, that binds the *named parties only* for both injunctive and compensatory remedies. It accepts the significant *power unbalances* of the contemporary society and the need for forms of litigation that *re-equilibrate* them. Simultaneously, and probably unwillingly, it also opens the door for enforcement processes that, despite concerning the general public, are conducted by private parties.

Considering the reluctance until the early 2000s (and more), for over half a century, to even contemplate this option, heavily criticising such 'almost-barbaric' practices of the common law world, the development is astounding.[183] It radically altered the traditional cornerstone of adjudication in the civil law world, in view of societal change and of the key objective of granting *effective* access to justice to everyone—a fundamental right itself, and among the most essential.[184]

Nonetheless, the result—as it often occurs when compromising—is quite unsatisfying, both from a procedural and a constitutional point of view. The most

---

used, the Directive's potential is not fully exploited due to a number of elements that it does not sufficiently address. The key shortcomings are its limited scope, the limited effects of injunction decisions on redress for harmed consumers and the cost and length of the procedure (see section 3 for an overview of the results)'.

[180] Added. Original wording: 'consumers', in RAD, Recital (1), which is coherent with its limited scope of application. The reflections therein, still, as we argue in these pages, have more general connotations.

[181] Id.

[182] RAD, Recital (5).

[183] See Cappalli and Consolo (1992).

[184] See *supra*, Chap. 4.

disappointing aspects, in this regard, are, on the one hand, the *limited scope of application* and, on the other hand, also as a consequence, the *failed attempt* to successfully *harmonise* the level-playing field for all EU countries and their citizens (here included, not the least, all the potential defendants).

5.3.3 Procedural Hallmarks and Constitutional Nuances

The essential features of the 2020 Directive, in comparative view to the above-depicted US model, will be hereinafter presented. The main constitutional and procedural issues stemming from the model at hand will also be underscored.

As addressed, said Directive 'sets out rules to ensure that a *representative* action mechanism for the protection of the collective interests of *consumers* is available in all Member States', by offering 'at least one procedural mechanism [...] for the purpose of both *injunctive* measures and redress measures' at national level.[185]

The key *representative function* from the common law class actions is hence confirmed, since the suits in question are 'brought by a qualified entity as a claimant party *on behalf* of consumers to seek an injunctive measure, a redress measure, or both'.[186]

The notion of '*qualified entity*' becomes particularly relevant to this regard, since they are the 'self-elected champions' who can file the class suits. The EU institutions, on this occasion, chose to abandon any reference to the 'natural or legal persons' from the 2013 Recommendation, as well as to turn in an opposite direction to the US model. The latter, as discussed above, attributed standing to sue to one or more *members* of the class, who became class representative(s). This figure is lacking under the EU Directive, which prefers to entrust the keys of (consumer) collective redress to *qualified* legal persons, either organisations or public bodies. A twofold set of problems immediately arises from a constitutional evaluation.

Primarily, Article 4 of the Directive sets an improper, confusingly unnecessary and dangerous *distinction* between qualified entities for *cross-border* and *merely domestic cases*. Requirements for the former are specified, whereas for the latter they are not. Such a differentiation can lead to absurd situations where the threshold for bringing a domestic action may be higher (or lower) than that for cross-border cases—thus pushing potential claimants to design on purpose merely formal cross-border cases—or where different states have different requirements—creating significant *disparities* in access-to-justice remedies between EU citizens. It also incentivises *forum-shopping*, both for plaintiffs and potential defendants when choosing their seats.

Another possible cause for concern is the potentially narrowing trend from a remedial standpoint represented by the choice to *prevent class members* from

---

185 RAD, Recital (7).

186 RAD, Article 3(5).

bringing the suits themselves. Under a comparative standpoint, this recalls in several ways the *collective complaints procedure* before the ECSR, where only selected organisations are entitled to do so.[187] One of the most treasured features of the class action model from common law is that *any* individual *directly* affected (any member of the class) can, potentially, file a collective claim. Taking this possibility away, might fundamentally cripple the effectiveness of the redress mechanism, obliging injured members to *always* find an intermediary. This places them at risk of exploitation, deprived from the *alternative* of leading the case themselves. Moreover, despite the Directive's requirement that qualified entities be 'independent and not influenced by persons other than consumers', in practice conflicts of interest may be difficultly perceived, as well as more likely to appear once such an '*oligopoly*' is generated.[188] Even in the best-case scenario, these qualified entities will only be interested in more mediatic, lucrative and larger cases (see *infra*, in relation to the 2019 Italian model).[189]

The possibility for *public entities* to file class suits, instead, should be favourably applauded, in light of the abovementioned positive Scandinavian experience with consumer ombudsmen, of possible connections with infringements already investigated by such authorities, as well as the general *regulatory pluralism* until now advocated (and partially lost with the exclusion of class members' standing to sue).

In respect to the US model, the *role of the lawyer* is evidently less central, partially clouded by that of the qualified entity—with which, still, they could collaborate. Interestingly, one of the much-criticised aspects of the common law class action, that of *contingency fees*, is not expressly prohibited by the Directive, nor any possible limit is mentioned. This goes beyond the 2013 Recommendation,[190] leaving Member States with the option of allowing the use of this particular, and incentivising, financing tool. In order to avoid abusive litigation—as stated in several provisions of the Directive—, a maximum threshold could have been set, as well as a clarification—like in the 2013 Recommendation—that 'The Member States that exceptionally allow for contingency fees should provide for appropriate national regulation of those fees in collective redress cases, taking into account in particular the right to *full compensation* of the members of the claimant party'. Punitive

[187] See, e.g., Palmisano (2022), Guiglia (2016), Lukas (2014), Cullen (2009), Churchill and Khaliq (2004).

[188] See, *infra*, next Chaps. 6 and 11.

[189] See, *infra*, next Chap. 6.

[190] See, *supra*, Commission Recommendation of 11 June 2013 on common principles for injunctive and compensatory collective redress mechanisms in the Member States concerning violations of rights granted under Union Law. See, e.g., its Article 29: 'The Member States should ensure that the lawyers' remuneration and the method by which it is calculated do not create any incentive to litigation that is unnecessary from the point of view of the interest of any of the parties'; see also its Article 30: 'The Member States should not permit contingency fees which risk creating such an incentive. The Member States that exceptionally allow for contingency fees should provide for appropriate national regulation of those fees in collective redress cases, taking into account in particular the right to full compensation of the members of the claimant party'.

damages, on the other hand, are explicitly forbidden by the Directive, in line with the Recommendation:

> It is important to ensure the necessary balance between improving consumers' access to justice and providing appropriate safeguards for traders to avoid abusive litigation that would unjustifiably hinder the ability of businesses to operate in the internal market. To prevent the misuse of representative actions, the awarding of punitive damages should be avoided and rules on certain procedural aspects, such as the designation and funding of qualified entities, should be laid down.[191]

To this regard, the rules on funding of representative actions do not appear currently sufficient, giving room to possible abusive use by competitors or third parties interested in their mere financial gain rather than the class redress. *Third-party litigation funding*, from an economic analysis viewpoint, presents positive incentives to overcome information and organisational asymmetries, high procedural costs and rational apathy, very similarly to contingency fees.[192] It has also been a phenomenon on the rise in recent years, currently esteemed to represent a 40–80 billion industry in the continent.[193]

Despite a Proposal for a Directive 'on the regulation of third-party litigation funding' from the EU Parliament from September 2022,[194] however, the landscape currently remains unregulated, although a study to map third party litigation funding has recently been ordered by the EU Commission. One of the main reasons for pausing discussions around such a Directive has been—it seems—the critical report from the International Legal Finance Association (ILFA) on the maximum limit—'Absent exceptional circumstances'—of 40%[195] as a share for third-party funders from the total award, as too low. This obstacle to regulation needs to be paired with the elimination from the RAD of the 2013 Recommendation's prohibition to 'base remuneration given to or interest charged by the fund provider on the amount of the settlement reached or the compensation awarded unless that funding arrangement is regulated by a public authority to ensure the interests of the parties'.[196] Both elements question whether the EU, while advocating on paper against abusive litigation, is leaving the door open to third, completely financial-oriented, parties to do so.

---

[191] RAD Directive, see, *supra*, Recital (10).

[192] See, e.g., Voet (2016) and Azar-Baud et al. (2024).

[193] See, e.g., Equal Times, 13 March 2023.

[194] European Parliament Resolution of 13 September 2022 with recommendations to the Commission on Responsible private funding of litigation.

[195] Id. See the proposed Article 14(4)—Invalid agreements and clauses: 'Absent exceptional circumstances, where a litigation funding agreement would entitle a litigation funder to a share of any award that would dilute the share available to the claimant and the intended beneficiaries to 60% or less of the total award, including all damages amounts, costs, fees and other expenses, such an agreement shall have no legal effect'.

[196] 2013 Recommendation, *supra*. See Article 32: 'The Member States should ensure, that, in addition to the general principles of funding, for cases of private third party funding of compensatory collective redress, it is prohibited to base remuneration given to or interest charged by the fund provider on the amount of the settlement reached or the compensation awarded unless that funding arrangement is regulated by a public authority to ensure the interests of the parties'.

The infamous 'toxic cocktail' from the EU Commission's Memorandum from 2008 in relation to the US class action model referred to a combination of several elements: among which, expressly cited, punitive damages, contingency fees and the opt-out regime. Accordingly, with regard to the *opt-in* 'ingredient' of such a cocktail, the 2013 Recommendation required that the class be formed on the basis of the '*express* consent of natural or legal persons claiming to have been harmed ('opt-in' principle)'.[197]

It is relevant to note today that, at odds with such a provision, the RAD, instead, chose to leave a margin of discretion to Member States: 'To best respond to their legal traditions, Member States should provide for an opt-in mechanism, or an opt-out mechanism, or a combination of the two'.[198] This regulation—which concerns only compensatory remedies (not injunctive ones, where no adhesion is required)—is certainly positive from an access-to-justice perspective, seeing how the opt-out regime was pivotal for the success of damages class actions overseas, since 1966.

At the same time, still, it requires appropriate safeguards from a notice-perspective, for ensuring clear understanding and acceptance from all the class members. The current regulatory framework does not appear to set them appropriately, leaving *all* discretion to national implementation. A previous assessment from judges, a maximum value or limited type of the claims could have been appropriate guiding parametres for Member States, as well as further regulation on notice, currently lacking.

Absent as well from the RAD's provisions is any reference to any *criterion* to identify the 'collective interests of consumers'. *Collective interests*, in the definitory article (Article 3), are described as 'the general interest of consumers and, in particular for the purposes of redress measures, the interests of a group of consumers', whereas a consumer appears to be 'any natural person who acts for purposes which are outside that person's trade, business, craft or profession'.[199]

Commonality and predominance (see *supra*, in relation to the US 'Rule 23' model) or the homogeneity test (see *infra*)[200] are examples of possible criteria for determining the presence of 'collective interests' stemming from 'the same unlaw-

[197] Id. See the provisions therein on 'Specific Principles Relating to Compensatory Collective Redress': Article 21. 'The claimant party should be formed based on the express consent of natural or legal persons claiming to have been harmed ('opt-in' principle). Any exception to this principle, by law or court order, should be duly justified for reasons of sound administration of justice'; Article 22. 'A member of the claimant party should be free to leave at any time before the final judgment or valid settlement, subject to the same conditions that apply to withdrawal in individual actions. This should not deprive them of the possibility to pursue their claims in another form, if it does not undermine the sound administration of justice'; Article 23. 'Natural or legal persons claiming to have been harmed in the same mass harm situation should be able to join the claimant party at any time before the judgment is given or the case is otherwise validly settled, as long as it does not undermine the sound administration of justice'; Article 24. 'The defendant should be informed about the composition of the claimant party and any changes therein'.

[198] RAD, Recital (43).

[199] RAD, Article 3.

[200] See, *infra*, next Chap. 6.

ful practice' harming a 'large number of consumers'. With the lack thereof, once again, the EU leaves determination to Member States. The goal of *harmonisation*, with the already mentioned perils, is thus not completely achieved, making the Directive at hand an improvable instrument.

The issue is proven also in relation to the notion of *consumer*, too wide as defined by the Directive itself and too flexible as bound by the hyper-connected society and economic global framework.[201] The references in the Annex to several other EU pieces of legislation—extremely varied—may cause some confusion on the exact scope of application of the Directive, too. On the one hand, it is not clear who is exactly a 'consumer', whilst on the other hand it is not specified how to narrow the collective interests that form the 'large number of consumers' harmed (since the term 'class', is obstinately avoided). Although, it must be said, such references from Annex I could also be an important 'trojan horse' to bring class actions in other fields of law, too.[202]

In addition, it should be underscored that the Directive, under Article 1, para. 2, *expressly* allows 'Member States from adopting or retaining in force procedural means for the protection of the collective interests of consumers at national level', as well as, *implicitly* for the enforcement of collective interests in other fields of law. Apart from constitutional doubts on the legitimacy of collective redress mechanisms only for certain infringements (to consumers and in competition law), analysed in the following,[203] the concern underlying the document at stake emerges once again: that is the concrete risk of a European Union running at very different paces, with completely different rules for each Member State.

5.3.4 *Current Implementation: Potential, Challenges and Open Questions*

The overall sensation analysing the Directive is exactly this: EU institutions finally realising the necessity to provide collective procedural paths to tackle the ever-increasing collective societal issues, but, due to competing lobbying interests, not completely achieving the desired results in such a delivery.[204]

The enforcement gaps left by the Directive can be subsumed under two paradigms.

First, the vagueness of the provisions set forth cannot be stressed enough. It is true that the instrument chosen is a Directive, which, pursuant to Article 288 TFUE, leaves to Member States the precise choice of form and methods to achieve the

---

[201] See, *supra*, Part I, in particular Chap. 2.

[202] See, *infra*, *Philips Respironics* case, in Chap. 7. See also Chap. 11.

[203] See, *infra*, Chap. 6.

[204] See also Azar-Baud and Sousa Ferro (2021). See also Azar-Baud et al. (2024).

bindingly-set result.[205] At the same time, nonetheless, the aimed result still appears too indefinite for national authorities to adequately and, most importantly, harmonically attain it. Furthermore, despite the much-depicted intention to leave no room for abusive use, the broadness of certain provisions or the complete lack thereof dangerously allows for pernicious conducts from business competitors, third-party funders or 'qualified entities' supposedly representing the interests of the class. Although in practice hardly achievable, a Regulation might be more suited to reach the proclaimed goals.

Second, in any case, the scope of application of the Directive appears too narrow, posing fundamental questions on the right to a judge and the principle of equality, under a constitutional viewpoint. Limiting collective redress to the consumer and competition sector (provided one can properly define the contours of such fields) does not appear justified nor by the historical evolution of group litigation nor by socio-legal evaluations of efficiency.

This '*silo approach*',[206] exacerbates the disparities in legal protection within the EU, since some fields of substantive law may count on a collective tool whereas others might not. Significant interpretative and 'access to justice' concerns inevitably arise, especially if the deficient fields involve fundamental rights (e.g. that to health or discrimination practices).

If the EU legislator deems it 'necessary to strengthen procedural mechanisms for the protection of the collective interests of consumers' through injunctive measures as well as redress measures and, thus, 'sets out rules to ensure that a representative action mechanism [...] is available in all Member States [...] to improve *consumers*' access to justice', it appears at least questionable that no such instruments are available for the safeguard of human dignity, the right to life, physical and mental integrity, proper education, health care and social assistance, environmental protection, freedom of thought and information, against inhuman or degrading treatment, unfair working conditions, and several more European 'common values'. Article 38 CFREU, on consumer protection, merely sets one right—and arguably, if a balancing were to be made, not the most important. The fact that it should be the only one granted with an 'effective remedy' (assumed, as the EU legislator does, see *supra*, that class actions concretely provide such an effectiveness) appears, at the very least, questionable. There is an evident contradiction with Article 47 CFREU, according to which, 'Everyone whose rights and freedoms guaranteed by the law of the Union are violated has the right to an effective remedy before a tribunal': *any*

[205] Still, the consolidate jurisprudence from the CJEU is clear in stressing that 'the national court is bound to interpret national law, so far as possible, in the light of the wording and the purpose of the directive concerned in order *to achieve the result sought by the directive* [...] The requirement for national law to be interpreted in conformity with Community law is inherent in the system of the Treaty, since it permits the national court, for the matters within its jurisdiction, to ensure the full effectiveness of Community law when it determines the dispute before it' (emphasis added), CJEU, Grand Chamber, Judgement of 5 October 2004, *Pfeiffer and Others*, C-397/01, §§ 113–114.

[206] See Voet (2025).

right guaranteed by EU law, not just consumer ones. Evidently, this only occurs in the fields of law covered by EU law.

Further doubts arise in relation to the considerable limitations to both *active and passive standing*, especially when matched with the (at least, at times) positive common law experience. This concerns the above reflections on the 'qualified entities', and those on the confinement of possible defendants to the business world (the so called 'traders', from Article 2 of the RAD). The administrative-jurisdiction tradition of civil law only partially justifies this choice, as subsequently addressed in relation to the Italian regime. This touches also cross-border enforcement, as shown by the so-far underwhelming case law.

5.4 Concluding Remarks. Bridging Opposite Enforcement Traditions

The transposition at national level of the RAD was due by 25 December 2022, with the entry into force of domestic procedural measures by 25 June 2023.

At the moment, almost all 27 Member States have transposed it.[207] By June 2027, and annually thereafter, each Member State should report to the Commission relevant information on the number and type of actions, infringements, parties and outcomes of the related proceedings. Commission's reports are also expected starting from the subsequent year.

Considering how most countries are—questionably[208]—adopting procedural instruments for conducts subsequent to the entry into force of said procedural mechanisms, it is expectable that it will take some time for the first case law to develop. Nonetheless, safe for significant exceptions, after almost two years the general numbers still seem low.[209]

It does not appear as a coincidence, however, that the most promising implementations come from jurisdictions which offer regimes with a *large scope of application*, if not fully general, and with—at least in certain cases—an *opt-out regime* (for compensatory relief). The Netherlands, that adopts both, is by all means the trailblazer within the EU,[210] with several US law firms specialised in class litigation and third-party funders opening offices therein.

Other Member States, for one reason or the other, appear to be lagging behind. Belgium and Portugal, for instance, present opt-out regimes, but limited scope of application. Italy, on the other hand, as will be analysed in the following,[211] presents

[207] See Azar-Baud et al. (2024).

[208] See, *infra*, next Chap. 6 in relation to Italy.

[209] See Azar-Baud et al. (2024).

[210] Kramer and Tzankova (2021).

[211] See, *infra*, next Chap. 6.

a promising remedy with a general scope, but confined—for the compensatory relief—to an opt-in regime.[212]

Furthermore, all EU countries appear to be lacking, even when standing is not too limited, the necessary proper *education* to class litigation.[213] This concerns both jurists—judges and attorneys—and civil society. Appropriate *funding* rules and good practices need to be developed, too.[214]

Such considerations link directly to the common law experience with group litigation, which was not introduced *ex abrupto*, but rather built on the, although not so efficient, previous experience of class actions. The breakthrough arrived in 1966 with the *amendments* to Rule 23 of the US Federal Rules of Civil Procedure, initially introduced in 1938. This means almost *three decades* to grow accustomed to the procedural technique at hand; that is without taking into account the previous legislative efforts of aggregate 'representative' litigation dating as far back as 1848 and 1921. Evidently, it is not an easy task; as such, it takes a long time. The civil law traditional binary mindset of litigation only heightens this issue.

At the same time, still, the knowledge provided by *almost 60 years* of class litigation from overseas cannot be disregarded, in its positive as well as in its negative aspects. It is too precious of a pool of data and lessons to pretend it does not exist (e.g., by refusing to use the name 'class actions' at EU level). Rather, *building* on it, judges and court auxiliary structures—centred around a dualistic concept of litigation—should be adapted to better deal with collective claims.

Judicial seminars and training courses should be offered to delve into the procedural and constitutional nuances of this complex kind of litigation.[215] It is naïve and counter-productive to expect that a first-instance judge, educated and used to binary litigation, who has only seen and studied such a type of cases, suddenly, on top of their ordinary workload, starts to efficiently manage collective cases, involving several stakeholders who are not parties to the proceedings and requiring very different reasoning and mechanisms for claim-admissibility, evidence, liquidation, and execution (as well as settlements, one of the most probable outcomes in the common law experience, after certification). Judicial training and case management,[216] therefore, are key aspects on which the EU needs to work, to truly develop effective class litigation techniques.

Concurrently, these aspects also apply to potential *class attorneys*, who may distrust the new procedural paths due to ignorance of the organisational, time and economic costs (especially, the latter, in case of loss), and not sufficiently advertised (or existing) incentives for them to bring the suit.

Finally, similar reflections can be put forth with regard to *civil society*, too.

---

[212] See Azar-Baud et al. (2024).

[213] Id. See also Randazzo and Maglica (2025).

[214] Azar-Baud et al. (2024).

[215] See *infra*, Chap. 11. See also Randazzo and Maglica (2025). Furthermore, in general on the issue of judicial training and education, see Rordorf (2020), p. 125.

[216] See Silvestri (2025).

On the one hand, especially in jurisdictions with opt-in regimes, potential class members need to be made aware of the existence of class suits. In the common law world people walking by are not surprised to find posters advertising class suits, which are, viscerally, an *inner* part of its *social texture* (see all the entertainment outputs portraying them, e.g. from the film industry). Individuals in Europe, instead, may be surprised, if not sceptical thinking it might be a scam, when notified with a potential class adherence.

On the other hand, common law, as discussed above, has a tradition of public interest litigation, of forms of private enforcement through the courts to promote social change.[217] This element is not extraneous to the civil law world. However, it pertains mainly to *different fora* (constitutional courts, the ECtHR, or the CJEU), rather than in front of ordinary, first-instance, judges. In these different fora the legitimacy of the complained norms or conducts to constitutional or supranational standards is mainly verified, thus spreading—in the former case—its *erga omnes* effects.

The effects of declarations of unconstitutionality are indeed *erga omnes*, that is on the *whole* community (and on *legislative acts*, especially). This is not the case of class litigation, in which the effects do fall in favour of (or against) more than one person, but still *not* in favour of (or against) *every* member of the society: rather in favour of (or against) a *minority* or a less-advantaged group (and concern specific, although possibly systemic or standardised, *conducts*).

Furthermore, similar types of *representative relationships* can be found in continental Europe in *other forms of association*: e.g., political parties, labour unions, churches or even families. The example of *labour unions* seems particularly pertinent, as will be analysed in the following,[218] comparing the stances brought, on the one hand, in the civil law world through negotiations of these entities on behalf of the workers and, on the other hand, those brought in the common law world through litigation. Likewise, significant civil rights achievements in the former jurisdictions have been obtained through *political representation*. This is the case, for instance, of same-sex couples or the right to abortion. Often, these political changes have been based on constitutional values or decisions; again, nonetheless, if any litigation was involved it was during the initial stages and in front of apex courts, stemming from individual cases.

Against such a backdrop, the absence of key actors from the common law system can be perceived in the civil law one. They are all those organisations and associations constituted specifically to *litigate* public interest claims. Very few, if any, exist with *that* principal focus in Europe. There is a number of no-profit entities dedicated to the judicial enforcement of *consumer* rights, but very few to *judicial* enforcement of *civil* and fundamental rights. In the same way, there is a number of no-profit entities devoted to the protection of human rights, but very few statutorily aiming to do so via *litigation*; rather, they act more through political advocacy and campaigning.

---

[217] See Cummings (2018).

[218] See, *infra*, Chap. 8.

This might also explain (not justify) the limited scope of application of the RAD and several domestic regimes, which in turn explains the lack of such types of organisations, in a viciously mutual cycle.

Under this standpoint, the US and common law social soil, instead, was much more fertile for group litigation, also from a funding perspective, with historic organisations such as, *in primis*, the Legal Defense Fund (which had brought the landmark *Brown v. Board of Education* case in 1954), and historic foundations *economically backing* them.

In conclusion, it can be assessed how the European Union is slowly, and drastically, changing course in relation to collective redress, accepting the need for new supra-individual procedural tools to tackle the supra-individual challenges of the contemporary world. Nonetheless, this process is proving to be dangerously short-sighted and unharmonised, thus exacerbating disparities between Member States' citizens and, in most cases, providing procedural redress only on paper, due to relevant regulatory obstacles or unaddressed gaps. The lessons from the previous and rich common law experience are not adequately taken into account.

The most important lesson from these being that mere procedural innovations are not sufficient, unless supported by concrete actions for change within the legal and social texture, too.[219]

References

Adler VO (1972) The viability of class actions in environmental litigation. Ecol Law Quart 2:533

Ancheta AN (1985) Defendant class actions and Federal Civil Rights Litigation. UCLA Law Rev 33:283

Andreotti T (2017) Dispute resolution in transnational securities transactions. Bloomsbury, London

Azar-Baud MJ, Sousa Ferro M (2021) Directive on consumer collective representative actions: a sheep in wolf's clothing?. EU Law Live, 5 December 2020

Azar-Baud MJ, Giannopoulou A, Maglica A, Tzankova IN (2024) Collective redress. A compare-and-contrast analysis of ten jurisdictions in the European Union. Digital Freedom Fund, Amsterdam

Bassett DL (2006) Constructing class action reality. Brigham Young Univ Law Rev 1415:33

Bognetti G (1998) Lo stato e i gruppi di interesse negli ordinamenti borghesi. Giuffrè, Milano

Born G, Salas C (2012) United States supreme court and class arbitration: a tragedy of errors, the symposium. J Dispute Resolution 1:21–48

Burns JW (1990) Decorative figureheads: eliminating class representatives in class actions. Hastings Law J 42:165–168

Caielli M (2015) Cittadini e giustizia costituzionale. Contributo allo studio dell'actio popularis. Giappichelli, Torino

Calabresi G (1970) The cost of accidents: a legal and economic analysis. Yale University Press, New Haven

Cappalli R, Consolo C (1992) Class actions for continental Europe? A preliminary inquiry. Temple Int Comp Law J 6(2):217–292

[219] See, *infra*, Chap. 11.

Cappelletti M (1975) Formazioni sociali e interessi di gruppo davanti alla giustizia civile. Rivista di diritto processuale:361–402
Cappelletti M (1976) Vindicating the public interest through the courts: a Comparativist's contribution. Buffalo Law Rev 25(3):643–690
Cappelletti M (1993) Alternative dispute resolution processes within the framework of the world-wide access to-justice movement. Modern Law Rev 56(3):282–296
Carroll M (2021) Civil rights, access to counsel, and injunctive class actions in the United States. In: Fitzpatrick B, Thomas R (eds) The Cambridge Handbook of Class Actions: An International Survey. Cambridge University Press, Cambridge, p. 25
Casavola F (1958) Studi sulle azioni popolari romane. Le 'actiones populares'. Jovene, Napoli
Chafee Z (1950) Some problems of equity. Michigan Law School Review
Chayes A (1976) The role of the judge in public law regulation. Harv Law Rev 89:1281
Churchill RR, Khaliq U (2004) The collective complaints system of the European Social Charter: an effective mechanism for ensuring compliance with economic and social rights?. Eur J Int Law 15(3):417–456
Cullen H (2009) The collective complaints system of the European Social Charter: Interpretative methods of the European Committee of Social Rights. Hum Rights Law Rev 9(1):61–93
Cummings SL (2018) Law and social movements: reimagining the progressive canon. Wis Law Rev:441–502
Cummings SL (2020) Public interest litigation in a comparative perspective. Aust J Hum Rights 26:184
Di Porto A (2013) Res in usu publico e 'beni comuni'. Giappichelli, Torino
Drahozal C (2001) Unfair' Arbitration Clauses. Univ Ill Law Rev 3:695–790
Elia L (1982) La Corte nel quadro dei poteri costituzionali. In: Barile P, Cheli E, Grassi S (eds) Corte costituzionale e sviluppo della forma di governo in Italia. Il Mulino, Bologna, p 489
Fadda C (1984) L'azione popolare: studio di diritto romano e attuale. Utet, Milano
Ford T (1966) The history and development of old rule 23 and the development of amended rule 23. Antitrust Law J 254
Gaboardi M (2019) New ways of protection of collective interests: the Italian class litigation and arbitration through a comparative analysis. J Dispute Resolution Univ Missour Law School 4
Galanter M (1974) Why the 'haves' come out ahead: speculations on the limits of legal change. Law Soc Rev 9:95
Goldsmith J (2013) European collective redress. The Law Gazette, 20 June 2013
Greenberg J (1997) Civil rights class actions. Procedural means of obtaining substance. Ariz Law Rev 39:575–586
Guiglia G (2016) Il ruolo del Comitato Europeo dei Diritti Sociali al tempo della crisi economica. Rivista AIC 2:1–22
Hanotiau B (2004) A new development in complex multiparty-multicontract proceedings: Classwide arbitration. Arbitr Int 20:1
Hazard G, Gedid JL, Sowie S (1998) An historical analysis of the binding nature of class suits. Faculty Scholarship 1423
Hensler DR (2001) Revisiting the monster: new myths and realities of class actions and other large scale litigation. Duke J Comp Int Law 11:179
Hess B (2014) European perspectives on collective litigation. In: Hàrsagi V, Van Rhee CH (eds) Multi-party redress mechanisms in Europe: squeaking mice? Intersentia, Cambridge
Hodges C (2010) Collective redress in Europe: the new model. Civil Justice Q 7:1
Hodges C (2013) Collective redress: a breakthrough or a damp Sqibb? J Consum Policy
Hodges C, Voet S (2018) Delivering collective redress: new technologies. Hart Publishing, Oxford
Holmes OW Jr (1897) The path of the law. Harv Law Rev 10:457
Homburger A (1974) Private suits in the public interest in The United States of America. Buffalo Law Rev 23
Issacharoff S (2012) Class actions and state authority. Loyola Univ Chicago Law J 44:369–390
Issacharoff S (2013) Assembling class actions. Wash Univ Law Rev 90:699

Issacharoff S, Zimroth P (2018) An Oral history of rule 23. An interview with Professor Arthur Miller. NYU Annual Survey Am Law 74:110

Joyce T (2014) Reining in crazy class-action lawsuits. National Review Online

Kavanagh A (2023) The collaborative constitution. Cambridge University Press, Cambridge

Kramer XE, Tzankova IN (2021) From injunction and settlement to action: collective redress and funding in The Netherlands. In: Uzelac A, Voet S (eds) Class actions in Europe. Holy grail or wrong trail? Springer, Cham, pp 97–130

Lester A (2016) Five ideas to fight for. Oneworld Publications, London

Lukas K (2014) The collective complaint procedure of the European Social Charter: Some lessons for the EU?. Legal Issues of Economic Integration 41(3):275–288

Marcus D (2011) Flawed but Noble: desegregation litigation and its implications for the modern class action. Florida Law Rev 63

Marcus D (2013) The history of modern class action, part I: Sturm und Drang, 1953–1980. Wash Univ Law Rev 90:587–652

Marcus D (2015) The public interest class action. Georgetown Law J 104

Miller A (2010) From Conley to Twombly to Iqbal. A double play on the Federal Rules of civil procedure. Duke Law J 60(1):6

Moore BC Jr (1977) Does it go far enough? Appl Bus Administration J 63:837

Mullenix LS (2014) Ending class actions as we know them: rethinking the American class action. Emory Law J 64:399–449

Murphy B, Cameron C (2006) Access to justice and the evolution of class action litigation in Australia. Melb Univ Law Rev 30(2)

Note (1978) Class actions under the truth in lending act. Yale Law J

Olson M (1965) The logic of collective action: public goods and the theory of groups. Harvard University Press, Cambridge

Palmisano G (2022) Collective complaints as a means for protecting social rights in Europe. Anthem, London

Pizzorusso A (1976) Intervento. In: Le azioni a tutela di interessi collettivi. Atti del convegno di studio. Cedam, Padova

Posner RA (1973) Economic analysis of law. Aspen, Boston

Randazzo B (2023) Access to justice in a multilevel constitutional system, protecting human rights. Giappichelli, Torino

Randazzo B, Maglica A (2025) La disciplina generale delle class action italiane alla prova delle garanzie costituzionali ed europee. Federalismi.it 5:158–196

Resnik J (2011) Fairness in numbers: comment on AT&T v. Concepcion, Wal-Mart v. dukes, and turner v. Rogers. Harv Law Rev 125(1):78–171

Rodotà S (1976) Le azioni civilistiche. In: Le azioni a tutela di interessi collettivi. Atti del convegno di studio. Cedam, Padova

Rordorf R (2020) Magistratura, giustizia, società. Cacucci Editore, Bari –

Rosenberg D (1987) Class actions for mass torts doing individual justice by collective means. Indiana Law J 62(3)

Sherman EF (2002) Group litigation under foreign legal systems: variations and alternatives to American class actions. DePaul Law Rev 52:401

Shlanger M (2006) Civil rights injunctions over time: a case study of jail and prison orders. N Y Univ Law Rev 81:550

Silvestri E (2025) Brevi note su case management e ricorsi collettivi. In: Randazzo B, Henke A, Voet S (eds) L'azione di classe italiana nel quadro europeo: profili sostanziali e processuali. Giappichelli, Torino

Sternlight J (2000) As mandatory binding arbitration meets the class action, will the class action survive? William Mary Law Rev 42(1):1–126

Taruffo M (2001) Some remarks on group litigation in comparative perspective. Duke J Comp Int Law 11:405–421

Trocker N (1990) Gli interessi diffusi e la loro tutela dinanzi al giudice civile. In: Various Authors (ed) Nuove dimensioni nei diritti di libertà. Scritti in onore di Paolo Barile. Cedam, Padova, pp 193–218

Uzelac A (2014) Goals of civil justice and civil procedure in contemporary judicial systems. Springer, Cham

Uzelac A, Voet S (2021) Class actions in Europe. Holy grail or wrong trail? Springer, Cham

Visscher L, Faure M (2021) A law and economics perspective on the EU directive on representative actions. J Consum Policy 44:455

Voet S (2016) The crux of the matter: funding and financing collective redress Mecchanisms. In: Hess B, Bergström M, Storskrubb E, Wahl N, Cramér P (eds) EU civil justice: current issues and future outlook. Hart Publishing, Oxford, p 201

Voet S (2017) Where the wild things are. Reflections on the state and future of European collective redress. In: Keirse A, Loos MBM (eds) Ius Commune Europaeum. Intersentia, Cambridge, p 138

Voet (2025) Introduzione. Sei suggestioni. In: Randazzo B, Henke A, Voet S (eds) L'azione di classe italiana nel quadro europeo: profili sostanziali e processuali. Giappichelli, Torino

von Bogdandy A (2022) Strukturwandel des öffentlichen Rechts. Entstehung und Demokratisierung der europäischen Gesellschaft. Suhrkamp Verlag, Berlin

von Bogdandy A (2023) Comparative public law for European Society. MPIL Research Paper 28

Waelbroeck D, Slater D, Even-Shoshan G (2004) Study on the conditions of claims for damages in case of infringement of EC competition rules. Comparative report. Ashurt, Brussels

Winkler WK, Perell PM, Kalaidzic J, Warner AM (2014) The law of class actions in Canada. Thompson Reuters, Toronto

Yan J (2011) A lunatic's guide to suing for $30: class action arbitration, the Federal Arbitration act and unconscionability after AT&T v. Concepcion. Berkeley J Employment Labor Law 32(2):551–567

Yeazell SC (1980) From group litigation to class action, part I. UCLA Law Rev 27(3):514

Yeazell SC (1987) From medieval group litigation to the modern class action. Yale University Press, New Haven

Chapter 6
The 2019 Italian Class Action Reform in an Integrating Constitutional Perspective

6.1 Premise. An Intertwined Procedural Tapestry

As anticipated, on 19 May 2021, Law No. 31 from 12 April 2019 came into force, introducing a *new dual class action* regime in Italy, under Title VIII-*bis* of the Code of civil procedure. The new regulations, characterised by compensatory and injunctive remedies, replace the previously underutilised Italian consumer class action, extending its original applicability both objectively and subjectively. The intent to '*bolster access to justice*' to all citizens for the protection of their rights and interests, even of constitutional relevance, in every sector is evident and has been repeatedly expressed, also in the preparatory works.[1] The legislative choice of setting a *general scope of application* presents it as a tool with disruptive potential.[2]

The new dual collective regime is extremely innovative also in reference to the other Member States' choices and to what has been advocated by the European Union itself, as discussed above.[3] In Europe, in fact, it is worth stressing again, class actions have always been viewed with considerable scepticism. Only in recent years, a worrying series of scandals harming consumers and users has led the various legislators—of individual Member States, autonomously and in parallel, on the one hand, and of the EU, on the other hand—to a gradual trend reversal. The last step of this legislative policy-*revirement* is marked by the already-mentioned recent RAD, focused on *consumer* collective redress. The Italian legislator from 2019, however, proposes a dual mechanism that significantly *surpasses* the protection threshold established by the EU legislator in 2020.

[1] Italian Parliament, Chamber of Deputies, report No. 53 from 1 October 2018.

[2] See Ruffolo (2021), p. 7.

[3] See *supra*, previous Chap. 5.

A. Maglica, *Collective Dimensions of Access to Justice*, European Union and its Neighbours in a Globalized World 23,
https://doi.org/10.1007/978-3-031-94522-9_6

The reasons for this choice—surprising, and bold, at first glance—from the Italian legislator are twofold.

It must be preliminarily recalled that the EU Commission's 2013/396 Recommendation 'on common principles for injunctive and compensatory collective redress mechanisms in the Member States concerning violations of rights granted under Union Law' provided for injunctive and compensatory collective mechanisms for *all* 'mass harm situations'.[4] The limitation to consumer protection came into play only subsequently with the RAD, after several lobbying interventions. It is, therefore, reasonably probable that the Italian legislator still had the 2013 EU Commission's Recommendation in mind when drafting the new domestic class action regime.

This links to the second reason, that is the *political parties* sitting in the Parliament's majority and leading the Italian government at the time of the implementation. The two main political parties then were MoVimento 5 Stelle and Lega Nord, both (especially the former) characterised by populist stances and an attention, in their electoral manifestos, for the most disadvantaged segments of the population, against institutional and corporate interests. A mention of the class action instrument appeared in their 'Contract for the Government of Change', presented to the Italian Parliament in May 2018, after winning the elections: among several commitments, that 'to implement the class action instrument, thereby enabling it to protect both private citizens and businesses against frauds or abuses committed by the same economic entity'.[5]

Such a commitment followed the long-standing effort of Alfonso Bonafede, the new Minister of Justice, to amend the until then scarcely-used 2010 consumer class action, since the previous parliamentary term.[6] The introduction of a bill regarding class actions by no other than then-deputy Bonafede dates back to 9 July

---

[4] Id. Commission Recommendation of 11 June 2013 on common principles for injunctive and compensatory collective redress mechanisms in the Member States concerning violations of rights granted under Union Law, Point I(1): 'The purpose of this Recommendation is to facilitate access to justice, stop illegal practices and enable injured parties to obtain compensation in *mass harm situations* caused by violations of rights granted under Union law, while ensuring appropriate procedural safeguards to avoid abusive litigation' (emphasis added).

[5] See the so-called 'Contract for the Government of Change' (*'Contratto per il Governo del Cambiamento'*) (2018), Ansa.

[6] See Silvestri (2021), p. 201, for a nuanced analysis of the 2019 Italian reform and according to whom, in relation to previous consumer-focused class action regime: 'Since 2010, the year when the rules governing class actions for damages entered into force, the number of class actions commenced and successfully brought to an end (meaning, with an award of damages granted, in general, to a small group of subjects) is just a handful. There are no official records. One can assume that probably 20 or 30 class actions were instituted, but the majority did not overcome the initial stage of the procedure, when the admissibility of actions is tested, and therefore it is impossible to track cases unless one has access to the records of the courts where they were brought'.

See also the report from the parliamentary discussions from 21 March 2017. According to Alfonso Bonafede, at the time still a Deputy (for MoVimento 5 Stelle), the reform to the previous class action regime that he had proposed, as a Deputy, in 2013, had failed after years of negotiations because of corporate and insurance companies' interests.

2013—incidentally *right after* the EU Commission 2013/396 Recommendation from 11 June 2013 (thereby revealing its close influence).[7] This proposal, however, foundered in the Parliament's Senate after initially receiving favourable consideration in the Chamber of Deputies. Still, the explanatory report for this bill is particularly revealing of the objectives underlying the 2019 reform, when Bonafede became Minister: in sum, 'to make the tool more usable and attractive'.[8] For this purpose, 'the first fundamental intervention' involved '*expanding* its potential users':[9] hence, in 2019, the general scope of application and the different legislative trajectory in relation to the 2020 EU Directive ('RAD').

The rest of the objectives will be further examined in the following.

In the meantime, it is worth highlighting the entry into force of the RAD, requiring Member States to implement it at national level by 25 December 2022. Despite the possibility of merely amending Title VIII-*bis* of the Code of civil procedure (embedding the 2019 class action provisions), however, the new Italian legislator—in a significantly different Parliament, with different majorities—in 2023 introduced an *additional* (dual, once again) consumer-limited regime.[10] A simple amendment would have been certainly advisable for a more coherent and harmonious system of collective enforcement, as well as admissible under the Directive itself.[11] Thus, in addition to the *two general* remedies—compensatory and injunctive—introduced in 2019 (effective from 2021) and included in the Code of civil procedure, there are now a *third and fourth* class action (compensatory and injunctive), dedicated to *consumer* protection, included in the Consumer code and in implementation of the EU Directive.

Furthermore, as if it were not complex enough, a *fifth* collective remedy before the administrative judge, from 2009, complements the framework. It is the so-called 'public class action', or 'action for the efficiency of administrations and public service concessionaires', pursuant to Legislative Decree of 20 December 2009, No.

[7] Italian Parliament, Chamber of Deputies, Proposal presented on the 9 July 2013.

[8] Id. This objective is sought 'through interventions on the extension of standing to sue, the introduction of incentives for use by actors and their representatives, the effectiveness of protection and guarantees in the overall conduct of the procedure, and a more detailed and precise regulation of such proceedings, also to avoid gaps and interpretative uncertainties' (translated from Italian).

[9] Id. 'The first fundamental intervention to extend the usability of the tool involves broadening its potential users. Extracting the class action procedure from the consumer code and more aptly placing it in the civil procedure code could prevent the exclusion from such a protection of all those subjects who find themselves, as consumers might, in a situation requiring access to justice characterised by modest compensatory claims caused by multi-offensive unlawful acts, or in a situation where, even if the claim is not modest nor the structural weakness established, they still intend to act collectively for procedural convenience. This would serve to enhance the deflationary effect of the tool and to reduce the risk of forming conflicting judgments in relation to the same conduct and homogeneous positions' (translated from Italian).

[10] The so-called 'representative actions for the protection of the collective interests of consumers', pursuant to Articles 140-*ter et seq.* cod. cons. (the Italian Consumer code), enacted by Legislative Decree from 10 March 2023, No. 28.

[11] Article 1, para. 2: 'This Directive does not prevent Member States from adopting or retaining in force procedural means for the protection of the collective interests of consumers at national level'.

198.[12] Although until now scarcely implemented, it may potentially overlap with the injunctive class action from the Code of civil procedure, as subsequently discussed.[13]

In this context of fragile certainties, the innovative Italian legislative intervention from 2019 is placed and will be herein analysed. It is worth stressing, once again, how the perspective adopted is not a civil-procedural one. Rather, it is a *constitutional* one, and, as such, it will concentrate only on certain aspects of the procedural remedies, relevant under an access to justice, fair trial and Italian constitutional legitimacy standpoint, as well as in line with the deep constitutional transformations highlighted in Part I.

6.2 The 2019 Italian Class Action Reform: Procedural Hallmarks, Innovations and Coordination Trajectories

Before delving into the main interpretative and applicative issues of the 2019 class action regime, a brief examination of its salient features is imperative. This dual—compensatory and injunctive—route of enforcement forms the core matter of the present research, necessitating an exhaustive presentation to facilitate subsequent constitutional discussions.

The limited success of the previous consumer tool, together with a unique political context, particularly favourable, has already been highlighted. As anticipated, the scarce use and scepticism towards the previous device—both from legal

[12] See, e.g., Fidone and Maltoni (2025), Campigli (2024), Gastaldo (2016) and Patroni Griffi (2010).

[13] At the same time, in addition to coordination with the supranational EU level and its implementations, an assessment of the national regulatory framework is necessary also in relation to the other, various, tools of collective judicial protection. Even before the previous consumer class action, in fact, several collective tools had entered the Italian legal system. Extremely sector-specific, they concerned, for example, the matter of abusive general contract conditions (Article 37 Consumer Code), the repression of anti-union conduct (Article 28 Workers' Statute), the repression of unfair conduct (Article 2601 Civil Code), and especially anti-discrimination (Legislative Decree No. 286 of 1998, on discriminations 'for racial, ethnic, linguistic, national, geographic origin or religious reasons'; Legislative Decree No. 215 of 2003 'for equal treatment of people regardless of race and ethnic origin'; Legislative Decree No. 216 of 2003, 'for equal treatment in employment and working conditions'; Law No. 67 of 2006, for the protection of 'people with disabilities victims of discrimination'; Legislative Decree No. 198 of 2006, 'Code of Equal Opportunities between Men and Women'). However, Law No. 31 of 2019 does not mention these tools, unlike what happens with the previous consumer class action (Articles 139, 140 and 140-bis Consumer Code), which is expressly repealed, and with the so-called administrative class action (or 'public', Legislative Decree December 20, 2009, No. 198, 'appeal for the efficiency of administrations and public service concessionaires'), which is expressly saved. To these, the new 'representative action for the protection of the collective interests of consumers, *ex* Articles 140-*ter et seq*. Consumer Code is now added. In the legislative silence, the doubt concerns the possible overlap with the new remedies of Articles 840-*bis et seq.* and 840-*sexiesdecies* of the Code of civil procedure. With this in mind, the main issues that the institute itself and its first applications raise from a constitutional perspective will be considered below. The analysis, in any case, will focus mainly on the discipline introduced by Law No. 31 of April 12, 2019.

practitioners and the general public—, coupled with a series of major economic scandals, led the parliamentary majorities at the time—characterised by a populist nature—to seek a remedy capable of 'bolstering access to justice'. The answer was found in a radical overhaul of the previous mechanism, set in the Consumer code since 2007, with relatively minor amendments from 2010 and 2012.

The most relevant choice was undoubtedly a full expansion of the *scope of application* of the class action regime. From *consumer*-limited it became *general*. Accordingly, from the Consumer code its regulation was transferred to the Code of civil procedure (hereinafter 'c.p.c.'), under the new Title VIII-*bis* ('On collective proceedings') of Book IV. The expansion regarded both the compensatory and the injunctive remedy, a dualism which was maintained: the former, for the enforcement of all 'homogeneous individual rights'; the latter, for any type of 'interest [...] of a plurality of individuals or entities'. This choice—innovative also with respect to the content of the RAD, as already mentioned—is undoubtedly one of the most significant of the 2019 Italian reform.

The existence of three other collective procedural models—the dual (compensatory and injunctive) *consumer* class action, under Articles 140-*ter et seq.* of the Consumer Code, in implementation of RAD, and the administrative class action of 2009—, as well as other minor sector-specific collective procedures already present in the Italian legal system, evidently necessitates an investigation into the relationships and coordination criteria between them.

In any case, this chapter concentrates, from a constitutional perspective, on the main issues raised by the *trans-substantive* framework established under Law No. 31 of April 12, 2019, and its initial applications. To this regard, since its entry into force on 19 May 2021, at least[14] fifty-four class actions have been brought (considering also the ones from the subsequent consumer model since 2023): twenty-four on consumer issues, eighteen on securities, six on employment and labour matters, four for the protection of the right to health and two (inadmissible) on tax matters.[15] The jurisprudence developed until now can, therefore, be described as still in an embryonic state, with several actions still pending.

In relation to the 2019 regime, the confirmation of the dual collective remedy is also extremely important: on the one hand, the compensatory *azione di classe* pursuant to Articles 840-*bis et seq.* c.p.c.; on the other hand, the injunctive *azione inibitoria collettiva* pursuant to Article 840-*sexiesdecies* c.p.c. Although most of the doctrinal debate and legislative focus so far seems to be on the compensatory class action, this duality is central.[16]

The two instruments are profoundly different. At times synergistic and complementary, they are still autonomous and the result of two opposing legal traditions.

---

[14] Until 31 December 2024. Not all of them are uploaded on the portal, see the subsequent discussion, also in Chap. 11.

[15] See, *infra*, Figures.

[16] Id.

As to the former model, the *compensatory* one is designed for the collective protection of individual rights *only*. Through it, the legislator mainly responds to the need to redress excessively-imbalanced economic/informational relationships in a global context, as demonstrated by the rich common law experience.

This type of action, governed by Articles 840-*bis et seq*. c.p.c., protects '*homogeneous individual rights*' (Article 840-*bis*, para. 1, c.p.c.). The legislator has dedicated most, if not nearly all, of the reform to this action, spanning fourteen articles. Through this mechanism, any 'member of the class,' as well as no-profit organisations or associations whose statutory purposes include the protection of such rights (provided they are listed in the public register established by the Ministry of Justice—raising constitutional legitimacy doubts, discussed later in para. 6.4.1), may bring an action for 'the determination of liability and an order for compensation or restitution'[17] against businesses or public utility service providers for acts or conducts performed in the course of their activities.

Once the admissibility phase is successfully passed—with a central focus on the requirement of homogeneity (see para. 6.3.1.1 below)—a first window opens (between sixty and one hundred and fifty days) for individuals holding homogeneous individual rights to join the action.

Regarding *class adhesion*, the decision to confirm the exclusivity of the so-called '*opt-in*' regime, which requires an *explicit* manifestation of intent to become part of the class and to be bound by the effects (both positive and negative) of the decision, has been maintained. Such a choice, promoted (but not imposed) at the EU level, clashes with the goal of *effective* access to justice in certain minor cases, but undoubtedly safeguards the principle of full participation of the parties in the process, as opposed to the 'opt-out' regime.

The *first window* for joining begins on the date of publication of the admissibility order on the telematic services portal; the application to join must also be submitted through this portal, in a dedicated area, and must meet the formal and substantive requirements outlined in Article 840-*septies* c.p.c. Moreover, under Article 840-*quinquies*, para. 1, c.p.c., those who join do not assume the status of a party.

Once proceedings are initiated, the court conducts the relevant fact-finding 'in the manner it deems most appropriate' (Article 840-*quinquies*, para. 2, c.p.c.), dispensing with any non-essential formalities to ensure due process. *Statistical data and presumptions* may also be used. Still under Article 840-*quinquies*, para. 3, c.p.c, unless specific reasons exist, the costs of any expert opinions commissioned by the court are borne by the defendant. Upon a well-founded request from the claimant, the court may order the defendant to disclose relevant *evidence* under their control, identifying facts and evidence reasonably available to them, with possible imposition of an administrative fine of up to €100,000 (to be allocated to a public fund)[18] for non-compliance. Alternatively, the court may consider proven the fact to which

---

[17] Article 840-*bis*, para. 2, c.p.c.

[18] The so-called '*Cassa delle ammende*'.

the requested disclosure pertains (Article 840-*quinquies*, paras. 5 and following, c.p.c.). This provision represents another advantage for the plaintiff.

At the conclusion of this phase, the court issues a *judgment* under Article 840-*sexies* c.p.c., determining the respondent's liability by verifying the infringement of homogeneous individual rights caused by the respondent's conduct. The judgment also defines the characteristics of these rights—thus delineating the 'class'—and specifies the documentation required to prove their holding, as well as a possible amount to be paid as a cost-fund to the plaintiff side by each adherent.[19]

At this point, a *second (and final) window* for joining the action opens, within a time that again varies between sixty and one hundred and fifty days.

Finally, a *delegated judge* and a *common representative* of the participants (the latter chosen from those qualified to serve as bankruptcy trustees) are appointed.

These two figures play a crucial role in the *liquidation phase*. Based solely on documentary evidence (in addition to what has already been established in the earlier phase), and with the possible assistance of '*experts* with specific technical expertise to assess the facts presented by participants as the basis for their claims,' the common representative prepares a liquidation plan, providing specific reasoning for each participant, which may be amended following written observations from participants and from the respondent.

The delegated judge, through a reasoned decree constituting an enforceable title, orders the defendant to make payments (or restitutions), approving the plan in whole or in part. Under Article 840-*novies* c.p.c., the defendant is also ordered to directly pay the common representative and the claimant's attorneys a performance-based fee, calculated progressively (ranging from 9% to 0.5%) depending on the number of participants and as a percentage of the total amount owed to them.

In contrast, the regulation of the *injunctive* collective action is significantly more concise, covered only by Article 840-*sexiesdecies* c.p.c. This action may be brought with respect to 'acts and behaviours harmful to a plurality of individuals' to obtain an 'order to cease or prohibit the repetition' of the harmful conduct, whether by omission or commission. It can be initiated by the same organisations or associations authorised to promote compensatory class actions (i.e., non-profits whose statutory purposes include the protection of such rights, provided they are listed in the public register established by the Ministry of Justice). It can also be brought, under Article 840-*sexiesdecies*, para. 1, c.p.c., by 'anyone with an *interest*' in obtaining the injunction. This expression, which lends itself to multiple interpretations, will require further examination (see para. 6.3.2 below).

It is worth emphasising again that the injunctive collective action is addressed in only one article. This choice stands out especially when compared to the compensatory class action, which is covered in fourteen articles. Such a numerical disparity in regulation heightens potential *coordination issues* between the two collective remedies.

[19] It is not specified in whose favour. It is deemed here to be in favour of the joint representative of the adherents, contextually appointed.

The former remedy (the compensatory one) could, in fact, appear as the general model to be analogically followed even for the latter (injunctive) action in circumstances not expressly regulated by the legislator. As will be discussed below, this could (and already does) prove particularly problematic, especially regarding admissibility conditions—specifically, the requirement of homogeneity—, with significant repercussions on the extension of the subjective and objective scope of application (see paras. 6.3 and 6.4 below). In this respect, it is worth noting that Article 840-*sexiesdecies*, para. 4, c.p.c., explicitly refers to a specific provision of the compensatory action ('Article 840-*quinquies* applies insofar as it is compatible'), relating to procedural aspects (terms, fact-finding acts, disclosure orders, and possible administrative monetary penalties). It will thus be necessary to determine whether this explicit reference should be understood as exclusive to the other provisions of the compensatory class action or analogically interpreted (see para. 6.3.2 below).

Common elements to both disciplines, in any case, are explicitly (*expressis verbis*) the *passive subjects* (companies or entities managing public services or services of public utility, concerning acts and behaviours carried out in the performance of their respective activities, as per Articles 840-*bis*, para. 3, and 840-*sexiesdecies*, para. 2, c.p.c.—see below, para. 6.4.2), and the *competent court* (the specialised business section from the Tribunal of the respondent's seat, under Articles 840-*ter*, para. 1, and 840-*sexiesdecies*, para. 3, c.p.c.—see below, para. 6.5).

Equal provisions and issues arise concerning the *transitional rules*. Pursuant to Article 7 of Law No. 31 of 2019, the provisions of the reform in question apply to 'unlawful acts committed after the date of entry into force' (May 19, 2021).

Furthermore, other significant novelties have been brought with the objective of adapting the procedural structure to the peculiarities of the new collective instrument, based on the (unsuccessful) previous consumer class action experience.

Among these, in particular, the establishment of the abovementioned new *telematic portal*, with a dedicated section in the public area of the telematic services website managed by the Ministry of Justice, stands out.[20] This official digital section is immediately assigned a key role, both for the *publicity* of the various proposed cases (through the publication within ten days, by the registry office, of the decree setting the hearing, as well as, subsequently, of other acts of the process), and for simplifying the procedure of *joining* the class, now exclusively online. This significantly reduces the burden on the court registries, but, above all, on the claimants, called upon to form the class. Moreover, *in theory*[21] it allows the general community to remain always informed about the class actions initiated and, through the elimination of paperwork, exponentially favours class adhesion. This clear simplification through the aid of new technologies represents in abstract, therefore, a significant step. In principle, joining the class is now one mere click away.

[20] Accessible here: < https://servizipst.giustizia.it/PST/it/pst_2_16.wp >.

[21] See, *infra*, para. 7. See also *infra*, Chap. 11.

As an incentive to propose more actions, the above-mentioned exceptional introduction of a *premium fee* for the plaintiff's lawyer should be noted, to be calculated as an additional percentage (between 9% and 0.5%) on the total amount due to all class members, progressively and varying based on their number. The percentages do not seem entirely convincing—they could be higher (especially in light of those, greater, intended for the 'common representative' of the class)—nor does the choice to limit such a premium compensation to compensatory actions. Given Italy's ban on contingency fees (in practice easily circumventable, through the coordination with non-attorney third parties), this provision nevertheless represents an important step forward in encouraging lawyers—the true engine of numerous class actions from overseas—to undertake actions with the new procedural instrument.

Finally, regarding *evidence*, the above-referred innovations introduced by Article 840-*quinquies* (applicable to the injunctive remedy, too, as per explicit provision) should be stressed. On the one hand, it imposes the obligation to advance the expenses for a possible technical consultant on the respondent and establishes that the judge may use statistical data and simple presumptions for the purpose of ascertaining responsibility.[22] On the other hand, it introduces a system of disclosure somewhat similar to the typical US discovery, also concerning confidential information of the defendant and supported by an administrative pecuniary sanction from 10.000 € to 100.000 € in case of non-compliance.[23] This system could greatly benefit the claimants, both from a strategic litigation perspective (thus, not necessarily aimed at a victory in the courtrooms) and in negotiating potential out-of-court settlements. At the same time, it is crucial to maintain adequate safeguards for defendants, ensuring *fair process guarantees* and protecting against meritless legal actions initiated by competitors, aiming to harm their business rather than addressing genuine grievances, or by 'buccaneering attorneys', looking for causes of actions and easy settlements in 'fishing expeditions'.[24]

6.3 The Objective Perimeter of Application

An element characterising both the compensatory and the injunctive mechanisms is their *representative* nature, i.e. the fact that legal situations (also) other than those of the parties are enforced and dealt with in court.[25] In other words, the case transcends the parties to the proceedings, extending the effects of *res judicata* to third parties.[26]

Also shared between the two instruments is the main novelty of the 2019 reform, namely the widening of the objective scope, which has become *general*. Both

---

[22] See, *infra*, Parts 3 and 4.

[23] Id., in particular Chap. 7 and the *Philips Respironics* case.

[24] See *supra*, previous Chap. 5.

[25] See Homburger (1974) and Cappelletti (1976).

[26] See Marcus (2014) and Subrin (2010).

actions are therefore so-called 'trans-substantial', as they are able to cover all areas of substantive law.

At the same time, as already mentioned, *significant differences* can be identified between them. In particular, the former serves as tool for protecting *homogeneous individual* subjective positions, whereas the latter seems to have a wider objective scope, by allowing the enforcement of *supra-individual* interests, too.

6.3.1 The Compensatory Class Action and the Enforcement of 'Homogeneous Individual Rights'

The compensatory class action under Article 840-*bis* of the Italian Code of civil procedure is aimed at enforcing 'homogeneous individual rights' by establishing liability and obtaining an order for compensation (or restitution) against the perpetrator of the harmful conduct.

This action is therefore used to protect *any* individual right. It is no longer limited to the consumer context, aimed solely at safeguarding so-called small claims, but it can now be employed in any area of law. This appears particularly significant from the constitutional perspective adopted here, as it potentially opens the door to a collective dimension of judicial enforcement for fundamental rights, too. For instance, it may apply to health, personal freedom, the protection of minorities, fair working conditions, other fundamental freedoms, and social rights.

It is important to emphasise that only active and full subjective legal positions, pertaining to a *single holder*, may be protected through this action—that is, individual rights. The role of the class action in this context, therefore, will be that to overcome practical barriers which concretely hinder the exercise of the right to legal action by individual claimants. These barriers include informational or organisational asymmetries, and insufficient economic or time incentives to initiate proceedings.[27]

The right to legal action for the defense of one's subjective rights, as already discussed,[28] is itself an inviolable right, 'protected by Articles 24 and 113 of the [Italian] Constitution [...] which characterise the democratic rule of law'. This right must be interpreted, in accordance with Article 6 of the European Convention on Human Rights (ECHR), as a 'concrete and effective' right, meaning that it guarantees a certain and tangible possibility to challenge an act that constitutes an unlawful interference with one's rights. Class actions thus become a key tool for ensuring—through *representative* mechanisms—this concrete possibility of obtaining compensation where it would not be feasible or practical to proceed individually.

Beyond the element of homogeneity, which will be addressed in the following paragraph (6.3.1.1), the legal framework under consideration does not impose

---

[27] See Cappelletti (1993).

[28] See, *supra*, Chap. 4.

objective limitations on the individual rights that may be collectively protected under Articles 840-*bis et seq.* of the Italian Code of civil procedure. Consequently, as anticipated, it appears permissible to bring a class action in any area of law. However, this raises a dual set of issues.

Firstly, it is necessary to ask whether the action under discussion can also be brought in areas governed by *specialised courts*—such as administrative, accounting, or tax courts—or in areas where *specialised sections*, such as the labour ones, are provided.

The applicability of the rules in question to disputes that fall under the jurisdiction of specialised courts is confirmed by the references to the Code of Civil Procedure found in the respective sector-specific regulations: Article 39, paragraph 1, of the Code of administrative procedure (Legislative Decree No. 104 of July 2, 2010); Article 1, paragraph 2, of the Code of tax procedure (Legislative Decree No. 546 of December 31, 1992); and Article 7, paragraph 2, of the Code of accounting justice (Law No. 197 of December 29, 2022). These external references apply wherever they are compatible and insofar as the matter is not already regulated by the relevant procedural rules.

Evidently, therefore, a collective action under Articles 840-*bis et seq.* c.p.c. will only be permissible for the compensation of subjective rights whose protection is already individually actionable before the relevant specialised court. With respect to administrative proceedings, for example, pursuant to Article 7, para. 5, of Legislative Decree No. 104 of July 2, 2010, this will only be possible in matters of exclusive jurisdiction as set forth under Article 133 of the same legislative decree, concerning acts committed by public administrations in the exercise, even indirectly, of public powers.[29] The fact that, pursuant to the same provision, claims can be brought 'even for compensation purposes' confirms the possibility of pursuing the compensatory class action remedy.

This interpretation finds further support in Article 1 of the same Code of administrative procedure, which states that 'Administrative jurisdiction ensures full and *effective protection* in accordance with the principles of the Constitution and European law'. In light of the above considerations regarding effective protection and the necessary adaptation toward a collective (or representative) dimension of judicial remedies, as required by Articles 2, 3, 24 (first paragraph), and 117 (first paragraph) of the Constitution—in relation to Articles 6 and 13 of the European Convention on Human Rights (ECHR) and Article 19 of the Treaty on the European Union (TEU) and Article 47 of the Charter of Fundamental Rights of the European Union (EUCFR)—it follows as a corollary that the dual general remedy provided by the Code of civil procedure should also be considered admissible before such special courts.[30] Analogous considerations must apply to tax and accounting jurisdictions.

[29] See Italian Constitutional Court, Judgement No. 178 from 2022, point No. 3.2. of the Points of law. On the compensatory remedy before the administrative judge, see also Italian Constitutional Court, Judgement Nos. 204 from 2004, No. 94 from 2017, No. 191 from 2006.

[30] See, *supra*, Chap. 4.

Of course, from a subjective standpoint, a significant issue arises as to whether, among the 'entities managing public or utility services'—which are designated as defendants alongside businesses—, public administrations and taxing authorities can also be included—under an extensive interpretation (see *infra*, para. 6.4.2).

As for the specialised sections of ordinary courts, such as the labour section, the collective remedy must be considered even more clearly admissible before them. Indeed, given the language of Articles 840-*bis et seq.* c.p.c, case law suggests that 'those connected to employment relationships do not appear to be excluded'.[31]

At most, as will be commented below, the issue to address is whether the specialised section in *business* matters, that holds exclusive jurisdiction over class actions pursuant to Article 840-*ter*, para. 1, c.p.c. (see below, para. 6.5),[32] should still have has jurisdiction over disputes in the special matters discussed until now.

Focusing on the *objective* scope of the collective compensatory action under the c.p.c., it is necessary, secondly, to assess the applicability of this general framework in relation to consumer law. This applicability should be considered excluded, in favour of the new (from 2023) consumer representative action governed by Articles 140-*ter et seq.* of the Consumer code (cod. cons.), as *lex specialis*, but only for authorised entities (see below, para. 6.4.2), and not for individual consumers.

This is explicitly established by Article 140-*ter*, para. 2, cod. cons., which provides that in the case of 'representative actions brought against professionals for violations of the provisions' listed in Annex II-*septies*, 'which harm or may harm the collective interests of consumers [...] authorised entities'—and thus *only* these entities (see below, para. 6.4.1, regarding other subjects, including individuals, who are entitled)—'cannot act through the class action provided for by Title VIII-*bis* of Book IV of the Code of Civil Procedure.'

This underscores the close connection between the objective and subjective scope of application, on the one hand, and the overlap between the 2019 class action under the c.p.c., analysed here, and the so-called 'representative' consumer action of 2023, on the other hand.

The potential conflict is significant, as the 2023 consumer collective action applies to violations of consumer law provisions listed in the annex to the RAD.[33] Given the broad definition of 'consumer'[34] in European law, it may happen—and has already occurred in early case law[35]—that violations of European rules listed in the annex also result in breaches of rights that are not strictly consumer-related, including fundamental rights, such as the right to health or that to live in a healthy

[31] See *Deliveroo* case, analysed *infra*, in Chap. 8: 'Among the individual rights that can be protected, it does not seem to be possible to exclude those related to labour relations' (translated from Italian).

[32] In relation to the compensatory class action. Equal exclusive jurisdiction is provided for, pursuant to Article 840-*sexiesdecies*, para. 3, c.p.c., in relation to collective actions for injunctions.

[33] See, *supra*, previous Chap. 5.

[34] Article 3 of the RAD: 'any natural person who acts for purposes which are outside that person's trade, business, craft or profession'.

[35] See *Philips Respironics* case, analysed *infra*, in Chap. 7.

environment.[36] This creates a risk of potential overlaps in terms of *subjective* standing—although only for authorised entities (see below, para. 6.4)—with the *objective* scope of the 2019 class action under the c.p.c. analysed here.

Furthermore, it is worth noting that the 2023 consumer framework includes numerous cross-references to the 2019 codified class action framework.[37]

6.3.1.1 The Homogeneity Requirement: A Key Issue

Article 840-*bis* c.p.c., in relation to the compensatory *azione di classe*, specifies that '*homogeneous individual rights*' can be enforced also through the class action, following the provisions of this title'. It is then followed by Article 840-*ter* c.p.c., which clarifies that 'the claim is declared inadmissible [...] when the court does not recognise the *homogeneity* of the individual rights protected under Article 840-*bis*'.

The notion of *homogeneity*, evidently, becomes the keystone of this compensatory class action, being decisive for its admissibility. Given the full extension of the scope of application in 2019, beyond the original consumer field, it is the only element—together with the subjective rules on standing to sue and to be sued, and the minor requirements under letters *c)* and *d)* of Article 840-*ter* c.p.c.—currently limiting the perimeter of (compensatory) class proceedings in Italy. It is, thus, essential to precisely clarify its meaning, given the vagueness of the term and the lack of legislative definitions.

Under a strictly literal standpoint, 'homogeneous' means 'of the same species, of the same nature, of the same character [...] by extension, similar, analogous, akin [...] figuratively, of a set composed of equal or related elements, or also well harmonised with each other'.[38] Etymologically, it stems from the ancient Greek '*ὁμογενής*', which translates as 'with the *same origin*'. In the context of Articles 840-*bis et seq.* c.p.c., therefore, it appears to signify 'individual rights' which are similar, but not completely identical, and which share same circumstances in relation to the action brough before the court.

The uncertainties and interpretative difficulties in approaching such an a-technical, 'meta-juridical' notion,[39] quite exceptional in the Italian civil-procedural panorama, are numerous and evident. They are also amplified by the fact that such a requirement for admissibility concentrates on how the dispute appears in the judicial and contentious dimensions, focusing on the concrete characteristics of the lawsuit, rather than on the nature of the rights asserted in the trial.[40]

Comparatively, the notion of 'homogeneity' finds parallelisms in the Portuguese and Brazilian class action regulations and—to a certain degree—analogues in the

---

[36] See *ILVA* case, analysed *infra*, in Chap. 7.

[37] See Giussani (2025) and De Dominicis (2025).

[38] See Treccani Vocabulary online.

[39] See Silvestri (2020).

[40] See Donzelli (2019).

'commonality' and 'predominance' requirements under the classic common law collective regimes.[41] As will be analysed, a large part of the Italian debate concerns precisely whether a meaning closer to 'commonality' or to 'predominance' should be adopted.

From a systematic viewpoint, 'homogeneity' is not a concept which finds other civil-procedural references in the domestic legal order. Its only use until now has been exclusively in relation to collective proceedings: within the initial consumer class action (now repealed), in substitution (since 2012) of the previous adjective 'identical'; in the here-analysed general class action pursuant to Article 840-*bis et seq.* c.p.c., from 2019 and in force since 2021; in the new consumer representative action, (unnecessarily, see *supra*) adopted in 2023 in enactment of the RAD. Its mention in the previous consumer class action offers, nonetheless, a decade of precious, yet far from unanimous, doctrinal and jurisprudential elaboration.

On the other hand, cautious yet precious considerations can be drawn from the use of such a linguistic term in the domain of *constitutional law*. This occurs namely in relation to referendum questions,[42] to the decree law and its conversion into law[43] and to federal systems' federal and federate constitutional provisions,[44] but also to describe similar but not identical situations under the principle of equality.[45] The contours of 'homogeneity' in such contexts are equally vague and uncertain. The understanding that can be drawn for the purposes of this research, nonetheless, is rather valuable. They confirm, in fact, the literal standpoint, which reads 'homogeneous' situations—especially for decree laws (and their conversion) and referendum questions—as situations not extraneous to each other's rationale or based on different objectives or objects.[46] This allows for a *degree of differentiation* among such homogenous situations, as long as they maintain an overall common ground; hence, by *no means* they should be conceived as *completely* identical.

Coming back to the current class action reform, the interpretative reconstructions from the previous regime (the consumer one, from 2007 onwards) must be gauged today in light of the parliamentary preparatory works from both concerned legislative periods (in particular the discussions from 2013 and 2018, see *supra*, para. 6.1), in coordination with the additional regulatory changes from the 2019 reform (primarily the new liquidation phase and its key players), as well as with the very first jurisprudential applications under the new 2019 general class action provisions. Only this way a proper understanding of such a key term for the success and viability of compensatory class actions in Italy can be fully grasped.

With this aim, the questions herein relevant are numerous.

---

[41] See, *supra*, previous Chap. 5.

[42] See Pace (2016a), Pace (2016b). Siclari (2016).

[43] See Filippi (2023), Lupo (2012).

[44] See Theilen (2021), Delledonne (2017), Caponi et al. (2014).

[45] See, e.g., Italian Constitutional Court, Judgement No. 40 from 2024, No. 108 from 2023, No. 270 from 2022 and No. 172 from 2021, finding a violation of such a principle whenever 'homogeneous situations are regulated in an unjustifiably different manner'.

[46] See Italian Constitutional Court, Judgement No. 149 from 2020, point No. 6.3 of the Points of law.

First, it needs to be clarified *what* exactly is to be conceived as 'homogeneous' today, in light of all the above-mentioned elements of evaluation. Is it required for the 'individual rights' to share the same cause of action ('*titolo*') or should other common elements be considered? And, if so, to which degree are personal (that is, non-common, or non-identical) elements allowed? Furthermore, following a relatively recent judgement from the Court of Cassation,[47] does this concern only pecuniary or also non-pecuniary damage?

Second, *when* should the assessment on homogeneity be conducted? At a preliminary (so-called 'admissibility') stage or after the court's determination on the defendant's liability? Evidently, the degree of in-depth of the assessment varies substantially in accordance with the procedural phase. In the former case, in fact, it could only be speculative.[48] Moreover, *who* should undertake it, to which degree and *where*?

Third, provided a degree of 'individualisation' is accepted among the individual rights of the class, it should be sorted out *how* to proceed for the quantification of damages. Different personal, or individual, elements within the subjective positions of the different class members lead to an entitlement to different sums as damages. *Who* should propose a method of quantification which considers both the common elements and the personal ones: the judge forming the class, the plaintiff with their lawyers, the delegate judge or the new figure of the 'common representative'? And, rather significantly, which quantification methods should—and *can*—be followed? The elimination of any reference to a 'homogeneous calculation criterion for liquidation' from the previous consumer class action (Article 140-*bis*, para. 12, cod. cons., now repealed), on the one hand, and the establishment of a whole new phase of 'project of the homogeneous individual rights of the adherents' (Article 840-*octies* c.p.c.), on the other hand, provide valuable interpretative indicators, as will be analysed. At the same time, the foreign experiences with class action litigation offer other criteria for quantification and diversification among homogeneous yet partially different individual rights: sub-classes, lump sums and *cy-près*, or fluid recovery, are some of the most notable mechanisms.

Last, the inevitable approximation in the quantification of individual damages given by the standardisation characterising—in any case—class proceedings needs to be evaluated against the backdrop of *fair trial guarantees*, both from the perspective of the class members who, despite adherence, are *not* parties to the proceedings (the right to a day in court, counter-balanced by the right to an effective delivery of justice, and the requirement—to some degree, criticisable—for an *explicit* adherence to the class, the so-called opt-in regime), and from the viewpoint, usually less regarded but not less important, of the defendant (equality of arms). The document-centred evidentiary regime, the rules on legal expenses and the provisions on execution of the liquidation project are closely linked, too. The repercussions of all these

[47] See, *infra*, *Trenord* case. Italian Court of Cassation, Section III, 31 May 2019, No. 14886.

[48] Donzelli (2019), p. 16.

issues on a constitutional level, foremost of access to justice and due process, are obvious.

As to the *first issue*, following legislative and jurisprudential developments, it is now undisputed that the expression 'homogeneous individual rights' indeed allows for differentiated traits within the mass of subjective positions composing the class.[49] In short, the individual rights whose enforcement is collectively sought *can* present, in addition to a necessary *common* (hence, identical) core, a *differentiated* (also referred to as 'personal', 'exclusive' or 'individualised') part between each other, that is a set of factual or legal issues which pertain to a single individual position rather than to the class as a whole.[50]

The initial, stricter, interpretation which required a *total* identity of the individual rights (that is of all the factual and legal issues related to each individual subjective position) should be, and has been, abandoned.[51] The legislative substitution in 2012, still with regard to the previous consumer class action (now repealed), of the adjective 'identical' with 'homogeneous' has clearly ended such a debate.

At the same time, also the doctrine proposing a 'predominance' test—that is finding homogeneity only when the common issues prevail over the individual ones—appears overcome today. On the one hand, it is complex to find solid criteria to equally determine predominance in concrete cases, as required by the principle of certainty and as shown by the US case law under Rule 23 (b)(3). On the other hand, it is, in any case, a test extraneous to the legislator's intention and to the literal meaning or systemic reading of the adjective 'homogeneous'. None of the recent cases mentions it.

Rather, the academic and jurisprudential elaboration is currently divided on the *perspective* to adopt. Whereas some propose to consider the *judicial claim*, and in particular the objective elements identifying it (the so-called '*causa petendi*' and '*petitum*', see *infra*), others stress the need to focus on the mere *factual situation* at the basis of the claim, and in particular on the fact *generating* the damage (rather than its consequences, the so-called 'event').

The consequences stemming from the adoption of one interpretative angle over the other are not irrelevant. The *former* requires the same '*causa petendi*' (that is the cause of action, in other words the set of facts and legal reasons underpinning the claim) and the same '*petitum*' (that is the specific type of relief or remedy requested to the court) for all the individual rights aggregated through the class action.[52] Following the *latter*, to find homogeneity it suffices to demonstrate (on evidence,

---

[49] See, e.g., *Telecom* case, Tribunal of Milan, Order from 15 February 2024, R.G. No. 21789/2023, or the *Millemiglia* case, Tribunal of Rome, Section XVII, Order from 8 November 2023, R.G. No. 1577/2023, and case law therein referred (i.e., Court of Appeal of Milan, Judgement from 6 June 2017, R.G. No. 385).

[50] Donzelli (2019), p. 13.

[51] See Poli (2012), p. 38, and Menchini and Motto (2010).

[52] See, *inter alia*, after the 2019 reform, Consolo (2020) and Donzelli (2019); see also Menchini and Motto (2010)—in reference, however, to the previous consumer class action, when the adjective 'identical' was still used.

see *infra*) that the action or omission (in short, the *conduct*) of the defendant that has given rise to a harm for which compensation or restitution is sought is common to all the individual rights presented as part of the class.[53]

The insistence on an identity of the *causa petendi*, under the former view, evidently encompasses *also* the facts *generating* the damage, whose mere identity is required according to the latter interpretative standpoint, too. Same cause of action, however, also means identity of the *other constitutive facts* of the compensatory (or restitution) legal situation, such as, e.g. under Article 2043 c.c., damage, causation, unlawfulness, fault or intent, or absence of excluding causes.

The requirement of the same causation (in Italian, '*nesso di causalità*') and of the same *damage* appears particularly onerous for the class plaintiffs, since they usually vary in cases of mass-harm conducts. It is extremely rare—e.g., in cases of mass incidents or defective products—that all the affected individuals have received the same type of harm and due to the same conduct. Cases concerning the right to health (e.g., due to environmental pollution, to a defective product,[54] to a mass incident or to a harmful medicine) are rather illustrative of how the damage suffered by each individual could be significantly different. Some may die, some may be permanently affected, whereas others could only be slightly injured. In addition, the way in which the damage has been produced could also vary within the group of affected people, for example considering other contributing causal factors (e.g., a physical or environmental predisposition, an unhealthy life-style or a scarce attention to the information folder).

The identity of the *petitum*, instead, could vary whenever a different type of relief is sought for different rights within the class: for instance, in some cases a restitution, in others a compensation for damages may be more appropriate to remedy the same harmful conduct of the defendant. Not always monetary redress is the only option to address a damage suffered. In some cases, for instance regarding fraud securities, the investors may seek different types of redress, according to their own different causes of actions: in some cases, simple restitution; in others, compensation for damages. Adopting this perspective would entail an inadmissibility of actions with *similar* sub-classes.

It is noteworthy that such a former viewpoint draws from, and in several stances was proposed before, 2012, during the validity of the initial consumer collective regulations, when the adjective 'identical' was still used instead of 'homogeneous', in relation to the class of individual rights.[55]

---

[53] See Giussani (2020), p. 359.

[54] See *infra*, Chap. 7, the *Philips Respironics* case.

[55] For instance, Menchini and Motto (2010) and Poli R. (2012), p. 38. See also Tribunal of Milan, Section X, order from 8 November 2013, *Associazione Altroconsumo c. Trenord s.r.l.*, one of the first cases after the substitution of the adjective 'identical' with 'homogeneous', which, despite finding an inadmissibility, unequivocally stated that 'This Court indeed believes that the damages claimed must present common basic characteristics (although not requiring the identity of the *petitum*)' (translated from Italian). This shift in perspective has also been clearly stressed by Caponi (2012), p. 151, right after the legislative substitution: 'With the second

Hence, even more today, the latter interpretation appears preferable, that is the one which identifies 'homogeneity' in the mere presence of a *common causative fact*. Furthermore, while not universally accepted, it is the prevailing one in the most recent jurisprudence.[56] The preferability is supported both by literal and systematic and logical-reconstructive reasons of the norm's *rationale*.

As anticipated, *etymologically*, 'homogeneous' derives from the ancient Greek noun '*ὁμογενής*', which translates as 'with the same origin'. Given the a-technicity of the concept, it seems correct to favour its most literal reading, rather than infer from it an additional burden of proof on the plaintiffs. *Comparatively*, this is also in line with those legal orders, such as the Brazilian and Portuguese one, from which the expression at hand was most presumably borrowed, which merely refer to the '*origen común*'.

Indeed, this concept appears to originate from Brazilian law, where the expression 'homogeneous individual rights' was first referenced in 1989 specifically in the context of class actions.[57] In this framework, Brazilian legal scholarship has clarified that homogeneity represents a legal fiction created by positive law 'with the sole and exclusive purpose of making possible the collective (molecular) protection of individual rights [the atoms] that possess a collective (mass) dimension'.[58]

Homogeneity, therefore, refers to the '*origem comum*' (common origin), as interpreted through an etymological-literal lens ('*ὁμογενής*', meaning 'with same origin'). This is to be understood broadly as a close connection that allows for the joint adjudication of the various subjective rights asserted in court. Unlike collective or diffuse positions—which are '*essentially collective*', by nature—these positions

amendment, the concept of 'identity' is replaced with that of 'homogeneity' of rights and situations protected by the class action. [...] From the wrongful act arise rights to compensation or restitution, linked by the commonality of the questions to be resolved to ascertain their existence. Therefore, neither the identity of the *petitum* nor that of the *causa petendi* is necessary' (translated from Italian).

[56] Court of Appeal of Milan, Judgement from 25 August 2017, R.G. No. 3756/2017. See also *Telecom* case, Tribunal of Milan, Order from 15 February 2024, R.G. No. 21789/2023, or the *Millemiglia* case, Tribunal of Rome, Section XVII, Order from 8 November 2023, R.G. No. 1577/2023.

[57] *Lei No. 7913 of 1989*, commented by Gidi (1995), p. 29. According to the same author, this expression, hitherto equally foreign to Brazilian procedural law, is due to a scholarly contribution by Barbosa Moreira, referring to "class actions for damages" in North American law. This expression was then re-proposed in Law No. 83 of 1995 on Portuguese popular actions and, most recently, in the Italian legal order with the former consumer class action (since 2009) and administrative class action 'for the efficiency of administrations before the administrative judge', pursuant to Legislative Decree No. 198 of 20 December 2009.

[58] Gidi (1995), p. 30 (translated Portuguese).

(the 'homogeneous' individual rights) should be understood as positions that are '*accidentally collective*', by infringement.[59]

Such a view is supported by the clear *rationale* of 'bolstering access to justice' of the 2019 class action reform, along with a series of *regulatory changes* in relation to the liquidation phase (subsequently analysed). The former, stricter, interpretation would, in fact, raise the *admissibility threshold*, by requiring a higher degree of common issues and, consequently, hindering in practice the legislative intent behind the recent reform.

A nuanced analysis, to this regard, cannot fail to mention an even broader, and more flexible, interpretation emerging from the parliamentary discussions ('*lavori preparatori*', in Italian) prior to the enactment of the 2019 reform.

As is known, the 2019 legislator missed once again the opportunity to shed light on the exact meaning of the 'homogeneity' requirement, if not—even better—to replace it with a more technical and objective legal criterion. It is superfluous to add that the same occurred in 2023, with the (last-minute) choice to refer once again to such a vague and confusing notion. It is also barely relevant to add that the reports from 2018 discussions show that a general amendment to include a definition of the term in the new regulations was proposed, however unsuccessfully.

Still, as discussed *above*, it is worth recalling that the Minister of Justice at the time of the 2019 reform (XVIII legislature), Alfonso Bonafede, during the previous legislature (XVII, from 2013 until 2018) had been the proponent of a bill for a class action reform which did not pass despite favourable and long parliamentary discussions, and which very much resembled the subsequent 2019 reform (enacted in the subsequent legislature, once Bonafede was Minister of Justice, after his political party included it in its electoral programme). Hence, the significance of reading the proposal for such a bill, from 2013, in which the future Minister of Justice himself gave indeed a definition of 'homogeneity':

> Homogeneity can, in other words, depend on the *identity of the good* (or service) being contracted by the different subjects, the *identity of the conduct* held by the professional towards multiple contractors, the identity of the consequences, *or* from the *fact of common relevance*. This complex and delicate operation defines the traits of the class, identifying its characteristics and potential number, allowing the judge with their assessment to determine either a restriction or an expansion of the evaluation of the class that the actor had proposed. In this sense, the attribution of a margin of discretion to the judge in the evaluation of the homogeneous character of the rights is fundamental, in order to allow them to clearly define the characteristics of the class and *ensure easy access* to the process and its *effective* unfolding.[60]

Although non-binding, this perspective appears particularly interesting for its flexibility: on the one hand, avoiding any reference to the claim and its cause of action ('*causa petendi*' and '*petitum*'), possible *alternatives* to the identity of the harm's '*generating fact*' (or 'origin', that is the etymological viewpoint) are offered in the 'identity of the *good or service*' (for contractual liabilities), in the 'identity of the

[59] Barbosa Moreira (1985), p. 195.

[60] Italian Parliament, Chamber of Deputies, Proposal presented on the 9 July 2013.

conduct' (also for extra-contractual, or tort, liability) and even the identity of the *consequences* or a mere, general, '*common relevance*'; on the other hand, a *margin of discretion* of the judge when determining the presence of homogeneity is stressed, with the clear intent to 'ensure *easy access* to the process' as well as its '*effective* unfolding'.

The rationale, evidently transferred during the subsequent legislature to the then-successful 2019 reform, is unmistakeably that of advancing concrete access to justice through the class action procedure. With this purpose, a broad (if not the *broadest* possible) interpretation of the concept of 'homogeneity' was proposed by the legislator.

Another highly-debated interpretative issue addressed by then-deputy Bonafede in his 2013 parliamentary-bill presentation was that of the *quantification* of damages. Following the initially stricter 'identical' requirement from the first consumer class action, some courts and minoritarian doctrine had been advocating for a need of identity not just of the '*causa petendi*' and of the '*petitum*', but also of the so-called '*quantum*', that is the precise monetary sum sought as indemnification for the incurred damages. After the 2012 substitution of the adjective 'identical' with 'homogeneous', nonetheless, the clear majoritarian approach (both doctrinal and, more slowly, jurisprudential) shifted in admitting a *differentiation* in the *quantification* of damages within the individual subjective positions composing the class. In short, different sums can now be awarded to different members of the class under the 'homogeneity' requirement. This is being absolutely confirmed by all the developing case law.[61]

Such a view was anticipately (in respect to the case law, at the time still rigid) proposed by Bonafede, who specified in the same occasion (2013) how 'the different extent of damage potentially suffered by individual consumers, to be calculated according to homogeneous calculation criteria, does *not* necessarily condition the admissibility of the claim. These criteria allow for satisfying diversified individual claims by applying the same calculation method'. The issue of the 'homogeneous calculation method' will be analysed in the following.

For now, with regard to the issue of diversified quantification, it is important to dwell on a key decision from the Italian Court of Cassation from 2019, in the *Trenord case* (one of the very few, so far, in relation to class action proceedings),[62] since, at first sight, it could misleadingly appear to propose a regression from such an interpretative stance, which admitted a different '*quantum*' within the class. The discussed statements from the Italian Higher Court are the following:

> the rights concretely prejudiced [... are] to be characterised [...] by the essential requirement of their relative homogeneity (pursuant to art. 140-*bis* cited), intended [...] as the distinctive trait of individual claims that, claimed by a set of consumers or users, are united by characteristics such as to justify a serial assessment and a joint procedural management, having to *exclude*, on the logical plane, even before the legal one, the compatibility of the procedural instrument thus outlined by the legislator with the execution of *assessments cali-*

[61] See, e.g., *Telecom* case, Tribunal of Milan, Order from 15 February 2024, R.G. No. 21789/2023.

[62] *Trenord* case. Italian Court of Cassation, Section III, 31 May 2019, No. 14886.

> *brated on specific personal situations* or with evaluations that dwell on the specific consistency of the emotional sphere or of the dynamic-relational experience of individual injured parties. In cases where, in fact, the complaints of the injured parties are such that they do not prefigure the possibility of a *tendentially standardised assessment* also of the related prejudicial consequences (both as regards specifically the *an* and the *quantum* of the damage), the class protection mechanism must be considered impracticable for this reason.
>
> [...] From these premises it follows that [...] the class action remains nevertheless *compatible* with the claim for compensation for *non-pecuniary damages*, where regarding the latter *the traits* in some way *common* to all members of the class are *strictly highlighted* (provided they are adequately specified and proven), with the consequence that the original proposer has the burden of requesting the repair of a non-pecuniary damage that is *not individualised*, but is based on circumstances common to all members of the class.
>
> [...] With the further specification, in cases of non-pecuniary damages claimed in the forms of class action (and precisely in order to *prevent an inadmissible punitive interpretation* of the compensatory responsibility, in the absence of legislative parametres capable of justifying it: see United Sections Judgment No. 16601 of 07/05/2017) of the allegation and proof of the concrete profiles of the prejudices complained of capable of enhancing the traits shared by all members of the class, *not personalisable* in relation to single injured parties, but united by characteristics such as to justify both the *serial appreciation* and the *jointly* claimed *procedural management*.[63]

As it can be read, the Court of Cassation directly addresses, for the first time, the notion of homogeneity specifying how it should be 'intended'. A potential ambiguity of the decision stems, however, from a possible contrast with the until-then (and subsequent) majoritarian view, according to which the quantification of damages within class actions can vary among the different subjective individual positions.

This is due to expressions such as 'having to *exclude*, on the logical plane, even before the legal one, the compatibility of the procedural instrument [...] with the execution of assessments calibrated on *specific personal situations*', or those stating how the class action mechanism cannot be employed in cases in which the injured parties' complaints do *not* 'prefigure the possibility of a *tendentially standardised assessment* also of the related prejudicial consequences (both as regards specifically the *an* and the *quantum* of the damage)', or, again, those stressing how the complainants should specify 'the traits shared by all members of the class, *not personalisable* in relation to individual injured parties'.[64]

Still, the Court does not move from the majoritarian approach, as confirmed by subsequent judgements of lower courts.[65] Apart from the arguments above, it should be considered, in fact, how the Court does require a 'standardised assessment', but only a '*tendentially* standardised' one. It excludes personalised evaluations in relation to injured parties, but only in relation to '*single*' individuals. It underscores indeed the importance of 'serial appreciation' and 'joint procedural management'. These are, however, as specified by the Court itself, logical assumptions before (or rather than) strictly legal ones.

---

[63] Id. (translated from Italian).

[64] Id.

[65] See, e.g., *Millemiglia* case. Tribunal of Rome, Section XVII, Order from 8 November 2023, R.G. No. 1577/2023.

It is conceptually *inherent* to the nature of collective proceedings, which, by definition, necessitate a collective (hence, joint) evaluation. It is a *technical necessity*, related to the court's *procedural* assessment, which in no way should influence the interpretation of the concept of homogeneity, instead related to the *substantive* positions (the 'individual rights') at stake. Under this perspective, the judgement at hand is indeed questionable. It appears also disputable in the part in which it seems to set the burden of proving—not homogeneity, but rather—the *feasibility* of joint procedural management on the class plaintiffs. Instead, as subsequently argued, once homogeneity is found and the claim proceeds as admissible, joint procedural management should *always* follow, *automatically*, under the judge's directions according to the concrete case's peculiarities.

A key additional aspect of the Cassation Court's findings in the *Trenord case* should be highlighted. It is the fact that the Court addressed the homogeneity test only in relation to the possibility of compensating *non-material* damages through the class action procedure. The principle of law declared by the Cassation Court, as a matter of fact, does not even mention the homogeneity concept, rather focusing on the central issue.[66]

Despite declaring, in abstract, the compatibility of class proceedings with the claim for compensation for non-pecuniary, the Court recalled its own, well-established principles on the matter: *(i)* the *constitutional relevance* of the interests violated (otherwise leading, in practice, to a repeal by interpretative means of Article 2059 c.c.—following which 'non-material damage must be compensated only in cases determined by law'—since any non-material damage, by the very fact of being such, that is, affecting personal interests, would be compensable); *(ii)* the *infringements' severity* (the offense should exceed 'a minimum threshold of tolerability', pursuant to Article 2 of the Constitution, which requires everyone, under the principle of solidarity, to tolerate a minimum, acceptable, degree of intrusions into their personal spheres, inevitably arising from being part of the same society); *(iii)* the *non-triviality of the damage* suffered (it should not consist of mere inconveniences, dissatisfactions, disappointments, anxieties or annoyances, nor in the infringement of 'entirely imaginary rights', like the right to quality of life or to happiness).

---

[66] *Trenord* case. Italian Court of Cassation, Section III, 31 May 2019, No. 14886, see, in particular, point No. 35: 'The assessment of non-material damage claimed in the context of a class action lawsuit filed under Legislative Decree No. 206 of 2005, Article 140-*bis*—in addition to the allegation and concrete proof of the ordinary requirements: 1) the constitutional relevance of the interests harmed; 2) the severity of the related injury; and 3) the non-triviality of the damages (i.e., that they do not consist of mere inconveniences, annoyances, disappointments, anxieties, or any other type of dissatisfaction concerning the most disparate aspects of life, in accordance with what was stated by Italian Court of Cassation, S.U., Judgment from 11 November 2008, No. 26972) – also requires the specific allegation and proof of the concrete profiles of the claimed prejudices, capable of enhancing the traits shared by all members of the class, not customizable in relation to individual injured parties, but united by characteristics such as to justify both the serial assessment and the jointly claimed procedural management' (translated from Italian).

The *Trenord case* was about a series of 'significant inconveniences' of extraordinary nature suffered by the users of the rail transport service managed by the defendant company, which, according to the Court of Appeal of Milan, justified granting them a generalised lump sum of 100 € for each user as non-pecuniary damage. According to the Cassation Court,[67] however, the Court of Appeal failed to adhere to the abovementioned three requirements—in particular to explain concretely and specifically how the gravity and seriousness threshold had been exceeded—, as well as the common traits justifying a standardised treatment. The impact on the future viability of class action suits in Italy is evident and significant, since such an interpretative perspective would severely raise the accessibility level, eliminating *de facto*, for most cases, the collective compensability of *non-pecuniary* damages.

For this reason, such a standpoint appears questionable. Pursuant to Article 24, in connection with Article 2, of the Italian Constitution, that is the above-discussed right to *effective* justice, which inevitably assumes *collective* connotations in light of societal developments, a *balancing* needs to be made.[68] On the one hand, the

[67] Id., see, in particular, point No. 17: 'In the case at hand, the Court of Appeal of Milan, far from adhering strictly to the principles so far mentioned, appears to have neglected both the aspect related to the identification of the constitutionally protected interest underlying the non-material prejudices compensated (except for a generic and abstract reference – moreover deduced for other purposes – to the 'limitations suffered in relation to one's free movement': see page 15 of the challenged judgment), and the specific identification and description of the forms and manners in which the non-material prejudices purportedly identified actually exceeded that threshold of sufficient gravity and seriousness identified interpretatively by the United Sections of 2008, as an essential limit of compensatory protection, failing to explain how the damages complained of, necessarily linked by a controllable material and legal causal connection to the contested non-performance, represented the outcome of a truly serious and grave offense to the interest protected at the constitutional level, without translating into mere inconveniences, annoyances, disappointments, anxieties or any other type of dissatisfaction concerning the most diverse aspects of life. [...] In fact, in the challenged judgment, the judge a quo appears to have limited their argument to the mere observation of 'prolonged delays, cancellations of runs, transfers from one train to another, changes of routes, overcrowded train conditions' which turned out to generate, in a purportedly uniform and generalised manner, 'a form of anxiety and intolerance for the inconveniences, annoyances, and difficulties, if not even the impossibility, of carrying out one's normal movements in order to reach workplaces, places of study, and so on', without taking on the burden of deducing and articulating in a concrete and specific manner the demonstration that such forms of anxiety, intolerance, annoyances, and difficulties/impossibilities are not reducible to those mere inconveniences, annoyances, disappointments, anxieties or any other type of dissatisfaction concerning the most diverse aspects of life that, as repeatedly emphasised, preclude, by virtue of the principle of social solidarity under Article 2 of the Constitution, the compensatory protection of non-material damage under Article 2059 of the Civil Code, to the extent that they express terms of an inadequately appreciable impact on the individual personal sphere, inevitably arising from the fact of social coexistence. [...] Nor are the profiles of the identified prejudices sufficiently alleged and proven in the challenged ruling, capable of enhancing the traits actually and concretely common to all members of the class, not customisable in relation to individual injured parties, but united by characteristics such as to justify both the 'serial' appreciation and the jointly claimed procedural management, in respect of Legislative Decree No. 206 of 2005, Article 140-*bis*' (translated from Italian).

[68] See *supra*, Chap. 4.

righteous and strict, well-established, jurisprudence on non-pecuniary damage, developed under the traditional *individual* civil-procedural litigative perspective. On the other hand, the urgency to provide the *possibility* (even with explicit adherence, given the opt-in regime) of compensatory redress for small claims which otherwise could (and would) not be pursued autonomously. The latter issue, coupled with the necessity of *deterring* wrongful conducts of large and repetitive players that systematically harm societal members without taking account (paying compensation, in short) for such negative externalities.

A constitutionally oriented reading, in light of the values at stake, might suggest a different consideration of the thresholds of 'gravity' and 'seriousness' necessary, according to the well-established Italian case law, for the compensability of non-material damage. They would still be present and would still need to be proven. However, this would not happen *individually*, by considering the sufficient gravity and seriousness in relation to the *single* homogeneous individual right. Rather, the territorial courts, in verifying such requirements, should make—precisely because of the constitutional values mentioned above—a *unified assessment* of the class as a whole. Thus, the gravity and seriousness of each single homogeneous subjective position (hence, with a factual 'common origin' and nothing else, see *supra*) should be *aggregated* to reach the total for the class. Even if the gravity and seriousness were not sufficient *individually*—and, therefore, assuming that the individual right holder sought non-material compensation through ordinary individual and autonomous judicial proceedings, it would be correctly denied redress for lack of reaching the minimum gravity and seriousness threshold—, *collectively* they could be reached. This way, with a constitutionally oriented reading, in light of Articles 24 and 2 of the Italian Constitution, the above-identified values could be balanced.

The alternative, otherwise, is the creation of a significant 'free zone' ('*zona franca*', borrowing an expression often used by the Italian Constitutional Court) of protection within the legal system, a free zone which, *inter alia*, the legislator of 2019 deliberately wanted to fill. In this sense, it is worth recalling that the decision of the Court of Cassation of 2019 regarded the legislation, now repealed, of the Consumer Code. The introduction of the new regime in 2019, into force in 2021, supports—with more force—the arguments set out above. Beyond the preparatory works and the full extension of the scope of application—quite indicative of the fundamental goal of expanding the paths of access to justice—, indeed, there are several provisions of the new discipline that, from a systematic perspective, favour a broader, more flexible approach.

In particular, regarding in general the quantification of damages, a further interpretative layer is offered also by the new internal discipline on the *liquidation phase*, introduced with the 2019 reform. Article 840-*octies* c.p.c. provides for a specific phase to examine class adherence and to draft a liquidation project (the so-called 'project of the homogeneous individual rights of the adherents'). This choice suggests that, beyond the initial phase of verifying the common ('homogeneous') features at the admissibility stage, a more *individualised* quantification among the different class components is still feasible.

This is supported by the fact that the individual tasked with such a liquidation (the so-called '*common representative of the adherents*'), pursuant to Article 840-*sexies*, letter *g)* c.p.c must meet the requirements for appointment as a bankruptcy trustee, a process in which *individualisation* is indeed allowed in the liquidation phase. According to Article 840-*octies* c.p.c., the common representative of the adherents can avail themselves of the support of *technical experts* for the evaluation of the facts. Furthermore, they must 'present their motivated conclusions for *each*' adherent, on the basis of (strictly) documentary evidence. Adherents and the respondent, within 30 days from the communication of the liquidation project, may deposit written observations and supplementary documents for a re-evaluation from the common representative. After a control from the judge, who can accept in whole or in part the adhesion, the respondent is ordered to 'pay the sums or things owed to *each* adherent as compensation or restitution'.

Such a wording of the norms clearly indicates room for an assessment '*individualised* in relation to single injured parties' (recalling the Court of Cassation's 2019 judgement).[69] Evidently, such an assessment will be *partially* (rather than 'tendentially') standardised. As stressed by the same Court, this is logically inherent to the nature of collective proceedings. The innovative stance, with which courts still need to get acquainted, is their fundamentally different role in this type of judicial setting. It is the *court*'s responsibility to identify the best technique to manage the joint claims. In doing so, they must consider the concrete features of the case at stake, adopting an active—even creative—stance, if necessary.

The Montesquieuian conception of the judge as '*bouche de la loi*', who passively interprets and applies the law to the facts presented by the parties, is definitively abandoned.[70] Instead, they become the main directors of proceedings of the highest

[69] *Trenord* case. Italian Court of Cassation, Section III, 31 May 2019, No. 14886. That is, in particular, already mentioned *supra*: the 'specific allegation and proof of the concrete aspects of the claimed prejudices, capable of enhancing the traits shared by all members of the class, *not* individualised in relation to single injured parties, but instead unified by characteristics such that they justify both the serial assessment and the jointly claimed procedural management' (translated from Italian).

[70] See already Calamandrei (1954), pp. 645–650: 'We no longer have any use for Montesquieu's judges, "*êtres inanimés*" made of pure logic. We want judges with a soul: *engagés* judges, who can bear with vigilant human commitment the immense weight of the great responsibility that is dispensing justice' [...] It has been said (as we have already seen) that democracy is a commitment, an *engagement*: "*faute de cet engagement la technique constitutionnelle est morte.*" The same can be said for the judicial technique. [...] the judge is not a mechanism: he is not a calculating machine. He is a living man: and that function of specifying the law and applying it to the concrete case, which *in vitro* can be represented as a syllogism, is in reality an operation of synthesis, carried out in the heat of the moment, mysteriously, in the sealed crucible of the spirit, where the mediation and welding between abstract law and the concrete fact require, to be accomplished, intuition and feeling, ignited in a diligent conscience. In short, the system of legality, and more generally the normative theory of law, is a didactic scheme, useful for jurists; but this logical breakdown of the judgment resembles the analyses of chemists, who, even when they have identified all the elementary substances of which a living organism is composed, have not managed to capture in formulae that spark from which, through the mysterious combination of these elements, life, has emerged. Moreover, even within the system of legality, it is the laws themselves that sometimes

complexity, due to the different interests at stake and voices to be heard, most of which not even formally participating to the trial. In most cases their control will continue also after the decision, to ensure a correct application of the tasks set therein (e.g., urging action from the legislative bodies, administrative agencies, corporations or other entities acting as defendants, but also from the claimants, for instance towards the rest of the community not formally involved in the proceedings). This may require creative thinking, even during the examination of the case, as well as an active check regarding adequacy of representation and lack of conflicts of interests among all the parties.[71]

Regarding quantification of damages, they need to learn to balance the exigence of *standardisation*, following the goal of judicial economy and the procedural limitations, with the necessity of providing a *minimum* degree of *diversification* in light of the different individual positions within the class, against the backdrop of *fair trial guarantees*, to be maintained in such a complex judicial setting.

The techniques for this purpose are numerous and largely tested in previous foreign experiences with collective proceedings, mostly from overseas. Among them, the most notable, are:

(a) the distribution of a *general lump sum* to all the class members:

Whenever no significant divergences can be found within the class in order to form two or more sub-classes, a mere lump sum may be individuated. In order to avoid the 'inadmissible punitive interpretation of the compensatory responsibility' (an issue—in part, questionably[72]—raised in the *Trenord Case*), a twofold preventive measure can be adopted: on the one hand, the *minimum individual damage* could be compensated to all the class members; on the other hand, preferably, the *overall damage* received by the class should be quantified and *divided by the total* number of the class members, the result of such an operation being the sum to which each individual member is entitled.

---

offer the judge a passage through which feeling can slip into the rigid formulae dictated by reason. It is the law that often grants the judge the power to decide according to equity, "according to the circumstances," "with fair appreciation of the circumstances of the case" […] In legislative technique, traditional expressions of generic and variable meaning ("good faith", "ordinary diligence", "diligence of a prudent family father") are frequently used. These have been metaphorically described as the respiratory organs or safety valves of the legal system, because through them, the judge—by assigning a concrete meaning to these flexible phrases case by case—manages to infuse the dead letter of the law with the vital air of social needs, which are in perpetual evolution. But even without considering these conscious technical expedients, by which the legislator himself causes the oxygen of the irrational to enter the"'rationalised" law, we must be persuaded that every interpretation is a recreation: and that in every interpretation individual inspiration is decisive' (translated from Italian).

[71] Quite skeptical, Uzelac (2014): 'The organisational design of the European judiciary the personal and organizational design of the European judiciaries in several aspects collide with the ideals of appropriate decision-making regarding claims affecting interests of large groups of people. The formalistic, lengthy, rigid and one-to-one traditional organisational design of the European judiciary is probably one of the highest obstacles for public interest litigation'.

[72] See Giussani (2020), p. 359.

The trouble with the latter approach would, however, be the impossibility of anticipately taking into account how many (and which) members will actually opt-in (or opt-out, under the regimes of other jurisdictions), provided their number can be concretely identified. This is certainly an argument in favour of an opt-out regime, at the very least for small-claims suits. Still, given that this 'collective quantification' criterion should be preferred only in cases in which the substantive positions forming the class hold no significant divergences, both defendant- and class-wise no substantial favourability should be found (in respect to a scenario in which all potential class members were to sue individually). Defendant-wise, hence, it can be argued that rather than *punitive* any such quantification might be *equitative*, under Article 1226 c.c.; at the end of the day, no additional damage in respect to the one concretely caused would be awarded.[73]

Class-wise, furthermore, given the double window to join the class pursuant to Article 840-*quinquies*, para. 1 c.p.c., and Article 840-*sexies*, para. 1, letter *e)*, c.p.c.,

[73] Cappelletti (1975), pp. 61–62, as always, particularly insightful and foresighted: 'the remedy that the judge can provide to those who seek protection for a diffuse or collective interest, appearing in court as the representative of a group or a collectivity [...] is a serious problem, another major issue that our code, our positive law, does not resolve. [...] Articles 2043 and 2059 of the Civil Code must be abolished and replaced, as they too are relics of an exclusively individualistic and rigidly "privatist" legal framework. [...] we must no longer look at *suffered damage* but at *produced damage*. In other words, in cases involving violations of collective interests, the judge should not necessarily limit the condemnation to the damage suffered by the parties in the case but must include in the ruling (which thus takes on an almost punitive character) the damage produced in its entirety. Otherwise, there could remain a sufficient margin of advantage for the repetition of the violation. If, for example, a polluting industry were only sporadically condemned to compensate for the damage suffered by a few individuals, the polluting behavior might remain advantageous because it entails a lower cost than what would be necessary to prevent it. [...] The most striking concrete examples once again come from the United States. Let us consider the famous *Eisen case*, which involved six million "parties", the vast majority of whom were "absent" and informally represented in court by a single *ideological plaintiff*, Mr. Eisen. In this case, although the parties were not present in the proceedings, they were nevertheless identifiable by name and address (approximately 2,250,000). They had suffered damages amounting, on average, to a few dollars each, for a total of several tens of millions of dollars. If the judge had been limited to ordering compensation only for the identified parties, the ruling would have had to be confined to that amount (not to mention that if the judge had restricted the ruling to the damage personally suffered by Eisen, it would have resulted in an award of only seventy dollars!). However, the total damage produced (to the six million affected individuals) was many times greater (and millions of times higher than the damage suffered by Eisen), and Judge Tyler deemed it appropriate to issue a ruling for the total sum, granting all absent parties, including those who had not been identified, a deadline to come forward and claim their minuscule share in the enforcement phase. [...] Here, then, a concept of compensation emerges that is not based on suffered damage but, as I mentioned, on produced damage, a concept that naturally raises the further question: what will the judge do with the *residual portion* of the damage (produced) that no one claims? This, in turn, generates a whole series of additional problems, to which the American judiciary has sought to respond with the concept of *fluid recovery*, a form of fluid compensation intended for purposes other than (but somehow connected with) the collective interest protected in the proceedings. This is yet another example of that judicial inventiveness and creativity, which, unfortunately, we do not even know where to find in our legal system' (emphasis from the original, translated from Italian). For further elaboration on the concept of *fluid recovery* see *infra*, technique of quantification d), in the following pages of this section.

the class members will still have clear knowledge of the class outline, with the alternative possibility of not adhering and proceeding individually with an ordinary action, should they consider the standardisation excessive. An illustrative use of this technique is once again the *Trenord Case*, in which the Court of Appeal of Milan, before the Cassation ruling from 2019, awarded 100 € of non-material damages to all the class members for distress caused by extraordinary train delays.

(b) the division into *sub-classes*:

In cases in which significant divergences do emerge within the class, two or more sub-classes should be formed, according to the harm suffered. The same reasoning above-depicted for the general lump sum applies for each sub-class. In the words of Rule 23 of the US Federal Rules of Civil Procedure letter C, section 5: 'When appropriate, a class may be divided into subclasses that are each treated as a class under this rule'. The present technique appears rather valuable to reduce the area of differentiation within the class, increasing effectivity of justice, class participation and, consequently, judicial economy.

So far, only one case in Italy—from the Tribunal of Cagliari, under the previous consumer-limited regime, against a water-supply company—has been registered to use this joint-management criterion.[74] In such a case, the court divided the class into three sub-classes:

> 1) The sub-class consisting of those who, in the territory of the municipality of Porto Torres and during the aforementioned reference period, have suffered the non-fulfillment in its *maximum gravity*, namely those who have not been able to use water for *all types of human use* on one or more occasions;
> 2) The sub-class consisting of those who, in the territory of the municipality of Porto Torres and during the aforementioned reference period, have suffered the non-fulfillment in its *intermediate gravity*, namely those who on one or more occasions have not been able to use water *for drinking and cooking*;
> 3) The sub-class consisting of those who, in the territory of the municipality of Porto Torres and during the aforementioned reference period, have suffered the non-fulfillment in its *minimum gravity*, namely those who on one or more occasions have not been able to use water *solely for drinking*.

Such a sub-division of the class members favours a '*tendential standardisation*', while also reaching the above-mentioned goals. It can be undoubtedly replicated in other types of cases, even ones in which the quantification of the damage might not be so immediate, as the comparative case law demonstrates: for instance, regarding securities or consumer issues, but also asbestos contamination and environmental pollution, prisoners or labour issues.

Furthermore, they can efficiently address classes of homogeneous individual rights in the strictly etymological sense (see *supra*), hence with different *causae petendi* or *petita*: for example, when despite the same origin, there are factual differences between the causes of actions (e.g., regarding causation), or in cases where

[74] Tribunal of Cagliari, Section II, Order from 17 November 2016, R.G. No. 10016/2015.

different groups of people seek different types of relief (e.g., some look for medical monitoring, others for immediate monetary compensation).

Pending cases in which this criterion has been proposed by the plaintiffs are further analysed in Part III.

(c) the identification of a lowest common denominator as a *multiplication parameter*.

Taking example from the previous consumer class action, a multiplication parameter, or 'homogeneous calculation criterion for liquidation' (Article 140-*bis*, para. 12, cod. cons., now repealed), can be employed. As stated by Bonafede in the above-mentioned speech from 2013, 'the different extent of damage potentially suffered by individual consumers, to be calculated according to homogeneous calculation criteria, does not necessarily condition the admissibility of the claim. These criteria allow the satisfaction of diversified individual claims by applying the *same calculation method*'.

Its main advantage is the fact that, potentially, it allows very diversified classes. It requires no identity at all between the damages concretely claimed by each class member. In abstract, they could all differ, as long as a minimum common parameter for multiplication is identified. At first sight, it seems only compatible with claims of mainly economical nature, that is, for instance, in the securities or consumer law field. Still, other litigation based on rights related more to the personal sphere, e.g., the right to health or other fundamental liberties, could also use this criterion for quantification of damages, provided a *mathematical* classification of the infringement is offered. This could occur, for example, by counting the *number of days* or, as already well-established in the jurisprudence, by taking into account the *percentages of disability* caused.[75] Accordingly, the damages stemming from a broader spectrum of violations could be quantified within class proceedings through this technique: e.g., for detention, degrading, unfair or discriminatory conditions, violations to the right to privacy, to the right to health, and several more.

Any explicit reference to this parameter is currently lacking under the 2019 general regime. There is no reason, however, to consider it cannot be used. On the contrary, given the access-to-justice approach of the reform, the lack of explicit reference could be perceived as a way as not to limit plaintiffs' and judges' attention to that sole technique of joint-management, granting them *maximum flexibility*.

This is supported by the most recent case law, under the new regime, which already offers a successful use of the present criterion. The Tribunal of Rome, for instance, in the recent *Millemiglia* case,[76] still pending, about a loyalty programme from the former Italian national flight company (Alitalia) with prizes offered in exchange for miles travelled/points, used this technique for admitting the compensatory *azione di classe* under Article 840-*bis* c.p.c. Evidently, each member of the

[75] See *infra*, Chap. 7.

[76] *Millemiglia* case. Tribunal of Rome, Section XVII, Order from 8 November 2023, R.G. No. 1577/2023.

loyalty programme had gathered a *different* number of miles, which entails the right to a different, from a *quantum* point of view, compensation. In order to 'tendentially standardise' the quantification, and hence give the admissibility green light due to a satisfaction of the homogeneity requirement, nonetheless, the court, following the plaintiffs' application, found that:

> It is *not preclusive* to the formation of a single class that the damages claimed by individual members are not susceptible to a unitary liquidation or require the application of different criteria or sub-criteria for liquidation. [...]
>
> The current *commonality* of positions among the claimants is determined by the *ownership of miles* and the fact that it entails the application of the Regulation of the prize competition named *MilleMiglia Program* [...]
>
> The Court concludes that, given the present circumstances, the claimants' subjective situations are *homogenous*, and there seem to be no differences between the positions of members who accumulated points in various ways. Concerning the *petitum*, the claimants formulated the request in a way that dispels any doubts regarding the homogeneity of their positions. They specifically asked that the compensation for the alleged suffered damage be *liquidated* in a manner correlated to the *number of points held by each*, making their positions, in the case of the claim's acceptance, definable uniformly. This involves identifying a *unitary parameter* that can determine the measure of restitution easily and serially, without the need for any individualised assessment.[77]

[77] Id. (translated from Italian). The fully relevant part of the Tribunal's order, albeit still based on the reference to the concepts of *causa petendi* and *petitum* (an approach, which, as discussed above, we deem incorrect and which is not shared by all courts): 'The homogeneity of rights, therefore, assumes the role of the main admissibility requirement for the action: its centrality is strictly related to the nature of the class action and its function, which is to allow the procedural aggregation of positions attributable to different subjects but susceptible, due to their serial nature, to be treated in a standardised manner. [...] The homogeneity of individual rights must be evaluated with regard to the 'causa petendi' of the action, so that rights based on the same action or omission of the same defendant can be considered homogeneous. This entails that the involved rights are characterised by a causal connection (identity of the title) or of an improper nature (identity of issues), as well as with reference to the 'petitum' (mediate and immediate). It is not preclusive to the formation of a single class that the damages claimed by individual members are not susceptible to a unitary liquidation or require the application of different criteria or sub-criteria for liquidation. It is necessary that the serial claims can be defined with a single decision and do not require individualized assessments, and this occurs when, due to the characteristics of the substantive case, the judge's decision can be based on common evaluations. This evaluation must be made based on the allegations of the parties, not on actual situations. Therefore, to satisfy the admissibility requirement of the action, the claimants must base the demand on aspects common to the injured parties, even if this means excluding certain aspects of prejudice not present in most positions. [...] In the present case, the claimants have alleged to be all members of the MilleMiglia Program, holders of a number of miles equal to or greater than twelve thousand as of October 27, 2021, the date of Alitalia's cessation of air carrier activity. They claimed to have suffered damage as a result of the respondent's conduct, which would have seriously prejudiced the rights they allegedly acquired through mileage accumulation. They asserted to act for the restitution of the suffered prejudice, explicitly requesting that it be quantified uniformly and correlated to each one's number of miles, without taking into account possible differentiations in positions resulting from some of them acquiring additional benefits related to the method of earning points. The Court, based on these allegations, finds that the subjective situations subject to the claim of the claimants against the respondent are homogeneous regarding the 'causa petendi.' The current commonality of positions among the claimants is determined by the ownership of miles and the fact that it entails

The 'unitary parameter' (the value of *one* point/mile), hence, serves as a unitary liquidation criterion, allowing the joint management of common and yet diversified (*quantum*-wise) subjective positions (that is, homogeneous in an etymological sense). In theory, more complex cases, could see a simultaneous use of more techniques, such as the present one and the above-mentioned sub-classes.[78]

(d) *cy-prés* or *fluid recovery* mechanisms:

A final, more creative, and by all means unorthodox (for civil law jurisdictions, at least) method of assessment of otherwise diversified subjective positions is that of *cy-près*, or fluid recovery.[79] It is a technique by several means extraneous to the Italian legal, and in general to the civil law, tradition. Its promising features—*in vitro*—and its partial success—*in concreto*—in the common law experience (especially US and Canadian) with class action litigation, nonetheless, demand special consideration. Against the backdrop of its functional features and potential, essential questions on its constitutional and regulatory legitimacy must be answered, too.

One of the most effective ways to explain how it works is to proceed by examples. The influential *Daar v. Yellow Cab Company* case, from 1969, reported by American scholarship,[80] stands as particularly illustrative. The case was a compensatory class action brought in front of the California Supreme Court for illegal

---

the application of the Regulation of the prize competition named MilleMiglia Program, the management and development of which, according to the respondent, has been entrusted to Italia Loyalty S.p.A. since 2012. The Court concludes that, given the present circumstances, the claimants' subjective situations are homogenous, and there seem to be no differences between the positions of members who accumulated points in various ways. [...] Concerning the petitum, the claimants formulated the request in a way that dispels any doubts regarding the homogeneity of their positions. They specifically asked that the compensation for the alleged suffered damage be liquidated in a manner correlated to the number of points held by each, making their positions, in the case of the claim's acceptance, definable uniformly. This involves identifying a unitary parameter that can determine the measure of restitution easily and serially, without the need for any individualised assessment' (translated from Italian).

[78] See *infra*, Chap. 7.

[79] On the difference between the two see Reddish et al. (2010), p. 620: 'While a broad definition of both concepts does render them largely equivalent, it is important to discern subtle but significant differences. As an abstract matter, both concepts refer to efforts to provide the 'next best' form of relief in cases where it is impractical or impossible to directly compensate the injured class members. In more recent times, however, the term cy pres has generally referred to an effort to provide unclaimed compensatory funds to a charitable interest that is in some way related to either the subject of the case or the interests of the victims, broadly defined. In contrast, 'fluid class recovery,' in the sense in which we use the term here, refers to efforts to fashion relief to those who will be impacted by the defendant in the future, in an effort to roughly approximate the category of those who were injured in the past. Thus, both concepts involve some form of 'second best' relief. However, [...] fluid class recovery represents a far more disciplined effort to indirectly compensate injured victims (through future approximations of who those victims were) than does cy pres, which in its modern form demands merely some generic link of the proposed recipient charity to the nature of the suit. Today, of these alternative methods, cy pres relief appears to be the one most often employed by federal class action courts'. See also Kalajdzic (2013), p. 173.

[80] Cited by Cappalli and Consolo (1992), p. 243; also in Hemker-Smith (1976), p. 811.

overcharges performed to its customers' fares by a taxi company, Yellow Cab, in the city of Los Angeles for a period of four years. Two sets of problems arose right away.

First, the homogeneity (for simplicity we shall refer to the current Italian terminology) was questionable, since—despite the common origin—the claims were based on *different factual elements*, ranging over several years. This issue, still, was easily surmountable, and surmounted, thanks to the above-discussed reasoning on a broader interpretation of that requirement, grounded on the *common origin*.

Second, most importantly, the *class members* were mostly *unknown*. To this regard, Yellow Cab, the defendant, argued that the class action could not proceed since the names of the cab riders could not be *identified*. Without knowing to whom any awarded damages should be distributed, how could the class be certified? Referring to the current Italian regime under Articles 840-*bis et seq*. c.p.c., can a class action be admitted for the compensation of 'homogeneous individual rights' if the holders of those rights—that is those entitled to damages—are unknown? How can someone join (through opt-in) the class if they are unable to submit 'the documentation [...] to provide evidence of the ownership of homogeneous individual rights', as required under Article 840-*sexies*, para. 1, letter *d)* c.p.c.? Article 840-*octies*, para. 3 c.p.c., stating 'In the adhesion procedure, means of proof other than *documentary* evidence are not admissible', also needs to be taken into account.

The court built its solution on the *exact knowledge* of Yellow Cab's *illegal gains*. Thanks to the company records, it was, in fact, possible to calculate the precise amount that the taxi company was—in *total*—bound to compensate. In practice, the issue on the impossibility of identifying the large majority of the *individual* cab riders from the *past* four-year period (very few had kept a receipt from their ride, provided it was ever given) was overcome by subsidising the lowering of *future* Yellow Cab rates. In other words, the damages' sum which could not be awarded to harmed past cab riders (that is unidentified class members) for lack of *individualised* (not total) documental proof, was awarded to a future, equally unidentified, class. The recovery was '*fluid*' since the compensation was not awarded *exactly* to those who had suffered the harm. The public interest and deterrent nature of this type of litigation thus emerges.

Similar solutions have been brought in a large variety of cases from common law jurisdictions, especially in consumer law, anti-trust, securities or employment issues. They have been particularly praised for very-small claim cases in which the incentive for the class to act is minimal. Through fluid recovery, by shifting the perspective and focusing on the total damages caused by the *defendant/injurer*, rather than on the single compensation for the *single member* of the class, an optimal *economic allocation* of the harmful activity can be reached. This way, it has been argued, the correct market value is assigned to such an injury-causing activity.

A similar approach makes even more sense for the protection of *diffuse rights*, given the hardship in identifying a single holder and the general—public—interest in curbing harmful conducts which affect a large part of, if not all, the society.[81] The

[81] Cappelletti 1976, p. 682.

main example, under this standpoint, is that of environmental pollution and climate change litigation, which could see the polluter investing the damage awarded in measures aiming at mitigating the effects of its polluting conduct, with a benefit for the whole community, rather than a mere compensation of hard-to-identify individuals.

Apart from a much-debated implementation of this technique even in the common law jurisdictions from which it originates, with a currently predominant use in settlement agreements rather than in judicial decisions, several concerns and points of discussion arise in relation to a possible use in the *current* Italian legal order.[82]

The initial argument against fluid recovery in Italy is the fact that it proceeds to compensate subjects that are *not parties* to the proceedings. It introduces in the—in theory—adversary bilateral adjudication process a *non-party* (or several, even unknown, non-parties), which is (or are) awarded damages despite not being *formally* involved in the judicial proceedings nor even being involved in the legally relevant *factual* circumstances which gave rise to the suit. Without a *clear regulatory provision* allowing it, it is difficult to argue for its use, given the current system of civil procedure in Italy.[83]

This raises fundamental questions regarding the role of the judge, too, who, rather than awarding compensation, ends up creating a new substantive remedy which, under different aspects, equals to an administrative sanction. The respect of the separation of powers principle is thus put at risk, especially considering the limitless discretion of the judge in determining the extent and features of the future *fluid* class. The key matter of *deterrence v. compensation* as the underlying justification of class litigation emerges, too. At the same time, the issue of *punitive damages* and its—partial—extraneity to the Italian legal order could be raised, too (although any critique on the matter would not hold, should the total amount awarded as damages equal the sum of all the individual injured members of the class adherent to it).

Furthermore, essential caveats stem from *fair trial* guarantees, both with regard to the defendant and the injured subjects who receive no compensation. In particular, the main obstacle for the current Italian legal order appears indeed to be the *opt-in* regime, which requires *explicit* adherence. To respect *due process* rights, the compensation awarded as full recovery should be only that resulting from the sum of all the adhering class members' entitlements to damages. Being them *unknown*, which is the reason behind fluid recovery, however, it results *impossible*. Hence, an apparent catch-22 situation, as long as opt-in is the only regime applicable.

---

[82] Caponi (2009), p. 383 seems quite open to this possibility: 'The theme of the liquidation of compensable damage is one of the most delicate aspects of the collective compensation action and would deserve a specific treatment. The problem would require a substantive law legislative solution. Civil procedure cannot renounce (at least de iure) to the precise implementation of substantive law, but it can conform and temper the latter, in the case of multi-offensive illicit acts, so as to make its faithful implementation possible even through mechanisms of collective liquidation of damage (for example, as happens in the American experience with *fluid recovery*)' (translated from Italian).

[83] See *infra*, Chap. 11.

All these issues, which fall outside the notion of homogeneity, will be further addressed in the conclusive Part IV of this work, dedicated to *de iure condendo* remarks.[84]

For the time being, regarding the four methods of *quantification* presented above, it seems appropriate to recall and stress that the homogeneity assessment, relevant for the admissibility of compensatory class actions pursuant to Article 840-*bis* and -*ter* c.p.c., is not an evaluation on the *merits* of the case. On the contrary, it is merely a 'determination of whether there are common issues' (factual or legal, i.e., a common origin) 'justifying representative litigation'.[85] Issues of quantification and liquidation, despite being crucial at the subsequent stage, should not be relevant for the verification of such a requirement. This is also due to the *prejudicial nature* of the *admissibility phase*.[86]

These considerations link directly to the *second issue* raised at the beginning of this paragraph, concerning homogeneity—that is, *when* should its determination be conducted, and *by whom*.

The one tasked with assessing it should be the judge, on the basis of the plaintiff's claim. Following Article 840-*ter* c.p.c., the decision on admissibility should be taken within thirty days from the first hearing. Evidently, the exam taken by the judge can only be approximate. This is supported by the other requirements for inadmissibility: 'a) when it is *manifestly unfounded*; […] c) when the petitioner is in a state of *conflict of interest* with the respondent; d) when the petitioner does not appear capable of *adequately representing* the homogeneous individual rights asserted in court'. None of them postulates an examination on the merits. Consequently, the homogeneity test ('b) when the court does not perceive *homogeneity* of individual rights protectable under Article 840-*bis*') should not presuppose either a thorough and comprehensive factual or legal analysis.

Rather, drawing from the account offered by the plaintiffs in their claim, the judge should declare the inadmissibility of the class action only when the individual rights enforced appear lacking a common link—that is a common *origin*, following the broad etymological interpretation herein proposed. Any evaluation on the merits, encompassing the defendant's liability, but also quantification and liquidation, should be *postponed*. This is in line with the assessments on admissibility before apex courts such as the Italian Constitutional Court or the ECtHR, where evidently no thorough examination on the merits is conducted during such a phase.

Class composition and the exact 'features of the homogeneous individual rights'—that is, 'the necessary elements for inclusion in the class of subjects […] holding homogeneous individual rights'—according to Article 840-*cinquies* c.p.c., are deferred to a *subsequent* phase, after the judge, with a judgement, has *accepted*

[84] Id.

[85] Kalajdzic (2021), p. 52: 'Ultimately, however, certification is not a test of the merits of the case but only a determination of whether there are common issues justifying representative litigation. Issues of liability alone would be sufficient to satisfy commonality'.

[86] See Donzelli (2019).

the class action and determined the respondent's liability for the conduct alleged by the plaintiffs.

Until then, therefore, the judge does not yet have to identify the criteria for joint-management and standardised liquidation. As a matter of fact, given the—dual—opt-in regime, they will probably be very far from even guessing the extent of the actual class (composed by those who concretely and explicitly adhere to the collective action, which is possible within a minimum of sixty days and a maximum of one hundred and fifty days both after the admissibility order and the 'acceptance judgement'—*sentenza di accoglimento* in Italian). This is another argument for the looser (yet literally more rigorous) interpretative standpoint on homogeneity.

As to the *third issue*, the different possible techniques for joint *quantification of damages* have already been presented. It has also been pointed out how Article 840-*octies*, para. 3, c.p.c., specifies that 'In the adhesion procedure, means of proof other than *documentary* evidence are not admissible'. Together with other normative choices from the 2019 regime—such as the regulation of the class proceedings by the summary judgement procedure ('*giudizio sommario di cognizione*') provided for by Article 702-*bis* c.p.c.—, the *complexity* of the dispute, particularly with regard to the *evidentiary* aspect, appears—according to some courts—to be a possible constraining factor for the examination of the suit.[87]

This is understandable from the perspective of *judicial efficiency*, less from the standpoint of *access to justice* (which, between the two, indeed seems to be the guiding objective of the reform, as discussed above). At the same time, if the evidentiary aspect has a limiting effect on the scope of application of the dispute, it is not clear why—if that is the case—the legislative choice does not *explicitly* include such a requirement (i.e., 'a lack of evidentiary complexity') among the grounds for inadmissibility under Article 840-*ter* c.p.c.

Moreover, from the *fair trial* lens, it must be noted how Article 840-*septies*, para. 3, c.p.c. allows the single *adherent* to submit, for an evaluation at the judge's 'prudent discretion', *statements from third parties*, whose identity is certified by a lawyer acting as public official pursuant to Article 252 c.p.c. This provision appears rather questionable, given the otherwise *strictly documentary nature* of the presentable evidence, as well as the fact that the third parties at hand don't appear to be possibly heard as witnesses nor to be bound by any oath to state the truth. Additionally, most importantly, under the *equality of arms* principle, it constitutes a manifest violation of the defendant's rights, given its apparent impossibility to present such third-party statements. Hence, a critical aspect under Article 111 of the Italian Constitution, as well as under Article 117, first paragraph, of the same Constitution, in relation to Articles 6 ECHR and 47 CFREU.

Apart from these evidentiary considerations, the subjects involved in the quantification and liquidation process should be highlighted. In particular, *new figures* emerge as protagonists under the 2019 regime: the '*common representative of the adherents*' and the '*judge delegated* for the adherence procedure'.

[87] See *infra*, Chaps. 7, 8 and 11.

Both are named at the time of the '*acceptance judgement*', when the court holds that the defendant, through the conduct alleged by the petitioner, has infringed a set of homogeneous individual rights, simultaneously defining their *features* and the *documentation* that must be produced, if necessary, by any adherent to provide proof of being holders of said homogeneous individual rights. Furthermore, raising doubts of constitutional legitimacy, it has been provided that, if necessary, the court in that instance may set a *monetary sum* to be paid by each adherent (including previous ones, from the first window to join-in, after the admissibility order) as a '*contribution to the expense fund*', presumably (but not clearly, per lack of specification of the norm) to be paid in favour of the common representative, therein named; the extent of such a sum, however, is, in theory, limitless.

As discussed above, the *common representative*, who must meet the requirements for appointment as a bankruptcy trustee, is in charge of drafting a *liquidation project* on the basis of the acceptance judgement's indications on the features of the homogeneous individual rights and class composition, as well as the documentation submitted by each adherent and the exceptions raised by the defendant, with a possibility for *written observations* from the parties for a re-evaluation. In this task, the common representative can avail themselves of the support of *technical experts* for the evaluation of the facts. Moreover, as anticipated, they must present their *reasoned* conclusions for *each* adherent, on the basis of *(strictly) documentary* evidence. It is not clear who should cover the costs of any such evidence, whenever obtaining it may pose an economic or even organisational burden on the adherent. This could be relevant, for instance, in relation to the right to health, in cases in which a medical evaluation may be required. Evidently, a centralised system of independent technical experts named, managed and paid by the common representative would be preferable.

The delegated judge is then tasked with verifying compliance and each adhesion. On the basis of the project of liquidation, with a motivated decree, they will finally order the defendant the payment of the sums or things owed to each adherent as a compensation or restitution.

As explained above, the wording of the norms indicates room for an assessment *partially individualised* in relation to single injured parties (as opposed to the Court of Cassation's 2019 judgement, referred to the previous consumer class action).[88] Still, as mentioned, given the collective nature of the proceedings, and the related goal of judicial efficiency, individualisation will necessarily have to be included in an *overall standardised* evaluation.

This is logically presupposed by the fact that the representative action entails a renunciation to individual and 'with full consideration' proceedings ('*a cognizione*

[88] *Trenord* case. Italian Court of Cassation, Section III, 31 May 2019, No. 14886. That is, in particular, once again, already stressed *supra*: the 'specific allegation and proof of the concrete aspects of the claimed prejudices, capable of enhancing the traits shared by all members of the class, not individualised in relation to single injured parties, but instead unified by characteristics such that they justify both the serial assessment and the jointly claimed procedural management' (translated from Italian).

piena', in Italian), in favour of a series of economic, organisational and time advantages for each adherent. *Pro quo*, pending (explicit) acceptance of the class member, the assessment on quantification is only partially individualised, and partially standardised. Hence, we return to the initial description (see *supra*) of the concept of homogeneity: in addition to a necessary *common* (hence, identical) core, a potentially *differentiated* part (also referred to as 'personal', 'exclusive'[89] or 'individualised') between each individual class member, that is a set of factual or legal issues which pertain to a single individual position rather than to the class as a whole.[90]

The role of the common representative does not seem sufficiently clear nor impartial. Given its public role in assisting the judge in the liquidation phase, an extension of said guarantees to this subject would seem necessary. An element of concern, in fact, together with the ambiguous possibility of a limitless 'contribution to the expense fund' for all adherents,[91] is the provision, under Article 840-*novies* c.p.c., para. 1,[92] of a *percentage*—calculated progressively on the basis of the

[89] See Menchini and Motto (2010), p. 5.

[90] See Donzelli (2019), p. 13.

[91] One must wonder whether this provision is necessary, also considering how Article 840-*quinquies*, para. 3, c.p.c states that: 'When an expert consultant is appointed, the obligation to advance the expenses and the fees for the latter are placed, unless there are specific reasons, on the defendant' (translated from Italian). At least a maximum limit should be defined by the legislator, as well as the conditions which allow its request and subsequent use.

[92] Article 840-*novies* (Costs of the proceeding): 'With the decree under Article 840-octies, fifth paragraph, the delegated judge also orders the respondent to pay directly to the common representative of the adherents, as compensation, an amount determined based on the number of class members on a progressive scale:

a) from 1 to 500, not exceeding 9 percent;
b) from 501 to 1000, not exceeding 6 percent;
c) from 1001 to 10,000, not exceeding 3 percent;
d) from 10,001 to 100,000, not exceeding 2.5 percent;
e) from 100,001 to 500,000, not exceeding 1.5 percent;
f) from 500,001 to 1000,000, not exceeding 1 percent;
g) over 1000,000, not exceeding 0.5 percent.

The percentages mentioned in the first paragraph are calculated on the total amount due to all adherents. The percentages can be modified by a decree of the Minister of Justice. The reimbursement of documented expenses is also due.

The judicial authority may increase or decrease the amount of compensation liquidated in accordance with the first paragraph by no more than 50 percent, based on the following criteria:

a) complexity of the assignment;
b) use of collaborators;
c) quality of the work performed;
d) diligence in conducting activities;
e) number of adherents.

For matters not provided for in the first and second paragraphs, the provisions on judicial costs apply. With the same decree mentioned in the first paragraph, the delegated judge also orders the respondent to pay directly to the lawyer who defended the plaintiff until the pronouncement of the judgment under Article 840-sexies an additional amount in addition to the sums due to each adher-

number of class members—on the total amount due to all adherents, to be paid by the defendant, in favour of said figure. This manifestly sets a significant and *direct interest*, for the common representative, on having more individuals adhere to the class as well as a higher sum awarded to them as damages. A potential conflict towards the *interests of the defendant* arises. This appears in potential contrast with Articles 3, 24, 111 and 117, first paragraph, of the Italian Constitution, the latter in relation to Articles 6 ECHR and 47 CFREU.

A pecuniary incentive is understandable, and to a certain degree laudable, for the *class attorneys* bringing the lawsuit. It recalls the contingency fees from the US class action model, with a narrow (probably *too* narrow) percentage rate in order to avoid 'fishing expeditions' and abusive litigation. Incentivised attorneys are, thus, vested with a *private enforcement function* for the public interest. On the other hand, however, it is not understandable *why the common representative*—who enters the proceedings only at a later stage, once the responsibility of the defendant has already been upheld—should have the same, if not higher (see percentages),[93] incentive. This clashes with the abovementioned provisions of the Italian Constitution, mainly the reasonableness principle under Article 3.

Being a subject charged with the task of drafting a project of liquidation, their *fees* should by no means be *dependent on the outcome* of the suit. Fairness and equality of arms demand *full impartiality*, which—as consolidated, also supranational, jurisprudence requires—encompasses also its *appearance* when objectively justified.[94] Such is the case of economic remuneration linked to the extent of damages awarded to one party.

Another reason to fear a possible conflict of interests of the common representative, this time towards the class, is their role in reaching a *settlement agreement*, pursuant to Article 840-*quaterdecies* c.p.c. After the acceptance judgement, with which the court holds the defendant liable for the harmful conduct claimed by the plaintiffs, the common representative can negotiate, on behalf of the adherents, a *settlement agreement* with the defendant. Pending authorisation from the delegated

---

ent as compensation and restitution. This additional amount, recognised as a premium compensation, is liquidated in accordance with the first paragraph. This premium compensation can be reduced by no more than 50 percent, based on the criteria established in the fourth paragraph' (translated from Italian).

[93] See also Id., para. 6, 'With the same decree mentioned in the first paragraph, the delegated judge also orders the respondent to pay directly to the lawyer who defended the plaintiff until the pronouncement of the judgment under Article 840-sexies an additional amount in addition to the sums due to each adherent as compensation and restitution. This additional amount, recognized as a premium compensation, is liquidated in accordance with the first paragraph. This premium compensation can be reduced by no more than 50 percent, based on the criteria established in the fourth paragraph' (translated from Italian).

[94] See, *infra*, Chap. 11. See also Italian Constitutional Court, Judgements No. 502 from 1991, point No. 4.1 of Points of law, Nos. 131 of 1996, point No. 3.2. of Points of law, No. 327 from 1998, No. 419 from 1998, point No. 2 of Points of law, No. 393 from 2002. See also CJEU, Grand Chamber, Judgment of 21 April 2021, *Repubblika v. Il-Prim Ministru*, C-896/19 and CJEU, Judgments of 24 June 2019, *Commission v. Poland*, C-619/18. See Randazzo (2023) and Bustos Gisbert (2022). See also, foresightedly, Onida (1982) and Calamandrei (1954), pp. 650 *et seq.*

judge, the settlement agreement is binding for the class adherents, safe for those that raise individual objections and, subsequently, after the judge's authorisation, decide—within fifteen days—to revoke the common representative's power to settle on their behalf. Such a short notice to decide whether to revoke and the fact that it is a subject which, once again, should be *impartial*—and instead negotiates vis-à-vis the other party, *representing*, as the name says after all, one party—leaves doubts on the appropriateness of the provision.

In sum, it is essential to ensure that this new *sphynx figure*—partially *representative of the class*, partially impartial *judicial auxiliary*—does not fall prey of *easy economic incentives*. At the moment, pending concrete jurisprudential development, the guarantees do not appear sufficient, as well as their overall role ambiguous and confusing. It seems that their partial representative functions towards the class—especially in smaller cases, with a more fiduciary base—could be taken by the plaintiff themselves with their attorneys (who, after all, brought and studied the case, until the court's holding of the defendant's liability), whilst the impartial judicial auxiliary duties could be entrusted to the delegated judge (already a second judge within the whole proceedings), or to court experts.[95]

Further issues pertaining to the respect of fair trial guarantees will be more exhaustively addressed in the following.

6.3.2 The Injunctive Class Action and the Enforcement of 'Meta-Individual' Positions

Despite its limited regulation, consisting of a single article compared to the fourteen dedicated to the compensatory remedy, the injunctive mechanism has a much broader scope of application. It not only protects individual rights, but also offers judicial protection for collective and diffuse rights and interests. As already argued in legal scholarship and partially demonstrated by early case law, this grants the mechanism a potential that is, at times, highly disruptive.[96]

An injunction, as is well known, refers to a judicial order imposing measures—provisional or definitive—intended to prohibit an act, either by commission or omission, which may not yet have been carried out, but which has caused or risks causing harm to one or more parties. It is, therefore, a measure that at times exhibits a quasi-interim nature, often requiring a more streamlined evidentiary process. At the same time, there is significant debate regarding the nature of the mechanism—whether it constitutes a mere ascertainment, a condemnatory measure, or is constitutive, particularly concerning definitive orders.

The innovations introduced by Article 840-*sexiesdecies* c.p.c. are numerous, significantly enhancing the scope and applicability of the mechanism to benefit various

[95] See also *infra*, Chap. 11.

[96] Ruffolo (2021).

parties, while also raising the risk of abuses detrimental both to defendants and to the multitude of individuals represented in court. The transition from a sector-specific remedy—scarcely used[97]—to a general tool reconnects the mechanism with the US legal experience, previously mentioned, which pioneered its full development, primarily for the protection of civil liberties and the promotion of substantive equality and social rights.[98]

In this context, US doctrinal developments, which frame injunctive class actions as a key tool of 'counter-majoritarian force',[99] find a meaningful parallel in the reflections of Italian constitutional scholars (among others, Leopoldo Elia). These scholars identify in the Italian Constituent Assembly's design—especially regarding the social formations mentioned in Article 2 of the Constitution—a pluralism aimed at creating 'genuine counterpowers or counterforces,' even in relation to state authority.[100]

Article 840-*sexiesdecies* c.p.c. establishes that any person with an 'interest' in obtaining an injunction against 'acts and behaviors carried out to the detriment of a plurality of individuals or entities' may initiate proceedings.[101] This confirms both the applicability of the mechanism across all areas of law, departing from the sectoral protection previously envisaged, and the ability to bring actions not only for the protection of individual rights but also for meta-individual positions.[102]

The latter aspect is highlighted by the general provision of Article 840-*sexiesdecies* c.p.c. ('interest in the decision'), as opposed to the express reference to the (collective) enforceability of 'individual (homogeneous) rights' in Article 840-*bis* c.p.c., concerning compensatory class actions. This allows—and has already allowed—the use of the new collective mechanism for the protection of legal situations across various fields, such as consumer protection, environmental law, health, or labour. In these domains, both subjective rights and collective or diffuse rights and interests have emerged as deserving of protection.

The exceptional nature of injunctive relief is particularly significant with respect to the latter category. On the substantive level, the fact that diffuse interests are 'ownerless' (in Italian, '*adespoti*')[103] and belong to communities that are, by definition, open, compels the legislator to adopt an equally open procedural approach regarding standing.[104] This ensures the availability of an effective tool for protection.

---

[97] Silvestri (2021).

[98] See, *supra*, Chap. 5.

[99] Issacharoff (2012), pp. 374 *et seq.*

[100] See, e.g., Tosato (1965), Barile (1984) and Elia (1992).

[101] Article 840-*sexiesdecies*, para. 1, c.p.c.

[102] See, *supra*, Chap. 4.

[103] Alpa (1993), Cudia (2012).

[104] Moreover, Article 840-*sexiesdecies* c.p.c. does not specify that the plaintiffs must necessarily be members of the class (nor that a class even needs to be defined, if possible at all). Once again, this represents an important difference from the compensatory class action under Article 840-*bis* c.p.c. and a further confirmation of the above-mentioned meta-individual nature of collective actions for injunctive relief. See *infra*, Chap. 4.

The 2019 framework thus intimately connects the *objective* scope of application to the *subjective* one (see *infra*, para. 6.4), as, for the first time, suits aimed at protecting diffuse situations can be brought by entities other than representative organisations advocating for such interests. Specifically, 'anyone,' *including individuals* (see *infra*, para. 6.4) may file these suits. This innovation will likely lead to the filing of multiple actions in the future, especially considering that other associations and organisations—even those not officially registered—may intervene in proceedings as procedural representatives of the individual petitioner.[105]

Compared to class actions for damages under Articles 840-*bis et seq.* c.p.c., collective injunctive actions are much more streamlined and accessible for claimants.

On the one hand, this mechanism only requires proof of potential harm. It is therefore sufficient for them to demonstrate the *current risk* of future damage, without the need to establish the occurrence of harm, its causal link, or intent or negligence. This 'lowering of the threshold for access to judicial protection'[106] constitutes a key distinction from class actions for damages.[107] It is corroborated, by analogy, by Article 140-*octies*, para. 4, of the Italian Consumer Code (introduced in 2023), which states that petitioners in collective injunctive actions (in this case, concerning consumer matters) 'are not required to prove the professional's [defendant's] fault or intent, nor the actual losses or damages incurred by individual affected persons'.[108]

On the other hand, Article 840-*sexiesdecies* c.p.c. does not require the court to assess the admissibility requirements imposed for damage-based class actions under Article 840-*ter*, paragraph 4, c.p.c. (see *supra*, para. 6.3.2).[109] This may result

---

[105] See, e.g. the *Philips Respironics* case, *infra*, Chap. 8.

[106] Id. (translated from Italian). In particular, *Philips Respironics* case, Tribunal of Milan, Section XIV, Order from 30 March 2023, R.G. No. 35350/2022. See also *infra*, Chap. 7.

[107] The express provision of Article 840-*sexiesdecies*, para. 5, c.p.c., according to which the court may make use of statistical data and simple presumptions, but also Article 8, para. 3, of the RAD, stands in this sense. On this matter, there is also a consolidated case law of legitimacy, specifically of the Italian Court of Cassation's United Sections, in relation to the injunction for anti-union behaviour pursuant to Article 28 of the Labour Statute: 'the injunctive nature of the action [...] leads to the conclusion that, for the purposes of the configurability of anti-union behaviour, the *psychological element* of the employer is irrelevant. What the judge must ascertain is the *objective suitability* of the conduct complained of to produce the result that the law intends to prevent' [Italian Court of Cassation, S.U., Judgement No. 5295 of 1997].

[108] *Philips Respironics* case, Tribunal of Milan, Section XIV, Order from 30 March 2023, R.G. No. 35350/2022 (translated from Italian). See also *infra*, Chap. 7.

[109] A decisive confirmation on this point comes again from the Tribunal of Milan, albeit in relation to another condition of admissibility, in the *ILVA* case, Tribunal of Milan, Section XV, Order from 16 September 2022, R.G. No. 10166/2021 (see *infra*, Chap. 7): 'It is significant, moreover, that for the action for an injunction there is no provision for the phase of admission of the application referred to in Article 840 ter of the Code of Civil Procedure and instead only the provisions of Article 840 quinquies of the Code of Civil Procedure, relating to the proceedings, are referred to, insofar as they are compatible. [...] Well then—apart from any consideration of expediency, which is not permitted here—, the state of the law seems, if anything, to signal the opposite will of the legislator to exclude, for the collective action for an injunction, the stages of admission and adhesion, thus precluding at root the possibility, in this regard, to proceed to analogical interpretations' (translated from Italian).

problematic with respect to the adequacy of the lead plaintiff to represent the group. At the same time, it is evident that the homogeneity requirement does not apply to this action (see *supra*, para. 6.3.1.1).

Article 840-*sexiesdecies* c.p.c., in fact, refers to the provisions governing class actions for damages only as far as Article 840-*quinquies* c.p.c. is compatible. Moreover, the absence of any reference to the concept of homogeneous individual rights, which is explicitly mentioned in Article 840-*bis* for damage-based class actions, is noteworthy. This interpretation is further supported by Article 840-*ter*, letter d), c.p.c. which mentions homogeneous individual rights as actionable solely 'pursuant to Article 840-bis,' without referring to Article 840-*sexiesdecies* c.p.c. By analogy, one may also invoke the 2023 consumer protection framework, wherein Article 140-*septies*, para. 8, letter c), cod. cons. identifies the homogeneity of individual rights as a prerequisite for admissibility exclusively for 'compensatory measures'.

Beyond its literal wording, an interpretation that disregards the criterion of homogeneity—and, consequently, the individuality of rights—appears preferable, particularly to fulfill the goal of 'expanding access to justice' underlying the reform under discussion.[110]

Indeed, such a reading, reliant on the homogeneity of individual rights, would exclude supra-individual positions from the scope of the injunctive action at issue. This outcome would clearly conflict with the *reasonableness* principle enshrined in Article 3 of the Italian Constitution, as it would fail to meet its objective and undermine the law's rationale.[111]

Moreover, a restrictive interpretation would lead to scenarios where 'the protection of certain fundamental rights—encompassed within the general and unified provision of Article 2 of the Constitution—develops unevenly, sacrificing other rights equally safeguarded by the Constitution and the European Convention on Human Rights'.[112] This would occur concerning supra-individual positions, for which injunctive relief through the general civil-procedural tool would not be guaranteed.[113]

The interpretation already provided in 2020 by the Plenary Assembly of the Italian Council of State regarding the (previous) class action under the Consumer Code (repealed in 2019) thus appears correct. The Council distinguished between individual positions (in that case, legitimate interests) attributable to individuals—where it is indeed possible to evaluate 'homogeneity'—and the supra-individual

---

[110] See *supra*, first paragraph of this Chapter.

[111] See Italian Constitutional Court, Judgement No. 43 from 1997.

[112] See Italian Constitutional Court, Judgement No. 317 from 2009.

[113] At present, there is a lack of cases envisaged in this sense, as all class actions with individuals rather than exponential entities as plaintiffs have so far always concerned individual rights; however, it cannot be ruled out that similar actions may be brought in the future—for instance in the area of climate change. See, for example, the well-known class actions in the Netherlands *Urgenda Foundation v. State of the Netherlands*, [2015] C/09/00456689, and *Milieudefensie et al v. Royal Dutch Shell*, [2021] C/09/571932.

('collective,' according to the Council) interests derived either from such individual subjective rights 'coalesced in their collective dimension' or from the 'aggregation of objectively similar diffuse interests',[114] that cannot be attributed to or actionable by a single entity. Unless opposing interests exist within the represented group, examining individual positions and categorising them into a specific group (or 'class') must, therefore, be excluded. Such an analysis is inherently irrelevant to the nature of the collective (not 'class') injunctive action, which is aimed at protecting meta-individual interests. A similar evaluation, based exclusively on individual subjective positions for subsequent compensatory purposes, is inconsistent with this action's essence and overall goal.

Similarly, referencing the concept of homogeneity in collective injunctive actions is also flawed from the perspective of coordinating with any subsequent class action for damages. If the homogeneity of individual rights was established in a collective injunctive action, such a finding could be used to determine the admissibility of a subsequent class action for damages.[115] However, the nature and purposes of collective injunctive actions—quasi-interim at times—are not always aligned with the assessment of homogeneity, which, while not prejudicial, entails greater complexity, historically and comparatively.[116]

---

[114] Italian Council of State, Plenary Assembly, Judgement No. 6 from 2020.

[115] As is well known, pursuant to Article 840-*sexiesdecies*, para. 9, the two actions must always proceed separately. Apart from the lack of appropriateness of the provision in question, it is relevant with regard to the extension of the effects of the judgement.

[116] *ITA Airways* case. Tribunal of Rome, Section XVI, Order from 13 December 2022, R.G. No. 3426/2022 (see also *infra*, Chap. 8): 'The purely preventive nature of the proceedings in question, in fact, is incompatible with the complex procedure aimed at the adhesion of the holders of homogeneous rights, which presupposes the publication of the order of admission of the class action, the latter phase not provided for collective actions for injunction. In fact, Article 840 sexiesdecies quinquies of the Code of Civil Procedure refers to the proceedings in chambers pursuant to Article 737 et seq. of the Code of Civil Procedure and only 'to the extent compatible' with Article 840 quinquies of the Code of Civil Procedure: it follows that, since the procedure of adhesion of the holders of rights similar to those at issue is not compatible with the collective injunction action, the request of the plaintiffs for the fixing of a time limit for adhesion to the requests they propose cannot be accepted' (translated from Italian). However, the possible treatment of only cases 'lacking in the complexity of the preliminary investigation', as set forth in the same order, does not appear to be acceptable in the light of the present analysis.

Lastly, in relation to the objective scope of application, in the temporal perspective, referring to both remedies, compensatory and injunctive, one cannot fail to consider the transitional rules of Law No. 31 of 2019, which establish the application of the new discipline only to 'unlawful conducts put in place' after its entry into force in May 2021. For relevant reflections, see *infra*, para. 6.2 of this chapter.

6.4 The Subjective Perimeter of Application for Both Class Actions

The limitations placed on the subjective scope of application by the rules of the Italian Code of civil procedure (c.p.c.) risk undermining, in practice, the significant objectives of effective protection pursued by the legislator in 2019. These objectives included extending the objective scope of application (see *above*, para. 6.3) of class actions and providing for a dual general remedy. In particular, serious doubts arise concerning the choices made by the legislator both regarding the *active parties* entitled to bring actions and the *passive parties*, which are concentrated in the business world.

Regarding the former, the new rules allow actions to be brought by both individual and collective entities.

On the active standing of individual parties, a distinction must first be made between compensatory class actions, under Articles 840-*bis et seq.* c.p.c., and collective injunctive actions, under Article 840-*sexiesdecies* c.p.c. While the former can be brought by 'any member of the class', the latter may be initiated by 'anyone with an interest' in the issuance of an injunction.

Therefore, to exercise the compensatory action, an individual proposer must necessarily demonstrate the existence and exact boundaries of a class and their membership in it. Additionally, as previously noted (see *above*, para. 6.3), under Article 840-ter c.p.c., the applicant must not have a conflict of interest with the respondent and must be able to adequately represent the rights asserted in court,[117] so as to overcome the hurdle of admissibility.

For the injunctive remedy, instead, it will only be necessary to demonstrate an interest to act under Article 100 c.p.c.[118] Consequently, for the action to be admissible, applicants will not need to assert or prove their effective entitlement to the substantive claim. Such a dual verification, moreover, would not be feasible in relation to diffuse situations, which cannot be tied to a single individual substantive position, as 'the substantive interest of the individual, understood as an individual component of the broader diffuse interest, [...] is not wholly or partially exclusive or capable of individual appropriation'. Once again, the confusion between the substantive and procedural levels, on the one hand, and the close connection between the objective and subjective scope of application, on the other hand, becomes apparent.

The prohibition under Article 81 c.p.c., which states that no one may assert a right belonging to another in their own name, does not appear to be violated. This is because the situation is expressly provided for by law and because—in relation to

---

[117] Mainly, the check carried out is on the plaintiff's financial means, such as to be able to bear the costs of the judgment.

[118] See Proto Pisani (2012) on the principle of atypicality of action in relation to Article 24 of the Constitution. See also Chiovenda (1903) and Andrioli (1955), p. 9.

the diffuse interests of a community or category—there is no single subject that holds full and exclusive title to those interests.

As is well known, administrative case law has filled this gap—in accordance with the combined provisions of Articles 2 and 24 of the Italian Constitution (the pluralist principle and the principle of effective judicial protection), as well as the supranational intermediate parameters (in particular, Articles 6 and 13 ECHR)—by granting standing to act for the protection of such supra-individual interests to collective entities that are sufficiently structured and strictly representative.[119]

In this context, the provision in Article 840-*sexiesdecies* c.p.c. is exceptional because, for the first time, it allows actions to protect diffuse interests to be brought (also) by *individual* subjects, and not only by representative entities. It is worth noting, as a confirmation of this exceptionality, that in the previous (dual) consumer class action (repealed in 2019), as well as in the subsequent (dual) consumer class action (introduced in 2023, in implementation of the RAD—see *above*, para. 6.1), active standing was granted exclusively to associations included in a specific list. This was a case of extraordinary standing for the protection of collective interests, aimed at 'pushing the threshold of protection forward, freeing it from the individual contractual bond, and conferring on it an injunctive characteristic capable of neutralising, at a general level, the acts and behaviors of the 'strong' private party likely to negatively affect the fundamental collective rights of consumers'.[120]

Evidently, despite the silence of the legislature, one cannot ignore, even systematically, the established administrative jurisprudence regarding the requirements to recognise standing to sue for non-registered associations, to be applied in this case to potential individual claimants. Primarily, there is the need for actual *representative* capacity and *adequate* suitability[121]—requirements that are, moreover, provided for, albeit in different terms, in letters c) and d) of Article 840-*ter*, para. 4, c.p.c. concerning class action claims for damages (see *above*, para. 6.3.1).

In cases involving non-diffuse interests, where the holder is an individual and, therefore, possesses parallel standing to sue as an individual, it seems appropriate to recognise the individual's capacity to initiate collective injunctive actions. This is justified both for reasons of procedural economy and in light of the principle of reasonableness under Article 3 of the Italian Constitution.

Beyond the already extensively cited principle of effective judicial protection under Article 24 of the Constitution,[122] which should prompt the interpreter to broaden the pool of eligible claimants (provided they are adequately representative, see *below*, para. 6.4.1), the principle of reasonableness under Article 3 of the Constitution must necessarily be read in conjunction with the principle of fair trial under Article 111 of the Constitution. This is further complemented by supranational

[119] See *supra*, Chap. 4.

[120] Id.

[121] See Italian Council of State, Section V, Judgement No. 253 from 1973; Italian Court of Cassation, S.U., Judgement No. 2207 from 1978; Italian Council of State, Plenary Assembly, Judgement No. 24 from 1979.

[122] See *supra*, Chap. 4.

standards, as interpreted by relevant courts, particularly Article 6 ECHR.[123] In fact, the very nature of injunctive measures—orders to cease or prohibit the repetition of certain acts or omissions—means their effects extend to all individuals substantively connected to the conduct, whether their interests are diffuse or not. Therefore, from the perspective of a fair trial and to ensure procedural balance, collective treatment appears more appropriate, as the effects themselves are collective. This approach aligns, among other things, with the practice and regulation of the so-called administrative class actions (see *above*, para. 6.1), which also provide for the active standing of individual users or consumers in a representative capacity concerning subjective positions (legitimate interests) which they hold (not diffuse ones, for which only representative entities may act in such cases).[124]

In this context, it is worth emphasising, again in light of the same internal and supranational parameters, the importance of developing appropriate tools and standards for verifying the *adequacy* of the (potentially, even individual) claimant to represent the asserted interests (and any opposing ones) in collective injunctive actions. To date, the limited case law on the matter currently points in the opposite direction.[125] This is particularly relevant considering the significant financial incentives a claimant may have in pursuing an action under Article 840-*sexiesdecies* c.p.c., through the potential use of economic sanctions (the so-called '*astreintes*') under Article 614-*bis* of the c.p.c.[126]

At the same time, it is important to consider how the injunctive order itself might harm other groups of individuals or entities (besides the claimants; for example, workers of a company polluting a portion of the territory). This necessitates, again under the same constitutional principles, the guarantee of appropriate opportunities for *adversarial proceedings*—not only for the parties, but for all stakeholders—to ensure adequate representation in the collective process. On the other hand, it will be necessary to balance these interests, by the ordinary judiciary with the assistance of the Constitutional Court and, if the matter falls under EU competence, also of the CJEU through preliminary rulings under Article 267 TFEU.[127]

Both actions—compensatory and injunctive—also allow for claims brought by '*organisations* or [...] *no-profit associations* whose statutory objectives include the protection' of the rights or interests harmed. However, it is established that 'only organisations and associations registered in a public list established at the Ministry of Justice'[128] may bring the action, pursuant to Articles 840-*bis*, para. 2, and 840-*sexiesdecies*, para. 1, c.p.c. Furthermore, Article 196-*ter* disp. att. c.p.c.[129] (the implementing provisions) stipulates that the Ministry of Justice, in consultation

[123] See Randazzo (2023).

[124] See *supra*, Chap. 4.

[125] See *infra*, Chap. 7.

[126] Referred by Article 840-*sexiesdecies*, para. 6, c.p.c. See also *infra*, Chap. 7.

[127] See *infra*, Chap. 7.

[128] Article 840-*bis* c.p.c. (translated from Italian).

[129] Also introduced, like the new Title VIII-*bis*, by Law No. 31 of 12 April 2019 (Article 2 thereof).

with the Ministry of Economic Development and after consulting the competent parliamentary committees, shall, by decree, establish 'the requirements for registration in the list referred to in Article 840-*bis*, para. 2, c.p.c., the criteria for the suspension and cancellation of registered organisations and associations, as well as the fee required for registration and its maintenance'.[130] This decree, effective from the 27 April 2022,[131] permits no-profit legal entities with statutory objectives aligned with the pursued protection to file claims.

Key requirements for registration include: establishment at least two years before the application for registration; headquarters in Italy or in another EU Member State; the statutory objective (even if not exclusive) of protecting homogeneous individual rights on a non-profit basis; a democratic organisational structure; continuous activity, demonstrated through local branches, public initiatives, and an updated website; statutory provisions for honorability requirements;[132] and, most importantly, administrative and accounting transparency, with annual publication and review of financial statements. On this point, there is a significant ruling by the Lazio Regional Administrative Court (TAR) from 23 June 2023, to be addressed later, as well as constitutional doubts about such restrictive and pre-established legal requirements (see *below*, para. 6.4.1).

Regarding the second aspect—*passive standing*—, both Articles 840-*bis* and 840-*sexiesdecies* stipulate that actions may 'be brought against companies or entities managing public services or utilities concerning acts and conducts carried out in the performance of their respective activities'.

Entities managing public services or utilities, as is well known, include those providing electricity, water, gas, telecommunications, transportation, or waste management, which may be private entities operating under concession or contract with the public and dealing with the community through agreements.[133]

This dual choice unambiguously confines the passive standing of the new mechanism to the entrepreneurial sphere, raising serious constitutional legitimacy concerns (see *below*, para. 6.4.2).

[130] Art 196-*bis,* see above. It further specifies how 'The contribution referred to in this paragraph shall be set at a level that in any case makes it possible to meet the costs of establishing, developing and updating the list. The requirements for registration include verification of the programmatic purposes, the adequacy to represent and protect the homogeneous rights acted upon and the stability and continuity of the associations and organisations themselves, as well as verification of the sources of funding used. The same decree establishes the modalities for updating the list' (translated from Italian).

[131] Decree of the Minister of Justice No. 27 of 17 February 2022, published in G.U. No. 86 of 12 April 2022.

[132] The requirement of honourability pursuant to Article 13 of Legislative Decree No. 58 of 1998 of all members (and not only of directors or representatives), referred to in subparagraph (g) of the Decree, appears to date to be excessive and, it is assumed, a mere typo.

[133] Greco et al. (2021), p. 490.

6.4.1 Active Standing: Doubts of Constitutional Legitimacy

With its judgement from 23 June 2023, the Lazio Regional Administrative Court (TAR Lazio) partially annulled the decree of the Minister of Justice dated 17 February 2022, No. 27, which regulated the public register of organisations and associations referred to in Articles 840-*bis* and 840-*sexiesdecies* c.p.c. The annulment specifically addressed the provision that barred *labour unions* from registering, since the requisite—now revoked—of operating as third-sector entities was deemed necessary (and labour unions in Italy do not operate as such).

In particular, the TAR highlighted that 'in exercising its regulatory discretion, the administration acted in a manifestly illogical and unreasonable manner' by restricting 'eligibility to initiate actions solely to those possessing the qualification of a third-sector entity'.[134] This, the administrative court noted, betrayed the spirit of the law, which instead aims to promote the broadest possible application for no-profit associations. The ruling further emphasised that 'the defence of the homogeneous individual rights of a specific category of individuals (in the case of the claimants, subordinate workers) is intrinsically connected to the typical associative purposes of unions [...]: hence, excluding such representative entities from the list of those authorised to initiate collective actions is irrational. Historically, the union's raison d'être lies in undertaking collective initiatives to defend the 'class' of workers (e.g., collective bargaining); therefore, barring such entities from collective judicial protection is antithetical to the general applicability of the remedy legislated'.[135]

This interpretation aligns with the reform's practical goal of facilitating access to justice, as well as with the understanding of the right to action under Article 24 of the Constitution, in light of other fundamental principles enshrined in the Italian Constitution, including the principle of horizontal subsidiarity (Article 118, fourth paragraph) and social pluralism (Article 2). The latter principle reflects the Italian Constituent Assembly's vision of social formations—such as labour unions—as entities aiming to 'transcend the atomistic limits of individual freedom [...] beyond the constraints stemming from public duties or commands of authority'[136] (authority—that is, sovereignty—to be read now, in an evolutive perspective, as encompassing also private entities, such as large multinational corporations).[137]

Among other requirements (see *supra*, para. 6.4), the provision that only entities established at least two years prior can register raises serious constitutional legitimacy concerns, despite being ostensibly aimed at ensuring the seriousness and reliability of claimants. This provision effectively precludes the initiation of collective

---

[134] TAR Lazio, Section I, 23 June 2023, No. 10653 (translated from Italian).

[135] Id.

[136] Italian Constitutional Court, Judgement No. 75 from 1992, point No. 2 of the Points of law (translated from Italian).

[137] See Pinelli (2016).

actions through *ad hoc* legal entities.[138] Coupled with the requirement of continuous activity (even with multiple territorial branches), it seems to foster the formation of a dangerous oligopoly of national organisations or associations dedicated to class actions. This is entirely at odds with the reform's intent and the pluralistic principle of Article 2 of the Italian Constitution, mentioned earlier. The associated risks are manifold: lack of diligence and bureaucratisation by registered organisations, conflicts of interest with potential claimants, inflexibility in responding to rapid societal developments, or specific needs of concrete or minor cases, and abuse of their dominant position over individual class members (e.g., through the imposition of onerous membership fees).[139]

It is worth noting the exponential increase in organisational and economic burdens of collective litigation compared to individual actions. Apart from so-called 'idealistic claimants', few individuals are incentivised to choose the collective route, and even if they wish to, they may lack sufficient resources to proceed. For this reason, it would be logical and reasonable to allow recourse in all circumstances—even those of a purely local nature—through flexible *ad hoc* legal vehicles capable of bearing such substantial burdens.[140] This approach aligns with the role recognised by the Constituent Assembly for intermediary bodies under Article 2 of the Constitution.[141]

Through the maintenance of other requirements and the judge's control at the admissibility stage, their independence and adequacy to represent the class would still be ensured. Alternatively, limiting the legal entities entitled to bring actions from the outset would represent a significant restriction in terms of effective access to justice, inconsistent with Article 24 and Article 117, first paragraph, of the Italian Constitution, in relation to Articles 6 and 13 ECHR and Article 19 TEU and Article 47 of the CFREU.

Furthermore, constitutional legitimacy concerns arise under Article 3, first paragraph, of the Italian Constitution with reference to individuals harmed by territorially confined conduct. These individuals, while constituting a class, may encounter greater difficulty in engaging nationally recognised organisations and associations already registered in the ministerial list. This would effectively limit the protection available to these individuals compared to those harmed by broader, numerically, economically, and media-significant cases.

The principle of horizontal subsidiarity, pursuant to Article 118, fourth paragraph, of the Italian Constitution, on the other hand, promotes the independent

[138] Kramer and Tzankova (2021), p. 100: 'The Dutch experience also demonstrates that ad hoc foundations are needed in a mature civil (law) justice system [...] Ad hoc organizations make sure that a proper system of checks and balances with respect to longstanding associations in collective redress remains in place'.

[139] See, more generally, Cappelletti (1993).

[140] This should create important incentives, making the application of the new discipline easier in practice. The European comparative perspective shows, in fact, that most class actions are brought by associations or organisations, rather than by individuals. See Azar-Baud et al. (2024).

[141] See Tosato (1965).

initiative of citizens, including in associative form.[142] This principle thus encourages the realisation of activities of general interest by entities that are, in practice, better positioned to provide protection or implement the rights and interests of citizens. Such an interpretation in terms of effectiveness is even more pronounced under Article 117, first paragraph, of the Italian Constitution, in relation to Articles 6 and 13 ECHR and Article 19 TEU and Article 47 CFREU. A regulation that, through excessively stringent requirements, deprives class members of the possibility of being represented in judicial proceedings by an organisation territorially closer to them appears inconsistent with these standards.

The public function and 'activity of general interest' performed by the organisation—under Article 118 of the Italian Constitution—would, in this case, correspond precisely to the exercise of the right of action (for the protection of collective or diffuse interests). This right, as previously noted,[143] is 'a component of a right protected by Articles 24 and 113 of the [Italian] Constitution and must be considered among those inviolable and characteristic of the democratic rule of law'.[144]

Further concerns about the reasonableness of the restrictions in question also emerge in relation to the well-known rule developed by administrative jurisprudence, known as the 'dual-track' rule. According to this rule, 'collective entities, and primarily associations, if they meet certain requirements, are entitled, independently and in addition to what is provided by specific legal provisions, to challenge before the administrative judge measures they consider harmful to the diffuse interests of the community they represent as an exponential entity'.[145]

According to the clear legal principle expressed by the aforementioned 2020 Plenary Assembly of the Council of State specifically concerning class actions (under the previous consumer protection legislation repealed in 2019), 'Associations are entitled to undertake actions to protect the collective legitimate interests of specific communities or categories, and in particular the general annulment action within the jurisdiction of administrative legitimacy, regardless of an explicit legal provision to this effect'.[146]

It is evident, therefore, that the disparity of treatment under the ministerial regulation in question becomes apparent when the same association brings an action before the administrative and ordinary courts, having active standing in the former case but not in the latter—pursuant to Articles 840-*bis*, para. 2, and 840-*sexiesdecies*, para. 1, c.p.c. (where they stipulate that 'only organisations and associations registered in a public list established at the Ministry of Justice may bring the action referred to in this article').

---

142 See also Italian Constitutional Court, Judgements No. 235 from 2009, point No. 9 of the Points of law, and No. 179 from 2019, point No. 12.3 of the Points of law.

143 See *supra*, Chap. 4.

144 Italian Constitutional Court, Judgement No. 26 from 1999 (translated from Italian), as well as No. 120 from 2014, No. 386 from 2004 and No. 29 from 2003.

145 Italian Council of State, Plenary Assembly, Judgement No. 6 from 2020 (translated from Italian).

146 Id. See *supra*, Chap. 4.

This appears even more unreasonable in relation to the specific case of the collective *injunctive* action, which, as is well known, is intended to prevent damage, including *potential* damage. It therefore requires prompt protection, for which access to a judge is a prerequisite, as clarified in the leading *Golder v. UK* case from 1975 before the ECtHR.[147] The necessary 'waiting' period of two years from the association's establishment before it can apply for registration on the ministerial list inevitably hinders any possibility of such a protection, clearly conflicting with the constitutional principles cited thus far.

To prevent the innovations introduced by the 2019 legislator from remaining purely theoretical or, worse, from giving rise to abusive practices, it is therefore desirable that the Italian Minister of Justice reconsiders opening the registration to recently established or strictly local organisations or associations, as advised by the positive comparative experience with the United States or with other European countries, such as the Netherlands or Portugal.[148] Alternatively, it seems necessary to partially annul the ministerial decree in question insofar as it requires, under its Article 3(1)(a), that organisations and associations must have been 'established at least two years prior to the submission of the application for registration on the list'. If this is not feasible, the constitutionality of Articles 840-*bis*, para. 2, and 840-*sexiesdecies*, para. 1, c.p.c. should be questioned, insofar as they stipulate that 'only organisations and associations registered in a public list established at the Ministry of Justice may bring the action referred to in this article.'

6.4.2 Passive Standing: Doubts of Constitutional Legitimacy

As clarified (see para. 6.4), Articles 840-*bis*, para. 3, and 840-*sexiesdecies*, para. 2, c.p.c. establish the passive standing of 'companies or [...] entities managing public services or services of public utility,' in relation to conducts carried out in the performance of their activities.[149] This provision also appears constitutionally questionable.

At first glance, it seems clear that the term 'companies' should be read extensively as including natural persons engaged in entrepreneurial activity. Consequently, all individuals who do not engage in business activities and do not fall within the category of 'managing public services or services of public utility' (for a definition of the latter, see para. 6.4 above)[150] are excluded from the list of potential defendants. This choice appears problematic for several reasons.

---

[147] ECtHR, *Golder v. UK*, No. 4451/70, 1975.

[148] Kramer and Tzankova (2021). See also Giussani (2019), p. 1574.

[149] Article 840-*bis*, para. 3, c.p.c.

[150] The latter must be understood, according to the case law formed with the previous consumer class action, as 'the private entrepreneurial subjects (with or without profit-making purpose) to which the PA [Public Administration], owner of the public service or public utility at a local level, delegates the relative management, but not already directly the Public Administration itself' (Court of Appeal of Rome, Order 21 June 2019, No. 6884/2019, R.G. No. 2398/2019, translated from Italian). For an in-depth study, see also Greco et al. (2021), p. 394.

First, while the restriction of passive standing to companies (alongside entities managing public services or services of public utility, see para. 6.4 above) might have been reasonable under the previous consumer protection framework repealed in 2019 or under the subsequent 2023 regime, the new *general*, trans-substantive scope of the reform from 2019 necessitates a corresponding general extension of the defendants' pool. This avoids creating unreasonable distinctions between similar or identical substantive situations based solely on the differing nature of the party responsible for the harmful (or potentially harmful) conduct in cases of injunctive class actions.

Particularly problematic is the exclusion of public administrations—as the alternative of the so-called 'public class action' under Legislative Decree No. 198/2009, concerning the 'remedy for the efficiency of public administrations and public service concessionaires' (see para. 6.1 above),[151] is unsatisfactory. It is worth recalling that this remedy, before the administrative court, is 'aimed at achieving a result beneficial, without distinction, to all co-holders of the diffuse interest in restoring [...] the correct provision of the service. In contrast, the class action [...] presupposes the exercise of an individual right, transposed into the hands of each individually identified holder'.[152] The collective proceeding before the administrative court against public administrations seeks to protect class members by requiring *specific performance* to address dysfunctions in administrative bodies or public service operators.[153] In contrast, the class action under Articles 840-*bis* and 840-*sexiesdecies* c.p.c. does not have direct remedial nature and does not allow for injunctive, much less compensatory, relief.[154] Reference is made to the above considerations on the possible use of the present rules before the administrative court, should an expansive reading of the concept of 'entities managing public services or services of public utility' be adopted (see para. 6.3.1 above).

The expression 'entities managing public services or services of public utility', and the interpretation that will be given by case law, are central to the future development of class actions analysed here in the Italian legal system. The inability to act against public administrations, following a restrictive interpretation, would create a safe zone for these public entities, in contrast with the principle of reasonableness under Article 3, first paragraph, of the Italian Constitution, as well as the previously mentioned constitutional and European parameters on the right of access to justice.

At present, the case law appears not well-established on the matter. These critical issues have been explicitly raised in recent cases. For example, in the context of an injunctive class action, the Rome Tribunal declared the lack of passive standing of the Municipality based on a strictly literal interpretation of Article 840-*sexiesdecies*

[151] See. *supra,* fn. No. 12.

[152] Italian Court of Cassation, S.U., Judgement No. 19453 from 2015 (translated from Italian).

[153] See Greco et al. (2021), p. 490. Article 1, para. 1, of Legislative Decree No. 198/2009 states: 'in order to restore the proper performance of a function or the proper provision of a service'.

[154] Id.

c.p.c.[155] Curiously, however, the same Rome Tribunal, in 2013, admitted two class actions against the Municipality under the previous consumer regime. In that case, the interpretation was evidently broader.

Further interpretative doubts arise concerning schools, hospitals, detention facilities, or religious institutions, whether private or public, with or without profit-making purposes. The lower courts have occasionally confronted this issue under the previous consumer protection regime (former Article 140-*bis* of the Consumer Code). In 2012, in the *Policlinico Universitario Agostino Gemelli* case,[156] the Rome Tribunal deemed a class action admissible based on a systematic interpretation of the term 'company,' considering 'the exercise of activity according to economic criteria, which includes, on the one hand, activities connected to intellectual professions traditionally excluded from entrepreneurial activities and, on the other hand, activities carried out by public entities,' including in this case 'a healthcare structure operating under an agreement with the National Health Service'.[157] Specifically, a joint reading of Articles 2082 of the Civil Code, Article 3 and Article 18 of the Consumer Code ruled out the restrictive interpretation of the term 'company' as necessarily linked to a for-profit aim, 'since the absence of such a purpose does not exclude the possibility of qualifying the activity as entrepreneurial', when carried out professionally and economically.[158] Today, with the inclusion of entities managing public services among those with passive standing, it seems even more logical to support their inclusion among potential defendants. This interpretation aligns

[155] Tribunal of Rome, Section XVI, Decree of 21 September 2021, No. 4274/2021, in relation to the new general discipline: 'This legislative choice, if it responds to a criterion of mere expediency that may not appear entirely convincing, insofar as it limits the operativeness of the institute to protection from 'enterprises' or bodies managing 'public services or public utilities' and not also from other subjects that do not carry out a business activity, even though their activity may damage 'a plurality of individuals or entities' and this in contradiction with the purpose inherent in the collective action for injunction - aimed at protecting against 'acts and conduct' carried out 'to the detriment of a plurality of individuals or entities', as specified in the first paragraph of Article 840-sexiesdecies c.p.c. - appears, on the other hand, justifiable in the part in which it excludes the public administration from the list of persons against whom the action can be exercised, since the latter is traditionally reserved a particular regime'.

[156] *Policlinico Universitario Agostino Gemelli* case, Tribunal of Rome, Order from 20 April 2012, No. 53276/2011, under the previous consumer-limited class action regime, in connection with an alleged tuberculosis infection of 1271 patients in the neonatal ward by a nurse employed there.

[157] Id. (translated from Italian).

[158] Id. The Tribunal held the action admissible also on the basis of the *homogeneity* of the individual rights asserted, underlining how 'the appreciation of the seriality that justifies the *joint procedural management* of the claims asserted by the individual members of the class, is correlated to the existence of *common characteristics* of the interests of the individuals, to the determination of which the Court is called upon to contribute with the order admitting the action by defining the characteristics of the individual rights subject to the proceedings. It must therefore be held that for the existence of the requirement it is necessary that the persons requesting protection are all consumers or users, that the same legal relationship or the same harmful conduct is pleaded as 'causa petendi', and that the claim asserted has as its object the restoration of the same injury, while the need to individualise the liquidation will not in itself be a limitation of the objective scope of the action' (emphasis added, translated from Italian).

with the rationale of the institution and the constitutional principles previously outlined in Articles 2, 3 and 24, as well as Article 117, first paragraph, of the Italian Constitution, in relation to Articles 6 and 13 ECHR and Article 19 and Article 47 CFREU.

Finally, further and more significant concerns arise regarding the exclusion of collective remedies, compensatory or injunctive, against the State. This appears relevant also due to the unreasonable disparity of treatment compared to actions against private legal entities wholly or substantially state-owned, against which the dual class action under the Code of civil procedure is undoubtedly admissible. Comparatively, the significant use of this instrument against public administrations and the State in jurisdictions where it is allowed, such as the Netherlands,[159] confirms the practical and effective necessity of collective protection even against these entities.

6.5 Jurisdiction and Competence: Doubts of Constitutional Legitimacy

The 2019 regulation establishes, in Articles 840-*ter*, para. 1, and 840-*sexiesdecies*, para. 3, of the Italian Code of civil procedure, that a class action must be filed by application 'exclusively before the specialised section for business matters, competent for the location where the defendant is based'.[160]

The legislator's choice to consolidate class actions in a single section of the tribunal can be understood if the aim is to ensure greater technicality, promoting the development of specific experience and expertise among judges, in the face of a procedural tool that is both new to the civil law legal culture and complex.

However, this option in favour of the *specialised* judge for business matters—although (partially) consistent with provisions regarding passive standing (see *above*, para. 6.4.2, and also see *below*, para. 6.6)—appears to be in clear contrast with the expansion of the objective scope of application underlying the reform, which is aimed—on paper—at providing a dual *general* remedy (see *above*, para. 6.1).

Therefore, it is necessary to reflect, firstly, on the constitutional legitimacy of the provisions in question—Articles 840-*ter*, para. 1, and 840-*sexiesdecies*, para. 3, c.p.c. and, secondly, on the possibility—overlooked by the legislator—that the defendant does not have a place of business in Italy.

As to the first issue, the attribution of *competence to the business section* of the tribunal could be understandable if businesses were the only eligible defendants. However, on the one hand, the class action regime introduced in 2019 is also available against 'entities managing public services or utilities', and on the other hand,

[159] See Azar-Baud et al. (2024).

[160] Article 840-*ter*, para. 1, c.p.c. (translated from Italian).

as mentioned earlier (see para. 6.4.2), such a *subjective* limitation raises doubts of constitutional legitimacy, at least in its restrictive literal interpretation.

Clearly, if a constitutionally-compliant, extensive interpretation of the concept of 'business' were adopted (see *above*, para. 6.4.2), the rationale behind the legislator's decision to assign competence to this specialised section would completely disappear, as contradicting Article 3, first paragraph, of the Constitution.

In any case, the attribution of competence in question appears, regardless of further considerations, to be of dubious constitutional legitimacy.

The first applications already show the emergence of actions for the protection of fundamental rights, such as the right to health,[161] to a healthy environment,[162] to fair working conditions,[163] and personal freedoms. At the same time, it is important to emphasise again the considerable variety of collective actions that could arise, and that have already arisen, in our legal system: just as examples, beyond the consumer sector, in addition to the already mentioned cases concerning the right to health, environmental law, and labour law, there are cases related to anti-discrimination law,[164] cryptocurrencies,[165] tax law, and banking law.[166] Moreover, comparative experience and the very origins of the institution demonstrate a significant use of collective proceedings for the protection of civil liberties and social rights, such as for the rights of migrants and prisoners, social housing policies and personal data protection.[167]

Judges in the specialised business section are now required to make decisions in areas vastly different from those they typically deal with, where their sensitivity and technical preparation will inevitably be inferior to the one of judges from other sections who deal with these matters daily. This results in a significant burden on the judges to study and, for the parties, in a risk of an improper decision; this contrasts with Article 24 of the Italian Constitution and Article 117, first paragraph, of the Constitution, the latter in relation to Articles 6 ECHR and 47 CFREU.

Furthermore, the specialised business section is now required, in addition to its regular workload, not only to familiarise itself with the significant peculiarities of the new collective procedural rules, but also to delve into extremely technical fields, including the particularly illustrative field of labour law.

In relation to the latter and to the practical difficulties that have already arisen, further constitutional doubts emerge about the current attribution of competence under Articles 840-*ter*, para. 1, and 840-*sexiesdecies*, para. 3, c.p.c. These are areas where other specialised sections already have competence for individual actions. It is evident that a judge specialised in one field (in this case, business law) cannot

[161] See, e.g., *Philips Respironics* case, *infra*, Chap. 7.

[162] See, e.g., *ILVA* case, *infra*, Chap. 7.

[163] See, e.g., *Deliveroo* and *Uber Eats* cases, *infra*, Chap. 8.

[164] See, e.g., *ITA Airways* case, *infra*, Chap. 8.

[165] See, e.g., *Binance* case, *infra*, Chap. 10.

[166] See, e.g., Tribunal of Venice, Order from 18 May 2023, R.G. No. 3/2023.

[167] See *supra*, Chap. 5.

have the same technical expertise as judges specialised in other fields (such as labour law) to adequately decide disputes related to the latter field, for which a different special procedure is already provided for individual suits.

This is precisely the case with the labour sector. Class actions already brought by workers against employers (e.g., those protecting food delivery riders)[168] clearly represent the challenges of assigning competence to the business court rather than to the labour judge, who would be competent in case of an individual claim filed by a single worker.[169] The irrationality of such a provision is evident.[170]

Similar considerations must also be made in relation to tax law (see *above*, para. 6.3.1), as well as, in general, in relation to disputes concerning substantive situations that would naturally fall under the competence of another judge if pursued individually.

Lastly, the second issue to analyse under a constitutional perspective is the case in which the defendant does not have a seat in Italy. This circumstance is not, in fact, contemplated by the legislator—hence, the possible reading that the Italian judge would have no jurisdiction for such defendants. An analysis of a pending case on this matter is offered *infra*, in Chap. 10.

6.5.1 Allocation of Jurisdiction

Also division of jurisdiction between ordinary and administrative courts becomes relevant, in Italy, in view of the possible exceptions of defendant companies, from two standpoints: on the one hand, in the event that the defendant company has carried out its acts in *conformity with an act of the public administration*; on the other hand, in the event that the case in question falls within the *exclusive jurisdiction of the administrative courts*.

With reference to the first problem, it is a well-established principle of the Italian legal system that any compliance with measures of the public administration is not sufficient to alter the system of attribution of jurisdiction, if this already pertains to

---

[168] See, e.g., *Deliveroo* and *Uber Eats* cases, *infra*, Chap. 8.

[169] The *Deliveroo* case, (id.) is particularly illustrative of the reluctance of the specialised business section to decide labour law issues on the merits. Specifically, the collective action for an injunction was rejected because, according to the Tribunal of Milan, the plaintiffs in the case at issue required an assessment 'well beyond the incidental nature of the recognition of the right asserted', contesting the contractual basis of the employment relationship and requiring a 'particular complexity in the correct identification of the actual injuries suffered and [...] the homogeneity of such injuries in relation to the subjects that would constitute the class to be defined' (translated from Italian). On this point, we should emphasise that it is not necessary to prove the homogeneity in the strict sense of the injuries, but rather the mere commonality of the acts causing injury to a plurality of individuals or entities; a commonality which is evident in the case in question, given the application of the same CCNL Ugl Rider and the distribution of work through the same algorithm. For further elaboration, see *infra*, specifically, Chap. 8 and, more generally, Chap. 11.

[170] See Donzelli (2019), p. 7, and Giussani (2019).

the ordinary judge. The Court of Cassation, in its jurisprudence of legitimacy, has recently reaffirmed this principle through a series of unequivocal rulings, in which it has definitively clarified that

> jurisdiction is determined on the basis of the request and, for the purposes of the division of jurisdiction between the ordinary judge and the administrative judge, it is not the prospect made by the parties that is relevant, but rather the substantive petitum, which must be identified, not only and not so much in function of the concrete pronouncement that the judge is asked to make, but, above all, in function of the causa petendi, i.e. the intrinsic nature of the position brought before the court and identified by the judge with regard to the facts attached.[171]

Therefore,

> the dispute in which the private individual, having ascertained the noise, nuisance and intolerability of the immissions produced by the wind turbines of a wind farm, as well as the detrimental effects caused by them on his own health and that of his family members and on the economic value of his property, has requested their cessation or at least their reduction within the limits of tolerability, together with compensation for damages, belongs to the jurisdiction of the ordinary courts, having regard to the substantive '*petitum*' of the claim, which does not concern the annulment of the administrative measure authorising the installation and operation of the plant for the production of electricity from wind power (nor does it presuppose the establishment of its unlawfulness), but concerns the protection of subjective rights to health and property, on the basis of the breach of the limits of tolerability laid down by Article 844 of the Civil Code.[172]

The case in question, therefore, gives continuity to the principle of law of the so-called 'substantial *petitum*' and reaffirms how the fact that a conduct is placed in conformity or not with administrative measures does not in any way affect the division of jurisdiction. When the plaintiff does not request the annulment of such measures, but rather the *protection of their own subjective position* (such as, for example, the right to health or the right to property, requesting compensation for damage, the total inhibition or the reduction within tolerable limits of a certain activity), the ordinary judge will still have jurisdiction. Already in 2006, the United Sections of the Court of Cassation affirmed how fundamental rights (such as—in the case then under consideration—that to health) operate in private relations and override the public administration, which 'has no power, not even in the public interest, not only to weaken them, but not even to prejudice them *de facto* and indirectly'.[173]

It follows, therefore, that both injunctive and compensatory relief are devolved to the ordinary courts irrespective of whether or not they comply with administrative acts. If the unlawful conduct *complies* with acts of the public administration, the ordinary judge will limit themselves to '*disapply* the aforementioned provision and impose the cessation or adjustment of the activity so as to eliminate the harmful consequences'—in the case of an action for an injunction—, or to decide on the claim for damages or for the restitution of property—in the case of an action for

[171] Italian Court of Cassation, S.U., Judgement No. 29298 from 2021 (translated from Italian).

[172] Id.

[173] Italian Court of Cassation, Judgement No. 23753 from 2006 (translated from Italian).

compensation or restitution. In the opposite scenario of *non-compliance* with acts of the public authority, on the other hand, the ordinary judge will simply *sanction the activity as non-compliant* with administrative regulation, inhibiting it or bringing it into compliance.

The second problem, on the other hand, as anticipated, concerns the relationship with the exclusive jurisdiction of the administrative judge, pursuant to Article 103, first paragraph of the Italian Constitution. Consider, for example, letter c) of Article 133 c.p.c., which, as is well known, sets out the matters falling within the jurisdiction of the administrative courts:

> 'disputes concerning public services relating to concessions of public services, excluding those concerning indemnities, fees and other consideration, or relating to measures adopted by the public administration or by the manager of a public service in an administrative procedure, or relating to the entrustment of a public service, and to the supervision and control of the manager, as well as relating to the supervision of credit, insurance and securities market, pharmaceutical services, transport, telecommunications and public utility services'.

In view of the fact that both Article 840-*bis* (class action for damages or restitutory relief) and Article 840-*sexiesdecie*s (collective action for injunctive relief) mention that they may also be brought 'against the managing bodies of public services or public utilities, in respect of acts and conduct committed in the performance of their respective activities',[174] doubts may arise as to the competent court for such matters.

On this point, the Tribunal of Rome has already had the opportunity to express its stance in the very first collective action brought under the new rules.[175] Recalling the orientation of the *Sezioni Unite* of 2015 in relation to the previous consumer class action pursuant to Articles 139 and 140 of the Consumer Code where it observed that

> 'it is not possible to derive from such norms the attribution to the court, competent to judge on the so-called class actions [...], of a jurisdiction extended beyond the limits that in general pertain to it, with the exception of the cases included in the exclusive jurisdiction of the administrative judge',[176]

it reiterated how:

> class actions would not have introduced a derogation, only because of the common nature to an indefinite number of possible users—and in this sense collective—of the interests affected, to the traditional division of jurisdiction between ordinary judge and administrative judge, based on the distinction between subjective rights and legitimate interests, [...] seeing no reason to differentiate, in class actions, as regards jurisdiction, the legal regime of matters reserved by law to the jurisdiction of the administrative court from those in which the jurisdiction of the administrative court is correlated to the legal nature of the asset being protected (legitimate interest rather than subjective right).[177]

---

[174] See Italian Constitutional Court, Judgement No. 35/2020 (translated from Italian). See also, *ex multis*: Italian Court of Cassation, SU, Judgement No. 25578 from 2020, Italian Court of Cassation, SU, Judgement No. 8092/2020.

[175] Tribunal of Rome, Section XVI, Decree from 21 September 2021, R.G. No. 4274/2021.

[176] Italian Court of Cassation, SU, Judgement No. 10095 from 2015 (translated from Italian).

[177] Id.

It concluded—with a thesis that appears reasonable—that the ordinary division of jurisdiction between the ordinary judge and the administrative judge must be maintained also in the application of the new (dual) instrument of collective judicial protection. Therefore, the general perimeter of application of the new collective discipline (homogeneous individual rights, under the compensatory and restitutory profile; in general, subjective, also super-individual, positions harmed by a common conduct, under the injunctive profile) necessarily reduces where the exclusive jurisdiction of the administrative judge is provided for.

Within the scope of the matters reserved to the latter, it will be possible to bring the aforementioned public (or 'administrative') class action pursuant to Legislative Decree No. 198 of 2009 ('recourse for the efficiency of public administrations and public service concessionaires'), aimed at 'restoring the correct performance of the function or the proper provision of a service', following the 'violation of deadlines or the failure to issue general administrative acts that are mandatory and do not have regulatory content [...], the violation of the obligations contained in the service charters or the violation of established qualitative and economic standards' by public administrations and public service concessionaires. This remedy, as already recalled, is the only one expressly preserved by the 2019 reform, which, however, has different compensatory and injunctive aims and, therefore, can be well coordinated with it.

An exception to the administrative court's exclusive jurisdiction over subjective rights, in matters where it is expressly provided for by the legislature, on the other hand, will be represented by disputes aimed at protecting rights of high constitutional rank, such as the right to health or equality. Notwithstanding the increasing number of rulings by the administrative courts concerning fundamental rights, the natural judge of these will still be the ordinary judge.

The harm of constitutionally protected rights by conduct in compliance with administrative measures will not, therefore, be susceptible of degrading them to mere legitimate interests; consequently, jurisdiction will in any case lie with the ordinary judge. A similar result will be reached in disputes in which there is no connection with the exercise of a discretionary power of balancing public interests by the public administration: even if they fall within the matters identified by the legislature as the subject matter of exclusive jurisdiction, the protection of these 'subjective rights which cannot be affected'[178] will in any event fall to the ordinary courts, with the consequent applicability of the new class action.

[178] See Italian Court of Cassation, SU, Judgement No. 1463 from 1979 (translated from Italian), and Italian Court of Cassation, S.U., Judgement No. 5172 from 1979.

6.6 Non-retroactivity of the New Provisions: Doubts of Constitutional Legitimacy

Article 7 of Law No. 31 of 2019, the one introducing the new class action regime, states that 'the provisions of this law shall apply to unlawful conduct put in place after the date of its entry into force'—that is, 19 May 2021. *Ad abundantiam*, the next sentence reiterates that 'the provisions in force prior to the same date of entry into force shall continue to apply to unlawful conduct put in place previously'. In case of offences relating to the consumer sphere or to the use of services, therefore, the previous rules pursuant to Articles 139, 140 and 140-*bis* of the Consumer code apply. In other non-consumer cases, however, the only remedy available will be the individual action.

In this regard, it is worth reflecting, first of all, on the *constitutional legitimacy* of this transitional rule and, secondly, on a case not regulated by the legislator, that is that of unlawful *conducts protracted over time* during the term of both regulations, on which a number of application uncertainties could develop.

6.6.1 Doubts on Constitutional Legitimacy

The letter of the law, on the one hand, and the preparatory works, on the other hand, irrefutably deny the applicability of the new procedural instrument to facts that occurred (and were fully concluded) before 19 May 2021. Such a provision of non-retroactivity—which is among other things the subject of much parliamentary debate—would undoubtedly be legitimate and appropriate in the event that the new rules had a *substantive* nature of regulating legal relations or made new rights or interests justiciable. However, numerous profiles lead to attributing to the new class action mechanism a mere *instrumental* nature with respect to subjective situations already protected previously.

This qualification—on which the majority of the doctrine, in the debate that has already arisen in relation to the previous consumer class action, agrees—would entail an 'unreasonable exception to the rule that, if new procedural rules are introduced, allows the deduction in court of rights arising at an earlier time than the one in which action is taken under the new rules',[179] according to the principle '*tempus regit actum*'.

Among the arguments that can be deduced in support of this thesis is the fact that the legal situations that can be protected through the new instrument pre-existed it. It did not introduce new substantive legal positions, but merely an *alternative* to the individual action, which was already previously available. This is evidenced by the literal fact of the new legislation, where it states that 'homogeneous individual rights may also be protected by class action' and that 'in any event, the right to

---

[179] Caponi (2009), p. 383 (translated from Italian), and, although more neutral, Pace (2011).

individual action remains unaffected'.[180] This interpretation is also supported by the rulings of legitimacy courts relating to collective action for environmental damage, introduced by Article 18 of Law No. 349 of 1986, in which the Constitutional Court pointed out that the notion of environment finds its '*genetic source*' not in the new procedural instrument, but in the pre-existing constitutional and primary provisions.[181] It appears, therefore, evident that the instrumental nature is also shared by the new class action, whenever it aims, in the same way, to protect the environment, other 'primary and absolute intangible public values' or other multiple 'homogeneous individual rights'.

One could, therefore, question the constitutional legitimacy of Article 7, para. 2, of Law No. 31 of 2019 in the part in which it does not provide that the provisions of that law also apply to unlawful conducts put in place prior to the date of its entry into force (19 May 2021) for breach of Articles 3 and 24 of the Italian Constitution. It should, nonetheless, be specified how the Constitutional Court's constant case law has recognised 'the legislature's wide discretion – subject to the limit of manifest unreasonableness – in establishing the transitional rules dictated to facilitate the transition from one regime to another'.[182] On several occasions, the Court has rejected questions of constitutionality raised on this point, reaffirming this principle. Therefore, it remains unlikely that such an issue would be upheld.

Nevertheless, when one considers the preparatory works, it is difficult to regard the current legislative choice as reasonable.[183] In fact, they clearly show how the legislature, in exercising its discretion, did not impose a temporal distinction with the intention of 'safeguarding the reliance on legal certainty' or to favour 'the gradual substitution of the new for the old discipline without identifying particular situations',[184] so as to avoid excessive initial litigation with repercussions on the principle of the reasonable duration of proceedings.

Quite the contrary, as clearly emerges from the parliamentary debate, the legislative choice is dictated by the desire to prevent the application of the new rules to certain *specific* facts prior to 19 May 2021 (in particular, the name of *Autostrade per l'Italia S.p.A.* recurs several times[185]—against which, among other things, an action pursuant to Article 840-*bis* has already been, unsuccessfully, brought),[186] as happened in 2009 with the previous consumer class action, in relation to scandals such as Parmalat, Cirio or Giacomelli.

---

[180] Article 840-*bis* c.p.c., respectively first and last paras. (translated from Italian).

[181] Italian Court of Cassation, Judgement No. 25010 from 2008.

[182] Italian Constitutional Court, Judgement No. 309 from 2008 (translated from Italian), Order No. 419 from 1990; Judgement No. 268 from 1986; Judgement No. 301 from 1986.

[183] The speech from On. Zanettin from report No. 53 from 1 October 2018, that from On. Bartolozzi from report No. 54 from 2 October 2018, that from Onn. Bartolozzi, Pittalis e Zanettin from report No. 55 from 3 October 2018 are particularly relevant.

[184] Id. (translated from Italian).

[185] Id.

[186] Declared inadmissible exactly since it regarded facts and conducts preceding the entry into force of the reform. See Tribunal of Rome, Section XVII, Order from 14 October 2022, No. 21595/22.

The time limitation introduced by the transitional rule does not, therefore, appear to pursue the general interest, but rather seems to be aimed at preventing *certain* companies from being exposed to claims for damages, hitherto hindered by the inefficiency of individual procedural instruments, but to which they would—in abstract terms—*already* be bound under substantive law.

In this context, the perplexity as to the reasonableness of the choice made by the legislator seems well-founded. Preventing the use of the new collective procedural instrument for events occurring before 19 May 2021 does not, in fact, protect the interest in legal certainty or other values of constitutional importance, but merely makes it more unlikely that guilty defendants will be called upon to answer in court for their violations of individual subjective positions.

6.6.2 Unlawful Conducts Protracted Over Time During the Two Regimes

Quite apart from the foregoing assessments on their constitutional legitimacy, the transitional provisions of Law No. 31 of 2019, in introducing the temporal distinction of application, have left some perplexity as to the 'unlawful conducts put in place' both before and after the date of entry into force. Three different cases are proposed below that could cause interpretative uncertainties, in addition to the, albeit limited, case law on the subject.

We shall assume, first, the case of the *same defective product* sold to some consumers *before* 19 May 2021 (date of the entry into force) and to others *afterwards*. Can the new class action under Articles 840-*bis et seq*. c.p.c. be used for all? This is a classic case of a tort repeated over time and the answer is certainly yes. The new discipline of the class action, in fact, does not present an '*atomistic*' conception of the various injuries, but constantly emphasises the collective and unitary nature of the multi-offensive tort.[187] Therefore, the multi-offensive conduct must be identified as a *unicuum* and, whenever even a portion of the unlawful activity (such as the sale of the defective product even to a single person, in our example) has taken place after the entry into force of the new discipline, the latter shall be applicable.

Second, we can think of a case of serious environmental pollution by a company, such as—according to the plaintiffs' claims—in the double injunctive *azione collettiva*, initially, and compensatory *azione di classe*, then, against *ILVA* and *Acciaierie d'Italia* (see *infra*, Chap. 7). In this circumstance, the right to live in a healthy environment, the right to individual health of many local residents, and their right to property would be infringed, due to a significant devaluation of the market value of property in the area. If the polluting activity started after 19 May 2021, no problem would arise, as the new class action, both compensatory and injunctive, would certainly be applicable. On the other hand, what if the polluting activity is *still*

---

[187] See Donzelli (2019).

continuing, but *started before* 19 May 2021? The conduct would qualify as a '*permanent tort*' and, even in this case, the answer must certainly be in the affirmative. In fact, it would be absolutely unreasonable, as well as contrary to the principle of equality pursuant to Article 3 of the Italian Constitution, to prohibit the use of the new procedural tool against a certain unlawful conduct merely because it has an origin dating back in time, almost as if this represented a shield of unprocedibility against them, whereas, if they had started later, the new rules would be applicable.

In relation to the limitation of (its) jurisdiction *ratione temporis*, *inter alia*, the European Court of Human Rights has also expressed itself extensively, coming to similar conclusions and elaborating the notion of '*continuous violation*', according to which the procedural law in force at the time of the last infringing conduct or, alternatively, even only at the time of an element of it, must apply.[188]

Therefore, the same considerations set forth above regarding the unitary conception of multi-offensive conducts apply. It should also be noted how this interpretation—so far widely shared by domestic doctrine and jurisprudence—is in line with the comparative experience of other European states on the subject of class actions.

Last, as a third possibly problematic case, let us assume—taking up the previous example concerning the pollution of a portion of territory by a company—that the activity is terminated before the entry into force of the new rules, but that the *effects* of the new rules (also) manifest themselves *after* 19 May 2021 (which is quite likely, especially for environmental or product damage, e.g., due to defective medicines): would the new collective procedural rules be applicable in these cases as well?

The limited domestic jurisprudence (not yet of legitimacy)—in relation to the previous consumer class action of 2009 (for which a similarly ambiguous provision was prepared)—has so far denied the application of the new discipline in the case of the so-called '*instant torts with permanent effects*', interpreting as 'unlawful conduct' only the facts and *not* also the effects of these. This interpretation is in line with the above-mentioned interpretation of the ECHR on the subject of *continuous violation*, which has determined on several occasions that the continuation of the effects of an act over time is not sufficient for the purposes of determining jurisdiction *ratione temporis*.[189]

However, in the case law so far examined by the Italian courts, a marked divergence in the factual reconstructions of the infringing conduct, when this has been protracted in time, should be noted. In particular, similar or even identical cases have been qualified as either an '*instant tort with permanent effects*', or as a '*permanent tort*' depending on the court or level of jurisdiction—without the adoption of any common criteria for determination. The different procedural rules that the courts have deemed applicable depending on the *qualification* within one or another case (on the one hand, the previous rules in the case of the 'instant tort with

[188] See Randazzo (2012), pp. 91 *et seq.*

[189] See ECtHR, *MELTEX LTD v. Armenia*, No. 37780/02, 2008, § 1; ECtHR, *Călin et autres v. Roumanie*, Nos. 25057/11, 34739/11 and 20316/12, 2016, §§ 58 *et seq.*; ECtHR, *Iordache v. Roumanie*, No. 6817/02, 2008, § 49.

permanent effects'; on the other hand, the new procedural rules, in the case of the 'permanent tort') carries obvious consequences in terms of *legal certainty*.

Pending a greater consolidation of the case law on the subject, also by means of further rulings from the Italian Court of Cassation, it remains, therefore and in any event, desirable for the courts to adopt an extensive reading of the concept of 'unlawful conduct', aimed at guaranteeing access to the procedural instrument to the greatest possible number of cases characterised by the same multi-offensive conduct protracted over time.

6.7 Publications on the Telematic Portal and Publicity

A minor, but still relevant, point of interpretative divergence regards the duty of court clerks to *publish on the public area of the telematic services portal* the files of injunctive class actions, in addition to those of compensatory ones.

For instance, while the Tribunal of Rome has already ordered the publication of the injunctive *azioni collettive* proposed before it, other territorial courts—at least the Tribunal of Milan three times and the Tribunal of Turin once, as informally gathered—have failed to do so. Such application uncertainties are constitutionally significant, given the important disparity of treatment between analogous situations. A prompt resolution is hence desirable.

The reluctance to publish presumably stems from the lack of an *explicit* provision imposing such a duty under Article 840-*sexiesdecies* c.p.c., the sole concerning the injunctive class action. Such a provision, nonetheless, refers, in its para. 4, to the regulations set for the compensatory class action and, in particular, to 'Article 840-*quinquies* c.p.c., to the extent compatible'. This latter provision, titled 'Procedure', refers to the publication on the telematic services portal (provided for also under Article 840-*ter* c.p.c.) both in para. 1 and, in particular, para. 14. Any direct reference to Article 840-*ter* c.p.c. (which does not directly touch the issue of the publication on the telematic portal, either) is evidently lacking from Article 840-*sexiesdecies* c.p.c., since the former provision regulates the 'form and admissibility' of the compensatory *azione di classe*, mentioning a phase (that of admissibility) and some requirements (e.g., homogeneity) which do not apply with regards to injunctive collective suits. Any reference to it under Article 840-*sexiesdecies* c.p.c. would have been otherwise rather confusing.

Consequently, the interpretation so far adopted by the Tribunal of Rome, which envisages a duty of publication of the case files *also* for injunctive class actions *ex* Article 840-*sexiesdecies* c.p.c., rather than only for compensatory ones *ex* Article 840-*bis* c.p.c., is to be preferred by all means. This appears necessary in light of a constitutional-oriented interpretation, pursuant to the reasonable clause under Article 3, first paragraph, of the Italian Constitution.

Not even the legislative choice to handle the collective injunctive actions through the forms of the in-camera proceeding under Articles 737 *et seq.* of the Code of civil procedure—quite surprising in itself—seems to justify the failure to publish on the portal. At most, this—questionable, but herein irrelevant—choice is due to the absence of formality (in terms of timing and assumption of evidence) from the in-camera proceedings. The lack of a public hearing typical of in-camera proceedings, indeed, does *not* conflict with the mere publication on the portal of the decree setting the hearing date or the subsequent decisions of the judge (and only those of the *judge*, since the parties' documents remain hidden from the public, safe for the introductory claim application, filed by the plaintiff—a choice which is also debatable, under an equality of arms perspective). Indeed, given the collective and potentially *superindividual nature* of the interests at stake, it seems reasonable—*rectius*, necessary—to inform society of the initiation, and conclusion, of collective injunctive proceedings, too.

Moreover, the appropriateness of publishing the decree setting the hearing is justified, in a systematic reading, also by the need to prevent further collective injunctive actions based on the same facts and against the same defendant, as expressly provided for by Article 840-*quater* with reference to the compensatory class action. Further reflections shall be spent on this particular choice in the last chapter of this work, under Part IV (Chap. 11).

6.8 Concluding Remarks. A Still Evolving Tapestry

This Chapter has tried to offer a closer look at the nuances of the 2019 dual class action regime in Italy, under a constitutional lens. As shown, and as declared in its premise, it is a quite intertwined procedural tapestry, situated in the already complex Italian constitutional fabric. It is, however, also an unfinished work, which will require serious interpretative effort from all the legal practitioners and social actors involved, to foster its use for more concrete access to justice for everyone, while ensuring the constitutional guarantees of the fair trial.

In these final reflections, it should be taken into account that the new regime entered into force only in 2021. It was, and still is, a 'wild thing',[190] very alien to the legal and social tradition in which it has been cast. Therefore, some time for adequate reception of the 'legal transplant' is only natural. After all, even in the US, where the current class action model emerged in 1966, several decades passed before the right formula was found by the legislator (considering that the then amended Rule 23 on class actions had first been introduced in 1938, with similar versions in place even before).[191]

At the same time, nevertheless, the contemporary social and constitutional transformations highlighted in Part I pose a series of radical and unprecedented challenges which require an urgent solution. Class actions may not be (are not) the

[190] Voet (2017), p. 115.

[191] And even today, as touched upon *supra*, in the previous Chap. 5, several commentators would argue that it is far from being an effective tool.

panacea, but could be a partial answer, at least to some of the issues we are, globally, and urgently, confronted with. For this simple reason, we cannot afford to miss on the correct implementation of this double-edged tool, nor to wait for several decades before seeing any concrete results in terms of effectiveness.

As a consequence, to facilitate a more nuanced analysis and future implementation, it becomes mandatory to study also its practical application, through the cases presented in the next Part III, as well as to propose the already evidently necessary changes, in the final Part IV.

References

Alpa G (1993) Interessi diffusi. In: Digesto delle discipline privatistiche. Sezione civile, 9th edn. UTET, Torino, p 609

Andrioli V (1955) La tutela giurisdizionale dei diritti nella Costituzione della Repubblica italiana: discorso inaugurale dell'anno accademico 1954-55. Nistri-Lischi, Pisa

Azar-Baud MJ, Giannopoulou A, Maglica A, Tzankova IN (2024) Collective redress. A compare-and-contrast analysis of ten jurisdictions in the European Union. Digital Freedom Fund

Barbosa Moreira JC (1985) Tutela jurisdicional dos intereses coletivos ou difusos. Temas de Direito Procesal 3:195

Barile P (1984) Diritti dell'uomo e libertà fondamentali. Il Mulino, Bologna

Bustos Gisbert R (2022) Judicial Independence in European Constitutional Law. Eur Const Law Rev 18:591

Calamandrei P (1954) Processo e democrazia. In: Cappelletti M (ed) Calamandrei P (1965) Opere giuridiche, I. Morano, Napoli

Campigli V (2024) Per una valorizzazione dell'azione di classe pubblica come strumento di tutela processuale dei diritti sociali. Il diritto dell'economia 70(115):310

Caponi R (2009) Il nuovo volto della class action. Il Foro italianoV 132:383

Caponi R (2012) Azione di classe: il punto, la linea, la discontinuità. Il Foro Italiano 135:151

Caponi G, Capuozzo V, Del Vecchio I, Simonetti A (2014) Omogeneità costituzionale europea e identità nazionali: un processo di integrazione circolare tra valori costituzionali europei e teoria dei controlimiti. Federalismi.it 24:1–34

Cappalli R, Consolo C (1992) Class actions for Continental Europe? A preliminary inquiry. Temple Int Comp Law J 6(2):217–292

Cappelletti M (1975) Appunti sulla tutela giurisdizionale di interessi collettivi e diffusi. Giurisprudenza italiana 127:49–63

Cappelletti M (1976) Vindicating the public interest through the courts: a comparativist's contribution. Buffalo Law Rev 25(3):643–690

Cappelletti M (1993) Alternative dispute resolution processes within the framework of the world-wide access to-justice movement. Mod Law Rev 56(3):282–296

Chiovenda (1903) L'azione nel sistema dei diritti. Zanichelli, Bologna

Consolo C (2020) L'azione di classe, trifasica, infine inserita nel cpc. Riv dir proc:714–751

Cudia C (2012) Gli interessi plurisoggettivi tra diritto e processo amministrativo. Maggioli, Rimini

De Dominicis F (2025) Un breve raffronto tra la Direttiva 2020/1828 (UE) e il d.lgs. 23 marzo 2023, n. 28: considerazioni in punto di attuazione. In: Randazzo B, Henke A, Voet S (eds) L'azione di classe italiana nel quadro europeo: profili sostanziali e processuali. Giappichelli, Torino

Delledonne G (2017) L'omogeneità costituzionale negli ordinamenti compositi. Editoriale Scientifica, Napoli

Donzelli R (2019) L'ambito di applicazione e la legittimazione ad agire. In: Sassani B (ed) Class action. Commento sistematico alla legge 12 aprile 2019, n. 31. Pacini Editore Srl, Pisa

Elia L (1992) Le norme sulle formazioni sociali nella Costituzione repubblicana. In: Various Authors (ed) Studi in onore di G. Vignocchi. Mucchi, Modena, pp 545–553
Fidone G, Maltoni A (2025) L'azione per l'efficienza delle amministrazioni e dei concessionari pubblici, 2024. In: Henke A, Randazzo B, Voet S (eds) L'azione di classe italiana nel quadro europeo: profili sostanziali e processuali. Giappichelli, Torino
Filippi S (2023) Gli ancora incerti contorni dell'omogeneità nella giurisprudenza costituzionale recente sul decreto-legge. ConsultaOnline 2:380
Gastaldo V (2016) La "Class action" amministrativa: uno strumento attualmente poco efficace. Federalismi.it 10:20
Gidi A (1995) Coisa julgada e litispendência em ações coletivas. Saraiva
Giussani A (2019) La riforma dell'azione di classe. Riv dir proc 6:1574
Giussani A (2020) Diritti omogenei e omogeneizzati nell'azione di classe. Riv dir proc:359
Giussani A (2025) Un breve raffronto tra la Direttiva 2020/1828 (UE) e il d.lgs. 23 marzo 2023, n. 28: considerazioni in punto di attuazione. In: Randazzo B, Henke A, Voet S (eds) L'azione di classe italiana nel quadro europeo: profili sostanziali e processuali. Giappichelli, Torino
Greco G, Cafagno M, Galetta DU, Ramajoli M, Sica M (2021) Argomenti di diritto amministrativo, 4th edn. Giuffrè, Milano
Hemker-Smith CE (1976) Consumer class actions in California: a practical approach to the problem of notice. Pac Law J 7:811
Homburger A (1974) Private suits in the public interest in the United States of America. Buffalo Law Rev 23:343
Issacharoff S (2012) Class actions and state authority. Loyola Univ Chic Law J 44:369–390
Kalajdzic J (2013) The "illusion of compensation": Cy près distribution in Canadian Class Actions. Can Bar Rev 92(2):173
Kalajdzic J (2021) Climate change class actions in Canada. Supreme Court Law Rev 100(2):52
Kramer XE, Tzankova IN (2021) From injunction and settlement to action: collective redress and funding in The Netherlands. In: Uzelac A, Voet S (eds) Class actions in Europe. Holy grail or wrong trail? Springer, Cham, pp 97–130
Lupo N (2012) L'omogeneità dei decreti-legge (e delle leggi di conversione): un nodo difficile, ma essenziale per limitare le patologie della produzione normativa. In: D'Elia G, Tiberi G, Viviani Schlein MP (eds) Scritti in memoria di Alessandra Concaro. Giuffrè, Milano
Marcus D (2014) Trans-substantivity and the processes of American Law. BYU Law Rev:1191
Menchini S, Motto A (2010) Art. 140 bis. www.judicium.it
Onida V (1982) Giurisdizione e giudici nella giurisprudenza della Corte costituzionale. In: Barile P, Cheli E, Grassi S (eds) Corte costituzionale e sviluppo della forma di governo in Italia. Il Mulino, Bologna, p 159
Pace A (2011) Interrogativi sulla legittimità costituzionale della nuova 'class action'. Riv Dir Proc 15:1
Pace A (2016a) Ancora sulla doverosa omogeneità del contenuto delle leggi costituzionali. Riv AIC 6:2
Pace A (2016b) I limiti alla revisione costituzionale nell'ordinamento italiano ed europeo Nomos. Le attualità del diritto 1
Patroni Griffi F (2010) Class action e ricorso per l'efficienza delle amministrazioni e dei concessionari pubblici. Federalismi.it:13
Pinelli C (2016) Oligarchie finanziarie mondiali, democrazie nazionali e la dicotomia pubblico/privato. Qualche riflessione per i giuristi. Costituzionalismo.it 1
Poli R (2012) Sulla natura e sull'oggetto dell'azione di classe. Riv dir proc 1:38
Proto Pisani A (2012) Introduzione sulla atipicità dell'azione e la strumentalità del processo. Il Foro italiano
Randazzo B (2012) Giustizia costituzionale sovranazionale: la Corte europea dei diritti dell'uomo. Giuffrè, Milano
Randazzo B (2023) Access to justice in a multilevel constitutional system, protecting human rights. Giappichelli, Torino

Reddish MH, Julian P, Zyontz S (2010) Cy pres relief and the pathologies of modern class action: a normative and empirical analysis. Fla Law Rev 62(3):620

Ruffolo U (2021) Interessi collettivi (e diffusi), azione inibitoria collettiva e "misure idonee" correttive. In: Ruffolo U (ed) Class action ed azione collettiva inibitoria. Commento sistematico alla legge 12 aprile 2019, n. 31. Giuffrè, Milano, p 7

Siclari M (2016) È possibile richiedere un referendum costituzionale parziale? Nomos. Le attualità del diritto 1

Silvestri E (2020) Nuovi orizzonti per l'azione di classe? Giustizia insieme 1299

Silvestri E (2021) Rebooting Italian class actions. In: Uzelac A, Voet S (eds) Class actions in Europe. Holy grail or wrong trail? Springer, Cham, p 201

Subrin SN (2010) The limitations of transsubstantive procedure: an essay on adjusting the 'one size fits all' assumption. Denver Univ Law Rev 87:377

Theilen JT (2021) European consensus between strategy and principle. Nomos, Baden-Baden

Tosato E (1965) Persona e bene comune nello stato contemporaneo. In: Tosato E (ed) (1989) Persona, società intermedie e Stato. Giuffrè, Milano, p 138

Uzelac A (2014) Why no class actions in Europe? A view from the side of dysfunctional justice systems. In: Hàrsagi V, Van Rhee CH (eds) Multi-party redress mechanisms in Europe: squeaking mice? Intersentia, Cambridge, pp 53–74

Voet S (2017) Where the wild things are. Reflections on the state and future of European Collective Redress. In: Keirse A, Loos MBM (eds) Ius Commune Europaeum. Intersentia, Cambridge, p 138

Part III
Collective Enforcement. Exercises of Change

Chapter 7
Case Study No. 1: Environmental 'Sacrifice-Zone' and Harmful Medical Devices—The *ILVA* and *Philips Respironics* Cases

7.1 Premise. Why Case Studies?

As anticipated above,[1] a fundamental assumption at the basis of this investigation is that only a connection with empirical reality allows for the development of a testable, relevant and valid theory.[2] Hence, the dedication of a whole Part of this work, the present one, to case studies, in order to concretely evaluate the implementation, the potential and the risks of the procedural device in question.

Through the following case studies the dynamics of class action litigation will be further understood. Concurrently, theories and ideas from the previous abstract analysis will be tested against the backdrop of concrete reality, of concrete people and of their rights enforced through the mechanisms in question.[3] For the purposes of this investigation, a *comparative multi-case study* approach has been selected.

As explained *supra*, out of the available jurisprudence, selection has moved under two directives: diversity and procedural comparativeness.

Diversity has been a guideline for choosing case studies in the sense of providing a limited, but still varied array of enforced fundamental rights, to ensure external validity:[4] *(i)* environmental harm and mass personal injuries; *(ii)* unfair working conditions; *(iii)* prisoners' and migrants' rights; *(iv)* cryptocurrencies, although in relation to specific access-to-court issues (class waivers, arbitration clauses and foreign defendants). Different rights and interests require different ways of enforcement. They present distinct features, in relation to justiciability, redressability, dimensions and commonality within a class. Different subjects—usually the public

[1] See *supra*, in Chap. 2.

[2] See Glaser and Strauss (1967).

[3] See Einsenhardt (1989).

[4] See Merriam (2002).

A. Maglica, *Collective Dimensions of Access to Justice*, European Union and its Neighbours in a Globalized World 23,
https://doi.org/10.1007/978-3-031-94522-9_7

administration or private corporations—can infringe them, with active conducts or omissions. Different remedies—at times not even judicial—may be sought by the claimants: i.e., injunctions, monetary compensation, so-called *cy-près* or 'fluid recovery' solutions, public and political attention. Evidently, these differences play a role when assessing the effectiveness of a procedural route in enforcing fundamental rights and moving social change. Hence, the necessity of taking into account different rights and circumstances for a more comprehensive assessment.

By *procedural comparativeness*, instead, a special attention to cases that have already been litigated through other procedural paths is meant, either in relation to the exact same case or through similar cases. A perfect example is the *ILVA* case, concerning the steel plant in the province of Taranto (Italy) recently labelled as a 'sacrifice zone' by the UN Special Rapporteur on Human Rights and the Environment, due to the high level of air pollution to which it exposes the local population. After being litigated at numerous stances in front of the Italian Constitutional Court, Court of Cassation, Council of State and even the European Court of Human Rights, in 2022 the case has been brought to the Court of Milan with the filing of an injunctive class action suit (and subsequently a compensatory one). Without anticipating the findings of the case study (see *infra*, paras. 3 and 4 of this chapter), this sets an ideal ground for comparative case study analysis. Furthermore, the much richer common-law experience with similar cases of local environmental pollution litigated via class actions will be taken into account (with the obvious institutional and regulatory differences with the Italian class action device, which will be adequately underscored), in order to consider possible trends and future developments.

As anticipated, apart from *(i)* environmental mass harm (including climate change) and other standardised violations of the right to health, the other case studies concern *(ii)* employment discrimination, *(iii)* unfair conditions within detention and migration centres and *(iv)* access-to-court issues via cryptocurrencies. Given the still forming case law on the matter, some of these case studies may not only concern Italian class actions. They will, also, draw from concrete cases litigated through other procedural devices to evaluate the possible use of class actions in this context. This exercise will only be possible with the invaluable assistance of, once again, the decades-long common-law class action case law on the matter, as well as that of other EU Member States that have implemented class actions under the new 'RAD' Directive.[5] Needless to state, the consideration of foreign cases will occur only by means of established regional legal scholarship.

Lastly, contaminating differences among individual cases have been considered to highlight *recurring patterns* or inevitably *unique findings* that separate the class action cases from those with other procedural devices. This analysis is conducted in a constitutional perspective, under the lens of fair trial and effective protection. While still pursuing a 'ground up' approach, a number of theoretical propositions—drawn from the study presented in the previous Part (concerned with the regulatory framework)—has been developed. They will emerge through the present Part's analysis, but also conclusively presented in the next, final, Part.

---

[5] See, *supra*, Chap. 5.

7.2 Environmental and Mass Health Injuries

That of collective environmental damage and mass harms to individuals' health is shown by the comparative experience as one of the possibly most impactful uses of the class action procedure for fundamental rights' enforcement. This kind of protection can be entailed both as a form of compensation for damages suffered and as a form of cessation and deterrence from dangerous activities. Notably, asbestos cases or cases related to defective products—usually medical or pharmaceutical—can be recalled to this regard.

For instance, the well-known *Agent Orange* litigation from the 1980s should be recalled, defined as 'perhaps the greatest Rule 23 adventure of all time, at least up to that point'.[6] The case concerned a highly toxic herbicide sprayed during the Vietnam War by US forces over Vietnam, Cambodia and Laos from 1961 until 1971, seriously affecting, immediately and long-term, the health of millions of people, including several US and foreign soldiers. The damage suffered from the inhalation of even a few minutes of such a herbicide—if not by eating food cultivated or animals living in the area where it was sprayed—was various and extensive: from short-term 'darkening of the skin, liver problems and severe acne-like skin disease' to 'type 2 diabetes, immune system dysfunction, nerve disorders, muscular dysfunction, hormone disruption and heart disease'.[7] In different cases, it could lead, and unfortunately led, to death. Moreover, its dangerous dioxin favoured miscarriages and several other diseases on developing fetuses.[8]

Stemming from it, after the successful use of the class action tool in the 1960s and 1970s mainly for civil rights litigation and for structural reform, several actions were brought in different jurisdictional avenues from the 1980s for personal mass harm cases.[9] In particular, a federal class action filed in 1979 on behalf of 2.4 million US veterans who had been exposed to the 'Agent Orange' toxic herbicide during the Vietnam War, after being certified, was settled for a record-award, at the time, of 180 million dollars.

The *judge* in this case, Judge Weinstein of the Eastern District Court of New York, was notably praised for his judicial creativity and tenacity in 'miraculously cabin[ing] the mass of 'Agent Orange' claimants into a single class suit, strong-arm[ing] a settlement and creat[ing] a bureaucracy to distribute the settlement fund to victims. As stressed by Weinstein himself, the class action device in this circumstance had the ability to avoid 'a tedium of repetition lasting well into the next century' (it was 1979).[10] In sum, the collective representative model promoted *judicial efficiency* and concrete *delivery of justice*.

---

[6] Marcus (2013), p. 646.

[7] History.com. Last update on 16 May 2019.

[8] Id.

[9] See Marcus (2013).

[10] Cappalli and Consolo (1992), p. 225. On the role of the judge, see also Chayes (1976) and *infra*, Chap. 11.

Several similar actions have been successfully brought in the common law world in relation to collective violations to the right to health from the 1980s, in *a new wave of 'mass personal injury' litigation*. They did not concern only mass harms related to environmental pollution, but also defective products, especially medical and pharmaceutical ones. Some of the most well-known cases are, for example:

> *a)* the *diethylstilbestrol (DES) litigation*, concerning a synthetic hormone designed to prevent miscarriage but causing very serious side effects in the reproductive organs of the future children (mainly female), sold from the 1940s until the early 1970s;
> *b)* the *Pfizer Heart Valve* litigation, related to a heart valve implanted in about 55.000 people around the world from 1979 to 1986 which presented a number of failures and fractures;
> *c)* the several *silicone breast implant* cases, purportedly increasing chances of several serious diseases in implanted women;
> *d)* the *Essure* litigation against Bayer, concerning a female sterilisation device which caused diseases and severe discomfort;
> *e) contaminated hemophilia blood products* cases, concerning the infection with HIV and hepatitis C of several thousands of hemophiliacs as a result of blood transfusions with a blood clotting product concentrate, sold in the 1970s and 1980s;
> *f)* the *tobacco litigation* which put pressure on the defendants, leading, *inter alia*, in 1998 to the landmark Tobacco Master Settlement Agreement (MSA) between the largest tobacco companies and the attorney generals of forty-six US States.

These cases—most of them concluded with settlements and, sometimes, with the involvement of public officials, too[11]—managed to effectively deliver redress to the millions of injured individuals. The relief obtained was both *compensatory*—often through settlement funds set up to cover medical screening and future medical costs, at times even not arisen yet—and *injunctive*. In connection to the latter, the hazardous products or conducts were taken off the market or ceased. Moreover, the astronomical costs covered by the defendant companies often raised standards of care for the future, thus creating a strong *deterrent effect* to avoid similar mass harms.

As a negative effect of the 'personal harm litigation' wave, the tendency to convey most of the compensation in the attorneys' pockets and in other administrative fees must be accounted, too. Judge Weinstein himself, in 1995, in relation to the above-mentioned *DES* cases, noted how 'Given transactional and other costs, somewhere in the order of 20 percent of each dollar paid by industry or society probably goes to the victim'. This was, and still is (see *supra* and *infra*), a strong argument against '*tort-lottery lump sum payments*'.[12]

As will be further argued, alternative dispute resolution 'fluid' arrangements *stemming* from class action suits and aiming at providing a sort of '*complete insurance policy*' should, rather, be preferred.

With these premises, the present chapter aims to focus on class litigation, under the 2019 Italian regime, relating to two cases of 'mass personal injury'. The first is the well-known *ILVA* case and concerns *environmental pollution* in the Taranto region, in the south of Italy, whereas the second is the *Philips Respironics* case, with regard to a *harmful medical device* for respiratory and sleep therapy. Both cases,

[11] See Kysar (2018), pp. 54 *et seq*, with specific regard to the tobacco litigation.

[12] Weinstein (1995), p. 4.

still partially pending and involving the claim for relief of both injunctive and compensatory nature, will be discussed below. A parallelism will be naturally drawn with the above-depicted types of litigation, the *Agent Orange* litigation in relation to the *ILVA* case and the other *defective health products* cases in relation to the *Philips Respironics* case.

7.3 The *ILVA* Case. Factual Contextualisation and Previous Litigation

As anticipated, the first case herein examined is the *ILVA* case.

ILVA is a company specialised in the production and processing of steel, firstly in the city of Genova in the beginning of the twentieth century and subsequently, since 1965, operating in the province of Taranto, too. At one point, it counted the Italian State as its main shareholder; it was then privatised and is now, since 2015, under '*extraordinary administration*' ('*amministrazione straordinaria*') due to its status of severe insolvency.

Over the years, the impact of emissions from ILVA's steel plants on the environment and on the local population have been debated extensively and object of long and harsh *legal* and *political battles*. Whereas the former have seen for several years litigation in a large number of, national and supranational, judicial fora, the latter have seen the involvement, in several stances, of the Italian Government, with purported attempts since the early 1990s to put into practice a de-pollution plan for the rehabilitation of the area, given the high risk of environmental crisis.[13]

In particular, numerous AIAs ('*Autorizzazione Integrata Ambientale*', that is 'integrated environmental authorisation' from the Environmental Ministry) and 'saving ILVA' decree-laws (repeated in time, and consequently constitutionally illegitimate, as found by the Constitutional Court itself in 2018)[14] have been proposed since 2011 to allow the continuation of the steel company's activity, judged as of '*strategic national interest*', while adopting purported measures to reduce the impact of polluting emissions on the environment and on the local population.

Despite the fact that the authorised emissions have been constantly exceeded, the administrative extensions and concessions have continued and are still continuing in the Tarantino area. This despite, *inter alia*, the UN Special Rapporteur on Human Rights and the Environment's precise and unequivocal definition of Taranto as a '*sacrifice zone*' in the world, in a recent report from 2023, due to the extremely high level of air pollution.[15]

---

[13] For a nuanced account, see Rizzo Striano (2021).

[14] Italian Constitutional Court, Judgement No. 58 from 2018.

[15] United Nations (2023) The right to a clean, healthy and sustainable environment: non-toxic environment. Report of the Special Rapporteur on the issue of human rights obligations relating to the enjoyment of a safe, clean, healthy and sustainable environment, para. 45.

It should be noted that the steel plant has for decades now compromised the residents' health and violated human rights by discharging vast volumes of toxic air pollution. Nearby inhabitants have suffered and still suffer from elevated levels of respiratory illnesses, heart disease, cancer, debilitating neurological ailments and premature mortality. For this very reason, the Genoa steel plant was closed in 2005, following court orders and agreements with the institutions, and relocated to Taranto, due to the high environmental damage and mortality rate. Some *epidemiological studies*, in fact, had shown a link between the particles emitted by the plant and the mortality rate of the population, much higher in the affected neighbourhood than that observed in other neighbourhoods of the city. Others, several scientific studies have shown a similar, if not stronger, link in the province of Taranto.[16]

Among the numerous *jurisdictional initiatives*, three call for special attention.

They are, *first*, the several *criminal, civil and administrative proceedings*, also in front of the Italian Cassation Court, which have, *inter alia*, led to the conviction of former owners and directors of the ILVA company (now Acciaerie d'Italia). Some of them are still pending. They have also seen an active role from public prosecutors and criminal judges in trying to stall the steel plants' activity—i.e., through emergency preventive confiscation, although never definitive—to protect the residents' and the workers' rights.[17]

The Government's intervention, through the means briefly depicted above, however, has until now managed to save ILVA from a full closure, that is a *ceasing* of the harmful conduct. The fact that it is the Government, entrusted with the executive power, rather than the Parliament, responsible of legislative functions, to stall the judiciary's initiative to enforce constitutionally-enshrined values raises essential questions on the separation of powers principle, too.

Moreover, despite the criminal conviction and ascertainment of the violation—in particular of the casual link between ILVA's activity and the numerous environmental, health and property (i.e., the value of the buildings) damages—safe for exceptional cases there has been no concrete *compensation*. Economic redress has indeed been sought in several stances and its legitimacy has been confirmed, *inter alia*, by the Court of Cassation.[18] The resources of the ILVA's *insolvency procedure*, still, quite brutally and simply, are declared by the extraordinary administration as not sufficient.

An additional aspect to take into account is that of accessing proceedings for single individuals. The *practical costs* may be, and are, too high for all the affected individuals to pursue damages in court, especially given the length and complexity of proceedings until now and the difficulty in establishing smooth mechanisms for compensation, even future one.

Second, there have been several proceedings in front of the *Italian Constitutional Court*, which have been taking place since 2003. None of them has managed,

[16] See Rizzo Striano (2021).

[17] Id.

[18] Id.

however, to effectively stop the steel plant's harmful activity. In 2013, in particular, the Court declared *inadmissible* the question of constitutionality raised by a criminal judge from Taranto, in the context of criminal proceedings for the extremely toxic emissions coming from the steel plant, with regard to the AIA (see *supra*) authorising ILVA to proceed with its activity and to regain possession of its property and factory, despite the ordered judicial confiscation.[19]

The criminal judge had raised doubts, *inter alia*, on the constitutional legitimacy on the merits of said decree-law with respect to the right to health and to a healthy environment, protected under Article 32 of the Italian Constitution (and, as regards the environment, since 2023, enshrined also under Article 9 of the Italian Constitution). The Italian Constitutional Court, however, replied as follows:

> The rationale of the censured regulation consists in achieving a *reasonable balance* between the fundamental rights protected by the Constitution, in particular health (Article 32 of the Constitution), from which derives the right to a *healthy environment*, and work (Article 4 of the Constitution), from which derives the constitutionally relevant interest in maintaining *employment levels* and the duty of public institutions to deploy every effort to that end.
>
> All the fundamental rights protected by the Constitution are in a relationship of mutual integration and it is therefore not possible to identify one of them as having absolute precedence over the others. Protection must always be 'systemic and not split up into a series of uncoordinated and potentially conflicting rules' (judgment no. 264 of 2012). If this were not the case, there would be the unlimited expansion of one of the rights, which would become a '*tyrant*' against the other constitutionally recognised and protected legal situations, which together constitute an expression of the dignity of the person.
>
> For the reasons set out above, it is not possible to share the assumption of the referring judge for preliminary investigations, according to which the adjective 'fundamental', contained in Article 32 of the Constitution, would reveal a 'pre-eminent character' of the right to health with respect to all the rights of the person. Nor does the definition given by this Court of the environment and health as 'primary values' (judgment no. 365 of 1993, cited by the referring court) imply a 'rigid' hierarchy between fundamental rights. The Italian Constitution, like other contemporary democratic and pluralist Constitutions, requires a continuous and reciprocal balancing of fundamental principles and rights, without any claim to absoluteness for any of them. The qualification of the values of the environment and health as 'primary' therefore means that they cannot be sacrificed to other interests, even if constitutionally protected, not that they are placed at the top of an absolute hierarchical order. The point of balance, precisely because it is dynamic and not pre-established in advance, must be assessed - by the legislature in laying down the rules and by the court of laws in its review - in accordance with criteria of *proportionality* and *reasonableness*, such as not to permit a sacrifice of their essential core.[20]

The Court, moreover, admitted that in a case of '*complete annihilation*'—as argued by the referring criminal judge from Taranto—of the right to health and to a healthy environment in favour of economic and productive interests there would indeed be a violation of Article 32 of the Constitution 'since no requirement, however constitutionally grounded, could justify the *total* impairment of health and the environment'.[21] However, the Court did not find that in the case at hand the *censured*

[19] Italian Constitutional Court, Judgement No. 85 from 2013.

[20] Id, points Nos. 9 *et seq.* of the Points of law (translated from Italian).

[21] Id.

provision—that is the authorisation to continue polluting production—*normatively* amounted to such a 'complete annihilation'.[22]

In particular, according to the Court, the path of environmental restoration and the taking into account, besides the right to health and the environment, of the *right to work*, guaranteed as well by the Constitution, from the AIA authorisation was deemed sufficient by the Court. The decision, very questionable, shed, in any case, light on a huge structural (and necessary) gap of the Italian constitutional review system: that is, the scope of the review limited to abstract *legislative acts*, not grounded to *factual* circumstances and conducts.

Subsequently, after further authorisations, a new ruling from the Constitutional Court in 2018 declared the new authorisation as constitutionally unlawful on the grounds that the authorities had ended up over-prioritising the interest of the continuation of *production activities* to the detriment of the protection of the constitutionally protected *rights to health and life*.[23] Yet, it still remained unconclusive as regards definitively stopping ILVA's harmful activity.

Third, another significant yet inconclusive step of the *ILVA* litigation saga was the application in front of the ECtHR from several residents from Taranto, in the *Cordella* case from 2019.[24] In such a case, the Strasbourg Court unanimously found a *violation* of Articles 8 and 13 of the ECHR, but also declared that the finding of an infringement is in itself sufficient to equitable satisfaction for the non-material damage suffered by the applicants. Moreover, the Italian State was to pay a mere 5.000 € to each of the *applicants* (not to all the *residents*, but just to the individual applicants in the proceedings at stake).[25] Furthermore, it dismissed the claim for equitable satisfaction. In relation to this decision two elements should be analysed.

On the one hand, there is, once again, a *clear judicial assessment* of a 'continuation of a situation of environmental pollution endangering the health of the applicants and, more generally, that of the entire population residing in the areas at risk'. The Court identifies 'the existence of a *causal link* between the productive activity of the company Ilva from Taranto and the compromised health situation'[26] and that 'Pollution has undoubtedly had a detrimental effect on the well-being of the claimants concerned'.[27] Furthermore, the Italian authorities, according to the ECtHR, 'have failed to take all the measures necessary to ensure *effective protection* of the right of the persons concerned to respect for their private life', whilst *no fair*

---

[22] Id.

[23] Italian Constitutional Court, Judgement No. 58 from 2018.

[24] ECtHR, *Cordella v. Italy*, Nos. 54414/13 and 54264/15, 2019. See the very recent ECtHR, *Cannavacciuolo and Others v. Italy*, Nos. 51567/14, 2025, too, a pilot-judgement which presents similar profiles in relation to increased rates of cancer and pollution of groundwater due to dumping and burying of waste on private land in the Campania region, affecting almost three million people living there. The Strasbourg Court unanimously found a violation of Article 2 ECHR (right to life).

[25] Id. See also Rizzo Striano (2021).

[26] Id., ECtHR, *Cordella v. Italy*, 2019, § 106 (translated from French).

[27] Id, § 107 (translated from French).

balance can be struck between any purported economic interest (e.g., economic production) and the extremely serious harm suffered by the residents of Taranto.

On the other hand, there is the inability—again, another *enforcement gap*—of the judicial authority at stake to provide *effective justice*, even in front of a blatant infringement to essential rights of a large group of people. The Strasbourg Court, in fact 'taking into account all the circumstances of the case and in particular the technical complexity of the measures necessary for the rehabilitation of the area concerned, which falls within the *competence of the domestic authorities*,' stated that 'it is *not for the Court* to address detailed recommendations with a *prescriptive content* to the Government'; rather, 'It is for the *Committee of Ministers*, acting under Article 46 of the Convention, to indicate to the respondent Government the measures which, in practical terms, must be taken by the latter in order to ensure the implementation of this judgment'.[28]

The applicants' request to apply a pilot-judgement procedure was therefore rejected. At the same time, however, after more than 5 years, the execution of the case is still pending, with ongoing supervision, as per official reports of the Department for the Execution of Judgements of the European Court of Human Rights. As a matter of fact, even the payment of the sums awarded for costs and expenses is still pending, as per the last reports.

7.4 The *ILVA* Case. Two Pending Class Actions

Shortly after the entry into force of the new trans-substantive Italian class action proceedings, in 2021, an injunctive *azione collettiva ex* Article 840-*sexiesdecies* c.p.c. was filed at the Tribunal of Milan (where the defendant company has its seat).[29] As discussed above, other proceedings had reached before other courts, even apex ones (i.e., the CJEU, the Council of State, the Court of Cassation), but all unsuccessfully.

The claimants of the injunctive class action are eleven residents from the city of Taranto, for many years (decades even) personally engaged as activists or even representatives of associations aiming at the closure of the ILVA steel plant. All of them, in different ways, with different harms, either directly or indirectly through close relatives, have been seriously affected by the defendant company's wrongful conduct.

With the class action at stake, they seek the protection of their 'right to health, to serenity and tranquillity in the conduct of their lives, as well as their right to a climate', alleging the current, malicious, continuous and no longer tolerable infringement by the defendants (ILVA and connected companies, i.e. Acciaerie d'Italia).

[28] Id, §§ 179 *et seq.* (translated from French).

[29] *Zaninelli* et al. c. *ILVA S.p.a., Acciaierie d'Italia Holding S.p.a. e Acciaierie d'Italia S.p.a.*, Tribunal of Milan, Section XV, R.G. No. 10166/2021.

The plaintiffs state, with the overwhelming support of several scientific reports and of all the previous judicial ascertainments—domestic and supranational (in particular the ECtHR judgement from 2019, commented above)—, that the pollution caused by the steel plants' emissions is exposing residents to death and severe additional diseases.

In concreto, for these reasons, they act on behalf of the approximately 300.000 residents in the Taranto area, for an order to close ILVA's activities. They seek a total closure or, in the alternative, a more limited closure aimed at decreasing in any case by at least 50% ILVA's emissions before 2026. In addition, they request that the respondents be ordered to give full effect to the measures invoked. Pursuant to Article 614-*bis* c.p.c., referred to in Article 840-*sexiesdecies* c.p.c., should the execution of the injunctive measures be delayed by the defendants, they ask that they are ordered to pay each of the applicants a 'just amount', as a measure of *indirect coercion*.

Moreover, from the outset, the plaintiffs reserved the right to institute a subsequent *compensatory class action* in order to obtain damages 'not for the personal injuries suffered individually, but for those *common* to the entire class, unjustly exposed, day after day, to the same risks as themselves'. As will be reported, the compensatory class action was indeed filed, once again in front of the Tribunal of Milan, in July 2023, three years after the injunctive one.[30]

Maintaining the focus on the injunctive *azione collettiva*, for now, it is important to note that, although the proceedings are still pending, two significant orders—of interim nature—have already been issued by the Tribunal of Milan, on the 16 September 2022.[31]

They entail, *first*, a rejection of all the defendant companies' exceptions on the inadmissibility of the application. This implies that such a rejection must be read solely with regard to the allegations and deductions related to the application, not with regard to their merits. Still, a rejection means that the collective injunctive application is deemed *admissible* by the court. The exceptions raised by ILVA and Acciaierie d'Italia, and therein rejected, were four.

(i) Regarding *jurisdiction*, the defendants argued that it pertained to the administrative judge, rather than to the ordinary one, as it concerned the non-exercise of a public power (that is the control on the respect of the AIA authorisation), as well as the overall adequacy of the AIA authorisation, that is an administrative act. This objection, however, was dismissed by the Tribunal of Milan, based on the well-established case law, recalled *supra*[32] that clearly admits the ordinary judge's jurisdiction *a)* on purported violations of administrative measures (the AIA authorisation, herein) by private individuals, under the perspective of the *injury* caused to the subjective rights of third parties and the consequences (compensatory or injunctive)

---

[30] *ILVA* case, compensatory class action still pending before the Tribunal of Milan, Section XV, R.G. No. 29261/2023, plaintiffs' application (translated from Italian).

[31] In particular, the admissibility order: *ILVA* case, Tribunal of Milan, Section XV, Order from 16 September 2022, R.G. No. 10166/2021.

[32] See *supra*, Chap. 6.

of that injury, as well as *b)* on private individuals' conduct in conformity with an administrative measure which is alleged to be unlawful and therefore susceptible to *disapplication*, once again in the perspective of the injury to the subjective rights of third parties and of the consequences (compensatory or injunctive) of such an injury.

(ii) Also *standing*, both active and passive, was contested by the defendant companies. As to the former—that is, the *legitimatio ad causam*—they argued that the plaintiff in a collective injunctive action pursuant to Article 840-*sexiesdecies* c.p.c. must be 'the holder of a subjective right concretely affected by the (necessarily unlawful) conducts alleged to be injuring the homogeneous rights held by individuals belonging to the same 'class''.[33]

The Tribunal of Milan, however, referred to the wording of the norm—'Whoever has an *interest in the issuance* of an injunction of acts and conduct'[34] (not an individual right)—to clarify that the assertion of a *concrete* and direct infringement of a subjective right of which the applicants claim to be homogeneous holders is *not* required for the injunctive class action at stake.

Rather, the reference to a '*prejudice*' in the rest of the norm, demonstrates that, to be entitled to bring an action, it is sufficient for the plaintiff to envisage 'a *present risk*—i.e. the danger of *future* damage—affecting his active subjective legal position and, like his own, also that of a plurality of other legal subjects belonging to the same 'class''.[35] Hence, the test is much more *flexible*, especially given the peculiar aim of injunctive actions to prevent *future* harm, for which the *casual link* is not yet foreseeable nor provable (thus, the explicit reference to statistical data and simple presumptions): not a concrete infringement, but a mere relevant (future) *risk*. The level of such a risk shall be addressed in the merits of the proceedings.

Moreover, in relation to a purported lack of representativeness of the class plaintiffs (a requisite under Article 840-*ter*, para 4, letter d), c.p.c. for the compensatory class action—regarding the admissibility phase), the Tribunal of Milan set a *crucial precedent*. It stated, in fact, as extensively argued *supra*, that the *admissibility* phase is not part of the injunctive *azione collettiva ex* Article 840-*sexiesdecies* c.p.c., but *merely* of the damages *azione di classe ex* Article 840-*bis* c.p.c.[36]

The Milanese judge is very clear. This interpretation is based on literal, analogical, systemic and historic/logical reasons. The result is much more flexible proceedings for the former type of procedural remedy. As shown later (in the next paragraphs—*Philips Respironics* case—and in the next chapter—*Deliveroo* injunctive class action—, ironically both in front of the Tribunal of Milan, in a different Section), this view is not yet consolidated.

---

[33] Id., Article 840-*sexiesdecies* c.p.c. (translated from Italian).

[34] Id.

[35] *ILVA* case, Tribunal of Milan, Section XV, Order from 16 September 2022, R.G. No. 10166/2021 (translated from Italian).

[36] Id. See also *supra*, Chap. 6.

(iii) The exception on the absence of *standing to be sued*, instead, will not be commented here, for a lack of relevance for the present analysis. It suffices to recall that is has been rejected, too.

(iv) The last exception from ILVA and Acciaierie d'Italia, rejected as well, instead, touched on the issue of *time*. According to the defendants, the conduct the claimants aimed to inhibit was prior to the date of entry into force of the law (May 2021). On this matter, too, we shall refer again to the reflections above,[37] on the hermeneutical issue, for the purpose of identifying the applicable discipline, of distinguishing between the types of conduct long identified by general legal theory: instant conduct, instant conduct with permanent effects and permanent conduct.

As explained therein, it is undisputed that, in the case of a *permanent violation* continuing beyond the relevant regulatory date of entry into force (May 2021, herein), the conduct in its entirety—not being divisible since it is permanent—is subject to the superseding provisions, namely here the new class action from 2019, with a general scope of application. In the case at stake, recalling the ECtHR judgement from 2019 and other previous domestic judgements, the Tribunal of Milan qualified the conduct whose inhibition was asked by the plaintiffs—that is, the exercise of the productive activity of the ILVA steel plants—as of permanent nature, rather than instantaneous with permanent effects.[38] Hence, the rejection of such an exception, too.

The *second order* from the Milanese judge concerns three questions referred to the CJEU for a *preliminary ruling*, pursuant to Article 267 TFEU.[39] According to such a tool, as is known, any court or tribunal of an EU Member State may, if it considers that a decision is necessary to enable it to give judgment, request the CJEU to give a preliminary ruling on an interpretation of the Treaties or on the validity and interpretation of acts of the institutions, bodies, offices or agencies of the Union.

All three questions, in this case, referred to the *Directive 2010/75/EU* of the European Parliament and of the Council of 24 November 2010 on industrial emissions (integrated pollution prevention and control)—in particular Recitals Nos. (4), (18), (34), (28) and (29)—, whilst the first also to the precautionary principle and the protection of human health set forth in Articles 191 TFEU. These supranational provisions enshrine environmental protection as a *fundamental objective* of EU policy, declaring that 'environmental damage should as a priority be rectified at source and that the polluter should pay'.[40]

Such questions put the ball in the CJEU's court, as regards the *merits of the case*. The Tribunal of Milan, in fact, basically asked whether the legislative and administrative acts allowing the continuation of a blatantly harmful activity, beyond EU environmental standards, as set out in the mentioned Directive, are legitimate.

---

[37] Id.

[38] Id.

[39] *ILVA* case, Tribunal of Milan, Section XV, Order from 16 September 2022, R.G. No. 10166/2021.

[40] Article 191(2) TFEU.

Specifically, it inquired whether the omitted health damage assessment ('*valutazione del danno sanitario*') for the purpose of granting the AIA authorisation and the consideration of merely one set of pollutants are in line with EU law. It also asked whether the extension of the initial deadline granted to adapt the industrial activity with sufficient environmental and health protection measures, for approximately seven and a half years and for a total duration of 11 years, is legitimate.

On the 25 June 2024 the much-awaited decision was published.[41] With it, the Grand Chamber from the Luxembourg Court sided with the class plaintiffs.

In particular, it ruled that Member States, when granting or reconsidering a permit to operate a polluting installation, pursuant to Directive 2010/75/EU, read in light of Article 191 TEU and Articles 35 and 37 CFREU, should (also) *priorly* assess—'effectively and in a timely manner'—the effects of such an activity on the environment and on human health. To this regard, *all* polluting substances which are the subject of emissions scientifically recognised as harmful, even those initially unforeseeable, should be considered for such an assessment: again, the perspective is a concrete and effective one.

The abovementioned provisions are recalled by the Court inasmuch as they set the aim of high environmental and high human health protection. In its reasoning, the Court also clearly linked the two objectives, by stressing how the latter, under the principle of sustainable development, cannot be achieved without the former. When the assessment reveals, as pointed out by the Tribunal of Milan, results 'showing the unacceptable nature of the danger to the health of a large population' exposed to the polluting emissions, 'the permit concerned must be reconsidered in a short time frame'.[42]

This interpretation lead to the conclusive reply of the Grand Chamber, which ruled that, under Article 8(2) of Directive 2010/75, national legislation which allows repeated extensions of the period granted to the operator of a polluting installation (in this case, ILVA) to comply with the protective measures should be precluded when 'serious and significant risks to the integrity of the environment and human health have been identified'. Under these circumstances, 'the operation of that installation [must] be suspended'.[43]

---

[41] See CJEU, Grand Chamber, Judgment of 25 June 2024, *Ilva and Others*, C-626/22.

[42] Id., § 104.

[43] The Court, hence, follows, the strong stance took by the Advocate General, Juliane Kokott (Opinion from 14 December 2023), in favour of the class claimants, according to whom: 'Article 11(a) of the Industrial Emissions Directive must therefore be understood to mean that all the appropriate measures must be taken to prevent or reduce recognised environmental risks from an installation. [...] Article 11(c) may nevertheless establish obligations to take protective measures going beyond the best available techniques on account of specific characteristics of the installation in question, in particular on account of on-site conditions. Under that provision, no significant pollution may be caused by the installation. If the installation causes significant pollution despite the application of the best available techniques, additional protective measures must therefore be taken to prevent that pollution. [...] Such protective measures are also to be considered appropriate within the meaning of Article 11(a), as the notion of 'significant pollution' imposes an *absolute limit* on the operation of installations. If protective measures to that effect are not possible, a permit

It is interesting to note how also the CJEU referred to the abovementioned *Cordella* judgement from the ECtHR, specific about the ILVA case, when discussing reliance on scientific studies on polluting effects. In such a way, the EU Court demonstrates an integrated and coordinating perspective with the CoE level of protection, as required under Article 52(3) CFREU. This is also rather evident from the two judgements' reasonings, in particular in the special attention which is offered by both Courts to the '*effective* [nature of the] protection' which national authorities should ensure, under their positive obligations, when controlling polluting activities from private actors.[44]

While still waiting for the decision from the Tribunal of Milan, it is evident that the judgement in question provides an extremely powerful infusion of *authority* to the local Italian judges. In light of the two European Courts' judgements a suspension of ILVA's activity—even a partial one—appears foreseeable, in what would become immediately an historic decision. Relevant considerations, in any case, in terms of evidentiary pieces and participation of the involved stakeholders (i.e., the steel plants' workers), would still be required, as argued in the following.

Concurrently, as anticipated, another *azione di classe*, a *compensatory* one, was filed in July 2023, pursuant to Article 840-*bis* c.p.c., with a first hearing in April 2024.[45]

The competent court is once again the Tribunal of Milan, section specialised in company matters.[46] With such an application, the plaintiffs, more than 100 residents from Taranto, argue that—pending the suspension of the injunctive collective action while attending the CJEU's preliminary ruling—'significant new developments' have occurred, both with regard to the increase in emissions of toxic and carcinogenic substances, and with regard to the defendant companies' actions, namely a purported application for a re-examination of the AIA authorisation for another 12 years, from which 'it is inferred that the pollution, instead of being reduced, will be further aggravated'. Their application is on behalf of all the residents from the Taranto area, 249.672 as per the last census from 2023.

---

may not be granted for the installation. [...] Human health protection therefore has particular importance, which can also justify significant economic disadvantages. [...] Irrespective of such a legislation, pollution is to be considered significant if, taking into account the circumstances of the individual case, it results in excessive harm to human health. Pollution which violates the fundamental rights of the persons concerned by causing harm to human health is always significant'.

[44] Id. In particular, see also the ECtHR in the *Cordella* Judgement, § 159, mentioned above, in relation to the violation of Article 8 ECHR: 'States have a positive obligation, particularly in the case of dangerous activities, to put in place regulations tailored to the specific characteristics of the activity in question, particularly in terms of the risk it may pose. These regulations must govern the authorisation, commissioning, operation, safety and control of the activity in question, and require all persons involved in the activity to adopt practical measures to ensure the effective protection of citizens whose lives may be endangered by the activity' (translated from French).

[45] *ILVA* case, compensatory class action still pending before the Tribunal of Milan, Section XV, R.G. No. 29261/2023.

[46] Once again Section XV, the same from the injunctive class action.

A 'parallel *deterrent function*' of the present class action for damages is hence underscored by the plaintiffs themselves, who clearly state their intention to put pressure on the 'stubborn' (*sic dixit*) defendant companies, trying to have them desist at least from their plan to increase production through anaerobic combustion of coal, 'knowing that, if they do not, they will also be called to account for the further damage resulting from the implementation of this ill-fated plan'.[47]

An interesting deterrent potential of compensatory class actions is thus presented as a secondary, *last-resort, injunctive attempt*. 'If substantive rights will not stop you, perhaps economic disincentives – since it is the economic compass to drive your actions – will', the plaintiffs, in sum, seem to say to ILVA and to the related companies.

The main legal battle, once again, will be that of *admissibility* and, in particular of *homogeneity*, given that the other possible exceptions have already in large part been rejected in the injunctive class action by the Tribunal of Milan. According to the claimants, such an issue should not be debated for long, since it has already been recognised by the Tribunal itself in one of its two orders from September 2022, when it referred to the CJEU for a preliminary ruling. In particular, the following statement from the Milanese court has been recalled:

> In the light of the foregoing, it appears that the applicants have standing to bring proceedings, since they have stated that - as a result of the polluting emissions of the ILVA plant - they are in a situation of significant risk to their health, to the tranquillity of their lives, and to their right to a climate, *a situation common to all persons residing, like them, in the municipality of Taranto*.[48]

The adjective '*common*' would, therefore, demonstrate an already ascertained 'homogeneity' of the individual rights enforced through the present class action. Nonetheless, being the order in question, from September 2022, an interim one, it holds little if any authority. It will be on the claimants, therefore, to fully demonstrate the homogeneity at stake.

They appear, in any case, conscious of a *crucial distinctive trait* within all the class members' subjective positions: that is, the different *degree of risk* based on the *distance of residence* from the steel plants. Those living closer to them, in particular those within the first 20 km radius (about 40% of the class members), in fact, present a higher occurrence of death or additional diseases connected to the inhalation of ILVA's emissions, as per the scientific reports presented.

According to the class plaintiffs, still, this differentiating element should not be accounted by the court since the workplace, schools, and, in general, every movement of Taranto's people 'in a *highly integrated urban fabric*' should be considered.[49]

---

[47] Plaintiffs' application (translated from Italian).

[48] *ILVA* case, Tribunal of Milan, Section XV, Order from 16 September 2022, R.G. No. 10166/2021 (translated from Italian).

[49] Plaintiffs' application (translated from Italian).

Hence, safe for a different opinion of the Tribunal, they do not request a differentiation in the *liquidation of damages* per each class member. The compensation they request is, therefore, based on Article 1226 of the Civil Code, pursuant to which 'if the precise amount of the damage cannot be proved, it shall be assessed by the court on an *equitable* basis'.

Interestingly, within this compensation, they ask to include also *future damages*. Such a request is based on a number of jurisprudential precedents, also from the Italian Court of Cassation, which have allowed the compensation of future injuries when there is a certainty or, alternatively, a *high degree of probability* of their occurrence, which has a 'reasonable basis in an injury that has already occurred, or in objective facts that are directly connected with the illicit conduct and represent a cause'.[50] In sum, the 'well-founded expectation',[51] according to the 'normality and regularity of the causal development' is required—and sufficient, according to said jurisprudence—to award immediate compensation for harm yet to suffer.[52]

From this point of view, a comparison with the settlement reached in the *Agent Orange* case litigation in the US and the setting up of foundations tasked with medical monitoring for future illnesses, may be relevant.

The explicit reference, under Article 840-*quinquies*, para. 4, c.p.c. to *statistical data* and *simple presumptions* 'For the purpose of establishing the liability of the defendant', appears rather welcoming towards this option. The *scientifically reported* emergence of diseases even years after the inhalation, even in future children, yet to be conceived or born, is a further element to take into account to this regard, as further elaborated in the following.

Additionally, recalling the decision from 2017 of the United Sections from the Italian Court of Cassation, which opened the door, in abstract, to *punitive damages*,[53] the class claimants seek this type of damages, too—underscoring a purported fraud from the defendant companies, as well as the seriousness of the harm caused. It seems unlikely, however, that the Court of Milan should award them, given how the same '*Sezioni Unite*' from 2017 underscored that further requirements must be met—namely typicality, foreseeability and quantitative limits, all of which currently seem lacking. Still, this request sets itself within a trend of questioning the traditional civil law conception of the damage as characterised by a merely remedial, post-factual, function, towards a more preventive, if not punitive, direction.[54] The remedies provided under Article 614-*bis* c.p.c. are indeed revealing of such a trend.

---

[50] Italian Court of Cassation, Section II, Judgement from 15 December 2021, No. 40120 (translated from Italian).

[51] Id.

[52] Tribunal of Milan, Section I civ., Judgement from 27 January 2015, recalling *ex multis*, Italian Court of Cassation, Judgements Nos. 1637/2000, 1336/1999, 495/1987 and 2302/1965 (translated from Italian).

[53] Italian Court of Cassation S.U., Judgement No. 16601 from 2017: 'It is therefore not ontologically incompatible with the Italian legal system the institution of US origin of punitive damages'.

[54] See Rordorf (2020), p. 120.

It only remains to wait for the Tribunal of Milan's decisions, which inevitably will be influenced by the CJEU Grand Chamber's preliminary ruling judgement *ex* Article 267 TFEU, delivered in June 2024.

7.5 The *Philips Respironics* Case. Factual Contextualisation

As commented above, the common law experience has shown a wide range of class actions connected to harmful products and devices, especially in the medical and pharmaceutical field. One particularly illustrative case—*Philips Respironics*, an injunctive *azione collettiva*—was decided in Italy, too, in 2023,[55] with a decision on appeal delivered recently, in January 2024.[56]

The case stems from a global alert, from June 2021, from the multinational company Philips on a 'serious accident' involving some of its medical respiratory devices, the use of which would have posed a serious health risk to patients using them for the treatment of sleep disorders and various respiratory diseases. Among the harmful consequences for the patients, cancers, lung problems and even death were accounted. According to evidence subsequently presented, however, Philips was aware of these risks since 2014, at least.

The problem, in particular, concerned the foam inside the medical devices used for sound-absorbing functions. Such a foam was made of poliurethane polyester, a material whose degradation causes the release of particles and toxic substances, which were easily inhaled or ingested by the patients using the devices, with consequent serious risks to their health. In Italy, those patients were approximately 100.000. In line with EU standards, namely Regulation 2017/745, Philips undertook to substitute, repair or, at least, recall the defective medical devices.

In Italy, this process of substitution started in December 2021 and was supposed to finish by the 31 December 2022, as per deadline set by the Italian Ministry of Health. However, after 15 months, only approximately 25% of the devices had been substituted, with previsions showing that full substitution would not be obtained before the end of 2024. Such a delay was exposing all the users of the medical device to severe health issues, since they could be unaware of the risks or, when they were aware but were provided with no alternative, they had to decide whether to undertake them or see their health deteriorate in the absence of a medical device capable to cure the illnesses that had initially brought them to buy the Philips' harmful product.

Moreover, a note from April 2022 of the President of the Italian Institute of Health, addressed to the Italian Ministry of Health, underscored the dangers stemming from the use of these medical devices, as they released carcinogenic and

[55] Tribunal of Milan, Section XIV, Order from 30 March 2023, R.G. No. 35350/2022.

[56] Court of Appeal of Milan, special business Section, Order from 29 January 2024, R.G. No. 1059/2023.

genotoxic volatile organic substances.[57] In such a note, he stated that the risk from the devices in question could be considered 'acceptable in the case of exposure for short-term use, with replacement within one year', while a longer period of use of the medical devices could not exclude 'potential unacceptable risks for human health'.

As a result, in September 2022, in the wake of foreign experiences (i.e., in the US), litigation started in Italy under the new class action regime.

7.6 The *Philips Respironics* Case Litigation

The case, as anticipated, started with an *injunctive* class action brought, once again, in front of the Tribunal of Milan in September 2022.

The class plaintiffs were two associations, *Associazione Apnoici Italiani APS* and *Adusbef APS*, acting as mandataries of a class member, a patient who was a former user of one of the harmful medical devices. Both associations were involved in the protection of patients with illnesses that required the use of the medical devices in question. Moreover, the individual patient was clearly a member of the class, since he had acquired for medical purposes one of the harmful devices in 2017 and had stopped using it in 2021, right after Philips' communication. When filing the suit, more than one year later, he had not received yet a substitutive device and, because of this, his health conditions were compromised.

The first-instance decision by the Tribunal of Milan in this injunctive class action was rather successful for the applicants. Their request was the issuance of an *order of cessation* of the defendant companies' violations in progress—both omissive and active—and the fulfilment of the obligations and deadlines imposed by the competent national authorities. Furthermore, the plaintiffs asked for the fixing of an appropriate *penalty in case of delay*, as well as the *publication of the order* and any other suitable measure aimed at ensuring its exact and timely implementation.

Based on '*multiple evidence*', on 30 March 2023, the court upheld the application for an injunction, by ordering the two defendant companies—Philips and Respironics—to *complete the corrective action* before 30 April 2023.[58] As a *penalty* for each day of delay, it further set a sum of 20.000 €. As further mentioned in the appeal proceedings, such payments were addressed to the *two plaintiff associations*. Finally, the Tribunal ordered, at the defendants' expenses, a publication of these decisions on their websites and on three of the most read Italian newspapers. The urgency to remove the sources of risk, identified by Philips itself, did not appear 'further procrastinable' in light of the fundamental interests at stake and of the time already elapsed, according to the first-degree judge.[59]

[57] As reported in Tribunal of Milan, Section XIV, Order from 30 March 2023, R.G. No. 35350/2022.

[58] Tribunal of Milan, Section XIV, Order from 30 March 2023, R.G. No. 35350/2022.

[59] Id.

The Court of Appeal of Milan was then seized with a complaint (‘*reclamo*’) from the defendant companies shortly after the first-instance decision. Out of the twelve reasons for complaint raised by Philips and Respironics, the Court of Appeal *partially upheld* only the last one, concerning the orders from the Tribunal of Milan.[60] Pursuant to the Court of Appeal, the deadline set by the latter—30 April 2023, set on 30 March 2023—, was excessively close. It hence allowed for two extra months, extending the deadline to 30 June 2023.

Regarding the penalty, the Court of Appeal confirmed it until its decision, on 29 January 2024.[61] For the future, it decreased it to 10.000 € for each further day of delay in completion of the corrective (i.e., substitution) measures. According to the second-instance judge, such a lower amount was justified based on the continuation of the remedial action by the defendant companies during the proceedings and the consequent reduction in the number of products to be remedied, thus finding a balance between a deterrent effect and the protection of health of the concerned individuals.

The remaining reasons for the complaint were deemed unfounded. As previously done by the first-instance Tribunal, the Court of Appeal of Milan stressed that any difficulties found by the defendant companies in providing the corrective measures in a timely fashion, even if dependent on third-parties, should be borne by them, as per EU Regulation 2017/745. Moreover, in any case, they could still substitute the defective products with those from other companies, if they truly did not have the industrial ability to do so; an ability which they had, nevertheless, demonstrated in other jurisdictions, were the corrective plan was more advanced.

Concerning the other reasons for complaint, the Court of Appeal in its decision mainly referred to the Tribunal of Milan’s previous order, which offered a preliminary *theoretical recognition* of the therein employed injunctive *azione collettiva* pursuant to Article 840-*sexiesdecies* c.p.c. and its preventive goals.

The most relevant takes from both courts’ orders, for the purposes of the present analysis, will be herein briefly mentioned.

First, like in the *ILVA* case, the *injunctive* class action is underscored as a tool ‘designed to provide protection for the goods of life that are being damaged, but which have not yet been lost’.[62] Even if the unlawful conduct is in place, it may not yet have caused any damage or, if it has, it may not yet have completely exhausted its harmful effects.

This brings a ‘*retreat of the threshold of access to judicial protection*’ to the moment preceding the occurrence of the damage, that is *before* the completion of such a damage.[63] It is, in sum, to be conceived as a means of *prevention*, through an order projected to the *future*, independent from the actual harm, but, rather, depen-

---

[60] Court of Appeal of Milan, special business Section, Order from 29 January 2024, R.G. No. 1059/2023.

[61] Id.

[62] Tribunal of Milan, Section XIV, Order from 30 March 2023, R.G. No. 35350/2022 (translated from Italian).

[63] Id.

dent from a mere wrongful act, posing a *serious risk*. As a 'restorative or reintegrative' measure, according to the Tribunal, the injunctive actions aim to re-establish an altered factual or legal situation, regardless of the damage that may have occurred.

Second, it insists on the element of *homogeneity*. The homogeneity of the interest integrates, 'a prerequisite for the individual to bring a collective injunction', according to the Tribunal of Milan in such an instance.[64] At the same time, still, it seems to read this requirement in a rather *extensive* way: 'since the injury must [...] be diffuse or collective, it is necessary that the individual's interest coincides with that of a group or class united by exposure to an identical or at least *analogous risk of harm*'.[65]

In the case at hand, the court still found the presence of homogeneity within the class. In particular, it was found in the fact that all class members had been '*equally exposed to the risk* of potential damage to health caused by the degradation of the polyurethane polyester sound-absorbing foam and the possible emission of harmful volatile particles and compounds to be inhaled during use'[66] and in their *common interest* in a timely and complete corrective action.

This occurred despite the *significantly different* types of—potential—diseases, the different illnesses as a reason for using the medical device (with consequent potentially different predispositions to certain further diseases), the different period of use of the medical device and even the different medical devices used (the case concerned more than one, all produced and commercialised by Philips and Respironics). Evidently, its interpretation of such a key concept—which, we insist, should be applied only to compensatory class actions—is a *very broad* and flexible one. This finding sets a *key precedent* for similar cases related to health injuries.

Third, the Tribunal of Milan stresses in its order the 'legislative will to regulate a streamlined procedural form *devoid of evidentiary complexity*',[67] justifying such an interpretation by recalling Article 840-*sexiesdecies*, para. 5 c.p.c., which provides the possibility for the judge to use *statistical data* and *simple presumptions*. As further argued, namely in the next c*hapter* in relation to the *Deliveroo* case (decided by the same Section of the Tribunal of Milan, Section XIV), this assumption appears questionable.

Fourth, in the case at stake, such a *lack of evidentiary complexity* was favoured by the global alert, from June 2021, of a 'serious accident', issued by Philips itself, as well as by the numerous scientific reports and statements both from Italian and foreign main institutional health authorities.

Additionally, with regard to the notion of 'serious accident' it is interesting to note that the Tribunal of Milan makes copious reference to *EU Regulation 2017/745* 'on medical devices' (namely Articles 2 and 87) for the qualification of such a concept in the field at hand and the necessary corrective actions to be expected in these

[64] Id.

[65] Id.

[66] Id.

[67] Id.

circumstances. The correctness of seeking a qualification within said EU Regulation is confirmed by the Court of Appeal in several parts of its decision, too:

> On the basis of that framework, it must be noted, as the Tribunal correctly did in the order complained of, that the health risks described in the safety warnings issued by the complainants themselves 'and the identification of possible toxic and carcinogenic effects related to the accidental inhalation or ingestion of particles and volatile organic compounds released by the deteriorating sound-absorbing foam undoubtedly fall within the concept of 'serious accident' provided by the European Union legislation, in the present case, an alteration of the characteristics of the medical devices capable of causing the death of the user or a significant deterioration, temporary or permanent, of their state of health'.
>
> Considering, therefore, that the concept of 'serious accident' is also linked to the mere injurious potentiality of the defect of the product and that such an injurious potentiality can be said to be recognised by the complainants themselves, who for that reason issued the warnings and initiated the corrective actions, the completion of which was deemed necessary by the Health Authorities of our country, the ground of complaint, aimed at claiming the non-existence of an ascertained dangerousness, is without foundation.
>
> By this ground the complainants claim, therefore, that the studies on the dangerousness of the devices are still in progress and have been entrusted to independent and authoritative subjects, contrary to what the complainants claim.[68]

A further point for consideration linked to EU Regulation 2017/745 is the fact that this regulation is explicitly mentioned in the Annex I, no. 57 of the RAD for the protection of the collective interests of *consumers*.[69] Pursuant to its Article 2, para. 1, the RAD applies to any infringement of the provisions of Union law referred to in said Annex I—hence, also those from Regulation 2017/745 on medical devices. This poses a twofold set of reflections.

On the one hand, it underscores the significance, and urgency, of coordinating the Italian *consumer-focused class action regime from 2023* (which implemented EU Directive 2020/1828, and which, hence, *in abstracto*, could have been used for the present case, too)[70] with the regime from 2019 from the Italian Code of civil procedure (with a general scope of application, and which was indeed used in the present case, *in concreto*). The scarce utility of such a procedural instrument (the one from 2023, consumer-limited), if not bearing the aim of generating further complexity and confusion in the Italian legal order, has already been pointed out. Its domestic implementation is sincerely difficult to understand.

On the other hand, such a final element for consideration recalls once again the question of what it really means to be a *consumer,* or a *user*, in the currently global and extremely interconnected reality. Reference to *Part I* of this work is thus appropriate.[71]

---

[68] Court of Appeal of Milan, special business Section, Order from 29 January 2024, R.G. No. 1059/2023 (translated from Italian).

[69] See, *supra*, Chap. 5.

[70] See, *supra*, Chap. 6.

[71] See, in particular, *supra*, Chap. 2.

Last, it must be accounted that in June 2024 a *compensatory class action* was filed on the same case, between the same parties.[72] Three categories, or *sub-classes*, of individuals were identified by the plaintiffs: those who have been exposed to the risk and may contract related diseases in the future; those who have already suffered a personal harm to their health as a consequence of the defective device; the family members of those who have died as a consequence of the related injuries.

The damage sought is both pecuniary and non-pecuniary.

In relation to the former, it is interesting to note the numerous references from the Italian class plaintiffs to the settlement agreement reached in the US within a class action about the same medical device. This is done to show the manageability of *collective* evidence-collection and liquidation, in a case where multiple and diverse types of diseases may arise, with the necessity hence to prove the causality link for each adherent. The solution proposed—convincingly, it seems—is that of working closely with *technical (medical) experts* and of presuming the causality link upon occurrence of a twofold circumstance: the prior use of the defective product, on the one hand, and the verification of an injury previously-determined as 'qualifying', on the other hand, due to the enhanced risk of its verification brough by the usage of the medical device in question. A scale of severity from one to five, based on the different harm, is then proposed in order to further sub-categorise the class and allow an 'homogenisation' of its members' subjective positions.[73]

As to non-pecuniary damage, instead, previous reflections in connection with the key Cassation '*Trenord*' case from 2019 should be recalled.[74] Furthermore, jurisprudential elaborations from the Italian Constitutional and Cassation Courts, as well as from the CJEU and ECtHR, are stressed in order to legitimise the compensability of all non-pecuniary consequences in relation to fundamental rights, such as the right to health or that to life, including that of a loved one.

Such a choice to bring a damages class action after the injunctive one follows *strategic trends* from foreign jurisdictions related to the same mass harm, which have already reached (partial) settlements of several hundred million dollars.[75] The case, nonetheless, is still pending.

---

[72] Tribunal of Milan, Section XIV, compensatory class action, pending, R.G. No. 23551/2024.

[73] See, *supra*, Chap. 6.

[74] See, *supra*, Chap. 6.

[75] In the US, for instance, a class action lawsuit against Philips was partially settled for 479 million dollars in September 2023, only as a coverage of monetary reimbursements to device users and sellers who might have anticipated a replacement to their clients. Furthermore, this amount is uncapped, meaning that it could (will) increase based on future adhesions. See, e.g., New York Times, 7 September 2023.

7.7 Lessons and Open Questions

Neither of the two Italian cases related to mass environmental and personal harms—*ILVA* and *Philips Respironics*—has completely ended. However, significant trends already emerge from the four judicial orders delivered so far, incidentally all by the Tribunal of Milan and its Court of Appeal. The reason for such a concentration of cases in Lombardy's regional capital is, as already addressed, the provision(s) establishing jurisdictional competence in the section specialised in company matters of the place where the defendant has its seat, pursuant to Article 840-*ter*, para. 1, c.p.c. and Article 840-*sexiesdecies*, para. 3, c.p.c., which in most cases—at least for large corporations—tends to be Milan.

The elements to highlight under the present analysis are the following.

(i) In the words of the Tribunal of Milan in the *Philips Respironics* case, the injunctive class action *ex* Article 840-*sexiesdecies* c.p.c., in respect to the damages class action *ex* Articles 840-*bis et seq.* c.p.c, constitutes a '*retreat of the threshold of access to judicial protection*' in a perspective which is *temporal* but also, we may add, strictly *regulatory*—in the sense that lower standards for its admissibility are required.

The *temporal* aspect has already been extensively commented as an anticipation of the moment considered: not necessarily the total completion and *effective* occurrence of a harm, but merely a (present) *serious risk* of such a(n even future) harm: in sum, a *prejudice*. On this stance, the courts in both cases agree.

As a consequence, they also agree on the latter—a lower *regulatory* threshold—aspect; this is almost by default, given that no causal link nor a concrete damage needs to be proved, in contrast with the compensatory *azione di classe ex* Article 840-*bis* c.p.c. However, as commented under the next point, a different view is given on the extension of the *admissibility* requirements set under Article 840-*ter* c.p.c. for the compensatory class action.

(ii) Section XV of the Tribunal of Milan, in the *ILVA* case, in fact, is quite explicit in stating that the *admissibility phase* regulated under Article 840-*ter* c.p.c. is *not* required for the injunctive *azione collettiva ex* Article 840-*sexiesdecies* c.p.c., but *merely* for the damages *azione di classe ex* Article 840-*bis* c.p.c. This procedural stage, as is known, encompasses several requirements, among which the 'homogeneity of individual rights'.

Section XIV of the same Tribunal, in the *Philips Respironics* case (as well as in the *Deliveroo* case, see *infra*—next Chapter), instead, conceives the presence of homogeneous individual rights as a requisite, 'certainly' (*sic dixit*), of the former—injunctive—procedural remedy, too.[76] As further argued *infra*, concerning the *Deliveroo* case, this view appears questionable. The different approach followed by the different judges—in this circumstance, even from the same Tribunal—appears rather confusing.

---

[76] Tribunal of Milan, Section XIV, Order from 30 March 2023, R.G. No. 35350/2022.

Conversely, as already underscored, it must be noted that the Tribunal of Milan's interpretation of such a requirement in the *Philips Respironics* injunctive class action is, in any case, very *broad*. Beyond the formal qualification attributed in each case, the interpretation largely coincides with that from the above-mentioned ILVA injunctive class action, where the court referred to a '*common* situation'.

Paradoxically, by qualifying such a commonality of circumstances as homogeneous, the Tribunal of Milan in the *Philips Respironics* injunctive class action exposes itself to having to accept the verification of such a test almost by default in a hypothetical subsequent *compensatory* class action, pursuant to Articles 840-*bis et seq*. c.p.c.

What appears more problematic, in any case, as will be further argued, is the '*individuality*' requirement (as in 'homogeneous individual rights'). In fact, this would exclude in principle the possibility of seeking protection via the injunctive class action of *supra-individual* positions, too: e.g., in relation to climate change or the environment, which cannot be linked to an individual holder as they are '*essentially* [*ab origine*] *collective*'.[77]

(iii) This latter reasoning paves the way to what appears as a possible consolidating *strategical trend* on the plaintiffs' side: that is, to start injunctive proceedings, as a first litigation step, and proceed with the compensatory ones only at a subsequent time. This could occur since the latter ones are more onerous, not only from a 'threshold of access to judicial protection' standpoint (see *supra*, point *(i)*), but also from an economic, temporal and organisational perspective.

(iv) Such a lower—regulatory—threshold for the injunctive remedy is deemed by Section XIV of the Milanese Tribunal, from the *Philips Respironics* and the *Deliveroo* (see *infra*, next chapter) cases, as a reason for admitting only cases with a 'lack of evidentiary complexity'. Again, Section XV of the same Tribunal, in the *ILVA* case does *not* embrace—at least explicitly—such an opinion.

This is clearly visible from the reference both sections make to the possibility of using *statistical data* and *simple presumptions*, under the new regime: according to the *former* Section XIV, this possibility underscores the '*simple*' (*sic dixit*)[78] evidentiary nature of the collective proceedings at stake; pursuant to the *latter* section XV—herein supported—such a possibility merely prefigurates a more *flexible* approach when considering the existence of a causal link between conduct and harm (even future ones). In no way should this theoretical construction become a hindrance to the admission of cases that are too complex, from an evidentiary standpoint; if anything, the opposite.[79]

(v) A related aspect on which both sections of the Tribunal of Milan seem to find agreement is the *recurring reference* to other normative—hard and soft law—and judicial sources. In particular, a strong attention to the *EU legal order* must be fundamentally underscored, i.e. by the explicit use of Directive 2010/75/EU of the

[77] See, *supra*, Chaps. 4 and 6.

[78] Tribunal of Milan, Section XIV, Order from 30 March 2023, R.G. No. 35350/2022.

[79] See, *supra*, Chap. 6 and, *infra*, Chap. 11.

European Parliament and of the Council of 24 November 2010 on industrial emissions (integrated pollution prevention and control) and EU Regulation 2017/745 'on medical devices'. In the former case the request by the Milanese Court to the CJEU to give a preliminary ruling pursuant to Article 267 TFEU is especially significative.

The proposed reading of such an—undisputable—*trend*, further developed in the conclusive chapter of this research, stems from the perception—which is also a self-perception, by the Tribunal itself—that a *first-instance* Tribunal may be lacking the necessary (democratic) *authority* to give a decision of such a magnitude, both from an economic and social perspective. Even the injunctive action can have disruptive consequences for a corporation and all of its workers and investors, at times even more than a compensatory one. The examples of ILVA—whose economic continuation, which could be completely and forever stalled, has been deemed 'strategic' by the Italian government itself—or of Philips—which has been ordered to pay 20.000 € per day until it completes its corrective plan—are quite illustrative.

In this sense, as further argued, its own deficiencies in *democratic authority* can be filled by the authority that descends from the supranational legislators and apex courts. These references, of course, tie in with the internal constitutional order—in the Italian case under Articles 117, 10 and 11 of the Italian Constitution, which 'open' the domestic legal system to the rules of international law. On the delicate (yet key) issue of the 'functional splitting' of the democratic machinery[80] mention should be made to reflections from Part I.[81]

This *modus operandi* does not limit itself to the EU legal order. Rather, especially for matters that do not fall within EU competence, it can be carried out by directing to the CoE system and, to a lesser extent, by comparative references. This can be seen, for instance, in the numerous references by the applicants and by the Tribunal itself in the *ILVA* case to the ECtHR *Cordella* judgment from 2019 and, during the oral discussions, to the recent and successful Dutch injunctive class actions *Urgenda v. the Netherlands* and *Milieudefensie v. Royal Dutch Shell*, respectively from 2019 and 2021, through which the plaintiffs obtained an order (directed, in the former case, to the State and, in the latter, to a major corporation) to significantly reduce carbon emissions.[82] Similar references can be found in the recent *Philips Respironics* compensatory class action with regard to the US settlements.

(vi) It has been recalled that Philips, in the *Philips Respironics* injunctive *azione collettiva*, has been ordered to pay a penalty (pursuant to Article 614-*bis* c.p.c., referred to by Article 840-*sexiesdecies* c.p.c.) of 20.000 € for each day of delay from 30 April 2023 until 29 January 2024, and 10.000 € from 30 January 2024 until it completes its corrective plan. This sum, acceptable whether considered daily, becomes much more relevant in the larger perspective, as underscored by Philips

[80] Elia (1982), p. 517.

[81] See, in particular, *supra*, Chap. 3.

[82] *Urgenda Foundation* v. *State of the Netherlands*, [2015] C/09/00456689; *Milieudefensie et al* v. *Royal Dutch Shell*, [2021] C/09/571932.

and Respironics in their complaint. A rough estimate, in fact, reveals that the defendant companies have already paid 5.480.000 € until 29 January 2024 and, since then, approximately 300.000 € per month.

To this regard, *first*, once again the significative potential *economic consequences* of the injunctive class action, too, must be noted.

Second, the issue of *who* is entitled to *receive* these sums is extremely relevant, and until now—it seems—scarcely addressed. The order of the Court of Appeal of Milan seems to show that they are to be paid to the associations who filed the claim as mandataries of a class member.[83]

On the one hand, doubts arise whether, since they were acting as his *mandataries*, it should not be the class member himself to collect these sums.

On the other hand, a significant question of legitimacy—*in primis* on constitutional grounds—surfaces vehemently: that is, whether a single *individual* member of the class is entitled to receive a sum which is due to a delay affecting the *whole class*, rather than just himself (or herself). What is more, as in the case at hand, it is possible for said single individual to receive, at a certain point, the (individual) *redress sought* for the harm suffered, which *ab origine* gave rise to the injunction order and related penalty: namely, in the *Philips Respironics* case, a substitution of the harmful medical device; hence, losing any direct interest in the injunctive suit.

The fact that an *association* collects the sums rather than a single individual member of the class may appear more in line with the constitutional *dictum* (i.e., with regard to the rationality and equality principles, under Article 3 It. Const., in connection to the pluralist principle under Article 2 It. Const.). This would occur especially when, pursuant to Article 840-*ter*, para. 4, letter d) c.p.c., the court has verified that they are 'able to adequately address the homogeneous individual rights asserted in the case'.

However, this requirement pertains to the *admissibility phase* and, as such, it is uncertain whether it relates at all to the injunctive *azione collettiva*, as extensively argued until now. Thus, the absence—at least pursuant to the current regulatory regime—of a *procedural requirement* pursuant to which the judge checks the *adequacy* of the receiver of the penalty payment, which can become rather significant, as the *Philips Respironics* case shows. The shadow of 'buccaneering' class actions[84]

---

[83] And, in fact, they have been. A different approach can be found under Article 140-*terdecies* cod. cons, regulating the 2023 consumer-limited class action, pursuant to which 'the court shall fix a time limit for the fulfilment of the established obligations and, also at the request of the party that has brought the action, orders, in the event of non-compliance, the payment of a sum of money ranging from 1000 euro to 5000 euro for each non-performance or day of delay in relation to the gravity and duration of the non-performance. These sums shall be paid to a specific chapter of the revenue of the State budget to be reallocated to the extent of 50 per cent per cent to the Ministry of Justice for the strengthening of offices and other institutional services and for the remaining 50 per cent per cent to the Ministry of Enterprise and Made in Italy for the improvement of the activities of the section established by Article 140-quinquies' (translated from Italian). See, applying this norm, e.g., Tribunal of Bolzano, Judgement from 31 October 2024, No. 3484/2023.

[84] See, *supra*, Chap. 5.

lingers against the backdrop of these, as well as subsequent, reflections on the Canadian system's cy-près distribution technique,[85] in relation to the *Brazeau* case.

Moreover, it is not really clear how these funds will be managed by the associations in question, nor whether a control on any management will be conducted and by whom.

Third, as is known, Article 840-*novies* c.p.c. innovatively sets a series of 'rewards', or *contingency fees*, calculated on a proportional basis for the plaintiff attorneys in case of successful outcome of the *compensatory azione di classe* under Articles 840-*bis et seq.* c.p.c. Following the same rationale, under Article 3 It. Const., it appears at the very least questionable that a similar occurrence is not provided for the *penalties* in injunctive class actions.

(vii) The last element to underscore from these two Italian class action cases is not intrinsic to the judicial proceedings or orders *per se*. Rather, it regards the publication of said orders on the *official ministerial portal*, a publication currently lacking. As stressed above,[86] this practice from the court registry offices is by all means *contra legem* (and *costitutionem*) and inconsistent with that from other Tribunals (i.e., that of Rome—whilst that of Turin, in at least one case, seems to follow the—incorrect—Milanese example).

Furthermore, it is fundamentally against the rationale of the reform and the desirable goal of sharing the outcome (and reasoning) of a *collective* case with all the concerned group, rather than the mere parties.[87] The final *una tantum* publication of the mere ruling (*sensu stricto*, not the full order, with the reasoning) on three newspapers is by no means sufficient to compensate such a crucial, permanent, shortcoming.

References

Cappalli R, Consolo C (1992) Class actions for Continental Europe? A preliminary inquiry. Temple Int Comp Law J 6(2):217–292

Chayes A (1976) The role of the judge in public law regulation. Harv Law Rev 89:1281–1316

Einsenhardt KM (1989) Building theories from case study research. Acad Manag Rev 14(4):532

Elia L (1982) La Corte nel quadro dei poteri costituzionali. In: Barile P, Cheli E, Grassi S (eds) Corte costituzionale e sviluppo della forma di governo in Italia. Il Mulino, Bologna, pp 515–536

Glaser BG, Strauss AL (1967) The discovery of grounded theory: strategies for qualitative research. Aldine Transactions, New Brunswick

Kalajdzic J (2021) Climate change class actions in Canada. Supreme Court Law Rev 100(2):31–58

Kysar D (2018) The public life of private law: tort law as a risk regulation mechanism. Eur J Risk Regul 9:48–65

---

[85] See, *supra*, Chap. 9. See, also *supra*, Chap. 6, and, *infra*, Chap. 11. See also Kalajdzic (2021), especially pp. 52 *et seq.*

[86] See, *supra*, Chap. 6.

[87] It is fairly obvious, but it may be worth stressing that—given the complexity and novelty of the new instrument—it could be (extremely) useful also for attorneys, and the uniform development of future case law.

Marcus D (2013) The history of modern class action, part I: Sturm Und Drang, 1953-1980. Wash Univ Law Rev 90:587–652

Merriam S (ed) (2002) Qualitative research in practice: examples for discussion and analysis. Jossey-Bass, Hoboken

Rizzo Striano M (2021) ILVA, lavoro e bugie contro salute e verità. Altrimedia, Matera

Rordorf R (2020) Magistratura, giustizia, società. Cacucci Editore, Bari

United Nations (2023) The right to a clean, healthy and sustainable environment: non-toxic environment. Report of the Special Rapporteur on the issue of human rights obligations relating to the enjoyment of a safe, clean, healthy and sustainable environment, para. 45.

Weinstein J (1995) Individual justice in mass tort litigation: the effect of class actions, consolidation, and other multiparty devices. Northwestern University Press, Evanston, e-book

Chapter 8
Case Study No. 2: Food-Delivery Riders and Fair Working Conditions—The *Deliveroo* and *Uber Eats* Cases

8.1 Premise. Employment Class Actions

As anticipated, at least six class actions[1] have already been brought in Italy under the new dual general regime from 2019, in force since 19 May 2021, for the protection of workers' rights. Four of them are injunctive *azioni collettive ex* Article 840-*sexiesdecies* c.p.c., whereas two, the most recent and still pending, are a compensatory *azione di classe ex* Article 840-*bis* c.p.c. Out of six, in chronological order of filing of the claims, one has been extinguished due to the subsequent cessation of the matter in dispute (otherwise, it would have been declared inadmissible), one has been rejected, one has been declared inadmissible, one has been settled and the last two (compensatory) are still pending.

At first glance, the count does not appear favourable to plaintiffs. Still, there are numerous points for reflection; first and foremost, the *non-trivial number* of actions involved, and, in any case, the fact that such a number is progressively growing in this specific sector of law. Under this perspective, the US trend of civil rights class actions against employment discrimination, highlighted above,[2] promises to be resumed on the other side of the Atlantic.

In addition, it is worth mentioning the expectable *adaptation time* for the host (legal) system to gradually incorporate the new model, like in any type of transplant, a legal one in this case. On the one hand, in fact, *attorneys* must get used to the new procedural instrument: hence, the wait for the first damages suit, more complex and probably for this reason only recently proposed and still pending; similarly, this could explain the possible declarations of inadmissibility or extinction. On the other hand, the *courts* themselves have to adjust to the new collective procedural context

[1] See, *supra*, Chap. 6. See also, *infra*, Figures.

[2] See, *supra*, Chap. 5.

A. Maglica, *Collective Dimensions of Access to Justice*, European Union and its Neighbours in a Globalized World 23,
https://doi.org/10.1007/978-3-031-94522-9_8

and learn how to cope with the new collective mechanisms and their regulatory and interpretative nuances. As further explained, this has given rise to questionable takes.

This Chapter will concentrate in particular on the *food-delivery riders* class actions that have been filed in Italy: for unfair working conditions (an *injunctive* action declared inadmissible) and for the unfair termination of their employment relationship (a *compensatory* one, still pending). A third injunctive *azione collettiva*, against ITA Airways, declared inadmissible, will be taken into account when relevant, too, although not central to the present analysis.

The extinguished injunctive action, against the Municipality of Rome, or the settled one, in relation to private security workers, instead, will not be discussed here as they have not entered the merits of the discussion as regards workers' rights. The former one, against the Municipality of Rome, is in any case very relevant from a passive standing perspective, as mentioned *above*.[3]

8.2 The *Deliveroo* and *Uber Eats* Cases. Factual Contextualisation

The first case, the *Deliveroo* case, was brought in representation of 8.000 food-delivery riders from Deliveroo Italy srl, a company leader in the meal delivery service (MDS) in Italy since late 2015. As is known, Italy saw in recent years, an exponential increase of demand of MDS services, globally boosted, among other factors, by the 2020 pandemic.

Last counts mention over 60.000 riders in the whole country, in charge of delivering food supplies all over Italian cities directly to the home or office of clients who ordered through a mobile application. Riders often move with (usually personal) electronic bikes, through traffic, and with high speed, as their performances are ranked by algorithms, based on criteria of efficiency—that is number of deliveries and speed of delivery—, with a tendency to exclude the least performing, according to a highly competitive logic. Such an organisation increases the pressure on workers and has been widely criticised as discriminating and a cause of road accidents.

This form of work generated from the beginning great controversy and legal mobilisation, increasingly since 2019. In particular, the most sensitive elements for discussion were the lack of any kind of guarantee for the riders.

Often migrants, although legally residents, were paid extremely low wages based on piecework, and they were usually tied to companies through an occasional self-employment relationship that did not provide any coverage for fiscal contributions, holidays, sickness, incidents or any other form of protection.

After a series of road accidents in 2019 which caused the death of riders, investigations from public prosecutors started in several Italian cities. Individual actions to demonstrate that they were not in fact self-employed workers ('*lavoratori*

[3] See, *supra*, Chap. 6.

autonomi'), but, rather, employed workers ('*lavoratori subordinati*') were filed, too. Notably, the Italian Court of Cassation in 2020 recognised hetero-organisation in this type of work relationship, classifying it as subordinate employment.[4] Hence the need to apply all the health and safety provisions of subordinate employment to riders.

At the same time, also in 2020, negotiations were held by the most representative labour unions in Italy with the employers' association, Assodelivery, to which all the main MDS companies belong, for the conclusion of a national collective agreement (CCNL) on riders, at the invitation of the Ministry of Labour. However—and this is where the present lawsuit arises from—, rather unexpectedly and while negotiations were pending, in September 2020 the same employers' association, Assodelivery, entered into an agreement with a newly formed association, purportedly representing the riders, called Ugl Rider.

The agreement with this interlocutor, later defined by the courts as an interlocutor '*of convenience*', took place without any verification by Assodelivery of its representativeness. The agreement was reached within a few days, without prior participation or any kind of involvement of the workers nor of the historic and fully representative labour unions, previously involved in the negotiations. It was criticised by, among others, the Ministry of Labour itself.

Among the unfavourable conditions provided for by this CCNL 'of convenience' were the non-recognition of paid holidays, of weekly rest periods, of paid leave, as well as the determination of hourly wages significantly lower than those provided for by the CCNLs of similar sectors signed by the most representative trade unions (e.g., CCNL Logistics or CCNL Tertiary Sector). This evidently hindered the rights, constitutionally enshrined (e.g., Article 36 of the Italian Constitution, but also Article 3 It. Const.), of the MDS riders.

Deliveroo Italy, together with other (but not all) companies from Assodelivery, nonetheless, started to apply said CCNL to its workers. In particular, it was noted that it pushed them to accept under threat of non-prosecution of the work relationship. Several protests and critiques from academia, from the Minister of Labour and from the most representative labour unions were constantly registered on the *lack of representativeness* of the association UGL Rider, which appeared to have been set up on purpose for that agreement and which had met most of the Assodelivery demands, leaving those of the riders mainly unattended.

In the subsequent months, several judicial decisions upheld the claims for anti-union conduct brought by trade unions and considered not effective said CCNL in individual disputes brought by individual riders before them. In particular, the Tribunal of Bologna in June 2021 found and declared the unlawfulness of the application of said CCNL to riders by Deliveroo Italy and *ordered it to refrain* from applying said agreement to its riders. It also ascertained and declared the discriminatory and anti-union character of the reasons referred to by Deliveroo Italy for the

[4] Italian Court of Cassation, labour Section, Judgement from 24 January 2020, No. 1663.

termination of the employment relation of the *single* rider who had brought, *individually*, the case before the court.

Still, despite other similar decisions in *individual* cases, Deliveroo Italy continued to apply said CCNL and its unfair conditions to the rest of its approximately 8.000 riders throughout all Italy. As a consequence, the first case at hand, an *injunctive azione collettiva* was brought in 2021, right after the entry into force of the new 2019 regime, against Deliveroo, in front of the Tribunal of Milan, to forbid the application of said CCNL, signed by Assodelivery and UGL Riders, towards all the riders of the MDS company. The action at hand was brought by an individual rider, hence a natural person member of the class, with the support of several labour unions, acting as his mandataries (not UGL Riders, but others, more representative ones, such as CIGL).

The second case considered, the *Uber Eats* case, instead, is a *compensatory* class action. It is a collective suit once again in the MDS sector, but this time against another company, Uber Eats Italy s.r.l., also a member of Assodelivery and employing around 4.000 riders, in about sixty Italian cities. The case has been brought in late December 2023, and it is currently, after the first hearing, pending a decision on admissibility. It stems from the sudden termination by Uber Eats Italy of the work relationship in June 2023 with all its riders. After seven years (since 2016) on the Italian market, in fact, the multinational company deemed the market insufficiently profitable and abruptly decided to cease all delivery activities in the country. The riders were given a mere one-month notification, after which they could no longer access the delivery application and, hence, continue, to work.

According to the data subsequently provided by Uber Eats Italy itself to the labour unions, 95,82% of its network of riders had carried out an average of 466 deliveries (that is 40 h/month, with peaks in almost 14,65% of the cases of 66 h/month) in the last 6 years of activity. The average monthly earnings for the 95,82% of the riders were € 549,83.[5]

No compensation was given by their former employer, despite the existence of a personal, continuous and coordinated form of work and despite the fact that Assodelivery itself, on behalf of its member companies (hence also Uber Eats Italy), had signed agreements with the most representative labour unions (with CGIL, in this case, contrarily to the previous CCNL agreement, which had been signed with the 'convenient' UGL Riders). Such agreements regulated working conditions with a view to combating digital *caporalato* and imposed information flows to the CGIL. They also set a specific obligation on riders to refrain from using third-party companies for the delivery of orders, recognising to the CGIL a specific action to protect riders through anonymous reporting mechanisms.

In September 2023, for these reasons, the Tribunal of Milan (labour section), on the basis of Article 28 of the Italian Workers' Statute, upheld the complaint for anti-union conduct of Uber Eats Italy, filed by trade union organisations, acting as

[5] As per plaintiffs' application.

mandataries.[6] Uber Eats Italy's decision to cease operations in Italy and to terminate the employment relationships of its 4.000 riders was declared unlawful for failure to activate the information and consultation procedures provided by the legislation (namely law no. 223/91, Article 1, paras. 224–236, and Law No. 234/21, Article 24).[7]

Moreover, the Tribunal of Milan ordered to Uber Eats, on this occasion, to revoke the terminations of its 4.000 employment relationships from June 2023, as they were implemented in breach of such a consultation, ordering the riders' reinstatement, as well as to initiate the prescribed comparative procedures with the labour unions before taking any unilateral initiative.

All the riders, subsequently, received the 'revocation' of the termination from Uber Eats Italy. Still, the revocation was merely formal since riders were not enabled by the MDS company to connect to its application platform and receive delivery offers. Hence, since the 15 July 2023, notwithstanding the formal revocation of the termination, the riders have not received any remuneration from Uber Eats Italy nor has any process of consultation concretely started.

On these bases, the class action at hand was filed, once again in front of the Tribunal of Milan (*company matters* section), by individual riders acting through the labour unions, as their mandataries. With such a collective suit, they seek an order against Uber Eats Italy to pay *damages* equal to the lost remuneration, to be determined *ex aequo*, in light of the average monthly remuneration and of the equiparable CCNL for commerce or logistics (given the current lack of a specific 'riders CCNL', see *supra*).

It is worth highlighting that both suits—*Deliveroo* and *Uber Eats*—follow in the wake of a global trend of class litigation in the food delivery sector, especially in common law jurisdictions (US, Canada and Australia), with very similar claims.

---

[6] Article 28 of the Workers' Statute has long been recognised as one of the first collective injunctive mechanisms in the Italian legal order, albeit limited to such a very specific field and type of relief. For further insights, see, e.g., D'Onghia and Recchia (2023). See also Italian Court of Cassation, S.U., Judgement from 12 June 1997, No. 5295, stressing how for such a procedure the 'intentional element' of the employer is irrelevant, as the judge must assess whether the employer's conduct was (is) '*objectively* capable of infringing trade union freedom' (emphasis added) even if in abstract lawful. This occurs, according to the same judgement, since—'as in all civil actions for injunctive relief' the evaluation on the subjective element (the employer's intentionality) 'would end up determining an unjustified unequal treatment of cases that present equal need for protection, inasmuch as the legally relevant interest, the inhibition of conduct detrimental to trade union freedom, is equal' to all the affected group, rather than just the single individual (translated from Italian). See, more recently, in a confirmative sense, Italian Court of Cassation, Section I, Judgement from 24 May 2016, No. 10713.

[7] Tribunal of Milan, labour Section, Decree from 28 September 2023, No. 6979/2023.

8.3 The *Deliveroo* Case Litigation

As anticipated, the first case, the *Deliveroo* case, was an *injunctive* class action against Deliveroo Italy.[8] It aimed to obtain a judicial order forbidding the MDS company to apply to all of its riders in Italy, more than 8.000, the conditions laid down in the CCNL ('National Collective Employment Contract') signed by Assodelivery with only one *manifestly unrepresentative* trade union organisation, UGL Rider. Among the unfavourable conditions provided for by this CCNL were the non-recognition of paid holidays, of weekly rests, of paid leave, and the setting of hourly wages significantly lower than those provided for by the CCNLs of similar sectors signed by the most representative trade unions (e.g., CCNL Logistics or CCNL Tertiary Sector). In this perspective, the plaintiffs sought protection through a collective injunction action pursuant to Article 840-*sexiesdecies* c.p.c.

The case was significant from several points of view. It was, in fact, the first real class action on labour matters in Italy, as well as one of the first under the new rules introduced by Law No. 31 of 2019. It represented, therefore, an opportunity to assess the operability of the new collective procedural tool both for more general profiles and, specifically, as a means of protection in the employment law sector.

The breadth of the 2019 legislative provisions—set under the new Title VIII-*bis* of the Code of civil procedure and in force since May 2021—until then seemed to legitimise collective actions to protect workers harmed by the same conduct, whether active or omissive. At the same time, nonetheless, (mainly) potential defendants argued that class actions in labour matters could not be brought since the competence for class actions under the 2019 regime was attributed to the specialised section in *company* matters of the tribunal, whereas labour matters pertained to the specialised section in *labour* matters. This was, as a matter of fact, one of the main arguments of Deliveroo Italy, thereby insisting on an inadmissibility of the claim, either on the aforementioned grounds or because the *azione collettiva* should have been proposed in front of the specialised section in labour matters.

The significance of the issue is evident. If confirmed by the courts, the scope of an applicative extension to the employment sphere would have been indeed extraordinary: at the level of *guarantees*, implementation of the right of defence and concrete access to justice, but at the *socio-economic* level, too, considering the consequences to which a possible exposure of companies also to 'internal' class actions (from their employees), could lead—from the point of view of market choices, but also of better working conditions, as a deterrent fringe-consequence. The common law experience, as discussed *supra*, has been particularly rich since the early 1960s in this sector, with numerous success and progress achieved in the

[8] *Deliveroo* case, Tribunal of Milan, Section XIV, Order from 13 October 2022, R.G. No. 33816/2021.

labour sphere precisely thanks to class actions.[9] One can refer, for instance, to the extensive case law on discrimination or exploitation in the workplace.[10]

For these reasons, the test faced by the Milanese court in the present case was certainly considerable. The decision, although reached in October 2022, was published in January 2023 by the Court of Milan, Section XIV specialised in company matters, through an *order of rejection*.[11]

The main themes emerging *before* the decision were several: *(i)* a confirmation of the applicability of the class action discipline to *labour matters*; *(ii)* the *competence* of the specialised section on company matters also for employment disputes, notwithstanding their attribution to the labour judge of Article 413 c.p.c.; *(iii)* the *standing to sue* of labour unions; *(iv)* the possible *coordination* with the other instruments of collective judicial protection already present in the system, such as the action for the repression of anti-union conducts under Article 28 of the Workers' Statute or, the anti-discrimination ones; *(v)* the actual scope of paragraph 7 of Article 840-*sexiesdecies* c.p.c. when it provides that 'with the sentence to cease the omissive or commissive conduct, the court may, at the request of the public prosecutor or of the parties, order that the losing party adopts *appropriate measures to eliminate or reduce* the effects of the violations ascertained', as requested by the applicants.

The response of the Tribunal of Milan to these issues, while presenting positive elements, is not entirely convincing. In particular, from the court's rejection order the following can be noted.

(i) and *(ii)* The applicability of the class action to *labour matters* is confirmed ('Among the individual rights that can be protected, it does not appear that those connected to employment relations can be excluded').[12] This interpretation is in line with the wording of the law and the legislator's clear intention, as depicted from the parliamentary discussion reports.[13]

An inadmissibility on these grounds, as proposed by Deliveroo, would have opened the door to manifest questions of constitutionality, given an irrational and unfair exclusion from collective means of protection of this specific sector of law and category of individuals (workers, whichever the qualification—self-employed or not), notably weaker in relation to their counterparties (employers).

Moreover, as is known, also other non-labour sections of the tribunal increasingly often are called to deal with labour matters, as is the case of the bankruptcy section. The assignment of a dispute to a section rather than another should not generate a question of technical competence, but a mere internal allocation of resources within the same judicial office, as observed by the United Sections of the

[9] See, *supra*, Chap. 5.

[10] See Greenberg (1997), for an extensive account on the matter, with several examples.

[11] *Deliveroo* case, Tribunal of Milan, Section XIV, Order from 13 October 2022, R.G. No. 33816/2021.

[12] Id. (translated from Italian).

[13] See, *supra*, Chap. 6.

Court of Cassation in 2019.[14] This still leaves concerns on the constitutional legitimacy of such a choice of competence, further developed (see *infra*, Chap. 11).

The confirmation in *Deliveroo*, in any case, is *landmark*, as it paves the way for a new line of collective litigation. As already stressed, the comparative experience from overseas has shown the class action model as cardinal in ensuring a substantial increase of protection for workers. At the same time, however, the Milanese tribunal in several passages seems to *improperly raise the standard* required for the proposition of lawsuits in this sector, thereby risking making meritorious actions impracticable in concreto. This occurs in two respects.

First, the injunctive class action pursuant to Article 840-*sexiesdecies* c.p.c. (brought in the present case) is equated to the compensatory class action pursuant to Articles 840-*bis et seq.* c.p.c. under a key aspect. The rejection order incidentally emphasises, in fact, the necessity to respect the requirement of *homogeneity* of the individual rights asserted in the class action. Such a requirement, nonetheless, is set forth under Articles 840-*bis* and 840-*ter*, governing the admissibility phase of the *compensatory* class action, not the injunctive one. The analogical extension of such a requirement to the injunctive remedy appears—by all means—*incorrect.*

From a strictly *literal* point of view, such a requirement ('homogeneous individual rights'), in fact, is expressly provided for only in respect to the compensatory model. Indeed, in relation to collective injunctions, the provisions mention the mere 'interest [in the decision]', thus favouring also the protection of collective or diffuse situations, and not necessarily of individual subjective rights.[15]

This is supported by an historical reading, in light of the origins—dating back to the Roman *actio popularis*—of the collective injunction, precisely for the protection of *supra-individual* positions. No reference to homogeneity is present in Article 840-*sexiesdecies* c.p.c. either. Furthermore, a systematic viewpoint favours this interpretation, by reason of the reference (insofar as compatible) of Article 840-*sexiesdecies* c.p.c. *only* to Article 840-*quinquies* c.p.c. (which relates to the *procedure* of compensatory class actions), but *not* to the previous articles in which the requirement of homogeneity is set (the already mentioned Articles 840-*bis* and 840-*ter* c.p.c.).

More correct appears the line dictated by the other Section specialised in company matters from the same Tribunal of Milan (Sect. XV), in the previous collective injunctive action—against *ILVA* and Acciaierie d'Italia, discussed in the previous chapter—, in which the applicability of admissibility conditions in compensatory

---

[14] Italian Court of Cassation, U.S., Judgment from 23 July 2019, No. 19882, holding that 'the establishment of the specialised section for the enterprise responds to 'the need for a better organisation and quality of the response of justice, which is not inherent in the profile of competence'', also considering that 'the option in favour of the configuration of the relations between the ordinary section and the section for the enterprise as of competence in a technical sense contrasts with the most recent choices of legislative policy, oriented in the sense of a drastic reduction of the questions of competence', as referred to also by the plaintiffs in the present case (translated from Italian).

[15] See, *supra*, Chap. 6, for a more thorough reflection.

class suits—herein included the requirement of homogeneity—was expressly excluded for collective injunctive actions.[16]

This reading is also supported by other injunctive class actions, albeit they have not dealt directly with the issue of homogeneity either. The Tribunal of Rome, in its inadmissibility order in the *ITA Airways* injunctive class action from December 2022 (but published later),[17] has been particularly explicit on this point, embracing the thesis here and hitherto argued:

> The purely *interim nature* of the proceedings at issue, in fact, is *incompatible* with the complex procedure aimed at the adhesion of the holders of *homogeneous rights*, which presupposes the publication of the order of admission of the class action, a phase *not provided* for collective actions for injunction.
>
> In fact, Article 840 sexiesdecies [quinquies] of the Code of Civil Procedure refers to the court proceedings referred to in Articles 737 et seq. of the Code of Civil Procedure and only 'insofar as compatible' with Article 840 quinquies of the Code of Civil Procedure: it follows that the procedure of adhesion of the holders of homogeneous rights to those at issue is not compatible with the collective injunctive action.[18]

Second, under another aspect, the concrete claim in *Deliveroo* was *rejected* due to the peculiar nature of the *chambers procedure* pursuant to Articles 737 *et seq*. c.p.c., provided for collective actions for injunctions. According to the Tribunal of Milan, in fact, such a 'streamlined procedural form' excludes assessments endowed with investigative complexity, being Article '840 *sexiesdecie*s c.p.c. focused on the ascertainment of the injury and not on that of the right asserted'.[19]

Hence the rejection, since the claimants in the present case requested an ascertainment 'well *beyond* the *incidental nature* of the recognition of the right asserted',[20] contesting the contractual basis of the employment relationship and requiring a '*particular complexity* in the correct identification of the actual injuries suffered and

[16] *ILVA* case, Tribunal of Milan, Section XV, Order from 16 September 2022, R.G. No. 10166/2021, analysed in Chap. 7; see also, *supra*, Chap. 6. The Tribunal of Milan, in this case, was dealing with the requirement of 'adequacy' of the name plaintiff to represent the homogeneous interests of the class, pursuant to letter d) of Article 840-*ter*, para. 3, c.p.c. In any case, the general assumptions about the applicability of this article and the admissibility phase to the injunctive model are to be considered relatable also to the homogeneity test under letter c) of the same provision.

[17] *ITA Airways* case. Tribunal of Rome, Section XVI, Order from 13 December 2022, R.G. No. 3426/2022.

[18] Id. (translated from Italian). At the same time, as a reason for its order of inadmissibility, the Tribunal of Rome refers to the decision of the Tribunal of Milan in the *Deliveroo* case (see above): 'In accordance with recent case law, the Court considers that the proceedings referred to in Article 840 sexiesdecies of the Code of Civil Procedure, in referring to the forms of the proceedings in chambers pursuant to Article 737 et seq. of the Code of Civil Procedure, with the application, in so far as compatible, of Article 840 quinquies c.p.c.—denotes a ratio legis in favour of a streamlined procedural form devoid of any investigative complexity (as underlined by the provision of the fifth paragraph of Article 840 sexiesdecies c.p.c. where it is provided that the Court may 'make use of statistical data and simple presumptions')' (translated from Italian).

[19] *Deliveroo* case, Tribunal of Milan, Section XIV, Order from 13 October 2022, R.G. No. 33816/2021 (translated from Italian).

[20] Id.

[...] of the *homogeneity* of such injuries in relation to the persons who would constitute the class to be defined'.[21] This view is embraced by the Tribunal of Rome in the abovementioned *ITA Airways* case (which—it must be said—seemed to require a much more, perhaps too, complex preliminary ascertainment).[22]

On this point, it should be emphasised—again—that it is not necessary to prove the *homogeneity stricto sensu* of the injuries, but rather the mere *commonality* (i.e., common origin) of the acts causing injury to a *plurality* of individuals or entities (see *supra*, Chap. 6); a *commonality* which is evident in the case in question, given the application of the same CCNL Ugl Rider and the distribution of work through the same algorithm.

---

[21] Id.

[22] *ITA Airways* case. Tribunal of Rome, Section XVI, Order from 13 December 2022, R.G. No. 3426/2022. The decision proceeds as follows: 'This hermeneutic analysis is corroborated by the envisaged separation of the collective compensatory action from the collective action for injunctive relief, where they are proposed with a single action (Article 840 *sexiesdecies* u.c. of the Code of Civil Procedure). The collective action for injunction therefore joins the collective action for damages, as it is provided for by Title VIII-bis of the Code of Civil Procedure, 'Of collective proceedings', constituting a completion in the function of protection against the continuation of damaging conduct (see Tribunal of Milan 13/10/2022, N.R.G. 33,816/2021). 4. On the merits, [...] take legal action against ITA Italiana Trasporto Aereo s.r.l. invoking the collective injunction protection under Article 840-sexiesdecies c.p.c. in order to obtain ascertainment of the takeover under Article 2112 c.c. of ITA—Italiana Compagnia Aerea S.p.A. to Alitalia—Società Aerea Italiana S.p.A, with the consequent ascertainment of the injury suffered by the employees of the aviation asset, whose interests they claim are homogeneous, as a result of the failure to continue their employment relationship with the defendant. The application as brought is inadmissible. [...] The action for an injunction brought by the plaintiffs does not in fact seek to obtain the protection of the infringement of homogeneous rights carried out by ITA S.p.A. by means of a *cease and desist order* or the *prohibition of the repetition* of omissive or commission-based conduct, but rather requires and presupposes the ascertainment that between Alitalia S. p.A. and ITA S.p.A. a transfer of business has taken place, with the consequent application of the protections provided for the workers of the transferred company, pursuant to and for the purposes of Article 2112 of the Civil Code which requires the continuity of the employment relationship of the employees of the transferred company and the preservation for them of the rights arising therefrom. The plaintiffs' requests therefore imply an *ascertainment exceeding the incidental nature* of the recognition of the right asserted, underlying the proceedings for collective injunction under Article 840 sexiesdecies of the Code of Civil Procedure, which is focused on the *ascertainment of the injury and not on that of the right asserted* (in terms of Trib Milano 13 October 2022 cited above), as inferable, inter alia, from the provision of the fifth paragraph of Article 840 sexiesdecies of the Code of Civil Procedure, which, for preliminary investigation purposes, provides for the use of statistical data and simple presumptions, incompatible with the preliminary investigation requirements aimed at ascertaining the existence of the *transfer of a branch of business* between Alitalia S.p.A. and ITA S.p.A., firmly contested by the latter and, consequently, the rights arising from it for the former employees of Alitalia S.p.A.. It is therefore a question of a *complex double assessment*, incompatible with the typical cognition of collective actions for injunctions, aimed at the sole purpose of inhibiting commission or omission of conduct prejudicial to a plurality of individuals or entities: and indeed, the plaintiff's request, although qualified as a collective injunction, in reality has as its object the condemnation of ITA S.p.A. to continue with the plaintiffs the individual employment relationships corresponding to those entered into with Alitalia S.p.A, as a result of the establishment of business continuity between the two companies, a ruling certainly to be referred to a trial on the merits before the labour court' (emphasis added, translated from Italian).

The homogeneity test is by no means part of the injunctive class action. Furthermore, also for the same reasons, the investigation of the case in question does not appear to be excessively complex—at least on a probatory level.

That being said, a purported complexity of the case does not appear by any means as a justification for exempting the court from making an assessment. A certain degree of complexity may, in fact, be considered *inherent* in the collective nature of the class action. Higher the degree of complexity, higher the *judicial economy* gained. This would otherwise appear unreasonable in relation to individual proceedings, and hence in contrast with Article 3 of the Italian Constitution.

Concurrently, to assess an injury to a subjective position (i.e., a right), such a subjective position must be preliminarily ascertained. The reference 'to *statistical data* and *simple presumptions*' (emphasis added) from Article 840-*sexiesdecies*, para. 5, c.p.c., recalled by the Tribunal of Milan in the *Deliveroo* case—as well as by the Tribunal of Rome in the *ITA Airways* case—to justify the 'legislative intention to regulate a procedural form streamlined and devoid of any evidentiary complexity',[23] appears improper and misleading.

On the one hand, it must be underscored how the use of statistical data and simple presumptions is a *mere (additional) possibility* set out by the legislator, not a standard evidentiary rule provided for class proceedings. As is known, pursuant to Article 2729 of the Italian Civil code, '*Presumptions* not established by law are left to the prudence of the judge [116 c.p.c.], who must admit only serious, precise and concordant presumptions'. To this regard, a well-established jurisprudence has long elaborated that 'Simple presumptions constitute complete evidence to which the court of merit may attribute relevance, *even exclusively*, for the formation of its own conviction'.[24] Also *statistical data*, although the explicit reference in class proceedings' regulation is not trivial, have been used by Italian judges in both civil and criminal proceedings for a significant time now, as is equally well known.

On the other hand, the *legislative intention* to create a streamlined and swift procedure certainly exudes from all of Title VIII-*bis* c.p.c.'s recent provisions. This objective, nevertheless, is instrumental to a much larger—and paramount, for the legislator—aim: that of 'expanding its potential users', 'to make the tool more usable and attractive' and, in sum, of 'bolstering access to justice' (as per the *travaux préparatoires* themselves).[25] In this sense, the choice of the *chamber procedure*—although highly debatable—should be intended as seeking more *flexibility* rather than *simplicity* in relation to the class assessments.

To this regard, although the chamber procedure is probably not the most appropriate, its rules do not exclude the possibility of carrying out investigative activities, possibly even complex ones. The goals of 'bolstering access to justice' and the collective nature of the action, indeed, should lead *judges* to a more *proactive role* in

[23] *Deliveroo* case, Tribunal of Milan, Section XIV, Order from 13 October 2022, R.G. No. 33816/2021 (translated from Italian).

[24] See, e.g., *inter alia*, Italian Court of Cassation, labour Section, Judgement from 21 October 2003, No. 15737 (translated from Italian).

[25] See, *supra*, Chap. 6.

ascertaining the subjective situations asserted and finding whether the 'cessation or prohibition of the repetition of the omissive or commissive conduct [...], carried out to the detriment of a plurality of individuals or entities,'[26] should be ordered.

In the case at hand, the conduct 'carried out to the detriment of a plurality of individuals or entities' was no other than the application, to its more or less 8.000 riders, of the unfair conditions set out under the CCNL signed by Assodelivery with the non-representative UGL Rider. Again, the substantial difference in treatment following the Tribunal's strict interpretation appears in contrast with the reasonability canon required under Article 3 of the Italian Constitution, in relation to the homogeneous (identical) situation of individual proceedings initiated by any class member.

It is also understandable, still, the hesitancy of a judge *specialised in corporate matters* to make ascertainments in a highly technical and specialised matter such as that of labour, to which they are *inevitably extraneous*. Hence, the fundamental need to reconsider the *appropriateness* of the legislative choice to attribute *exclusive jurisdictional competence* to this section, even for *labour matters*.[27]

Proper means to increase *participation* from all the involved stakeholders, as already mentioned, should be offered by the legislator, too. This seems especially relevant in injunctive cases, given that the effects of the decision fall on everyone 'objectively',[28] without a chance of opting-in or even opting-out (like in compensatory suits).

(iii) The *Deliveroo* decision also found the *lack of standing to sue* on the part of the applicant labour unions, since they were not in the *public list* established at the Ministry of Justice (Decree No. 27 of 17 February 2022) to which Article 840-*sexiesdecies*, para. 2, refers. In that decree, fixing the criteria for inclusion in the list, labour unions were expressly excluded, by means of a reference to 'third sector entities' pursuant to Article 4 of Legislative Decree No. 117 of 3 July 2017. The ministerial choice was questionable, also from a constitutional point of view, since these are exactly those '*social formations*' that are often better placed to represent the collective protection instances of workers, as well as better able to bear the costs (including media costs) of any collective action than an individual worker. Given the letter of the decree, however, the court's decision seemed mandatory, safe for the possibility of raising a question of constitutionality to the Constitutional Court on Article 840-*sexiesdecies*, para. 2, or to seek the annulment of that part of the ministerial decree in front of the administrative judge.

The latter path was indeed followed, as a subsequent ruling of June 2023, from the *Regional Administrative Court (TAR)* of Lazio, appealed by labour unions, *annulled the provisions* of the same ministerial regulation that established the requirements for registration in the special register of the Ministry of Justice of the

---

[26] Article 840-*sexiesdecies*, para. 1, c.p.c. (translated from Italian).

[27] See, *supra*, Chap. 6, and *infra*, Chap. 11.

[28] Italian Court of Cassation, S.U., Judgement from 12 June 1997, No. 5295.

entities qualified to bring class actions, effectively excluding labour union organisations.[29]

The Regional Administrative Court pointed out that, 'in exercising its regulatory discretion, the administration had acted in a clearly illogical and unreasonable manner, circumscribing the legitimacy of the action to the mere possession of the qualification of third sector entity',[30] betraying the spirit of the law, which, on the contrary, is intended to favour the widest possible scope of action for no-profit associations.

It also recalled that 'the defence of the homogeneous individual rights of a specific category of subjects (in the case of the applicants, subordinate workers) is *intrinsically inherent* to the associative purposes typical of labour unions: the exclusion of such exponential entities from the list of those entitled to collective action is, therefore, irrational',[31] underscoring how 'on the other hand, historically, the birth of trade unions is functional to the exercise of collective initiatives in defence of the 'class' of workers (e.g. collective bargaining)'.[32]

Such a reading appears in line with the concrete *access to justice aim* of the reform, as well as with the interpretation of the right to action in light of the principles set out in the Italian Constitution, as discussed above.[33]

(iv) Concerning the *coordination with other instruments* of collective protection, the court recalled the last paragraph of Article 840-*sexiesdecies*, which states 'without prejudice to the provisions laid down on the subject by special laws', to exclude the possibility of resorting to injunctive collective actions against the repression of labour union conducts, for which the remedy of Article 28 of the Workers' Statute already exists.

In the present case, according to the court, it was not possible to examine the possible anti-union nature of Deliveroo's conduct. Recalling the jurisprudence of legitimacy, in any event, the Tribunal of Milan emphasised how the infringement by the employer of the employee's individual rights—as in the case under consideration—does not constitute trade union conduct. Such an interpretation, if extended also to discriminatory actions (for example, by giving preference to the action established under Article 44, paragraph 10, of Legislative Decree No. 286 of 1998), could *considerably reduce* the scope of application of the new Italian class action.

(v) Lastly, given the rejection of the appeal, it was not possible to ascertain the actual scope of the expression '*appropriate measures* to eliminate or reduce the effects of the violations ascertained'[34] set forth under paragraph 7 of Article 840-*sexiesdecies* c.p.c.

---

[29] TAR Lazio, Section I, Judgement from 23 June 2023, R.G. No. 10653.

[30] Id. (translated from Italian).

[31] Id. (emphasis added).

[32] Id.

[33] See, *supra*, Chap. 6.

[34] Emphasis added.

This is a very interesting provision, since—if understood in an extensive form, concerning also *economic* measures—it could allow overcoming, by means of the injunctive class actions, certain criticalities of the more complex class actions for damages, pursuant to Articles 840-*bis et seq.* c.p.c. Another general profile to be considered in future cases will be that of *passive standing*, given the limitation to companies and entities managing public services or public utilities, of dubious constitutional legitimacy and, still, recalled several times in the *Deliveroo* case order.[35]

8.4 The Pending *Uber Eats* Case Litigation

As anticipated, the second class action for the enforcement of MDS riders rights is still pending. The first hearing took place in April 2024, in front of the Tribunal of Milan, section XIV (the same as *Deliveroo*, but with a different President and judicial composition). To date, no decision has been communicated by the court. This is despite the provision from Article 840-*ter*, para. 3, c.p.c. which sets a deadline of 30 days from the first hearing by which the tribunal should decide on the admissibility. It is not a strict deadline, but still such a lengthy wait appears excessive and against fair trial guarantees, as interpreted by domestic and supranational Courts.[36]

It is a compensatory *azione di classe* seeking an order against Uber Eats Italy to pay damages for the abrupt and unfair termination of the work relation with its approximately 4.000 riders. Such a compensation, according to the claimants, should be equal to the lost remuneration of the riders, to be determined *ex aequo*, in light of the average monthly remuneration and the equiparable CCNL for commerce or logistics (given its current lack, see *supra*).

The key foreseeable elements of discussion, relevant for the present analysis, on which the court shall rule, are the following: *(i)* inadmissibility of the action for lack of *competence* of the specialised section in company matters; *(ii)* inadmissibility of the class proceedings for non-fulfilment of the *homogeneity* requirement; *(iii)* the issue of *time*, that is the inadmissibility of the 2019 regime, into force since May 2021 and only for subsequent conducts (see *above*), given that several workers might have started operating as Uber Eats riders before that date; *(iv)* in case of admissibility, how to ensure adhesion and liquidate the damages—that is, the *quantum* for each adherent rider.

---

[35] See, *supra*, Chap. 6, and *infra*, Chap. 11.

[36] See, e.g., ECtHR, *Scordino v. Italy (no. 1)* [GC], No. 36813/97, 2006, § 224: 'The Court emphasises once again that Article 6 § 1 of the Convention obliges the Contracting States to organise their legal systems so as to enable the courts to comply with its various requirements. It wishes to reaffirm the importance of administering justice without delays which might jeopardise its effectiveness and credibility'.

(i) Given the precedent of the same Tribunal of Milan in the *Deliveroo* case,[37] it is unlikely that *competence* should be declined in favour of the specialised section in labour matters of the Tribunal. This is also supported by the other case law in employment matters, for instance in the *ITA Airways* case,[38] in which the defendant company had preliminarily objected the 'functional incompetence', too, of the section specialised in company matters in favour of the labour judge, only to see such an exception rejected by the court:

> As is well known, the distribution of business within the same judicial office does not pose a problem of jurisdiction, since there is no possibility of choice between two different judges belonging to different judicial offices abstractly competent to judge the dispute, with the consequent inadmissibility also of the regulation of jurisdiction on the relative issue (see Civil cassation, No. 4889 of 2001). It has thus been reiterated that the nature of the labour dispute is capable of influencing only the *applicable proceedings* and not the competence, with the consequence, moreover, that where the court of merit has assessed the recurrence of the factual conditions for the traceability of the dispute within the scope of Article 409(3) of the Code of Civil Procedure, the ground of appeal objecting to the lack of jurisdiction of the court hearing the case is inadmissible, as it translates into a request for a different assessment of the facts as opposed to that made in the judgment under appeal (Civil cassation, No. 189/2011; Civil cassation, No. 12753/2003).[39]

Still, despite the nature of the labour dispute influencing merely the applicable proceedings rather than the competence, there are arguments to insist on the appropriateness of a discussion before the *labour judge*, certainly more sensitive to certain issues and armed with the, sometimes essential (see *Deliveroo* case),[40] expertise, as already argued and further presented in the following. One cannot help by wonder, in fact, whether the current delay in the execution on admissibility might be induced by these circumstances.

(ii) and *(iv)* That of homogeneity will probably constitute the legal battle on which the procedural victory will be played out, similarly to the abovementioned *ILVA* compensatory class action,[41] pending as well in front of the same tribunal, that of Milan. As extensively argued,[42] *homogeneity* of individual rights should be conceived *in primis* under an etymological standpoint (i.e., 'same origin'), as a *commonality* of the fact or conduct generating the harm; and nothing more. Once (if) demonstrated such a common origin, the plaintiffs—but, following the principle

---

[37] *Deliveroo* case, Tribunal of Milan, Section XIV, Order from 13 October 2022, R.G. No. 33816/2021.

[38] *ITA Airways* case, Tribunal of Rome, Section XVI, Order from 13 December 2022, R.G. No. 3426/2022.

[39] Id. (translated from Italian).

[40] *Deliveroo* case, Tribunal of Milan, Section XIV, Order from 13 October 2022, R.G. No. 33816/2021.

[41] *ILVA* case, compensatory class action still pending before the Tribunal of Milan, Section XV, R.G. No. 29261/2023.

[42] See, *supra*, Chap. 6.

'*iura novit curia*', the judge, too[43]—will need to devise an efficient criterion for joint management and liquidation of the damages due.

It is important to stress how the *common origin*, under a constitutionally-oriented (but also historical) interpretation, should be conceived *elastically*: in the present case, as a work relation with Uber Eats Italy and its abrupt termination in June 2023. As to evaluating efficiency of *joint management* and *liquidation*, again, we must underscore (see *supra*)[44] that such a determination does not pertain to the *admissibility* phase.

This phase—it must be recalled—is a fundamental yet merely *pre-judicial* and, thus, *speculative* stage of the proceedings. Management and liquidation, therefore, should not determine the admissibility of the claim, but rather be discussed at a subsequent procedural moment (that is, after the judge eventually issues the 'acceptance judgment'—'*giudizio di accoglimento*', pursuant to Article 840-*sexies* c.p.c.—, in which he/she 'defines the characteristics of the homogeneous individual right [...] specifying the elements necessary for inclusion in the class' of their holders).

In any case, *(iv)*, should the claim be declared *admissible*, it will undoubtedly be a challenging task.

First, it will be necessary to find all the riders. As anticipated, many of them are migrants and often do not speak the language; they rarely follow the news. A proper system of *publication and notice*—including translators—to allow them to properly understand the extent of the decision and to *opt-in*, whether interested, should be set up.

Cases like the present one raise doubts on the efficiency of the opt-in mechanism. An *opt-out* one, on the contrary, would have given more power to the class attorneys in negotiating a *settlement* for the whole class, once (if) the claim is deemed admissible. This would follow the common-law usual practice of settling once the class action is certified. Such an incentive to settle, given that, statistically, significantly less members adhere in opt-in systems, might be substantially hindered in cases like the present one.

Second, attributing to each rider the *same* compensation, determined *ex aequo*, in light of the average monthly remuneration and the equiparable CCNL for commerce or logistics, does not appear like a viable option (nor one currently sought by the claimants in the present case).

A different criterion for the determination of the *quantum* should, therefore, be identified, taking into account the possibility of dividing the riders into *sub-classes* and/or of using a lowest common denominator as a *multiplication unitary parameter*, like in the *Millemiglia* case, concerning a loyalty programme, as discussed above.[45] Such parameters and sub-division could be based on the number of hours worked per month by each rider, as well as on the number of months worked for the

[43] Cappelletti (1969), pp. 459 *et seq.*

[44] See, *supra*, Chap. 6.

[45] See, *supra*, Chap. 6. *Millemiglia* case, Tribunal of Rome, Section XVII, Order from 8 November 2023, R.G. No. 1577/2023.

company. An economic value should be attributed to these minimum parameters, within the 'acceptance judgment', pursuant to Article 840-*sexies* c.p.c., and then multiplied for each rider during the liquidation phase by the 'common representative of the adherents', acting as a public officer.[46]

(iii) In relation to a *potential inadmissibility* of the 2019 regime, into force since May 2021 only for conducts subsequent to such a date, given that several workers might have started operating as Uber Eats riders before, the reflections and case law on the 'permanent tort' scenarios can be recalled here, too.[47]

Pursuant to Article 3 It. Const., even if the activity started out before the entry into force of the new collective procedural instrument, no impediment to its application could be raised, given that it took place also after May 2021.[48] In any case, it should be noted that the activity started out before the entry into force is the *working relation*, not the harmful conduct, to which the 'permanent tort' jurisprudence refers. Such a harmful conduct is the one from June 2023 (and afterwards), consisting in the abrupt and *unfair termination* of the work relation, as described above.

8.5 Lessons and Open Questions

In conclusion, employment disputes through class actions still have to fully develop in Italy. While lawyers and—most importantly—judges have to adjust to the new procedural tool, important cases have been filed in this field, with the potential to advance fundamental rights' enforcement.

The causes for uncertainty still shrouding the institution, in force for four years now, are various.

First and foremost, the pervading *legislative confusion*, which leaves a powerful instrument of general application in the hands of *judges specialised* in a single and different subject—company matters—, overburdened and limited by interpretative and procedural uncertainties should be underscored.

Also, the *reluctance of the judge*s themselves should be accounted, however. They are the ones who must—and can, accompanied by other legal practitioners—embrace the new rules and become protagonists, even creatively and innovatively (from a procedural point of view). This occurs in a process and in a society that is increasingly calling upon them to take decisions with a strong social impact, in the face of blatant legislative inertia and of increasing disparities between individuals and large private actors. The rejection order in the *Deliveroo* case[49] seems particularly illustrative—and concerning—to this regard: it shows an improper reference to

[46] See, *supra*, Chap. 6.

[47] Id.

[48] Id.

[49] *Deliveroo* case, Tribunal of Milan, Section XIV, Order from 13 October 2022, R.G. No. 33816/2021.

compensatory provisions in injunctive class proceedings (the homogeneity test), on the one hand, and an unjustified rejection for purported 'particular complexity' in the identification of the harm suffered, on the other hand.

These judicial interpretations cause worry and also make one wonder whether the, *natural, labour judge* should not be more suited for deciding such employment claims.[50] It would indeed be interesting to see future class action claims in labour matters filed in front of the specialised section in labour matters, rather than in front of the company one. Should the former doubt (as they should) on their *competence* to decide, in favour of the latter, there would be cause for raising a *question of constitutionality* in front of the Constitutional Court. This way, given legislative inertia, a coordination of the different paths of judicial protection would be put into practice.

Furthermore, different types of proceedings, rather than the *chambers procedure* pursuant to Article 737 *et seq.* c.p.c., could be provided for by the legislator in the future, to discard a certain judicial *perception* that complex matters cannot be brought through a class procedure. Perception, it must be stressed, and not firm belief, given how other decisions in injunctive *azioni collettive* have been successfully discussed on the merits, in spite of any purported over-complexity of the matters. A clear example is the abovementioned *Philips Respironics* case, in front of the same Section XIV of the Tribunal of Milan (with a judicial composition equal in two thirds to that from the *Deliveroo* case), confirmed in appeal by the Court of Appel of Milan; also the injunctive action in front of the Tribunal of Turin for an unlawful marketing campaign can be noted.[51]

It must be stressed how the latter two cases were not related to employment matters, but rather to defective products or misleading corporate practices. This implies an encompassment within 'corporate matters', certainly more akin—rather than more complex, one might hypothesise—to the specialised section in corporate matters, than the employment cases herein examined. Hence, an argument once again in favour of a rethinking of the determination of the *jurisdictional competence*, either through legislative change, currently improbable although preferable, or through constitutional review.[52]

Second, the upcoming decision on *homogeneity* from the compensatory class action in the *Uber Eats* case, together with that in the *ILVA* case, promises to be crucial for the future development of collective suits in Italy. A high degree of flexibility and, in part, also of procedural creativity will be required from all parties involved.

Third, the actors involved are indeed the key pieces of the intricated class action puzzle in Italy. Judges, as much-underscored, defendants, but also potential claimants need to be proactive and understand the procedural and interpretative nuances of the new regime. Specific *training*, of judges and legal practitioners in general

---

[50] See, *infra*, Chap. 11.

[51] Tribunal of Turin, Section I, Order from 21 April 2023 (R.G. No. unavailable).

[52] See, *infra*, Chap. 11.

could be highly beneficial to this regard—as well as necessary legislative and regulatory amendments, further presented in the next, conclusive, Part IV.[53]

Last, a growing trend can be envisaged of labour unions—that is, 'old' actors, or 'social formations'—using the 'new' procedural paths to pursue their battles.[54] It can thus be registered a transformation, or even a *transmigration*, of intermediate social bodies (labour unions, in this case) from their previous old forms to new, evolved and transitory ones (class actions) to cope with the systemic voids and growing power-inequalities brought by the contemporary transformations.

References

Cappelletti M (1969) Processo e ideologie. Il Mulino, Bologna

D'Onghia M, Recchia GA (2023) Processo del lavoro e Sindacato: l'art. 28 St. lav. come apripista della riforma del 1973. Lavoro Diritti Europa (special issue):2

Greenberg J (1997) Civil Rights Class Actions. Procedural means of obtaining substance. Ariz Law Rev 39:575–586

Randazzo B, Maglica A (2025) La disciplina generale delle class action italiane alla prova delle garanzie costituzionali ed europee. Federalismi.it 5:158–196

[53] See, also Randazzo and Maglica (2025).

[54] See, *supra*, Chaps. 3 and 4.

Chapter 9
Case Study No. 3: Systemic Inhuman and Degrading Treatment of Prisoners and Migrants. Room for Future (Class) Actions?

9.1 Premise. Inhuman and Degrading Treatment of Prisoners and Migrants

Article 3 of the ECHR and Article 4 of the CFREU clearly state that 'No one shall be subject to torture or to inhuman or degrading treatment or punishment'.

The Grand Chamber of the ECtHR even defined it as 'one of the most fundamental values of a democratic society' and 'a value of civilisation closely bound up with respect for human dignity'.[1] Under such a system, the prohibition in question is to be conceived as an *absolute* one, even in the event of a public emergency threatening the life of the nation or in the most difficult circumstances—i.e., in the fight against terrorism, organised crime, severe economic burden, or potentially overwhelming migrant fluxes—, whichever the conduct or alleged offence committed.

Similar provisions and developments can be found in other national and supranational constitutional texts and jurisprudence.

For instance, the Italian Constitutional Court, in relation to prisoners, has long recognised the 'constitutional nature' of punishment,[2] under Article 27, third paragraph, of the Italian Constitution,[3] stressing how prison treatment 'must conform to

[1] ECtHR, *Bouyid v. Belgium* [GC], No. 23380/09, 2015, § 81.

[2] In Italian, '*volto costituzionale*' (literally: 'constitutional face'). Italian Constitutional Court, Judgement No. 50 from 1980, point No. 4 of the Points of law; referred to in Judgement No. 179 from 2019, point No. 4.4 of the Points of law, and, recently, in Judgement No. 10 from 2024, point No. 4 of the Points of law.

[3] Article 27, third paragraph, of the Italian Constitution ('Punishments may not consist of treatment contrary to a sense of humanity and must aim at the re-education of the sentenced person'), as well as Article 13, fourth paragraph, of the Italian Constitution ('All physical and moral violence against persons subjected to restrictions of liberty is punishable'), and the general principles set under Articles 2 and 3 of the Italian Constitution.

A. Maglica, *Collective Dimensions of Access to Justice*, European Union and its Neighbours in a Globalized World 23,
https://doi.org/10.1007/978-3-031-94522-9_9

humanity and must ensure respect for the dignity of the person',[4] under the 'guiding principles' of *individualisation* in relation to the specific conditions of the persons concerned and of the '*minimum means*', whereby restrictions may be adopted only if justified by the need to maintain order and discipline and, in relation to defendants, only if indispensable for judicial purposes.[5] Furthermore, as developed by constant case law from the same Constitutional Court, the principle of *proportionality*, pursuant to Article 3 of the Italian Constitution, is to be read as a prerequisite of and in conjunction with Article 27, third paragraph, and Article 3 of the Italian Constitution, in the sense of proportionality of the punishment, 'between [its] quality and quantity […], on the one hand, and the offence, on the other'.[6] Such principle, long 'part of the heritage of European legal culture',[7] now also under Article 49, para. 3, CFREU, applies simultaneously to the legislator as much as to the judges, of cognition, execution and supervision, as well as to the prison authorities themselves.[8]

This is a paramount corollary, after all, of the primacy of the human person and of their rights within the Italian constitutional order. The dignity of the person, enshrined under Article 3, first paragraph, the Italian Constitution, is protected 'through the baggage of inviolable human rights',[9] *ex* Article 2 of the Italian Constitution, even in cases of deprivation of liberty in execution of a prison punishment, 'indeed: especially in this case, whose distinguishing feature is the precariousness of individuals, deriving from the lack of freedom, in conditions of environment by their nature destined to separate them from civil society'. Even (most importantly) detainees should maintain such a baggage of inviolable human rights throughout the course of criminal execution, in accordance with Article 1 of Law no. 354 of 1975 on the Italian prison system.

Still, severe and *systemic* violations to such a right are periodically accounted all over Europe (and beyond), under numerous aspects. The present Chapter, in particular, will concentrate on two types of infringements: those concerning *prisoners and detainees*, on the one hand, and those related to *migrants and asylum seekers* and their reception (or, rather, lack thereof), on the other hand. Italy, specifically, has

[4] Citing Article 1 of Law No. 354 of 1975, as one of the 'guiding principles' of the penitentiary system.

[5] Italian Constitutional Court, Judgement No. 10 from 2024.

[6] Italian Constitutional Court, Judgement No. 313 from 1990.

[7] Id.

[8] Id. See also Italian Constitutional Court, Judgements No. 28 from 2022 and No. 40 from 2019.

[9] Italian Constitutional Court, Judgement No. 26 from 1999, point No. 3.1 of the Points of law.

a negatively impressive track record with regard to both these selected matters. Despite judicial and political reprimands at all levels for several years, decades even, the situation does not seem to improve, but, rather, it appears quite stagnant.

At the moment, no class action—injunctive or compensatory—has been brought in this field in Italy under the new regime, from 2019. This occurs despite significant litigation having been brought in recent years for the protection of prisoners and migrants, both in front of Italian courts, namely, the Constitutional Court, and, in front of supranational apex courts, namely the ECtHR. The Strasbourg Court, in particular, backed up by institutional and non-governmental reports, has repeatedly condemned Italy for violations of Article 3 of the ECHR, also pointing out on multiple occurrences the existence of unaddressed systemic and structural deficiencies in the country in relation to this field.[10]

A comparative assessment, on the contrary, reveals a remarkable use of the class action procedural device in the *common law experience* for the enforcement of prisoners' and detainees' rights. Jack Greenberg, the well-known Director (and legal counsel) of the NAACP Legal Defense Fund from 1961 until 1984, for instance, when discussing in a 1997 paper three relevant areas of civil rights litigation through class actions, chose precisely, as the first one, that of 'prisoners' rights':

> Class actions have played a major role in securing the rights of prisoners. Since the federal class action rule was revised in 1966, prisoner rights litigation has utilized the mechanism of class action to bring broad relief to inmates and detainees throughout the country. Prisoners' rights litigation has thoroughly reformed entire state prison systems in Texas, Florida and Georgia. In cases which lasted for years, those and other systems have been placed under judicial management for long periods of time. Less far-reaching cases have involved class action relief from double ceiling, religious discrimination, due process violation in parole standards, restrictions on an inmate's right to marry, solitary confinement, and denial of contact visits.[11]

Similar accounts can be found in other scholarly and non-governmental output from common law, when commenting class actions brought in the interests of disadvantaged groups or, in general, as a public interest litigation tool.

For these reasons, the present Chapter will, *firstly*, briefly recall the factual background of the violations of the fundamental right to not be subject to degrading or inhuman conditions, suffered by prisoners and detainees, on the one hand, and by migrants and asylum-seekers, on the other hand, in Italy. For this purpose, it shall refer to significant cases brought before domestic and supranational courts—mainly the Italian Constitutional Court and the ECtHR—, as well as recent reports and scandals.

Secondly, a selected number of cases from common law jurisdictions—namely US and Canada—will be described. In this part, the most relevant aspects, from a procedural standpoint, shall be highlighted. Such an exercise will draw from local scholarship's valuable insights and comments.

---

[10] See *infra*, next paragraph.

[11] Greenberg (1997).

Lastly, an *in vitro* evaluation on the possible future use of the dual Italian class action device from 2019—injunctive or compensatory, or both—shall be conducted, building on the previous analysis. A comparison with other non-class action procedural paths—i.e., in front of the ECtHR—will be proposed, too. As will be argued, there is indeed room for bringing collective suits to judicially address these relevant issues, although some regulatory and interpretative obstacles may stand in the way. These lessons will be included in the subsequent conclusive Chapter, when addressing the next possible steps for allowing a more efficient use of the class action model in Italy, specifically, and in Europe, more generally.

9.2 Factual Contextualisation. Systemic and Structural Violations: The Italian Case

As anticipated, Italy—alike numerous others European countries, and beyond—has a bleak history of fundamentally degrading treatment of prisoners and detainees, on the one hand, and migrants and asylum seekers, on the other hand. Such a history is not confined to the past, but, rather, well-rooted in the present and, unless the trend is substantially reverted, part of the future, too.

Regarding the former issue, that of prisoners and detainees, a first notable judgement for Italy is that from the ECtHR from 2009, in the *Sulejmanović* case.[12] In this instance, the individual applicant lamented having been confined, from January until April 2003, in the Roman Rebibbia penitentiary, in a jail cell of 16.20 m^2 with five other people, resulting therefore in a personal living space available for each of them of 2.70 m^2. From April until October 2003, he was placed in a different cell with only four people, resulting in a personal living space available for each of them of 3.40 m^2. This kind of detention conditions was common throughout all the Rebibbia prison, which accommodated a number of individuals between 1,456 and 1,660 while its maximum capacity was for 1.271.[13]

These concrete conditions contrasted with the minimum standards set in 2006 by the European Committee for the Prevention of Torture and Inhuman or Degrading Treatment or Punishment ('CPT', instituted by the CoE system, as is known). Pursuant to them, the space available per prisoner in the cells should be at least 7 m^2,

[12] ECtHR, *Sulejmanovic v. Italy*, No. 22635/0, 2009. The issue of overcrowded prisons had been presented to, yet not directly analysed by, the Italian Constitutional Court already in Judgements No. 6 from 1975 and No. 510 from 19995. After Law 1 August 2003, No. 207 on the conditional suspension of the execution of the judgement, whose rationale was 'prison deflation, aimed at mitigating the serious problem of prison overcrowding' (Italian Constitutional Court, order no. 346 from 2005), the Constitutional Court dealt with the problem more, but still not directly (see, e.g., also Order No. 351 from 2005, Order No. 276 from 2006, Order No. 103 from 2009). The first time was with Judgement No. 279 from 2013, after the *Torreggiani v. Italy* pilot-judgement from the same year from the ECtHR (see *infra*, in the text). See also Judgement No. 1 from 1969.

[13] ECtHR, *Sulejmanovic v. Italy*, No. 22635/0, 2009.

with a minimum distance of 2 m between the walls and 2.50 m between the floor and the ceiling. Moreover, each prisoner should be able to spend at least eight hours a day outside his or her cell, another element conflicting with the facts reported by the individual applicant, in the case at hand. Such parametres, it must be recalled, were presented as 'desirable' by the CPT; still, as pointed out by the applicant, the Court had already referred to them on multiple occasions.[14] Today, especially after the ECtHR Grand Chamber *Muršić v. Croatia* judgement, from 2016, these standards have been lowered, as 3 m^2 of surface area per detainee in a multi-occupancy cell appears to have become the applicable minimum standard to strongly presume a violation of Article 3 ECHR.[15]

In its decision from 2009 against Italy, the Strasbourg Court found a violation for the period of detention from January to April 2003, stating that 'the applicant's flagrant lack of personal space constituted inhuman or degrading treatment'.[16] It also recalled the *absolute* nature of the prohibition set by Article 3 ECHR, stressing that the serious repercussions that prison overcrowding can have on prisoners' rights, including the right not to be subjected to inhuman and degrading treatment, should not be underestimated. It also noted that a problem of overcrowding undoubtedly existed in the Roman Rebibbia penitentiary at the time of the applicant's deprivation of liberty.

After the ECtHR judgement, the overall situation—which regarded the Rebibbia penitentiary, but, in general, all the Italian prison system—did not improve in subsequent years. If anything, it was exposed even more.

In January 2013, it was the landmark *Torreggiani* case, once again in front of the ECtHR, to bring the focus back to the issue.[17] This time, however, the Strasbourg Court did not decide on an individual application. Quite extraordinarily it employed the so-called '*pilot-judgement procedure*', first introduced jurisprudentially in 2004 to deal with systemic and structural deficiencies within a national legal order.[18] After a previous case against Russia, this was the second-ever time that such a complex procedure was used against one of the 47 CoE Member States (now 46, after Russia's expulsion in 2022) for the violation of Article 3 ECHR.

The case stemmed from seven applications against Italy, from individuals complaining in particular about the conditions in which they had been held in the Busto Arsizio and Piacenza prisons for different periods of time, between November 2006 and June 2011. The Court considered that the applicants were not provided with a living space that complied with the parametres it had found acceptable in its jurisprudence; in all the cases, in fact, it was inferior to 4 m^2, exacerbated by a lack of hot water for a long period of time and inadequate lighting and ventilation. The

[14] See ECtHR, *Kalashnikov v. Russia*, No. 47095/99, 2002.

[15] ECtHR *Muršić v. Croatia* [GC], No. 7334/13, 2016.

[16] ECtHR, *Sulejmanovic v. Italy*, No. 22635/0, 2009, § 43.

[17] ECtHR, *Torreggiani and Others v. Italy*, No. 43517/09 *et al.*, 2013 (pilot-judgement).

[18] See Lemmens and Van Drooghenbroeck (2023), Glas (2019), Kurban (2016), Randazzo (2012), p. 123, Garlicki (2007).

Court considered that such detention conditions, having regard also to the length of the applicants' imprisonment, 'subjected them to an ordeal of an intensity which exceeded the *unavoidable level* of suffering inherent in detention',[19] therefore finding a violation of Article 3 ECHR.

Furthermore, the Court, based on the information received, found that prison overcrowding in Italy did not exclusively concern the applicants' cases. In particular, it noted that the *structural* and *systemic* nature of prison overcrowding in Italy was clear from the *statistical data* referred to above and from the terms of the declaration from 2010 of a national state of emergency by the President of the Italian Council of Ministers himself, already extended (at the time, January 2013) twice. As of 13 April 2012, Italian prisons housed 66.585 inmates, representing an overcrowding rate of 148%; 42% of the inmates were awaiting trial and held in pre-trial detention.[20]

Taken together, these facts showed, according to the Strasbourg Court, that the violation of the applicants' right to adequate conditions of detention 'was not the result of isolated incidents but stemmed from a *systemic problem* resulting from a chronic malfunctioning of the Italian prison system which had affected and was likely to continue to affect many people'.[21] This practice was incompatible with the Convention and confirmed by the several hundred applications against Italy, constantly increasing, already received by the Court.

As a consequence, the Court decided to apply the pilot judgment procedure to facilitate the *quickest and most effective* resolution of such a systemic malfunction. In doing so, it reiterated that, 'in view of the non-derogable nature of the right protected by Article 3 of the Convention, the [Italian] State is under an obligation to organise its penitentiary system in such a way that the dignity of prisoners is respected'.[22]

In particular, it recalled that it is not up to the Court itself to indicate the specific necessary actions. Pursuant to Article 46 ECHR, this task was incumbent on the Italian State, under the supervision of the Committee of Ministers, either by reducing the prison population, by building new penitentiary centres and by introducing new remedies or amending already-present ones for allowing preventive and compensatory redress. They were to be put in place within one year from the date on which that judgment was to become final. It especially underscored that, in matters of prison conditions, "*preventive*' and '*compensatory*' remedies must co-exist in a complementary manner'.[23]

Such a landmark judgement was followed by several others in front of the Strasbourg Court. Among them, for instance, the Court found violations of Article 3 ECHR in the *Viola* case, from 2019, in relation to the so-called '*ergastolo*

[19] ECtHR, *Torreggiani and Others v. Italy*, 2013, § 19 (emphasis added).

[20] Id. (emphasis added).

[21] Id.

[22] Id.

[23] Id.

ostativo' (irreducible life sentence), or in the very recent *Libri* case, from January 2024, concerning inadequate health care for a prisoner in serious need. Another application, stemming from the death of nine inmates in March 2020 in the Modena prison during a covid-related riot (thirteen deaths in total in Italy), is currently pending before the ECtHR, too.[24]

These cases demonstrate how the apparently positive reaction from the ECtHR in the *Stella* case, from 2014, one year after the *Torreggiani* pilot-judgement, has not found support in subsequent actions.[25] In sum, the problem still seriously persists.[26]

This is substantiated by the last report, from 2023, of the National Guarantor of the rights of persons deprived of their personal liberty ('*Garante nazionale dei diritti delle persone private della libertà personale*') to the Italian Parliament. The report is rather striking, while painting an ongoing bleak picture of the current conditions of the overall Italian prison system:

> A decade after the ECHR Court's ruling in Torreggiani and others v. Italy, our country does not seem to have resolved many of the critical issues that characterise its prison system. A clear symptom of this is the general increase in critical events that represent a sort of thermometer of the quality of the prison system and in particular of hetero- or self-directed ones, such as suicide acts, which in recent years have shown an increasing trend. The widespread structural degradation, the precarious hygienic and sanitary conditions of many detention areas, the absence in many cases of premises for treatment activities, the inadequacy of space, resources and personnel necessary to meet the numerous needs of health care needs of detainees, just to mention a few of the critical issues underlying the condition of widespread malaise, in the majority of cases have not yet found a solution, while, on the other hand, the chronic phenomenon of prison overcrowding is still present and extremely influential.[27]

These words make obvious, once again, the need for a structural reform in this sector in Italy. *Systemic* and *continuous* violations to the fundamental right to live in

---

[24] Ansa, 20 October 2022.

[25] ECtHR, *Stella and Others v. Italy* (dec.), Nos. 49169/09, 54908/09, 55156/09 *et al.*, 2014. In such a case the Court found an inadmissibility of applications lamenting the lack of effective remedies in respect to prison overcrowding in Italy, following the *Torreggiani* pilot-judgment: 'Following the communication of the applications to the Government, the Court had applied the pilot-judgment procedure in the case of Torreggiani and Others v. Italy, in which it had noted that prison overcrowding in Italy represented an endemic and structural problem. [...] Following that judgment, the Italian State had enacted a number of legislative measures aimed at resolving the structural problem of overcrowding in prisons and, in parallel, had reformed the law to allow detained persons to complain to a judicial authority about the material conditions of detention and had also introduced a compensatory remedy providing for damages to be paid to persons who had been subjected to detention contrary to the Convention. [...] The respondent State's domestic authorities had thus complied with the principles established in the Court's case-law in this area, and with the findings set out in the pilot judgment under Article 46 of the Convention'.

[26] To be fair, initially there was a drastic drop in the occupancy numbers of Italian prisons, as in March 2016, when the Committee of Ministers closed the execution phase of Torreggiani v. Italy, there were only 49.504 inmates for 52.846 spots (see Antigone Report (2024)).

[27] Italian national guarantor of the rights of persons deprived of their liberty ('*Garante nazionale dei diritti delle persone private della libertà personale*'), Report to the Parliament (2023), p. 100.

basic human conditions are currently in place—and have been, for decades—for the 62,445 prisoners and detainees from all over the country, as per the last census (from 30 April 2025), with a current overcrowding ratio of 133%.[28] Furthermore, the overall ineffectiveness of the attempts—judicial and not—to fill the mass gaps in the enforcement of 'one of the most fundamental values of a democratic society'[29]—borrowing once again the words of the ECtHR Grand Chamber from 2015—manifestly emerges from them.

The situation is further exacerbated by the high rate of suicides among inmates, with 88 cases in 2023 and again 88 in 2024. Episodes of torture and violence against inmates are also regularly reported.[30]

These simple yet crude figures clearly depict the *gap in the enforcement* process of traditional paths of enforcement.

On the one hand, the ECtHR shows its inability to indicate specific necessary actions and, most importantly, to effectively supervise, at least down the line, its own judgements, even when delivered in response to such a blatant systemic and structural violation to an absolute right.[31]

On the other hand, the *Italian Constitutional Court* itself in the same year as *Torreggiani* (2013), recognised 'a phenomenon that, albeit with different intensities, has been affecting the Italian prison system for some time and has resulted in a situation that cannot be prolonged', in light of how prison overcrowding 'undermine[s] the constitutionally imperative features of criminal enforcement and [...] affect[s], by compressing it, the irreducible 'remnant' of the prisoner's personal freedom',[32] both expressions of the personalistic principle at the basis of the Constitution.

In the same case, from 2013, however, the Constitutional Court declared the inadmissibility of the questions of constitutional legitimacy raised before it on the provision of the Italian criminal code (Article 147 c.p.) insofar as it did not provide the possibility of a postponement of the execution of a judgement when it was to be carried out in conditions 'contrary to humanity'. The inadmissibility was found by the Court due to the *plurality of regulatory solutions* that could be adopted, and not just the one proposed by the tribunals raising the question (that is, the postponement of the execution). As a consequence, according to the *Giudice delle leggi*, the path of 'additive intervention', through the so-called 'mandatory rhymes' technique, was to be excluded since it would have meant encroaching upon the *legislator's discretion*. This clearly depicts a fundamental limit of constitutional review, on specific legislation, in Italy.

The same judgement urged the legislator to act in their prioritary assessment on the appropriateness of means, in order to achieve what was (is) undoubtedly a

[28] See the last census from the Antigone Association (Antigone Report (2025), available here), with certain prisons (such as San Vittore in Milan), arriving to an overcrowding rate of even 220%.

[29] ECtHR, *Bouyid v. Belgium* [GC], No. 23380/09, 2015, § 81.

[30] See Antigone Report (2024).

[31] See Lemmens and Van Drooghenbroeck (2023).

[32] Italian Constitutional Court, Judgement No. 279 from 2013, point No. 6 of the Points of law.

'constitutionally necessary end',[33] affirming 'how excessive legislative inertia with regard to the serious problem identified in the present ruling would not be tolerable'.[34] Other decisions followed,[35] but none of them managed to overcome such an enforcement gap, ontologically intrinsic—for valid and obvious reasons—to constitutional review: that is, the possibility to add a normative criterion 'not inferable from the regulatory fabric'[36] when faced with a plurality of alternatives, whose choice should compete to the Parliament.[37]

Furthermore, as regards other types of proceedings, Articles 35-*bis* and 69, para. 6, b) o.p. (the Italian law on the penitentiary system) set the possibility of a 'jurisdictional complaint' ('*reclamo giurisdizionale*') against the 'non-compliance by the administration with the provisions [...] and the regulations relating thereto, as a result of which *the prisoner or inmate* suffers actual and serious prejudice to the exercise of his or her rights' (emphasis added). The right to health and to not be subject to inhuman or degrading conditions, also as a result of overcrowded prisons, should be herein accounted.

However, such a procedure regards only the specific *individual* subjective positions of the complainant. As found in recent case law, it is, 'in fact, impossible to ensure to the complainant *uti singulis* a restoration of a situation of full execution not contrary to the sense of humanity *without first resolving the general problems* affecting the entire building from the structural and hygienic-maintenance point of view' (emphasis added).[38] In the case at hand, from May 2024, the judge, tasked with supervision of the execution of the criminal sanction, ordered, firstly, general measures to the prison administration and, only subsequently, in case of inertia for sixty days, the transfer of the complainant to a different institution. Evidently, the general measures were not followed, and it seems rightfully so, since the *complaint* was an *individual* one and since Article 69, para. 6, b) only refers to *individual prejudice*. Rather, any order encompassing his personal and individual sphere in favour of a *collective redress*, should be granted within the scope of *collective proceedings* (see *infra*, next paragraphs).

The second type of cases for which the use of class actions is hereby proposed is that of *migrants and asylum seekers*. These infringements are strictly connected to those of prisoners' and detainees' rights. As a matter of fact, the same report from

[33] See also Italian Constitutional Court, Judgement No. 23 from 2013.

[34] Id.

[35] For instance, Italian Constitutional Court, Judgement No. 179 from 2017.

[36] Italian Constitutional Court, Judgement No. 32 from 2016.

[37] See, on the so-called *Cappato* case, before the Italian Constitutional Court, Randazzo (2023), p. 131, and Zanon (2021).

[38] Supervisory judge ('*magistrato di sorveglianza*') from Florence, Order from 22 May 2024, No. 2179/2024. It further proceeds: 'and thus with extraordinary maintenance and rehabilitation measures, which is why, in the event of inertia on the part of the administration that has continued beyond the deadline for such general measures, in order to ensure the prisoner's primary right, there is no alternative but to order him to be transferred to a different institution where the minimum living conditions mentioned above are guaranteed' (translated from Italian).

the Italian National Ombudsman of the rights of persons deprived of their personal liberty spends significant words on the increasingly worse and, to some degree, less talked-about conditions in the Italian 'Detention centres for repatriation' ('*Centri di permanenza per il rimpatrio*'—'*Cpr*'—, substituting the previous '*Centri di identificazione ed espulsione*'—'*Cie*'—, that is 'centres of identification and expulsion'), as well as in the 'Reception centres for asylum seekers' ('*Centri di accoglienza per richiedenti asilo*'—'*Cara*') or in the so-called 'hotspots', acting as 'suitable premises' to be used only—more in theory than in practice—as a kind of back-up of *Cprs* at police headquarters.

Said report from the National Ombudsman, as well as the specific ones for individual centres, underscores an equally dramatic picture in such centres, where fundamental rights—namely that to a judge, to health and to 'relational connections'—are often deprived from migrants. In sum, once again Italy appears to be violating in a systemic and structural manner the prohibition from Article 3 ECHR, to avoid inhuman and degrading treatment; a prohibition which, as already stated, amounts to one of the most cardinal values of any democratic society, and is also set forth in the CFREU and in the Italian Constitution itself, as illustrated above. In the words of the Italian National Guarantor of the rights of persons deprived of their personal liberty:

> This absence of connection is plastically represented by these places being emblematic of emptiness, both spatial and temporal.
> Spaces often designed only to contain, without any activity or meaningful internal relations, in a flow of time characterised by the indeterminateness of the outcome of its unfolding. A reality in which strongly harbours anger, failure, the desire for destruction and self-destruction.
> […] three aspects of protection because I believe that the shortcomings of each of them in the present context give the physiognomy of the current form of administrative detention: ever more extensive, in ever more varied places with little or no openness to the outside world, always lacking in fundamental safeguards. The risk is that it tends to legitimise itself more as a reassuring measure for the community rather than as an effective component for a strategy that, as has been repeatedly affirmed, including in recent times, succeeds in reducing situations of irregular presence on national territory and the consequent risks, also in terms of possible criminal connections.[39]
> […] On the de facto deprivation of liberty, the regulatory perspective is still lacking, especially with regard to detention practices in hotspots or in the waiting areas of airport transit zones.[40]

Furthermore, with regard to *Cprs*, the report stresses how, in 2022, out of 6,383 individuals detained in the Cprs only 3,154—that is, 50.60%—have been effectively repatriated in the end. This makes, in practice, the deprivation of liberty of the

[39] Italian national guarantor of the rights of persons deprived of their liberty ('*Garante nazionale dei diritti delle persone private della libertà personale*'), Report to the Parliament (2023), pp. 47 and 48.

[40] Id., p. 78.

remaining 49.40%—an 'inviolable' right, as per Article 13 It. Const.—in most cases, at the very least, questionable.[41]

These data are aggravated by recent protests in numerous *Cprs*, for the unbearable treatment received by migrants every day, with harsh videos surfacing of them being beaten down by public officers with truncheons, practically naked, under the heavy rain and covered with mud.[42]

Evidently, these issues are much wider and regard all European countries. This has been recently highlighted, for instance, in a recent article from March 2024 by Dunja Mijatović, then still Council of Europe Commissioner for Human Rights:

> Europe's insistence on looking tough on migration is endangering rule of law across the Continent. Pursuing ever more stringent asylum and migration policies, European countries are not only perpetuating human rights violations against asylum seekers and migrants; they are also dismantling collective human rights safeguards, as well as eroding wider legal and democratic checks and balances that protect all our rights.[43]

The ECtHR itself has repeatedly condemned Italy for its violations of Article 3 ECHR in relation to migrants' degrading and inhuman treatment in its reception centres. Three recent notable cases against Italy, for instance, are *J.A. and others*, *M.A.*, and *A.B.*, all from 2023, in all of which the Court held—unanimously—that there had been a violation of Article 3 ECHR for the conditions in which the migrants were subjected while in the Lampedusa hotspot. In its assessment, the ECtHR gave great relevance to the reports from previous years of the already mentioned National Guarantor. It also acknowledged how, in general terms, living conditions in hotspots were criticised by the UN Committee against Torture in its 2017 reports on Italy.[44]

In conclusion, to this day, as shown, no concrete substantial improvement seems to have occurred in relation to either of the two issues until now raised.

9.3 The Common Law Experience with Prisoners' Class Action Litigation. The *Plata*, *Ashker*, and *Brazeau* Cases

As mentioned, the common law experience with class actions offers a large number of cases related to detention conditions in prisons. As accounted by local scholarship, these cases have been successfully brought for decades now, mainly in relation to prison overcrowding. Recent years, furthermore, have seen a filing of class suits by migrants, too, i.e., in relation to the unhealthy and degrading conditions in detention centres.

---

[41] Id, p. 46.

[42] Milano Today, 11 February 2024.

[43] Politico, 6 March 2024.

[44] See Zirulia (2023).

Given the more established case law to this regard, as well as the existence of a considerably more developed academic scholarship, the present paragraph will merely concentrate on cases related to *prisons and penitentiaries*. Still, as resulting from the examination of the Italian system, it can be argued that these cases share numerous similarities with the ones of *migrants and asylum seekers*. Hence, the lessons derivable from studying the former will be applied also to assessing the future viability of class actions in Italy for the enforcement of the latter's rights. Any relevant differences will, however, be reported in the concluding paragraph when relevant.

The chosen cases pertain to the US and Canada jurisdictions. They have managed to successfully improve the conditions of inmates, achieving both structural reform and injunctive and compensatory relief.

The first illustrative one, on which we shall concentrate in depth, is the *Brown v. Plata* case. *Brown v. Plata* started as a lawsuit filed in 2001, in the US Northern District Court of California, initially named *Plata v. Davis* and then *Plata v. Schwarzenegger*, which reached the US Supreme Court in 2010 (decided in 2011). Due to its massive proportions and ramifications, it has been described by academic commentators as 'the most significant class action litigation of the past decade'.[45]

It stemmed from the unbearable overcrowding of California's state prisons, which were accommodating approximately 150,000 inmates despite being designed to hold a maximum of approximately 80,000 people. While the numbers increased, the conditions of incarceration worsened for all the inmates, from the quantity of personal space available, to basic systems of health, lightning, ventilation, control and security. This caused a surge also in the number of accidents, suicides, fights and physical and mental illnesses, with several deaths reported, too.

Special attention to the *lack of adequate health care*—or delay in its provision—was initially stressed by the applicants in the class action. As accounted, an *unnecessary inmate death* once every six or seven days on average was being reported because of such systemic failures.

The plaintiffs were ten inmates from different California state prisons who had been 'seriously injured because of the defendants' deliberate indifference to their serious medical needs in violation of the cruel and unusual punishment clause of the Eighth Amendment to the United States Constitution'.[46] A *subclass* was also presented, encompassing prisoners with disabilities.

The class action was an *injunctive* one, under Rule 23(b)(2) of the Federal Rules of Civil Procedure, on behalf of the class of all the prisoners with serious medical needs who were then, or would have been in the future, under the custody of the CDC (California Department of Corrections), excluding prisoners from Pelican Bay State Prison. The reasons for class treatment, apart from a purported commonality of questions of law and fact, were the numerosity of the class, which made joinder

---

[45] Issacharoff (2012).

[46] Plaintiffs' application.

of all members impracticable, and the risk of inconsistent or varying adjudications establishing incompatible standards, should the class members proceed separately.

The plaintiffs sought a declaration on the unconstitutionality and unlawfulness of the conducts suffered, as well as an injunction from subjecting the *whole* class to said 'acts, omissions, policies, and conditions'. Monetary damage was sought only for the named plaintiffs. The class was filed against the Governor of California, the California Department of Corrections (CDC) and several Directors and public officials therein connected, in their official capacity.

In 2002, a *settlement* was successfully negotiated between the parties and subsequently approved as fair, reasonable and adequate by the Court. This order, however, was *appealed* by the defendants, with a consequent continuation of the litigation. It must be noted that the litigation is still ongoing today, although with very positive progress, as accounted by the Court itself (i.e., in 2012).

The first relevant result of the litigation was the court appointment, in 2005, after six continuous days of evidentiary hearings, of a *Receiver* 'to take control of the delivery of medical services to all California state prisoners confined by the California Department of Corrections and Rehabilitation ('CDR')'. Based on the abovementioned statistics of a preventable inmate death every six to seven days due to constitutional deficiencies in the CDR's medical system, the court found that a 'dramatic overhaul' was necessary. The situation, according to Judge Thelthon Henderson, could not be 'more grave, and the threat of future injury and death is virtually granted in the absence of drastic action'. He also stated: 'By all accounts, the California prison medical care system is broken beyond repair'.[47] The Receiver was bound to give a report initially twice (subsequently three times) a year and had extraordinary power to implement a plan for action. Such a power was also *economic*, with orders of payment of millions of dollars and the possibility of constructing new buildings or hiring new personnel.

It was on the wake of this plan and of the Receiver's reporting, that the problem of *prison overcrowding* and its interfering effect on overhauling the prison health care system emerged. These led to a plaintiffs' motion to convene a new three-judge district court to impose a *population cap*, with consequent reduction of the number of inmates in the CDR prison system.

As a result of such a motion, a new litigation path emerged which led to the above-referred Supreme Court decision in 2011.[48] With a five-to-four majority this Court affirmed the previous injunction order to reduce the prison population by releasing approximately 46,000 inmates. According to the Court, said order was an *extrema ratio* due to the legislative and executive powers' longstanding unwillingness or inability to find the financial resources necessary to remedy the systemic and structural problem. Since no other relief could have remedied the violation and substantial flexibility had been given to the State in determining its execution, the order was affirmed by the Supreme Court.

---

[47] Opinion from 3 October 2005.

[48] *Brown, et al. v. Plata, et al.*, 563 U.S. 493 (2011).

Subsequently, in practice, as expectable, a substantial restructuring of the prison system was enacted by California legislature, with the passing of new regulations, the redefinition of several felonies and the moving of numerous inmates from California prisons to county jails.

Today, as per the last official report from the CDR, from 6 December 2023, California's adult prison population is 91,429, occupying 121% percent of its current design capacity.[49] Considering the almost 200% capacity from 2001, when the first *Plata* injunctive class action was started, the outcome has been, by all means, massive.

Other cases to account, briefly, are *Ashker v. Brown* and *Brazeau v. Canada*.

Ashker v. Brown was another class action suit filed against the California state prison system, this time in relation to solitary confinement in the Pelican Bay Security Housing Unit. Similarly to the *Plata* case, it started out, in 2012, as an *injunctive* suit, with ten named plaintiffs who had been placed in solitary confinement for over a decade on the basis of a purported gang-association or membership.

The class included all the approximately 1,100 inmates serving indeterminate SHU sentences at the Pelican Bay SHU on the basis of gang validation. Also in this case, a *subclass* was proposed, including all inmates who were then, or in the future, imprisoned at the Pelican Bay SHU under the same conditions and policies for longer than ten continuous years, in violation of the Eighth Amendment. They sought declaratory and injunctive relief, including an order compelling the defendants (i.e., the Governor of California and several other related state authorities)[50] 'to swiftly develop constitutionally-adequate procedures for reviewing ongoing placement in the SHU, to release from the SHU those prisoners who have languished under the cruel conditions there for over a decade, and to alleviate the conditions of confinement for all Pelican Bay SHU prisoners'.[51]

In 2014, the case was *certified* by the Court as a class action. Interestingly, the main issue was the *commonality* test. According to the defendants, 'a host of individual questions not subject to classwide proof' was present. In the court's view, nonetheless, such a requirement was met, since, to satisfy it, 'a plaintiff need only show that his or her claims raise *some* questions that are amenable to classwide adjudication'.

In particular, the common questions of law and fact raised by the plaintiffs were identified *(a)* in the long-term confinement inside the Pelican Bay SHU, exposing inmates to a 'sufficiently serious' deprivation of basic human needs and *(b)* in the defendants' common conduct, in assigning inmates to the SHU for indefinite terms acted with a 'sufficiently culpable state of mind'. The fact that the conditions in the SHU and the mental health risk were *common* was deemed sufficient, whereas the

[49] Report from the CDR, 6 December 2023.

[50] Namely CDCR's Secretary, Pelican Bay's Warden, and the Chief of CDCR's Office of Correctional Safety, each of whom was sued in his official capacity. This is why the suit, originally 'v. Shwarzenegger', was later amended in 'v. Brown', upon the changing of the California State Governor.

[51] Plaintiffs' application.

fact that different inmates may exhibit *different symptoms* was not sufficient to exclude commonality. Pursuant to the Court, individual factual differences were even less decisive for this test, in class actions challenging a '*system-wide*' policy.

After certification, a *landmark settlement* was reached in 2015 that fundamentally altered the nature of SHU confinement in California.[52] It dramatically reduced it, changed it from a status-based (gang affiliation) to a behaviour-based system, proposed valid alternatives, allowed more out-of-cell time and introduced constant monitoring. It was approved by the Court.

For the sake of completeness, it must be pointed out that the execution of this settlement has not, to date, been fully respected by the defendants and that, therefore, the litigation is still ongoing. Nevertheless, like in the previous *Plata* case, significant progress has already been made.

Finally, the last case reported is *Brazeau v. Canada (Attorney General).*[53] This Canadian class action shares elements of both previous US class actions in *Plata* and *Ashker*. Contrarily to them, however, it introduces the issue of *damages* and *compensatory* collective relief. Rather than from a single action suit, it stemmed from a multiplicity of suits (apart from *Brazeau*, also *Reddock v. Canada (Attorney General)* and *Gallone c. Canada (Attorney General)*), in front of the Ontario Superior Court of Justice and of the Superior Court of Québec, subsequently united in a jointly written decision. The reason for this was the fundamental intertwining between them.

The main facts of the case involved once again inmates of penitentiaries, this time operated by the Correctional Service of Canada ('CSC'). In particular, in the original *Brazeau* class action suit, filed in 2015, the plaintiffs sued the Government of Canada (represented by the Defendant Attorney General of Canada) for breaches of ss. 7 and 12 of the Canadian Charter of Rights and Freedom. They lamented the conditions of their administrative segregation—i.e., solitary confinement, very similarly to the *Ashker* case—, *systemic failures* in providing them with the necessary health care and, as a consequence, a worsening and further developing of serious medical illnesses (physical and, mainly, mental). Moreover, they alleged that they had been deprived of necessary medications for long periods of time and that they had suffered *damages* due to the systemic abuses perpetrated by Canada, for which they sought compensation.

After a series of amendments, the original *Brazeau* class was *certified* in 2016 as composing:

> All offenders in federal custody, who were placed in administrative segregation in a federal institution situated outside Québec after February 24, 2013, or who placed in administrative segregation in *a federal institution anywhere in Canada* before February 24, 2013 were diagnosed by a medical doctor with an Axis I Disorder (excluding substance use disorders) or Borderline Personality Disorder, who suffered from their disorder, in a manner described

[52] Settlement agreement from 31 August 2015, US District Court, Northern District of California, Oakland Division, C09-05796 CW.

[53] *Brazeau v. Canada (Attorney General),* 2020 ONSC 7229 (CanLII) and *Brazeau v. Canada (Attorney General),* 2021 ONSC 1828 (CanLII).

in Appendix A, and reported such during their incarceration, where the diagnosis by a medical doctor occurred either before or during incarceration in a federal institution and the offenders were incarcerated between November 1, 1992 and the present, and were alive as of July 20, 2013.[54]

At this point, after certification, the parties tried to *negotiate*, as required, the so-called Distribution Protocol and of the Individual Issues Protocol, in order to determine the procedure for assessing individual issues of damages, given the individual difference between each inmate. These differences regarded, for instance, the number of days under administrative segregation or the type and seriousness of the illness suffered as a result, or worsened after such a segregation. Since no agreement was found, the Superior Courts of Ontario and Québec agreed to hold a joint hearing to determine themselves such criteria.

We shall not go currently into detail on such complex determinations. Merely the following elements, of interest for the present analysis, shall be considered.

First, the class action regards, with specifications, inmates from federal penitentiaries '*anywhere in Canada*'. Such an amplitude of the class is key. The courts of Ontario and Québec certified the class in spite of evident *differences* in the questions of law and fact. These different legal and factual elements stemmed also from the different time frame and personal illnesses reported by each individual inmate, in each prison.

Evidently—and we agree—the courts deemed this lack of identity of the questions of law and fact not decisive for the future joint management of the class nor relevant for determining commonality. This is in line with the definition of '*common issues*' under the Canadian Class Proceedings Act, from 1992, as '(a) common but *not necessarily identical* issues of fact, or (b) common but not necessarily identical issues of law that arise from common but not necessarily identical facts' (emphasis added). This point raises important interpretative questions, in relation to the *homogeneity* requirement in Italy, already mentioned above (Chap. 6) and to which we shall return below.

Second, the class action was a *damages* one. The damages sought were Charter and punitive ones, to be awarded, firstly, in the *aggregate* (as a base award) to the class and, then, through an *individual damages* assessment, as compensation for pecuniary and non-pecuniary personal injury sustained by each class member.

Again, this follows the Canadian Class Proceedings Act, from 1992, which, in Section 24, establishes the possibility for the court to determine the *aggregate* or a part of a defendant's liability to class members where 'no questions of fact or law other than those relating to the assessment of monetary relief remain to be determined in order to establish the amount of the defendant's monetary liability' and 'the aggregate or a part of the defendant's liability to some or all class members can reasonably be determined without proof by individual class members'. In this case, the court may also order that such an award be shared by individual class members on an average or proportional basis. In this circumstance, the court also determines

[54] *Brazeau v. Attorney General (Canada)*, 2016 ONSC 7836 (CanLII).

non-complex procedures for individual class members to present their claims, i.e. by using standardised proof, receipts or other documentary evidence—with the audit of claims even on a sampling basis.

Furthermore, pursuant to Section 27.2 of the same Act:

> The court may order that all or part of an award under section 24 that has not been distributed to class or subclass members within a time set by the court be paid to the person or entity determined under subsection (3) on a cy-près basis, if the court is satisfied that, using best reasonable efforts, it is not practical or possible to compensate class or subclass members directly.

The person or entity determined under subsection (3), to whom payment of non-distributed damages, should be made on a *cy-près* basis are:

> (a) a registered charity within the meaning of the Income Tax Act (Canada) or non-profit organization that is agreed on by the parties, if the court determines that payment of the amount to the registered charity or non-profit organization would reasonably be expected to directly or indirectly benefit the class or subclass members; or
> (b) Legal Aid Ontario, in any other case.

The issue of *cy-près* and *fluid recovery* schemes has been already discussed in detail as a valuable distribution alternative, at the moment alien to the Italian system but certainly to be considered for the future.[55]

In the case at hand, 20 million $ were awarded as an *aggregate damages* award, to be subsequently distributed with a specific and detailed scheme to the *class members*, as a partial remedy for their unlawful placement in administrative segregation, contrary to ss. 7 and 12 of the Canadian Charter of Rights and Freedoms.[56] The class members were also granted judgments to have their *individual damages* determined. Proportionally similar judgements were also awarded in the *Reddock* and *Gallone* cases, whose decision were subsequently joined to *Brazeau*.

Third, after judging on the common issues, the court had to set out the procedure for the *individual issues* determinations. This phase, subsequent to the ruling on the common issues of the class, regards issues that require the participation of individual class members, which, as a consequence, shall be determined individually.[57] In doing so, the court, pursuant to the Canadian Class Proceedings Act, Section 25(3), has a great margin of *flexibility* in determining the procedure. This can be done either by dispensing unnecessary procedural steps and by authorising any appropriate special procedural steps, also relating to discovery and proof. Furthermore, a reasonable time frame within which individual class members can present their claim is set, too. Naturally, an adequate plan for *dissemination of notice* has to be provided, too.

---

[55] See *supra*, Chap. 6.

[56] This was the result of an overturning in appeal. In the initial summary judgment decision, in fact, the 20 million $ award less Class Counsel's fee were to be paid by Canada for additional mental health or program resources at its penitentiaries.

[57] Sections 11 and 25, Canadian Class Proceedings Act.

In the case at hand, without entering into details, it should be noted that the courts, after taking into account the plaintiffs' and defendants' proposals (since they could not reach a settlement), drafted a rather *articulated plan of distribution*. As summarised by the courts themselves, this plan had nine major elements. The ones we shall highlight are two.

On the one hand, individual class members were provided with a 'claims form' in which they could select one of *three different tracks* to make their claim for individual compensation. Each track entailed a different, progressively more complex, assessment procedure, as well as a different, progressively higher, monetary range of the individual damages sought.

On the other hand, the key involvement of a so-called '*Administrator*' and of a '*Roster of Managers/Experts*', named by agreement of the parties or by order of the court, must be noted. These managers/experts were not appointed as referees with adjudicative authority. They had, nevertheless, the key function of determining the individual class member's *eligibility* to receive a share of the distribution of the aggregate damages award by reviewing the claims form and their file, reporting to the administrator. They were also in charge of determining, for track 2 claims, the *quantum* of the individual class members' claims by reviewing the claims form, their individual file, the affidavit material, the transcripts, and facts filed by both the individual class member and the defendant, reporting to the Ontario Superior Court of Justice or to the Superior Court of Québec.[58]

Rather significantly, these managers/experts were required to have *proven medical knowledge*.[59] Moreover, also relating to experts' contribution, as set forth under Section 23 of the Canadian Class Proceedings Act, for the purposes of determining issues relating to the amount or distribution of a monetary award, 'the court may admit *as evidence statistical information* that would otherwise not be admissible as evidence, including information derived from sampling, if the information was compiled in accordance with principles that are generally accepted by *experts* in the field of statistics' (emphasis added). The explicit reference to the possibility of using *statistics* has been repeatedly mentioned in the Italian cases commented in the previous two Chapters, although with contrasting interpretative views. On this, we shall return in the following.

Last, the conclusive aspect to underscore about the *Brazeau* class action is shared with the previous two US cases commented, the *Plata* and *Ashker* Californian class actions. It is the question of who the class *defendants* were: in *Brazeau*, the Attorney General of Canada; in *Plata* and *Ashker*, the Governor of California, the California

[58] Track 3 claims, instead, were presented, for individual damage, to a judge of the Ontario Superior Court of Justice or of the Superior Court of Québec who would determine the class members' claim pursuant to a summary judgment procedure or an analogous procedure.

[59] '(a) a person licensed to practice medicine in any Canadian jurisdiction; (b) a person licensed to practice psychology in any Canadian jurisdiction; (c) a person registered as a psychotherapist in any Canadian jurisdiction; (d) a person registered as a psychiatric nurse in any Canadian jurisdiction; or (e) a person licensed as a psychiatric social worker in any Canadian Jurisdiction.' (para. 110 of the Court's judgement, from 2020).

Department of Corrections (CDC) and several Directors and public officials therein connected (i.e., also prisons' wardens), all in their official capacity. The relevance of this element is cardinal when assessing the possibility of similar class actions in Italy.

9.4 Comparative Evaluations and Room for Future (Class) Actions

The three reported class actions related to prisoners' rights in US and Canada are particularly illustrative to show the potential of this type of litigation in the field. They have been selected among a large array of cases in order to extract lessons that may prove valuable to anyone evaluating the viability of similar proceedings in Italy (or Europe), pursuant to Title VIII-*bis* c.p.c. (or similar trans-substantive models), herein analysed. Both *practical and procedural advantages* emerge, under a perspective (and objective) of structural change, in relation to other litigation paths followed until now, i.e. the above-referred individual applications or the pilot-judgement procedure before the ECtHR, but also constitutional review itself. At the same time, also *potential obstacles* arise that may hinder an efficient use of the class action mechanism in this particular field. It is hereby relevant to highlight them, too, in order to suggest—especially in the next, conclusive, Part—interpretative, institutional and regulatory solutions.

With this aim, the present paragraph shall concentrate on the following issues.

(i) The main question mark concerning prisoners' and migrants' rights class actions in Italy, under the 2019 regime, is that of the *standing to be sued*. As presented, Articles 840-*bis*, para. 3 and Articles 840-*sexiesdecies*, para. 2 c.p.c. establish that both compensatory and injunctive class actions in Italy can be brought against companies or against entities managing public services or public utility services, in respect of acts and conducts in the performance of their respective activities. The notion of '*entities managing public services or public utility services*' is therefore crucial.

In fact, one should wonder if—recalling the US and Canadian cases—the state attorney general, the governor, the national department of corrections, the single penitentiary entity and the directors and public officials connected to them, all considered in their official capacity, may be called as defendants under the Italian provisions, too.

By all means, it seems that all these subjects—especially the single penitentiaries—can be encompassed under the notion of entities managing public services or public utility services. Their *public nature* is highlighted by the fact that they are all called as defendants 'in their official [that is, public] capacity'. Their role is that of ensuring penitentiary treatment and the execution of criminal judicial decisions (in the case of prisoners and detainees). Criminal law, as is known, has, *inter alia*, general-preventive and deterrent functions, which seek the benefit (hence, utility) of the whole society (hence, the public). Criminal sanctions, as set forth under Article 27, third paragraph, of the Italian Constitution, furthermore, must aim at the re-education of the convicted person. Such a re-education, as specified by Article 1, para. 2, of the Italian law on the penitentiary system (Law no. 354 of 1975), should aim, also through contacts with the outside, to social reintegration.

As per Article 15, para. 1, of the same law, the treatment of convicts and inmates should be carried out 'through education, vocational training, employment, participation in projects of *public utility*, religion, cultural, recreational and sporting activities'. Moreover, pursuant to Article 20-*ter*, para. 1, of the same law, they may even work voluntarily and free of charge within the framework of *public utility* projects, both internal and external. Hence, the close connection with *public utility services* and *public services* which are indeed part of the activities carried out by penitentiary centres and their officials.

In addition, as discussed above,[60] the Italian jurisprudence, albeit very limitedly, has already confronted this issue under the previous consumer-focused class action regime of Article 140-*bis* of the Consumer Code. In 2012, in the *Agostino Gemelli* case,[61] before the Rome Tribunal, standing to sue was admitted against a hospital, which—for several degrees—may be equated to a prison. In that case, the court deemed the class action admissible based on a systematic interpretation of the term 'company', which included 'activities connected to intellectual professions, traditionally excluded from business activities, and activities carried out by public entities', as well as 'the healthcare facility operating under an agreement with the National Health Service'.[62]

Specifically, by combining Articles 2082 of the Civil Code and Articles 3 and 18 of the Consumer Code, the Rome Tribunal rejected the restrictive interpretation of 'company' necessarily connected to the 'for profit' purpose, 'since the absence of such an *aim* does not in itself *preclude* the possibility of qualifying the activity as entrepreneurial', as long as it is based on *professionalism* and *economic efficiency*. The same reasoning can be applied to the case of prisons, since their activity is also based on these objectives.

(ii) Slightly more complex may appear (but only at first sight) the issue of coordination with the so-called *administrative* or *public class action*, pursuant to legislative decree 198/2009, in front of the administrative judge. Said action, as anticipated above, concerns 'appeals for the efficiency of administrations and public service concessionaires'. As discussed, these provisions are preserved pursuant to Article 840-*bis* c.p.c., with an express reference, and Article 840-*sexiesdecies*, which refers in general (and more confusingly) to 'special legislation'.

---

[60] See *supra*, Chap. 6.

[61] Id.

[62] *Agostino Gemelli* case. Tribunal of Rome, Order from 20 April 2012, No. 53276/2011. See, *supra*, Chap. 6.

The conflict, nevertheless, is only apparent. In fact, as developed *supra*,[63] the goal of the—three—class action models is rather different:

(a) the *compensatory* device, under Articles 840-*bis et seq.* c.p.c., aims at economic redress or restitution after a suffered *harm*;
(b) the *injunctive* one, pursuant to Article 840-*sexiesdecies* c.p.c., seeks an order to *cease* an activity which is causing prejudice, to be conceived elastically, thus also as the *risk* of a *future* harm;
(c) the *administrative* one, as per l.d. 198/2009, focuses on achieving a *specific result*, corresponding to the correct performance of services, respect of standards or deadlines set by law, regulations or charters.

The admissibility of each action, as a consequence, depends on the specific formulation of the *claim* by the class plaintiffs. The strategy, evidently, will be closely connected to the concrete nuances of each case.

(iii) To this regard, the *injunctive* class action appears particularly powerful, and feasible, for cases of prison overcrowding or of migrants' mistreatment in Cprs and hotspots in Italy. A *collective* suit could indeed be effectively brought on behalf of all the inmates subjected to the same degrading and inhuman treatment seeking the *ceasing* of the conducts causing it (i.e., filling cells with too many inmates, but also a lack of appropriate health care in Cprs or migrants' hotsposts). In this perspective, Samuel Issacharoff's comment on the *Plata* case seems applicable to the Italian situation, too: 'Absent unitary treatment through a class action, no prisoner would have a claim as to the *systemic* violations caused by overcrowding, but only standing to seek legal redress for his or her *individual* harms'.[64] This is exactly the issue depicted above in relation to the jurisdictional complaint pursuant to Articles 35 and 69, para. 6, b) o.p., in which it is, 'in fact, impossible to ensure to the complainant *uti singulis* a restoration of a situation of full execution not contrary to the sense of humanity *without first resolving the general problems* affecting the entire building from the structural and hygienic-maintenance point of view' (emphasis added).[65]

This portrays, on the one hand, the capacity of the injunctive *azione collettiva* from Article 840-*sexiesdecies* c.p.c. to provide enforcement for meta-individual positions, too, which otherwise could not be directly sought by a single person within individual proceedings.

On the other hand, the relief it grants is disruptive but also singular: in the sense that it does not entail a choice from the courts over a plurality of options. It is merely, at its primary enforcement-core, the ceasing of the (even potentially) harmful activity. The upper layers of enforcement are merely optional; this is the case of the specific restorative or preventive measures to be implemented, whose plurality of options indeed could clash with the legislator's discretion.

---

[63] See, *supra*, Chap. 6.

[64] Issacharoff (2012).

[65] See Supervisory judge (*'magistrato di sorveglianza'*) from Florence, Order from 22 May 2024, No. 2179/2024, mentioned *supra*.

Their optionality, still, is essential, as it allows the judge to avoid any formulation on the matter: should the judges believe this would infringe the principle of separation of powers, they can simply stall the (potentially) harmful conduct.

The order in *Plata* imposing a mere population cap, but not clarifying how specifically it should be reached, is rather illustrative to this regard. Evidently, if backed by adequate public and procedural fora, as well as procedural *astreintes*,[66] this could indeed create—and has created in the cases mentioned above, *Plata* and *Ashker*—a bottom-up push to involve—often extra-judicially but still judicially-supervised—legislative, executive, civil and other political actors (see *infra*, for further related reflections).[67]

The traditional paths' inability to provide concrete *structural* redress, could be overcome by the simplicity and yet profound force of the class injunctive tool. The (correctly) broad readings developed until now by the Italian courts (namely the Tribunal of Milan), especially in the *ILVA* and *Philips Respironics* cases, when assessing the admissibility of the suits bodes well with an access to justice perspective. This is relevant both in relation to the commonality/homogeneity[68] of the subjective positions prejudiced, but also to the very concept of prejudice. The latter, according to the Tribunal of Milan in the abovementioned cases can entail a mere *risk* of a *future* harm.

The representative character of the class suit, on the one hand, and the lack of any adhesion phase for the injunctive action (no necessary opt-in or opt-out phase), on the other hand, makes the procedural instrument's potential extremely disruptive. In fact, in its decision, the court would need to evaluate the interests of the whole class. As such, very much alike the *Plata* or the *Ashker* case, it would inevitably need to adopt a *systemic* view. A systemic standpoint which, it could be argued, is by a certain degree *intrinsic* to the very nature of the injunctive class action, given the two elements recalled above: the *representative* nature, and the *erga omnes*—or, at least, *ultra partes*—effects, due to the lack of adhesion.[69]

(iv) The ECtHR and constitutional case law, nevertheless, may still prove crucial for the litigation at hand, at least in Italy. The constant search for *authority support*, highlighted above, in relation once again to the *ILVA* and *Philips Respironics* cases, may be fulfilled through it. A declared infringement of systemic nature by the supranational and domestic *apex courts* certainly eases the work of the first-degree judge, called to an order of such a potential magnitude. The backup of other institutional documents and reports can be paramount, too (e.g., see those, *above*, from the

[66] See Article 840-*sexiesdecies*, para. 6, c.p.c., for the Italian injunctive collective remedy, allowing the fixation of a sum of money to be paid (pursuant to Article 614-*bis* c.p.c.) by the defendant should they fail to comply with the court's order of cessation or prevention for each subsequent breach or non-compliance or for each day of delay in performing the measure. See *supra*, Chap. 7, in relation to the *Philips Respironics* case.

[67] See, in particular, *infra*, Chap. 11.

[68] See, *supra*, Chap. 6.

[69] Id. See also, *supra*, Chap. 4.

National Guarantor for the rights of the persons detained or deprived of their personal liberty).

(v) The possibility of using *statistical data* and simple presumptions, as discussed *supra*, has been mentioned by some courts (e.g., *Philips Respironics*, *Deliveroo* or *ITA Airways* cases—not the *ILVA* one) as interpretative evidence of the non-complex nature of the evidentiary assessments that class actions can perform. On the one hand, it must be noted that the common law experience makes a key use offers of such data, especially in prisoners' rights cases, as commented above. On the other hand, the complexity of these cases—still ongoing, in the *Plata* case for more than two decades—should be taken as a model by judges.

(vi) The role of *judges*, indeed, as argued in the next Part,[70] is crucial. In these types of proceedings—of high complexity, of high stakes and of high flexibility—they become the leading directors. As such, they need to embrace their newfound function and the procedural flexibility awarded to them, in terms of evidence and structuring of the proceedings. In this role, it becomes fundamental that they seek the support of experts to share the otherwise unsurmountable managerial burden and any technical deficiencies—e.g., in the *Brazeau* case—, not eschewing from inviting the parties to settle when necessary and, most importantly, from elaborating articulated plans or creating technical support groups. The division into several ranks of the different potential individual claims and the presence of a *roster* of medical managers/experts (and one administrator) in the *Brazeau* compensatory class action needs to be underscored once again.

(vii) The compensatory relief, observed in *Brazeau*, deserves a final reflection.

First, any pondering on limiting the application of the 2019 damages class action in Italy, contrarily to its access-to-justice rationale, on the basis of a strict interpretation of the homogeneity requirement should consider this case. In fact, it brilliantly demonstrates how the possibility of a '*tendentially standardised assessment*' (recalling the words of the Italian Cassation's judgement from 2019)[71] exists practically in any collective proceeding stemming from common (but not necessarily identical) issues of law or fact. The complexity of the distribution and management in *Brazeau* was considerable. Yet, with the abovementioned technical support and articulated planning any difficulty was overcome.

Furthermore, the opening of another phase for individual distribution, after judging on the common issues and the aggregate damages award, radically contrasts with the view of the Italian Cassation's judgement from 2019, which argued that the compatibility of 'assessments calibrated on *specific personal situations*' (emphasis added, recalling the exact words) should be excluded 'on the logical plane, even before the legal one'.[72] On the legal plane, such an argument is poorly convincing both under a literal and under a systemic interpretative standpoint (see *supra*, Chap. 6). On a logical plane, it is now refuted by the concrete and successful example of

[70] See, *infra*, Chap. 11.

[71] See *Trenord* case, Italian Court of Cassation, Section III, Judgement No. 14886 from 2019.

[72] Id.

the *Brazeau* case (*inter alia*), which proves that joint 'assessments calibrated on *specific personal situations*' is indeed possible.

What is more, such an evaluation, as demonstrated in the same Canadian class action, is indeed possible also concerning *non-pecuniary* damage. Once again, the assistance of technical experts—in this case medical experts—can be key to this regard.

Second, the possible *parallel deterrent, or even injunctive, function* of compensatory class actions was advanced while commenting the *ILVA* case.[73] It is possible that both prisoners' and migrants' rights cases may see the use of such a procedural tool in addition to the injunctive one for this purpose—to put further pressure on the defendants; further pressure that may be fueled also by a system of so-defined '*integrated advocacy*'.[74] To increase such a parallel deterrent and injunctive function, however, probably regulatory amendments should be introduced, too: for instance, concerning adhesion (opt-in v. opt-out), the system of dissemination of notice (see *supra*, *Brazeau*) or a distribution of damages through fluid recovery or *cy-près* mechanisms (again, see *supra*, in relation to Section 27.2(3) of the Canadian Class Proceedings Act, while discussing *Brazeau*).

The last institute—fluid recovery or *cy-près*—, in particular, could provide the sort of desirable '*complete insurance policy*' mentioned at the beginning of this Part[75] while discussing Judge Weinstein's considerations, from 1995, on personal harm class litigation and, specifically, on the *DES* cases.

The focus on these concluding reflections, however, pertains to the next Part IV.

References

Antigone Report (2024).

Garante nazionale dei diritti delle persone private della libertà personale, Report to the Parliament (2023).

Garlicki L (2007) Broniowski and after: on the dual nature of 'Pilot Judgments'. In: Caflisch L, Callewaert J, Liddell R, Mahoney P, Villiger M (eds) Droits de l'homme – Regards de Strasbourg: Liber Amicorum Luzius Wildhaber. NP Engel, Kehl, pp 177–192

Glas LR (2019) The execution process of Pilot Judgements before the committee of ministers. Human Rights Int Legal Disc 13(2):73–97

Greenberg J (1997) Civil rights class actions. Procedural means of obtaining substance. Ariz Law Rev 39:575–586

Issacharoff S (2012) Class actions and state authority. Loyola Univ Chicago Law J 44:369–390

Kurban D (2016) Forsaking individual justice: the implications of the European Court of Human Rights' pilot judgment procedure for victims of gross and systematic violations. Human Rights Law Rev 16(4):731–737

Lemmens K, Van Drooghenbroeck S (2023) How "Systematic" is the European Court of Human Rights' approach to "Systemic" violations of the convention? Germ Law J 24(6)

[73] See the previous Chap. 7.

[74] See, *infra*, Chap. 11.

[75] Id. See also, *supra*, Chap. 7.

Randazzo B (2012) Giustizia costituzionale sovranazionale: la Corte europea dei diritti dell'uomo. Giuffrè, Milano
Randazzo B (2023) Access to justice in a multilevel constitutional system, protecting human rights. Giappichelli, Torino
Zanon N (2021) I rapporti tra la Corte costituzionale e il legislatore alla luce di alcune recenti tendenze giurisprudenziali. Federalismi.it 3:86–98
Zirulia S (2023) Il favoreggiamento dell'immigrazione irregolare. Tra overcriminalisation e tutela dei diritti fondamentali. Giappichelli, Torino

Chapter 10
Case Study No. 4: Arbitration Clauses, Class Waivers and Foreign Defendants. The *Binance* Case

10.1 Premise. Arbitration Clauses, Class Waivers and Foreign Defendants

As anticipated above,[1] one of the main issues partially stalling the success of class actions in the US is that of arbitration clauses in standard contracts. Such clauses select individual arbitration as a forum for resolving disputes arising from said contracts, which are mainly in the consumer and securities field. Similar contractual provisions are also common, nonetheless, in employment matters, with some notable cases in the area of professional sports, too.[2]

As reported by American scholarship, the trend to insert mandatory arbitration clauses in adhesion contracts was started by corporations in many ways exactly with the objective of avoiding class suits and the inherent risks for their business. This occurred, initially, under the assumption that arbitration always and only encompasses individual bilateral disputes. For some time—notably with the *Keating v. Superior Court* decision, from 1982 in front of the Superior Court of California, and with the *Green Tree v. Bazzle* decision from 2003 in front of the US Supreme Court—the majoritarian jurisprudence allowed class proceedings in front of the arbitrators, provided they were not explicitly excluded pursuant to the arbitral tribunal's own interpretation of the contract.[3]

This seemed in line with 'the importance of the class action device for vindicating rights asserted by large groups of persons', as it 'both eliminates the possibility

[1] See, *supra*, Chap. 5.

[2] The so-called *NFL Concussions* case, accounted in Issacharoff (2021) and Cabraser and Issacharoff (2018). See also the notable *Wal-Mart v. Dukes* case for employment matters (see, *supra*, Chap. 5).

[3] See Born and Salas (2012).

A. Maglica, *Collective Dimensions of Access to Justice*, European Union and its Neighbours in a Globalized World 23,
https://doi.org/10.1007/978-3-031-94522-9_10

of repetitious litigation and provides small claimants with a method of obtaining redress for claims which would otherwise be too small to warrant individual litigation'.[4] Moreover, 'denial of a class action in cases where it is appropriate may have the effect of allowing an unscrupulous wrongdoer to 'retain the benefits of its wrongful conduct".[5] Furthermore, it followed doctrinal and jurisprudential voices that had remarked how adhesion contracts were characterised by one party having substantially more power than the other and, therefore, easily dictating the terms and conditions, identical for all the adherents and without a concrete negotiation, *i.e.* banks, insurance companies, securities, consumer and employment ones.[6]

Still, corporations quickly adapted by inserting explicit exclusions. Additionally, changes in the US Supreme Court's composition led to a resounding turn-around in what has been defined as 'a tragedy of errors'.[7] To this day, several commentators agree that this is the main hurdle hampering class adjudication in such a jurisdiction.[8]

A case brought in front of the Tribunal of Milan—the *Binance* case—, already decided and now appealed, has offered the opportunity for Italian—and European—judges to confront themselves on this key issue. The main difference between the legal orders at stake, however, is the far-reaching protection ensured to consumers, to be conceived as 'weak parties', in adhesion contracts, under *EU standards* and related domestic implementations.[9] In particular, the guarantees set by the so-called EU 'Unfair terms' Directive 93/13, regarding the formation phase of the contract, should be accounted.

The same *Binance* case, hereinafter analysed, is particularly valuable since it raises another crucial matter (anticipated above)[10]: that of the *competent court for foreign defendants* not having a seat in Italy, as, under a strict interpretation of the 2019 regime, it appears that 'the Italian judge lacks jurisdiction in respect of class actions brought against defendants having their seat only abroad'.[11] Evidently, such a reading, based on the normative criterion that individuates the competent judge in the specialised business section of the Tribunal where the defendant has its seat, if

[4] *Richmond v. Dart Industries, Inc* case (1981).

[5] *Vasquez v. Superior Court* case (1971).

[6] See, *supra*, Chap. 4.

[7] Born and Salas (2012).

[8] See, e.g., Issacharoff (2021), pp. 164–165, Mullenix (2014), Gilles and Friedman (2012), Yan (2011), Sternlight and Jensen (2004), Sternlight (2000).

[9] E.g., in Brussels I bis Regulation (EU) No. 1215/2012 of the European Parliament and of the Council of 12 December 2012 on jurisdiction and the recognition and enforcement of judgments in civil and commercial matters (recast), Recital (18): 'In relation to insurance, consumer and employment contracts, the *weaker* party should be protected by rules of jurisdiction more favourable to his interests than the general rules' (emphasis added). See also the recent CJEU, Judgement from 11 April 2024, *Air Europa Líneas Aéreas*, C-173/23, § 27 (discussed *infra*).

[10] See, *supra*, Chap. 6.

[11] *Binance* case, Tribunal of Milan, Order from 17 August 2024, R.G. No. 44534/2021, p. 11 (translated from Italian).

confirmed, would substantially impair the right to effective judicial protection, under Articles 2, 3, 24, and 111 of the Italian Constitution, as well as Article 117, first paragraph, of the same Constitution in relation to Articles 6 and 13 of the ECHR and Article 19 TEU and Article 47 of the CFREU.

10.2 The *Binance* Case. Factual Contextualisation

The lawsuit at hand, in front of the Tribunal of Milan, originates from a series of so-called abnormal 'black-outs' on the platform Binance Futures, lasting for several hours, in four different dates between February and June 2021. The Binance group, as is known, is a global leader in the exchange of cryptocurrencies, with—as reported—over 19 billion dollars moved daily on a worldwide scale. Binance Futures, in particular, is specialised in the exchange of highly speculative derivative financial tools.

As a result of said abnormal 'black-outs', the users of the platform were systematically prevented from accessing their accounts in a time of severe market turbulence (coinciding with a 'tweet' from multi-billionaire Elon Musk and related prohibitions from the Chinese Republic), and, thereby, had their ability to modify their strategies and thus to avoid the liquidation of their positions irreparably compromised. This was due to the attainment of margins on the derivative products (margins that were retained by the platform, with the consequent crystallisation of the loss for users).

A relevant anomaly of the 'black-outs' lies, furthermore, in the fact that the Binance platform continued to operate during their occurrence. This allowed the variation of the products' prices, even though users were not able to access nor manage their so-called 'wallet' and the leverage applied, by liquidating or correcting their positions or, at least, supplementing the margins to cover them.

As a consequence, numerous users lamented having suffered severe losses in the value of the crypto-products part of their portfolio on Binance Futures. A group of Italian ones, in particular, decided to file a compensatory class action lawsuit on behalf of the Italian users of the platform, since the compensation offered by Binance—only to some of them—was deemed inadequate.

To this regard, before addressing the nuances of the lawsuit, it must be noted that the contract in question—between Binance and the users of the platform—was an adhesion one, concluded online through the so-called 'point and click' formula, by merely accepting the terms and conditions on the Binance website. The main peculiarity, to this regard, is the fact that such terms and conditions provided for a resolution of any dispute arising from the Contract to *foreign individual arbitration*. The seat of such an individual arbitration was, initially, at the time of the abnormal 'black outs', Switzerland, whereas since March 2021, after the first episode, it became Hong Kong, due to a unilateral modification of its own Terms and Conditions by Binance itself. Similarly, in March 2021 the Terms regulated the choice of applicable law by mentioning that of Hong Kong, whereas previously there was no express choice.

Lastly, it should be noted that Binance, being operative digitally, has no seat in Italy.

10.3 The *Binance* Case. Litigation and Pending Appeal

The present class suit was brought in November 2021 by a group of Italian users of Binance futures for the losses suffered as a consequence of the abnormal 'black-outs' on the platform and the related significant decrease in value of their crypto-products.

In particular, it seems relevant to stress that each user, evidently, suffered a different loss, on the basis of the different products and different amounts invested.

As to the notion of investment, it became immediately relevant in the litigation in question whether the users of the platform were to be qualified as consumers or professional investors. This, in fact, would have resulted in the application or not of the Directive 93/13/CEE on unfair terms in consumer contracts, according to which 'A contractual term which has not been individually negotiated shall be regarded as *unfair* if, contrary to the requirement of good faith, it causes a *significant imbalance* in the parties' rights and obligations arising under the contract, to the detriment of the *consumer*'.[12] In particular, 'A term shall always be regarded as not individually negotiated where it has been drafted in advance and the consumer has therefore not been able to influence the substance of the term, particularly in the context of a *pre-formulated standard contract*',[13] such as in the case at stake.

Evidently, such a Directive, as interpreted by the CJEU (see *infra*), together with its domestic implementations, sets a series of fundamental guarantees which, as will be argued subsequently, cannot be disregarded.

The fact that the Annex of the Directive, referred to in Article 3, para. 3, as containing an indicative and non-exhaustive list of the terms which may be regarded as unfair, specifically mentions clauses that require the consumer 'to take disputes exclusively to arbitration',[14] makes the verification of this qualification evermore relevant.

Still, the Tribunal of Milan did not follow this line of reasoning. Quite surprisingly, in August 2024, it declared its lack of jurisdiction in favour of the competent foreign arbitral tribunal.

This decision was justified on the grounds that, according to said Tribunal, the *New York Convention* (on the recognition and enforcement of arbitral awards, from 1958) should be applied to evaluate the validity of the arbitration clause within the contract. According to the court, the *formal validity* would then be met merely by the written form, as per Article II, paras. 1 and 2, of the Convention, whilst the

[12] Council Directive 93/13/EEC of 5 April 1993 on unfair terms in consumer contracts, Article 3(1).

[13] Id., Article 3(2).

[14] Id., Annex, paragraph 1, letter q).

substantial validity, pursuant to Article V.1.a of the same Convention, would require that the arbitration clause is not valid under the law of the country where the award is made—hence, either Swiss or Hong Kong law (the Tribunal does not clarify which one).

As a consequence, the national provisions providing special protection for consumers—Articles 1341 and 1342 c.c. and Articles 33–36 cod. Cons., the latter implementing Directive 93/13—according to the Tribunal of Milan, could not be applied, since they 'are not characterised by express indications of mandatory binding force in Italy with respect to different applicable foreign regulations, *nor* can they be considered as falling within the category of those of *domestic public order*'.[15]

As will be argued in the next paragraph, these arguments appear extremely flawed, as well as the references to the New York Convention (and its specific provisions recalled), and, in general, the solution given to the possible conflict between said Convention and EU provisions—Directive 93/13—protecting consumers. It particular, this passage from the decision seems rather questionable:

> Finally, the applicants referred to Directive No 93/13/EEC on unfair terms in consumer contracts. However, *irrespective of the assessment of the merits of the alleged qualification of the applicants as consumers*, it must be considered that - the source in question, being a directive, is *expressly addressed to the Member States*; - the directive was adopted in Italy, as evidenced by all the rules of Italian law designed to protect consumers and to guard against the introduction of unfair terms into contracts, so that it is *not apparent*, nor have the plaintiffs pointed out, what scope for *immediate and independent application the directive* in question may have in relation to the question of the validity of the arbitration clause at issue - nor have the plaintiffs argued, *nor does there appear* to be any room for interpretation to that effect, that the *directive at issue takes precedence over the 1958 New York Convention* and the rules interpreting international treaties.[16]

As will be commented below, all these arguments are refuted by consolidated CJEU and Italian constitutional case law.

Finally, the last problematic aspect from the decision at stake is the '*ad abundantiam*' statement provided by the same court, as a further ground for inadmissibility. This regards the abovementioned issue of jurisdiction of Italian judges for class actions filed against defendants that do not have a seat in Italy. Since Article 840-*ter*, para. 1, c.p.c., provides that the competent judge is the one from the specialised business section of the Tribunal where the defendant has its seat,[17] it would follow, according to the reasoning of the Milanese court, that no judge exists in Italy with jurisdiction over class actions against such foreign subjects.

If confirmed, as further analysed, this interpretative stance would pose a great number of issues under a constitutional point of view, in relation to the abovementioned provisions, namely with regard to the right to an effective remedy and to the

---

[15] *Binance* case, Tribunal of Milan, Order from 17 August 2024, R.G. No. 44534/2021, p. 11 (emphasis added, translated from Italian).

[16] Id. (emphasis added).

[17] See *supra*, Chap. 6.

principles of equality and reasonableness. At the same time, the need to look for a constitutionally-acceptable filling criterion would still be paramount (see *infra*).

In any case, it must be reported that the decision in question has now been appealed, in front of the Court of Appeal of Milan.

10.4 Doubts of Constitutional Legitimacy and Open Questions

Pending the decision on the appeal, a number of considerations already emerges as paramount from this key case, which clearly demonstrates how procedural nuances can concretely impinge on the enforcement of fundamental rights, hereincluded first and foremost that to effective judicial protection.

(i) The *right to effective judicial protection*, as discussed,[18] stands 'among man's *inviolable rights*, which the [Italian] Constitution guarantees in Article 2, as it can also be deduced from the consideration given to it in Article 6 of the European Convention on Human Rights',[19] being 'intimately connected with the very principle of democracy to ensure to all and always, for any dispute, a judge and a judgment'.[20] As observed by the Italian Constitutional Court, 'the recognition of the holding of rights cannot but be accompanied by the recognition of the power to assert them before a judge in a judicial procedure'.[21] Consequently, 'taking legal action to enforce one's rights [...] is itself the content of an inviolable right', 'protected by articles 24 and 113 of the [Italian] Constitution [...] characterising the democratic rule of law'.[22] These arguments have long been expressed by the ECtHR, too, according to which, in relation to Article 13, the requirements therein included, enshrining the right to an effective remedy, 'take the form of a guarantee and not of a mere statement of intent or a practical arrangement. That is one of the consequences of the rule of law, one of the fundamental principles of a democratic society'.[23]

Such a core principle, evidently, cannot be challenged even by the norms of international treaties and their interpretative rules, such as the New York Convention or the Vienna Convention, contrarily to the Tribunal of Milan's assessment.[24]

---

[18] See *supra*, more in detail, Chap. 4.

[19] Italian Constitutional Court, Judgement No. 98 from 1965, point No. 2 of Points of law (translated from Italian).

[20] Italian Constitutional Court, Judgement No. 18 from 1982 and No. 82 from 1996 (translated from Italian).

[21] Italian Constitutional Court, Judgement No. 98 from 1965 (translated from Italian).

[22] Italian Constitutional Court, Judgement No. 26 from 1999 (translated from Italian), as well as Nos. 120 from 2014, 386 from 2004 and 29 from 2003.

[23] ECtHR, *Čonka v. Belgium*, No. 51564/99, 2002, § 83.

[24] See *Binance* case, Tribunal of Milan, Order from 17 August 2024, R.G. No. 44534/2021.

As repeatedly affirmed by Italian constitutional jurisprudence, in fact, 'Even with a view to achieving the objective of maintaining good international relations, inspired by the principles of peace and justice, in view of which Italy allows limitations of sovereignty (art. 11 Const.), the *limit* that marks the openness of the Italian legal system to the international and supranational system (Articles 10 and 11 Const.) is constituted [...] by *respect for fundamental principles* and inviolable human rights, identifying elements of the constitutional system'.[25] The principle of effectiveness of judicial protection is thus unmistakably linked to the supreme principles.

Furthermore, the Italian Supreme Court of Cassation has also clarified that the *general clause of public order*, 'represents a mechanism for safeguarding internal harmony and a curb against the entry of values incompatible with the inspiring principles' of the constitutional order,[26] among which—evidently, for the above reasons—effective judicial protection must be accounted. Moreover, as clarified by the same Court, 'international public order has also acquired a promotional function, aimed at fostering the dissemination of principles recognised at supranational and international level', including that of *effective judicial protection*, to be understood as 'the right to a remedy adequate to satisfy the need for protection of that specific, unique, sometimes unrepeatable substantial situation of legally protected interest'.[27] In this sense, travelling individually to Hong Kong for an arbitration, in order to obtain compensation for, possibly, just a few hundred euros, is certainly not an adequate path of protection—whichever the subjective position enforced (e.g. even minor economic redress), since the interest at stake, it should be stressed, is the larger one of concrete *access to a court*.

The equivalence between public order and effective jurisdictional protection is further confirmed by Italian constitutional jurisprudence,[28] which includes both among the 'supreme principles of the constitutional order': *on the one hand*, the former as a set of 'fundamental rules laid down by the Constitution and the laws at the basis of the legal institutions into which the positive order is articulated in its perennial adaptation to the evolution of society'; *on the other hand*, the latter as the fundamental rule of every democratic society.

It is, thus, possible to subsume the latter—the inviolable right to a judge, declined in a 'practical and effective' manner, in accordance with the Strasbourg case

[25] Italian Constitutional Court, Judgement No. 238 from 2014 (translated from Italian), in relation to the right of judicial enforcement, a judgement which cites 'with regard to Article 11 of the Constitution: Judgments No. 284 from 2007, No. 168 from 1991, No. 232 from 1989, No. 170 from 1984, No. 183 from 1973; with regard to Article 10, first paragraph, of the Constitution: Judgments No. 73 from 2001, No. 15 from 1996 and No. 48 from 1979; also Judgment No. 349 from 2007'.

[26] Italian Court of Cassation, S.U., Judgement No. 38162 from 2022 (translated from Italian).

[27] Italian Court of Cassation, Section III, Judgement No. 21255 from 2013 (translated from Italian).

[28] Italian Constitutional Court, Judgement No. 18 from 1982.

law[29]—within the notion of '*constitutional public order*', as a system of values and mandatory principles that historically inform the general order of the state community.[30]

The consequence of such a subsumption is the impossibility in the case in point to apply, via Articles 10 and 11 of the Italian Constitution, the rules of the New York Convention from 1958 on arbitration agreements over this *essential limit*, which constitutes an identifying element of the Italian constitutional system, as per Article 2 of the Italian Constitution.[31]

(ii) Similar conclusions stem from the *CJEU consolidated jurisprudence*, which has long clarified that Member States are obliged, by virtue of the principle of sincere cooperation under Article 4(3), TEU, to ensure, within their territories, the application of and respect for EU law and therefore, 'as provided for by the second subparagraph of Article 19(1) TEU, Member States are to provide remedies sufficient to ensure effective judicial protection for individual parties in the fields covered by EU law. It is, therefore, for the Member States to establish a system of legal remedies and procedures ensuring effective judicial review in those fields'.[32]

It follows from the well-established guidelines of European case-law that the *obligation of interpretation in conformity with EU law* requires the national judge to prefer the interpretation that allows it to declare of its own motion that it has jurisdiction whenever the only ground for declining jurisdiction is an unfair term (the arbitration clause, in the *Binance* case at hand).

Again, in more general terms, it has been emphasised that 'It is the responsibility of the national courts in particular to provide the legal protection which individuals derive from the rules of Community law and to ensure that those rules are fully effective'[33] and that this applies '*a fortiori* […] when the national court is seised of a dispute concerning the application of domestic provisions which, as here, have been specifically enacted for the purpose of transposing a directive intended to confer rights on individuals'.[34] This would be exactly the case of those Italian domestic rules implementing the Unfair terms Directive (Articles 33–36 cod. Cons.).

Thus, in the application of national law, including the provisions of private international law, 'the national court is bound to interpret national law, so far as possible, in the light of the wording and the purpose of the directive concerned in order *to achieve the result sought by the directive* […] The requirement for national law to be interpreted in conformity with Community law is inherent in the system of the Treaty, since it permits the national court, for the matters within its jurisdiction, to

[29] See, *supra*, Chap. 4.

[30] Crisafulli. (1956), p. 71.

[31] See again Italian Constitutional Court, Judgement No. 238 from 2014.

[32] CJEU, Grand Chamber, Judgement of 27 February 2018, *Associação Sindical dos Juízes Portugueses*, C-64/16, §§ 34 *et seq*.

[33] CJEU, Grand Chamber, Judgement of 5 October 2004, *Pfeiffer and Others*, C-397/01, § 111.

[34] Id., § 112.

ensure the full effectiveness of Community law when it determines the dispute before it'.[35]

It must then be emphasised that the principle of interpreting national law in conformity with European law 'requires the national court to consider national law as a whole in order to assess to what extent it may be applied so as not to produce a result contrary to that sought by the directive'.[36]

In that regard, where national law, including private international law, 'the application of interpretative methods recognised by national law', including interpretation in conformity with European law as well as interpretation in conformity with the Constitution 'enables, in certain circumstances, a provision of domestic law to be construed in such a way as to avoid conflict with another rule of domestic law or the scope of that provision to be restricted to that end by applying it only in so far as it is compatible with the rule concerned, the national court is bound to use those methods in order to achieve the result sought by the directive'[37] and, more generally, by EU law.

This explains how, contrarily to the Tribunal of Milan's reasoning, the EU Directive *by all means takes precedence* over the New York Convention, and thereby the domestic rules transposing the former (Articles 33–36 cod. cons.) take precedence over the domestic rules adhering to the latter (for Italy, Law 19 January 1968, no. 6).

Additionally, the case law from the CJEU clearly refutes the Tribunal of Milan's reasoning in relation to Articles 33–36 cod. cons., in implementation of Directive 93/13/EEC. The CJEU just recently, in fact, reaffirmed in the judgment *Air Europa Líneas Aéreas*, from 11 April 2024, that 'Article 6(1) of Directive 93/13 must be regarded as a provision of equal standing to national rules which rank, within the domestic legal system, as rules of *public policy*'.[38]

It follows that, 'in accordance with the principle of equivalence, where, under domestic law, the national court has discretion or the obligation to assess of its own motion whether a contractual term is contrary to national rules of public policy, it must also have discretion or the obligation to assess of its own motion whether such a term is contrary to Article 6 of Directive 93/13, where it has the legal and factual information necessary to that effect'.[39] According to Article 6 para. 1 of Directive

[35] Id., § 113–114 (emphasis added). See, to that effect, also, cited therein, 'Von Colson and Kamann, paragraph 26; Marleasing, paragraph 8, and Faccini Dori, paragraph 26', as well as 'Océano Grupo Editorial and Salvat Editores [2000] ECR I-4941, paragraph 30; and Case C-408/01 Adidas-Salomon and Adidas Benelux [2003] ECR I-12537, paragraph 21, Case C-160/01 Mau [2003] ECR I-4791, paragraph 34'.

[36] Id., § 115. See, to that effect, also, cited therein, 'Carbonari and Others, paragraphs. 49 and 50'.

[37] Id.

[38] Emphasis added. CJEU, Judgement of 11 April 2024, *Air Europa Líneas Aéreas*, C-173/23, § 34, recalling 'judgments of 6 October 2009, Asturcom Telecomunicaciones, C-40/08, EU:C:2009:615, paragraph 52, and of 17 May 2022, Unicaja Banco, C-869/19, EU:C:2022:397, paragraph 24'.

[39] Id., § 35 (emphasis added), recalling 'judgment of 17 May 2022, Unicaja Banco, C-869/19, paragraph 25 and the case-law cited, judgments of 6 October 2009, Asturcom Telecomunicaciones, C-40/08, paragraph 52, and of 17 May 2022, Unicaja Banco, C-869/19, paragraph 2'.

93/13, 'Member States shall lay down that unfair terms used in a contract concluded with a consumer by a seller or supplier shall, as provided for under their national law, not be binding on the consumer and that the contract shall continue to bind the parties upon those terms if it is capable of continuing in existence without the unfair terms'. In particular, again according to the CJEU, this rule is to be understood as 'That is a mandatory provision which aims to replace the formal balance which the latter establishes between the rights and obligations of the parties with an effective balance which re-establishes equality between them'.[40] Again: 'according to the Court's settled case-law, the system of protection introduced by Directive 93/13 is based on the idea that the consumer is in a *weak position* vis-à-vis the seller or supplier, as regards both his or her *bargaining power* and his or her level of knowledge'.[41]

In this regard, it must also be recalled the established European case law according to which, pursuant to the principle of effectiveness, national laws and their interpreters must not 'make it in practice impossible or excessively difficult to exercise the rights conferred on consumers by European Union law (principle of effectiveness)'.[42] The role of the national judge is to 'assess for those purposes whether the seller or supplier, dealing fairly and equitably with the consumer, could reasonably assume that the consumer would have agreed to such a term in individual contract negotiations';[43] it is thus an essential one.

This case law plainly contradicts the order of inadmissibility from the Tribunal of Milan, which states, instead, that 'the relevant imbalance is that which arises from the discipline envisaged by the clause, not that which allegedly exists in the positions of the parties'.[44]

Equally undisputable is the non-applicability of the law of a third country pursuant to Article 6(2) of Directive 93/13/EEC, which states that: 'Member States shall take the necessary measures to ensure that the consumer does not lose the protection granted by this Directive by virtue of the choice of the law of a non-Member country as the law applicable to the contract if the latter has a close connection with the territory of the Member States', a link restored in the present case by the residence in Italy of the consumers within the contract (purportedly, the class plaintiffs).

Therefore, contrary to the findings of the Court of Milan, an abusive or vexatious arbitration clause—insofar as drafted by a single contracting party and determining a significant *real imbalance to the detriment of the consumer*—cannot be

[40] Id., § 28, recalling 'judgments of 26 October 2006, Mostaza Claro, C-168/05, paragraph 36, and of 17 May 2022, SPV Project 1503 and Others, C-693/19 and C-831/19, paragraph 52'.

[41] Id., § 27, recalling 'judgments of 27 June 2000, Océano Grupo Editorial and Salvat Editores, C-240/98 to C-244/98, paragraph 25, and of 17 May 2022, SPV Project 1503 and Others, C-693/19 and C-831/19, paragraph 51'.

[42] CJEU, Judgement of 14 March 2013, *Aziz*, C-415/11, § 50; see also CJEU, Judgement of 26 October 2006, *Mostaza Claro*, C-168/05, and CJEU, Judgement of 6 October 2009, *Asturcom*, C-40/08.

[43] Id., § 69.

[44] *Binance* case, Tribunal of Milan, Order from 17 August 2024, R.G. No. 44534/2021, pp. 9–10 (translated from Italian).

considered valid merely as a result of the application of a foreign law, given the fact that it is contrary to the domestic and European public order, also configured by the consumer guarantees under consideration here (Articles 33–36 cod. cons., implementing Directive 93/13).

As to the notion of significant imbalance, it should be recalled that—again according to the consolidated case-law of the CJEU it 'must be assessed in the light of an analysis of the rules of national law applicable in the absence of any agreement between the parties, in order to determine whether, and if so to what extent, the contract places the consumer in a less favourable legal situation than that provided for by the national law in force'. In addition, 'in order to assess whether the imbalance arises 'contrary to the requirement of good faith', it must be determined whether the seller or supplier, dealing fairly and equitably with the consumer, could reasonably assume that the consumer would have agreed to the term concerned in individual contract negotiations'.[45]

In this regard, it seems impossible to argue that a reasonable consumer would have acceded the arbitration clause at hand, in favour of *individual* arbitration—in Switzerland and now even in Hong Kong—, had they been able to have full knowledge of it in the context of a *fair* negotiation with the other party.

Contrarily to the Tribunal of Milan's findings, an evaluation of the *qualification as consumers* of the class plaintiffs seems by all means fundamental, as it would imply the extension of EU guarantees and, consequently, the non-bindingness of the arbitration clause as unfair, pursuant to Article 6 of Directive 93/13 (and the domestic provisions: Articles 33–36 cod. cons.).

(iii) A consequence of the qualification as consumers of the class plaintiffs—which seems indeed correct, in light of the EU's consolidated case law and provisions until now recalled—poses nonetheless a new set of problems.

In particular, it seems relevant to consider whether the new consumer-focused class action regime, from 2023, implementing the RAD Directive,[46] should be used. In fact, the RAD itself in Article 2(1), clarifies that it 'applies to representative actions brought against infringements by traders of the provisions of Union law referred to in Annex I, including such provisions as transposed into national law, that harm or may harm the collective interests of consumers'. In the Annex I, the very second provision of EU law listed is Directive 93/13 'on unfair terms in consumer contracts', the one at stake in the present *Binance* case. This is also reiterated in the domestic regime from 2023, which, under Article 140-*ter* cod. cons., para. 2, specifies that 'The provisions of this Title shall apply to representative actions brought against traders for infringements of the provisions listed in Annex II-septies, which affect or are likely to affect the collective interests of consumers' and, most importantly, that in such a case, 'the qualified entities may not bring class actions as provided for in Title VIII-bis of Book IV of the Code of Civil Procedure [the 2019 trans-substantive regime]'.

---

[45] CJEU, Judgement of 14 March 2013, *Aziz*, C-415/11, § 76.

[46] See *supra*, Chap. 6.

Since the Annex II-*septies*, point 2), cites once again Directive 93/13 and its national transposition (Articles 33–38 cod. cons.), there seems at first reading to be a contradiction in the *Binance* case from the plaintiff's side: *either* they are consumers who, therefore, benefit from EU guarantees as set under Directive 93/13, *but* in that case they should file a class action under Articles 140-*ter et seq*. cod. cons. (the 2023 consumer-focused regime, transposing the RAD), *or* they can proceed via the general regime from 2019 under Articles 840-*bis et seq*. c.p.c., *but* without qualifying themselves as consumers.

However, such an assertion appears, at deeper analysis, incorrect. Two arguments support this view.

First, the temporal aspect. As is known, the new 2023 consumer-related regime applies only to actions aiming at obtaining redress against violations subsequent to its *entry into force*—that is, 25 June 2023, pursuant to Article 4, para. 2, of d.lgs. 10 March 2023, no. 28. The *Binance* case, instead, refers to conducts (the so-called abnormal 'black-outs') occurred between February and June 2021.

The 2019 regime, instead, applies to conducts subsequent to its entry into force, on 19 May 2021, according to Article 7, para. 2, of law 12 April 2019, no. 31. The fact that at least three, out of four, of such 'black-outs' took place after the entry into force,[47] makes the 2019 discipline certainly applicable.

In any case, it seems like the infringement in question could be qualified as a continuous violation, or 'permanent tort', following the Italian case law (see *supra*, Chap. 6), thus encompassing also the conducts from February 2021, by proving that it was part of a larger scheme, or a standard practice, against the platform's users.[48] The relevance of this inclusion stands, obviously, in relation to the quantification of damages.

Second, the issue of standing. Article 140-*ter* cod. cons., para. 2, states that, in cases pertaining violations of the provisions listed in the Annex, 'the *qualified entities* may not bring class actions' (emphasis added) *ex* Articles 840-*bis et seq*. c.p.c. Clearly, such a prohibition only regards qualified entities (i.e., associations or organisations), but not *individual consumers*, who do not have standing under the 2023 regime but who do have it under the 2019 one.

A restriction of the right to action, enshrined under Articles 2 and 24 of the Italian Constitution, would appear unreasonable, under the paradigm set by Article 3 of the same Constitution, in relation to other individuals acting outside the consumer sphere.

Furthermore, this reading seems supported by Article 140-*ter* cod. cons., para. 2, itself, when it subsequently specifies that 'The contractual and non-contractual remedies in any event provided for in favour of consumers shall remain unaffected': among these remedies, one must consider also the collective one from 2019.

---

[47] *Binance* case, Tribunal of Milan, Order from 17 August 2024, No. 44534/2021, p. 3. The exact dates were: 8 February, 19 May, 28 May and 4 June 2021.

[48] Italian Constitutional Court, Judgement No. 53 from 2018, point No. 3 of Points of Law.

(iv) the differences among the two regimes—the trans-substantive one from 2019 and the consumer one from 2023—appear relevant under a constitutional perspective for another matter, too. This is an issue which could come up in the *Binance* case herein analysed, should it proceed on the merits after an overturn in appeal.

Considering the *statute of limitations* in Italy (5 years for extra-contractual liability and 10 years for the ordinary one), in fact, there is the serious risk that by the time the (double) adhesion phase opens such a period has expired. This would occur for extra-contractual damages sought after February or June 2026 and contractual ones after 2031, thus hindering in concrete the application of the class action mechanism.[49]

This significant hurdle has been addressed by the EU legislator with the RAD and by the Italian one while transposing it, with the 2023 dual consumer-focused remedy. Article 16 of the RAD and Article 140-*duodecies* cod. cons. state, in fact, that the applicable limitation period is *interrupted* in respect of *all the consumers* concerned by the collective action by the mere filing of it.

It must also be mentioned that the RAD in its transitional provisions clarifies that 'Member States shall ensure that laws, regulations or administrative provisions on suspension or interruption of limitation periods transposing Article 16 only apply to claims for redress based on infringements [...] that occurred on or after 25 June 2023. This shall not preclude the application of national provisions on suspension or interruption of limitation periods which applied prior to 25 June 2023 to claims for redress based on infringements [...] that occurred before that date'.[50]

Similar provisions, however, are lacking in relation to the 2019 general regime. The only reference is that from Article 840-*sexies*, para. 7, c.p.c., pursuant to which 'The request for adhesion produces the effects of a judicial claim': some authors have inferred from this norm that the interruption (or suspension) of the limitation period for future adherents follows only from their adhesion.[51]

Still, even though the interruption of the limitation period is indeed one of the effects of the judicial claim, it does not appear likely that the Italian legislator had this prohibition in mind, since otherwise they would have explicated it. Moreover, as analysed above,[52] the Italian legislator used as a model the Commission Recommendation from 11 June 2013 when drafting the 2019 regime: in said EU text, albeit not expressly related to adherents, the rationale of suspending the limitation period, in order to preserve the right of access to a court, clearly emerges with respect to the provisions on 'Collective alternative dispute resolution and settlements' and 'Collective follow-on actions'.[53] It seems, therefore, that the Italian 2019

[49] And, thereby, fundamentally clashing with the principle of effective legal protection, in favour of a purported legal certainty. See *supra*, Chaps. 3 and 6.

[50] Article 22, 'RAD'. See *supra*, Chap. 5.

[51] See De Dominicis (2025) and Giussani (2025).

[52] See *supra*, Chap. 6.

[53] Commission Recommendation of 11 June 2013 on common principles for injunctive and compensatory collective redress mechanisms in the Member States concerning violations of rights granted under Union Law (see *supra*, Chap. 5), respectively para. 25 and paras. 33 and 34.

provision in question refers, more generally, to the instauration of the *lis pendens* and the future extension of the *res judicata* effects with and on the adherents.

This would also be in line with a constitutionally-oriented interpretation, to be favoured, and specifically with the already much-mentioned principles of reasonabless and effective judicial protection. In the alternative, it would appear questionable whether such a regime (from 2019) is constitutionally legitimate in the part in which it does not provide for an interruption or suspension of the limitation period.

It must be recalled how according to the consolidated jurisprudence from the Italian Constitutional Court, 'when it comes to the regulation of proceedings and the configuration of *procedural rules*, the legislator has wide discretion, with the only limit of manifest unreasonableness'.[54] However, it is disputed whether the limitation period has substantive or procedural nature.[55] As the well-known *Taricco* case clarified, albeit in relation to criminal law, the limitation period has a substantive nature. In relation to civil law, the fact that it is regulated in the Civil Code, under Article 2934 c.c., rather than within the Code of Civil Procedure, appears as an additional indicator of a possible substantive nature (an issue still debated).[56]

In any case, it seems relevant to note that, pursuant to the Italian Constitutional Court's case law there is a violation of the principle of equality 'when *substantially identical situations* are regulated in an *unjustifiably different* manner'.[57] In the case at hand, an interpretation, or a circumstance, in which only adherent consumers enjoy the interruptive effect of the limitation period for class actions, whereas other individual adherents do not, appears unjustifiable. This occurs given the substantially identical situation regulated by the two class action regimes, an identity which touches even the individual person at hand, since that of 'consumer' is a transient quality: one subject can contemporarily be consumer and at the same time not.

Beyond this argument, which is significant but not decisive on its own, the fact that acting as a consumer does not appear to present significant differences with respect to acting in other areas of life, or at least differences such as to justify greater protection for infringements suffered in that area, and thus 'render the legislator's choice not censurable in terms of reasonableness, seems instead diriment'.[58] On the contrary, an opposite discipline would seem appropriate, in favour of greater safeguards for subjective positions closer to the fundamental core of the individual, such as the right to health, to non-discrimination, to live in non-degrading conditions and so on, already extensively cited in the above—all rights that can indeed be protected by the 2019 collective remedy, and not by that from 2023.

---

[54] Italian Constitutional Court, Judgement No. 155 from 2014, point No. 7 of Points of Law (translated from Italian). See also, *ex plurimis*: Judgements No. 10 from 2013, No. 17 from 2011, No. 82 and 50 from 2010, No. 221 from 2008.

[55] Travaglino (2017), p. 50.

[56] Id.

[57] *Ex plurimis*, see Italian Constitutional Court, Judgement No. 171 from 2022 (translated from Italian), No. 71 from 2021, No. 85 from 2020, No. 13 from 2018, No. 71 from 2015, No. 108 from 2006, No. 340 and No. 136 from 2004.

[58] Italian Constitutional Court, Judgement No. 216 from 2014 (translated from Italian).

At most, one should discuss the extension of this interruptive effect to all adherents for actions *commenced* before 25 June 2023, date of the entry into force of the *tertium comparationis* of the reasonableness evaluation under Article 3 of the Italian Constitution (that is, the 2023 consumer regime), or simply consider constitutionally legitimate the extension for *adhesions subsequent* to such a date, despite the moment in which the collective action was filed. In light of Articles 2 and 24, as well as Article 117 of the Italian Constitution, in relation to Articles 47 CFREU and 6 and 13 ECHR, the latter view appears more correct, for reasons of effectiveness in the access to a court, which, under the former reading would be substantially impaired.[59]

(v) Beyond the considerations outlined hitherto, it bears recalling the reflections from above[60] on the (necessary) collective dimension of access to justice, which were briefly reiterated under point *(i)* in relation to the 'constitutional public order' and the limits to the application of international treaties, such as the New York Convention in the case at hand.

This brings to the conclusion, driven by ECHR guarantees and ECtHR case law, that the qualification as consumers of the plaintiffs is only relevant up to a point (that is the application of Directive 93/13). In assessing the voluntariness and full knowledge of the choice to adopt arbitration clauses, in fact, the consistent case law of the Strasbourg Court pays attention to the *specific qualities* of the contracting parties.

For example, clauses concluded by commercial companies, even in adherence to the general terms and conditions of others, have been held to be lawful and 'freely' accepted: 'It is difficult to believe that the company [...], which is very active in the sector of civil engineering but also in that of private housing, would be obliged to accept arbitration clauses in order to exist as a construction company', given that 'a decision to renounce [...] could have repercussions in terms of its turnover but probably not in terms of its capacity to thrive in the construction business'.[61]

However, as illustrated by the same Court, a difference must be struck between commercial B2B contracts and non-commercial arbitrations, between a company and individual persons, without any individual negotiation, where any refusal would *concretely* prevent the individual from accessing the services offered by the company.[62]

---

[59] On the balancing with the opposing principle of legal certainty see considerations, *supra*, Chap. 4.

[60] Id.

[61] ECtHR, *Mutu v. Switzerland*, No. 40575/10, 2018, § 107, commenting on previous case law on commercial arbitration.

[62] Id. See also ECtHR, *Pfeifer and Plankl v. Austria*, No. 10802/84, 1992, § 38: 'Mr Pfeifer as a layman [non-professional] was not in a position to appreciate completely. A waiver of rights expressed there and then in such circumstances appears questionable, to say the least. The fact that the applicant stated that he did not think it necessary for his lawyer to be present makes no difference. Thus even supposing that the rights in question can be waived by a defendant, the circumstances surrounding the applicant's decision deprived it of any validity from the point of view of

In this regard, it is evident how the absence of individual negotiation, according to the *practical and effective* interpretation promoted by the ECHR,[63] once again renders the arbitration clause at issue null and void, depriving individual adherents of judicial protection before their own natural courts. There is therefore room to argue, it seems, that the scope of *application of these principles should be extended beyond the consumer discipline*—as long as an imbalance between the parties is proven. In sum, besides the formal qualification of the parties, it should be assessed whether *concretely* there was a significant imbalance which makes the whole negotiation process—and thus the waiver of the right to an ordinary tribunal—invalid. This fundamentally responds to the rationale of the collective instrument at hand, that is to overcome otherwise unsurmountable power asymmetries.[64]

(vi) The argumentative passage '*ad abundantiam*' from the Tribunal of Milan in its inadmissibility order from August 2024, currently appealed, poses similar critical issues, in the part in which it states that, in any event, Article 840-*ter* c.p.c. would not allow a class action to be brought in Italy 'against defendants having their seat only abroad, since not even in the abstract is a specialised section on company matters competent to hear that case'.[65] This would occur since, it is worth reminding, pursuant to said provision class actions (under the 2019 regime) should be brought 'exclusively before the specialised section on company matters competent for the place where the defendant has its seat'.

According to the Tribunal of Milan in the *Binance* case, therefore, even if Italian law was abstractly applicable and the arbitration clause was null and void, the plaintiffs could not bring the case before any Italian court, since the defendant company has no seat or domicile (or establishment or representative) in Italy. The Court has reached this conclusion without carrying out the necessary attempt to interpret the norm in conformity with the Constitution and the ECHR, nor, if impossible, without questioning its constitutional and European legitimacy.

The paradoxical consequence of this strict interpretation, if confirmed on appeal, is that any foreign operator who decides to operate in Italy without opening any office would secure a veritable 'immunity' from Italian jurisdiction in respect of class actions.

The court appears to base its reasoning on the aim to 'avoid forum shopping' by consumers.[66] However, it fails to consider the *forum shopping* incentive in the opposite sense for potential defendants, who would evidently be encouraged not to be based in Italy, thus avoiding collective actions.

Although it is true that the Brussels I *bis* Regulation (1215/2012), referred to in the inadmissibility order, does not consider class actions (understandably, being

---

the Convention. In conclusion, the Court rejects the Government's preliminary objection and considers that there has been a violation of Article 6 para. 1 (Art. 6-1)'.

[63] See *supra*, Chap. 3 of Part 1.

[64] Id.

[65] *Binance* case, Tribunal of Milan, Order from 17 August 2024, R.G. No. 44534/2021, p. 11 (translated from Italian).

[66] *Binance* case, Tribunal of Milan, Order from 17 August 2024, R.G. No. 44534/2021, pp. 10 and 11.

earlier than the RAD and even than the Commission Recommendation), it is worth recalling how that regulation is based on the principle of *protection of the weaker party*, which 'should be protected by rules of jurisdiction more favourable to his interests than the general rules' ('In relation to insurance, consumer and employment contracts', Preamble no. 18).

Also, under an analogical perspective, the 2023 consumer-focused regime appears once again a precious model for interpretation. Art. 140-*septies*, para. 4, cod. cons., in fact, provides that 'If the domicile is also unknown, the court of the place *where the plaintiff* has its seat shall have jurisdiction'. Hence, it can be inferred that when the domicile of the defendant is unknown (and therefore inaccessible)—or foreign—it is indeed possible to refer to the forum of the plaintiff (in the case of Art. 140-*septies* cod. cons., a 'qualified entity' representing consumers). The rationale of this provision is evidently the one argued so far: not to leave plaintiffs without a forum for collective actions when the defendant is not established in Italy.

This analogical interpretation appears the only one capable of bringing the discipline of Article 840-*ter*, para.1, c.p.c. in line with Italian and European constitutionality and compatibility, to guarantee the 'supreme principle of the right to judicial protection',[67] including collective protection and respect of the principle of equality (in relation to consumer matters, under the 2023 regime). It is, in fact, precisely Art. 140-*septies*, para. 4, cod. cons., from the 2023 regime, that provides that 'constitutionally necessary filler criterion'[68] to avert the risk of an 'impaired protection of fundamental rights (which is also likely to be prolonged over time, in the continuation of legislative inertia)'.[69] Therefore, in the present *Binance* case, it appears as the specialised business section from the Tribunal of Milan may very well be the competent court, provided the name plaintiffs are domiciled in Milan.

In view of the seriousness of the matter, a timely intervention by the legislator to fill the gap appears, in any case, highly desirable. The only alternative to this constitutionally-oriented interpretation, otherwise, seems to be the raising of a question on the constitutional legitimacy on Article 840-*ter*, para. 1, c.p.c., with reference to Articles 2, 3, 24, 111 and 117, first paragraph, of the Italian Constitution, the latter in relation to Articles 6 and 13 ECHR, Article 19 TEU and Article 47 CFREU, in so far as it does not provide that, in the absence of a seat in Italy of the defendant, the competence criterion of the residence of the name plaintiff is applicable.

---

[67] See *supra*, Chap. 4.

[68] Italian Constitutional Court, Judgement No. 242 from 2019, point No. 4 of Points of Law. See also Italian Constitutional Court, Judgement No. 40 from 2019, No. 233, No. 222 from 2018 and No. 236 from 2016.

[69] Italian Constitutional Court, Judgement No. 242 from 2019, point No. 4 of Points of Law (translated from Italian).

References

Born G, Salas C (2012) United States supreme court and class arbitration: a tragedy of errors, the symposium. Journal of Dispute Resolution 1:21–48

Cabraser E, Issacharoff S (2018) The participatory class action. N Y Univ Law Rev 92:846–877

Crisafulli V (1956) La scuola nella Costituzione. Rivista trimestrale di diritto pubblico

De Dominicis F (2025) Un breve raffronto tra la Direttiva 2020/1828 (UE) e il d.lgs. 23 marzo 2023, n. 28: considerazioni in punto di attuazione. In: Randazzo B, Henke A, Voet S (eds) L'azione di classe italiana nel quadro europeo: profili sostanziali e processuali. Giappichelli, Torino

Gilles M, Friedman G (2012) After class: aggregate litigation in the wake of AT&T Mobility v. Concepcion. Univ Chicago Law Rev 79:623–676

Giussani A (2025) Un breve raffronto tra la Direttiva 2020/1828 (UE) e il d.lgs. 23 marzo 2023, n. 28: considerazioni in punto di attuazione. In: Randazzo B, Henke A, Voet S (eds) L'azione di classe italiana nel quadro europeo: profili sostanziali e processuali. Giappichelli, Torino

Issacharoff S (2021) Rule 23 and the triumph of experience. Law Contemp Probl 84:161–182

Mullenix LS (2014) Ending class actions as we know them: rethinking the American class action. Emory Law J 64:399–449

Sternlight J (2000) As mandatory binding arbitration meets the class action, will the class action survive? William Mary Law Rev 42(1):1–126

Sternlight J, Jensen EJ (2004) Using arbitration to eliminate consumer class actions: efficient business practice or unconscionable abuse? Law Contemp Probl 67:75–103

Travaglino G (2017) Le stagioni della prescrizione estintiva. Questione e giustizia 1:48–75

Yan J (2011) A lunatic's guide to suing for $30: class action arbitration, the Federal Arbitration act and unconscionability after AT&T v. Concepcion. Berkeley J Emp Labor Law 32(2):551–567

Part IV
Conclusive Assessment

Chapter 11
Final Constitutional Assessment and Forward Look

11.1 Premise. Picking Up the Threads

The current research is based on a few cardinal pillars. Building on them, the central thesis has been developed.

As a preliminary foundation, the need for a comprehensive reassessment of the constitutional framework has been highlighted as of the outmost urgency in the contemporary, constantly shifting, evading and intertwining socio-economical skein. *Globalisation* and *technological innovation*, as reported in Chap. 2, are fundamentally *transforming*—if they have not already, irremediably, transformed—the context in which we live. Such a context, under a different layer of perspective, is also the setting in which our rights and interests are enforced—or supposed to be enforced.

These shifting trends are not necessarily negative. Progress not even conceivable until a few decades ago has been reached in different areas of science and life. This regards several sectors: from medicine and health to transportation and communications, with an enriching and continuous exchange of ideas, people and knowledge (which, among other things, also makes this research possible).

At the same time, nevertheless, new challenges have emerged, too. Their distinctive and salient feature, if one was to be sought, while beginning to adopt the perspective of the constitutionalist, is probably their utter impinging on *power*. To this fascinating yet complex issue is dedicated—albeit briefly, in an instrumental fashion to the subsequent discussion—Chap. 3. Such a dwelling is crucial for the subsequent reflections, although merely transient, for obvious necessities of not diverting too far from the main perimeter of the research. Drawing from well-established academic constitutional scholarship has been foundational for this purpose.

The resulting picture is one where *new centres of gravity* emerge, propelled by evolving centrifugal and centripetal forces, where the dichotomy between private

A. Maglica, *Collective Dimensions of Access to Justice*, European Union and its Neighbours in a Globalized World 23,
https://doi.org/10.1007/978-3-031-94522-9_11

and public law becomes the ever more blurred,[1] much in the same way as the borders between national states. As accounted, sovereignty from the traditional Westphalian state is increasingly shifting towards new actors. Supranational systems and international organisations emerge, while multi-located and veiled transnational corporations and their supply chains cross the original national state's ground.

These tensions and power migrations create open fractures in which single individuals more easily fall. Such cracks are characterised by a collapse of the traditional (under the civil law tradition) mechanisms of *responsibility* of the subjects concretely holding power. Elusive, punctiform, crossing borders and legal orders, riding new, often unregulated practices and devices, it becomes extremely difficult to hold them *accountable* for their conducts.[2]

The traditional paths of democratic *representativeness*—the so-called intermediate bodies, *in primis* political parties and labour unions—struggle, with legislative and executive actors, consequently, often being unable or even disinterested in pursuing the interests of all the population. Even when they are, they might lag behind for lack of resources—also economic ones—or technical abilities. *Inequalities*, as a result, are exponentially increased.[3]

Despite their enshrinement on paper—in several constitutional charts, national and supranational—, *systemic* and *standardised* violations of the most basic rights occur on a daily basis. The systemic and structural character, on the one hand, and the massified and standardised nature, on the other hand, of these infringements is key. They are the result of those very phenomena which fueled, and keep fueling, the constitutional transformations: globalisation and new technologies.[4]

Conducts of the new powerful actors tend to take place in such a way: a systemic one, operating through all the social tissue, dealing with people not one at a time, but as infinitesimal *nameless*—'unseen'[5]—*fragments* of their major—or mass—scale activities. From *citoyens*, they become mere consumers, or users. The individual is left naked, unrepresented and unable to make his or her voice heard whenever a violation from these much more powerful actors is suffered. New 'meta-individual' positions, worthy of protection, steam into the legal order, as well.[6]

A goal for those studying the evolutions of power, its limitations and the guarantees of rights, becomes that of finding *new paths of enforcement*.[7] To this regard the

[1] See, *supra*, Chap. 3.

[2] Id.

[3] Id.

[4] See, *supra*, Chap. 2.

[5] 'Millions of spiritual Creatures walk the Earth / Unseen, both when we wake, and when we sleep', Milton (1667), Book IV, lines 677–678. See, *supra*, Part I, especially Chap. 3.

[6] See, *supra*, Chap. 4.

[7] See Barile (1984), p. 95: 'There are two fronts on which work needs to be done in this field: the side of concepts [...] and the side of judicial protection (which individuals or social formations are entitled to enforce them, and before which courts', translated from Italian, first cited in Trocker (1990), p. 193.

present research has focused on the judicial one. However, the abovementioned fractures in the social and constitutional context, evidently, cannot be filled with the ordinary litigation models (nor even by litigation alone, see *infra*).

New challenges require new responses. Another foundational point of this work, to which Parts II and III have been dedicated, is exactly this: to identify and foster new legal—specifically, herein, procedural—approaches that can efficiently confront the new type of injustices embedded within our society.[8]

For this purpose, the *class action* mechanism has been analysed, especially in the Italian legal order, as part of the larger multilevel European constitutional system.[9] The main challenge for this book was to evaluate it in a *constitutional perspective*: as an instrument of more effective *access to justice*; as a potential tool of disorder and constitutional illegitimacy by infringing *due process guarantees*; and its use for enforcing not just consumer rights but *fundamental* ones, too.[10]

Particular attention has been paid to the regulations introduced in 2019 in the new Title VIII-*bis* of the Italian Code of civil procedure. The extension of the scope of application set forth therein, from a perimeter previously limited to consumers to, now, a general one, in fact, requires careful consideration also of constitutional nature, given the disruptive potential of the new dual (injunctive and compensatory) device. This has been the central focus of Chap. 6.

Preliminarily, instead, a general overview of the class action model has been provided under Chap. 5, dedicated to its US and (common law) origins and to how, only in recent years, after heated debate, it was legally transplanted in Europe, too. The implementation of the so-called 'RAD' Directive has been discussed, to this regard. In particular, it has been worth recalling that, after the well-known US amendments from 1966, the first wave of class action litigation was for the enforcement of *civil rights*, and against racial segregation specifically. The EU focus on collective redress so far, instead, has been on *consumer* and competition law, i.e. through the RAD Directive.

Part III, finally, with its four Chapters, has been dedicated to a more practical (and, hence, 'effective')[11] approach. Through case studies, the practical application

[8] Impossible not to quote again Mauro Cappelletti's ground-breaking research on access to justice, and in particular the Florence Project from the 1970s. See, e.g., Cappelletti (1978). For further references, see, *supra*, Chap. 4. On the 'close links that unite procedural law to constitutional law […] [since] all freedoms are empty if they cannot be enforced and defended in court', see, instead, Calamandrei (1953), pp. 576–577, cited *supra*, in Chap. 2.

[9] See Randazzo (2023).

[10] On the close connection between constitutional law and procedural paths of enforcement, see again, *supra*, Cappelletti (1993) and Calamandrei (1953). Apart from Cappelletti's foresighted studies, previous attention from Italian constitutional scholarship, albeit limited and brief, on this specific procedural model (although at the time still consumer-limited) can be found also in Mezzanotte (2022), Pace (2011) and Rordorf (2010). Already anticipatorily stressing the importance of the phenomenon, together with Cappelletti, see also Rodotà (1976), Pizzorusso (1976), Trocker (1990), Bognetti (1998) and Taruffo (2001).

[11] ECtHR, *Scordino v. Italy (no. 1)* [GC], No. 36813/97, ECHR 2006, § 192; ECtHR, *Prince Hans-Adam II of Liechtenstein v. Germany* [GC], No. 42527/98, ECHR 2001, § 45.

of the class action instrument in Italy has been analysed, both for the enforcement of (fundamental) rights and for the concretisation of a fundamental right itself (the principle of effective legal protection): in *environmental matters* and *mass health harms* stemming from a medical device; in *discriminatory matters* and unfair exploitation in gig-economy *labour* contexts; for inhuman and degrading treatment, due to systemic dysfunctions, of *prisoners*, detainees, *migrants* and asylum seekers; in crypto-currency matters, with highly relevant profiles of *class waivers through arbitration clauses* and foreign defendants' incentives to forum shopping.

In most cases, the approach, although always focused on the Italian constitutional system, has also been *comparative*: towards other procedural instruments (in a vertical way, too, e.g. mainly towards the ECtHR paths of enforcement), but also in relation to other jurisdictions (in particular US and Canada, offering a richer class action litigative experience, especially in Chap. 9).

It is exactly this element of comparison, coupled with that of *coordination*, to convey the keystone with which we wish to propose, at present, a closing for the research: that is, the crucial elements of *pluralism* and *integration*. Pluralism and integration assume relevance from multiple standpoints: of ideas, models, interpretations, techniques, provisions, structures, practices; between jurisdictions, courts, plaintiffs, attorneys, judges, defendants, civil society (academics, too) and other powers (the legislative and the executive).

For these reasons, the implementation in Italy of a class action technique with a general scope of application must be evaluated *extremely positively*. It enhances the *access-to-justice* potential through judicial action, with a tool capable of rebalancing again power *equilibria*, of enforcing new 'meta-individual' positions: in other words, of overcoming otherwise unsurmountable legal and practical barriers, by filling otherwise too deep gaps in enforcement and representation processes.[12]

The multiple lessons conveyed by the case studies leave optimism.

At the same time, however, the dual Italian mechanism, although a fundamental step forward, is *far from perfect*. It lends itself to abusive practices and, moreover, presents rather problematic provisions, whose constitutional legitimacy should be questioned.[13]

To tackle these issues, *interpretative and practical* attention must be paid while implementing the *current* mechanisms. The next paragraph will be dedicated to a brief recapitulation on this matter.

Active changes in the legislation, still, will be necessary, too. The current regulatory provisions can and, therefore, must be *improved*, also to overcome such serious doubts of constitutional legitimacy. This holds special importance given their disruptive potential to influence the positions of several individuals, and with mass economic impact, too. Lessons from the first developing case law and from successful experiences from abroad should be taken into account, too. The aim of this Chapter is also to recall the most relevant among these reflections.

Last, a final consideration on *pluralism* and *integration* shall be offered.

---

[12] See, *supra*, Chap. 4.

[13] See, *supra*, Chap. 6, as well as, more generally, the reflections through the case studies in Part III.

11.2 Integrating Regulations, Constitutional Principles and Case Law: A Conclusive Reflection *de Iure Condito*

First and foremost, the lack of clear interpretative certainty surrounding the key concept of *homogeneity* has been extensively debated throughout this work, in several circumstances.[14]

As explained, said test should merely be applied to compensatory class actions as depicting (in a broad view) 'a common origin'.[15] The Tribunal of Milan, in the *ILVA* injunctive class action, has provided an order confirming this view, with particular reference to its limitation to compensatory actions. At the same time, however, the same Tribunal of Milan and—less explicitly—other courts in other cases (e.g., the *Philips Respironics* or the *Deliveroo* cases, in Milan, or the *ITA Airways* injunctive class action, in front of the Tribunal of Rome) present different readings.[16]

As argued, the latter standpoint may paradoxically prove more favourable to plaintiffs planning to proceed with an injunctive action, initially, and a damages one, subsequently. In fact, should homogeneity be declared in the injunctive *azione collettiva*, it may be easier to proceed at a later time with the compensatory *azione di classe*. This could become an important *strategical trend* for class plaintiffs.[17]

In particular, actions concerning serious and *continuous harms* seem to see the consolidation of this trend. The interpretative inclusion of the 'homogeneity' test, as part of the admissibility phase, within injunctive collective actions, too, does not appear to be a decisive factor for this trend, either.

After all, this tendency is only logical. The developing jurisprudence significantly appears, in fact, to be distinguishing the injunctive instrument from the damages one in relation to the type of infringement suffered.

The former is evaluated by the courts as a lawsuit aiming to stop a *potentially* harmful conduct or situation. The *effective* harm is not necessarily an element to prove for the plaintiffs. It is sufficient to demonstrate the existence of a *serious risk* that an injury will occur. Or, in the case of continuous violations, to show that they have not ended yet. Thus, in sum, the completion of the harm is not *per se* required for seeking this particular type of relief.[18]

In the latter class action model, aiming at compensatory redress, instead, plaintiffs need to present adequate proof of all the elements of the injury, included the harm itself, its *quantum* and the specific *causal link* between the conduct and the exact harm. There is, consequently, a significant difference concerning the *evidentiary threshold* expected for each action. This threshold, as argued above, is lower for the injunctive *azione collettiva*, in light of the elements underscored.[19]

---

[14] See, *supra*, in particular, Chap. 6.

[15] Id.

[16] See *supra*, Part III.

[17] Id., especially Chap. 7.

[18] Id.

[19] See, *supra*, in particular, Chaps. 6 and 7.

Contrarily to the statements of some courts (i.e., see *supra*, the *Philips Respironics*, *Deliveroo* and *ITA Airways* cases),[20] however, such a lower threshold does not exclude *per se* the admissibility of injunctive class actions for particularly *complex* matters. It merely regards the evidentiary *onus* on the plaintiffs. The judge will have to balance, on the one hand, the need to prevent irreparable harm with the necessity of not issuing unjustified measures, which could harm in turn the defendants. In complex circumstances, the judge can, and should, make use of *auxiliary tools*, such as the hearing of experts[21] or the request for technical reports to better understand the matter and assess the applicability of the injunctive action.

The explicit reference to the possibility of using *simple presumptions* and *statistical data* is a further support for him (or her) while completing such a delicate assessment, in order to have a more nuanced view and flexibility.[22] Certain courts' view that the provisions expressly recalling this possibility actually demonstrate the Italian legislator's intention to exclude the admissibility of injunctive class actions for evidentiary complex matters does not seem convincing.[23] Not only since such a possibility already existed in the Italian legal order, but because, on the contrary, this explicit reference reiterates the core *access-to-justice goal* of the reform.

Statistical data and simple presumptions, in other words, are underscored by the Italian legislator simply as additional means for demonstrating the risk of *future* harm. Given the possible lack of such a concrete injury, it is rational to expect the use of presumptions and statical analysis for determining its probability in light of a specific conduct. Any complexity in ascertaining, previously, that the conduct concretely took place, or the correctness of the statistic, does not pertain the *admissibility* of the action at stake.[24]

Limiting the perimeter of application—both for injunctive and compensatory actions—for a purported evidentiary complexity on the basis of this, rather questionable, reasoning empties the 2019 class action provisions of their true rationale. It is, in fact, in particular complex cases that a unitary assessment may be more beneficial: both for *judicial efficiency* reasons (i.e., avoiding the evidentiary assessment on the same complex matters repeatedly, in potentially hundreds of thousands of proceedings) and on the grounds of the *higher* economic, temporal and organisational *costs* that may prevent a single individual from acting alone (thus, *in concreto* denying him, or her, justice).[25]

This regards also non-material damage in the constitutionally-oriented interpretation of the jurisprudential thresholds of 'gravity' and 'seriousness', proposed above.[26] As such, it has been discussed, a *unified assessment* of the class as a whole,

[20] See, *supra*, in particular, Chaps. 7 and 8.

[21] See, *supra*, in particular, Chap. 9.

[22] See, *supra*, in particular, Chap. 6.

[23] See, *supra*, in particular, Chaps. 6 and 8.

[24] Id.

[25] See, *supra*, Chap. 4.

[26] See, *supra*, Chap. 6.

rather than the mere individual members would occur. The gravity and seriousness of each single homogeneous subjective position (hence, with a factual 'common origin' and nothing else, see *supra*) should be *aggregated* to reach the total for the class. Even if the gravity and seriousness were not sufficient *individually*—i.e., if the individual right-holder sought non-material compensation through ordinary individual and autonomous judicial proceedings—, *collectively* they could be reached. This way, with a constitutionally oriented reading, in light of Articles 24 and 2 of the Italian Constitution, the above-identified values could be balanced.[27]

These reflections, which are necessary, should not distract us from the final point of arrival of the present considerations: spurious of these interpretative limits, in the light of a purely literal, systematic and historical interpretation, the 2019 Italian injunctive *azione collettiva* has an extraordinary potential, dictated by its expressive simplicity (it is regulated by only one article, it should be recalled).

Furthermore, the possibly enormous economic impact of the sanctions *ex* Article 614-*bis* for this action, as an instrument of indirect coercion, boosts its potential. The *Philips Respironics* case, in particular, has shown that said penalties—so-called '*astreintes*'—are apparently paid directly to the class plaintiffs. This sets, on the one hand, huge incentives for this type of action—even more than the compensatory one, to a certain degree, where contingency fees are capped—, but also, on the other hand, raises several concerns on the suitability (if not legitimacy) of said provision, given that the lawsuit is in principle on behalf of a *group* of people, not just the single plaintiff ('anyone with an interest') who recovers the sums.[28]

The crucial difference between the compensatory remedy, *ex* Articles 840-*bis et seq*. c.p.c., and the injunctive one, *ex* Article 840-*sexiesdecies* c.p.c., still, as much underscored until now, lays in the objective scope of application. While the former allows the collective, via representation, enforcement of individual subjective positions (rights), the latter protects also supra-individual interests, not *directly* linked to an individual subject, not even necessarily held by *any* individual.[29] A prime example is that of climate change suits or the environment, where no single holder can be found, but rather they are goods or interests pertaining to the society as a whole, or at least to a large group.

In the words of the United Sections from the Italian Supreme Court of Cassation in a landmark case from 1979 (reiterated in 2006), 'The perspective that there is legal protection *only* in the case of exclusive connection between a good (or a fraction thereof) and a single specific individual, or a personified group—and thus assimilated to the individual—, is conditioned by a patrimonial approach to legal protection and risks of mortifying by reason of such a conditioning the irresistible

[27] See, *supra*, Chap. 4.

[28] See, *supra*, Chaps. 6 and 7.

[29] Id. See also, *supra*, Chap. 4.

tendency to the actionability of claims that is the cornerstone of our Constitution (Article 24 of the Constitution)'.[30]

The *ILVA* case, in relation to the right to health and to a safe environment, demonstrates this fully: it aims to stop an activity declared, on several occasions, by various governments, even as being of 'strategic national interest', with the incredible economic consequences—for the company as much as for its workers—that a possible closure would entail.[31] The high sum the defendants would have to pay, under the collective action at stake, as a penalty for the delay in executing the court's order should be accounted, too—as illustratively shown in the *Philips Respironics* case.[32]

In this sense, given how in several injunctive class actions the delicate issue of the separation of powers could arise, the other *trend* that is developing appears rather reasonable. This is the key tendency of the courts—especially first instance ones, when confronted with the most delicate cases, with the most far-reaching consequences—to seek support in institutional reports, in supranational legislation and in previous decisions of supranational courts, like the CJEU and the ECtHR. This could be seen also as way of enhancing *authority* and seeking more *democratic legitimacy*.[33]

Once again, therefore, we return to the theme of *coordination* through the concept of *integration*; integration, in this case, between sources and courts within a common multilevel constitutional architecture, in order to attribute the necessary *authority* to an ordinary national (Italian) judge of first instance—of a specialised section—in making decisions that may cause *profound societal effects*.[34]

---

[30] Added emphasis, translated from Italian. Italian Court of Cassation, S.U., 6 October 1979, No. 5172, which notably also stated that the right to health, under Article 32 of the Constitution, 'presents itself not only as a mere right to life and physical safety, but (also) as a real right to a healthy environment'. See also Italian Court of Cassation, S.U., 1 August 2006, No. 17461, and Italian Court of Cassation, S.U., 27 July 2022, No. 23436. See also more thoroughly, *supra*, Chap. 4.

[31] See, *supra*, Chap. 7.

[32] Id.

[33] Id., in relation to the *ILVA* case and the recent decision from the Court of Justice (GC) in response to the preliminary ruling sought within such a case. See CJEU, Grand Chamber, Judgement of 25 June 2024, *Ilva and Others*, C-626/22.

[34] On the issue of judicial activism and its relationship towards other forms of direct democratic representation, see Angiolini (2012), pp. 202–205, translated from Italian: 'Of course, since it is probable that the courts and judges are not all 'wise' like Solomon, and that not all parties to a dispute are inclined to cooperate in 'justice', all the above does not detract from the hope that, for the protection of human rights, a more robust contribution can come from the exercise of democratic political participation, through majority deliberations or the election of representative bodies to deliberate. Democratic participation, however, cannot be absolutely relied upon. Democracy, even where it exists, now has macroscopic gaps and shortcomings. In particular, given the fragility of other manifestations of democracy, especially at supranational and international level, it remains for the most part caged within states, within which 'peoples', 'nations' or other collectivities, selected with arbitrary criteria by the 'sovereign', deliberate or elect representatives to deliberate, by majority vote, what is easy to have effects and constraints on others. [...] Since, with all the reservations that must be maintained [...] justice cannot be reduced, or at least it may be not

The common law experience shows, instead, a far greater ease from the courts in making use of the class action instrument. While still considering the particularities of the Italian legal and cultural tradition (i.e., in relation to punitive damages), the Italian judges should follow their example, supported by technical experts and data.[35]

In direct connection with the issue of sharing and increasing knowledge and good practices among courts is the fact that the publications of decisions on the *ministerial portal* are only partial. In some cases, key information is lacking. In most injunctive class actions, no news on their filing—hence, *existence*—is even given. Furthermore, with the introduction in 2023 of the consumer representative action, those cases are thrown into the mix, too. The result is a confusing potpourri of *partial information* which assists in no way the courts and the legal practitioners, as well as potentially interested members of the class. Paradoxically, in the *ILVA* and *Philips Respironics* injunctive class actions, the members themselves of the class could not access the orders already issued by the courts (in the latter case even of appeal). This practice does not seem to align with the values set forth in the Italian Constitution, regarding the *publicity* of the hearing as a core pillar of the fair trial (Articles 111 and 117, first paragraph, in relation to Article 6 ECHR, especially),[36] which evidently needs to be proportionally enhanced to the *collective dimensions* of the proceedings.

Finally, maintaining an access to justice perspective, one should refer to the reflections from above on the *non-retroactivity* of the new provisions for unlawful conducts preceding 19 May 2021 (date of the entry into force of the 2019 class action regime),[37] on jurisdiction over foreign defendants[38] and on *standing to be sued*.[39]

Regarding the last point, the importance of encompassing among potential defendants *public entities* such as hospitals, penitentiaries or schools has been

---

reduceable, to a mere and generic 'counter-power' of a 'normative' nature, which only serves to give back a chance to those who have been defeated in democratic deliberation. Insofar as it succeeds in reversing the objective intervention of an independent and impartial third party to resolve a dispute between disputants who are guaranteed equality of arms, justice is not only an alternative means of balancing human rights to the political and democratic one, but the specific garrison to ensure that human rights are not 'destroyed' or unduly taken away in their exercise, in the absence of others' positions worthy of protection, from the freedom and responsibility that each person has for himself'. The core issue, hence, appears to be, on the one hand, that to identify when a judicial decision is a necessary '*garrison*' and, on the other hand, that to ensure appropriate *guarantees* (of fair trial) in front of such judicial authorities, even and especially when operating under new (collective, in this case) dimensions of justice.

On the delicate issue of judicial review—specifically in relation to the Italian Constitutional Court—and democratic legitimacy, see also, already referred to *supra* in Chap. 3, e.g., Crisafulli (1978), p. 73, Elia (1982), p. 515, Rodotà (1982a), p. 489, Mezzanotte (1984), Cappelletti (1994), p. 157, Cheli (1996), Fioravanti (1999), Mezzetti (2007, 2010) and Morrone (2019).

[35] See, *supra*, particularly emblematic, Chap. 9.

[36] See Randazzo (2023), p. 107.

[37] See, *supra*, Chap. 6.

[38] Id. See also, *supra*, Chap. 10, in relation to the crucial *Binance* case, still pending on appeal.

[39] See, *supra*, Chap. 6.

stressed, also in relation to the potential class actions for the protection of prisoners' and migrants' rights.[40] In addition to what has already been asserted, it appears mandatory to include them in consideration of the principle of equality set under Article 3 of the Italian Constitution, too. Otherwise, as already stressed, an unreasonable difference of treatment would occur between private entities operating said public service and the public ones: e.g., between private and public hospitals or schools (but also detention centres, should such a service be entrusted to a private entity). The former could potentially be sued in a collective suit, whereas the latter would be unreasonably shielded from such a possibility. Municipalities and Regions should be included, too.

11.3 The Pivotal Role of the Judge

The role of the judge must be underscored as a key—probably *the* key—factor for the success of collective judicial proceedings, in Italy and everywhere.

As it has been discussed until now, the potential of this new type of enforcement is significant, since it promises, at least on paper, to re-equilibrate otherwise unbalanced power-dynamics. Under this perspective, as demonstrated, it is a clear concretisation of the principle of effective legal protection and of the *equality of arms*, as set forth under Article 6 ECHR, in the sense of a 'fair balance' between them.[41]

At the same time, however, a twofold series of issues arises.

The first inherent risk is that of falling prey of *formalistic interpretations*, which, in practice can hinder the concrete use of the tool.

The *Binance* case, analysed under Chap. 10, is particularly illustrative to this regard, as it shows how a strict reading of norms, not constitutionally-oriented, can concretely preclude collective access to justice, as discussed in Chap. 4.

Similar hermeneutical approaches have been shown in employment matters—for instance, in the *Deliveroo* case from Chap. 8—, towards which judges from the specialised business section evidently have reluctance: this has led to the highlighted questionable interpretative solutions, such as those insisting on the inadmissibility of cases of 'particular complexity' or on a rigid reading of the 'homogeneity' test. The 'practical and effective' approach promoted by the Strasbourg Court, which enters the Italian constitutional order through Articles 11 and 117, first paragraph, of the Italian Constitution, is once again rather precious to this regard.[42]

In other words, one cannot expect collective litigation to (effectively) work in a given jurisdiction because of the mere implementation of related provisions. These provisions, which fundamentally shift the dimension and way of delivering justice,

[40] Id. See also, *supra*, Chap. 9, in relation to the possible use of class actions for the (collective) protection of prisoners' and migrants' rights.

[41] See *supra*, Chap. 4.

[42] Id.

require a flexible outlook, which inevitably needs to be tailored to the specific circumstances of each case. Such a flexibility needs to be brought also towards the reading of the norms and of the traditional (binary) structures of civil proceedings, understanding that they need to be adapted, too, in order to ensure the enactment of the reform's rationale (and comply with fundamental constitutional principles): that is to overcome the 'atomistic limit of individual' enforcement[43] in order to ensure effective judicial protection—'itself the content of an inviolable right', 'protected by articles 24 and 113 of the [Italian] Constitution [...] characterising the democratic rule of law'.[44]

The second risk is that of *abuses*. They can regard *defendants*, potential subjects of extorsive or anti-competition practices, but the most important challenge appears to be towards the *members of the class* (for the compensatory tool) or the *whole group*, if not society (for the injunctive remedy). Class actions, in fact, push—and break—the boundaries of litigation as a two-party affair, by making it a multi-party and, therefore, potentially, multi-interest affair.

Such a balancing of competing interests at stake may even recall, in some ways, that of constitutional courts or, even more, that of the administrative judge 'between solidarity and inviolability',[45] when appreciating the legitimacy of the weighing of interests that the administrative authority itself has established. The main difference being, of course, that the object of collective actions is not a legislative or administrative act, but rather a *conduct*, most often from a private subject (even though, as discussed above, also entities managing public services, or services of public utility, have passive standing).[46]

The element to stress, still, it appears, is that of the potential *competing* nature of the *internal* positions of the members of the class, who are not necessarily parties to the proceedings. Hence, the fundamental role of the judge in ensuring the respect of the *adversarial principle*, as part of the right to a fair trial, under the collective dimension, too: that is, by considering the possible adversities also *within* the class, in a one-sided perspective, too. All members of the class, therefore, should have the possibility to familiarise themselves with the evidence before the court, as well as the possibility to comment on its existence, contents and authenticity 'in an appropriate form and within an appropriate time'.[47]

This, evidently, implies the creation—and the judicial predisposition, in terms of attitude, first and foremost—of structures and procedural moments in which such a possibility can be realised. It also makes *publicity* of the proceedings—and of the

---

[43] See, e.g., Italian Constitutional Court, Judgement No. 75 from 1992. We return, in sum, to Calamandrei (1953), pp. 576–78, and (1954), p. 650 *et seq.*, see *supra*, Chap. 2.

[44] Italian Constitutional Court, Judgement No. 26 from 1999, translated from Italian, as well as No. 29 of 2003, No. 386 of 2004 and No. 120 from 2014.

[45] Scoditti (2022), p. 162.

[46] See *supra*, Chap. 6.

[47] ECtHR, *Krčmář and Others v. the Czech Republic*, No. 35376/97, 2000, § 42; ECtHR, *Immeubles Groupe Kosser v. France*, No. 38748/97, 2002, § 26.

reasoning of the decisions reached therein—a key element not currently sufficiently taken into account nor by the legislator nor by the judicial machinery, as abundantly discussed above.[48]

11.4 Integrating Findings and Doubts of Constitutional Legitimacy: A Conclusive Reflection *de Iure Condendo*

The present paragraph aims at discussing *regulatory hurdles* that substantially hinder the use of the class action device in Italy. In such an evaluation, it suggests elements for future improvement. In particular, it focuses, *(i)* on the *competent court*, that is—currently—the section of the tribunal specialised in company matters, *(ii)* on the rules on *standing to sue*, limited to certain subjects and thereby dangerously hampering the effectiveness of the dual collective remedy at stake, and, finally, *(iii)* on possible amendments regarding the *distribution of damages*, especially considering the comparative experience, and *class definition*.

11.4.1 Competent Court

As is known, the 2019 Italian regime establishes that 'the application for a class action shall be brought by means of an application exclusively before the specialised section on company matters competent for the place where the defendant has its seat'.[49] It also sets forth that the action 'may be brought against companies or against entities managing public services or public utilities, with regard to acts and conducts carried out in the performance of their respective activities'.[50] This choice, on the one hand, tends to *narrow the passive scope* of the new procedural institution to the world of companies and, on the other hand, precisely because of this, hinges the jurisdiction at the *specialised section* on company matters of the tribunal where the defendant has seat.

Doubts as to the constitutional legitimacy or, in any event, as to the necessary constitutionally oriented interpretation, in relation to *potential defendants domiciled only abroad,* have already been discussed at length in Chap. 10.

---

[48] See *supra*, Chap. 6.

[49] Article 840-*ter*, para. 1 c.p.c., with similar provisions for the injunctive class action pursuant to Article 840-*sexiesdecies* c.p.c.

[50] Article 840-*bis*, para. 2 c.p.c., with similar provisions for the injunctive class action pursuant to Article 840-*sexiesdecies* c.p.c.

The already mentioned doubts as to the constitutional legitimacy of the provisions limiting *passive standing* to the business world[51] also affect the present provisions on *competence*. This choice appears particularly problematic.

One can certainly understand the legislator's decision to bring class actions to this specialised section of the tribunal to ensure greater *technicality*, as well as to increase over time the *expertise* of judges, faced with a procedural instrument as new to civil law legal culture as it is complex. One cannot deny, however, the challenging nature of the current competence. It is, in fact, discordant to delegate to judges *specialised* in a given subject (company matters) the decision of disputes with a *generalised* scope of application.

In relation to the constitutional perspective of the present research, further concerns arise.

If, as hitherto hypothesised, collective actions were to be brought in connection with fundamental rights related to the individual's *personal sphere* ('private life', borrowing ECHR vocabulary), such as that to health, to a healthy environment or personal freedoms, the judges of the specialised business section would be required to decide matters *extremely different* from those dealt with on a daily basis, in which their sensitivity and technical preparation would inevitably be less than that of their colleagues in other sections, with a significant increase in the burden of study for the judges themselves and the risk of an improper decision for the parties. The case studies analysed already show a trend in this direction.[52]

At the same time, it is urgent to emphasise once again the considerable *variety of fields* of law in which class actions could appear (and are already appearing) before the judges.[53] And it must not be forgotten how, in addition to having to familiarise themselves with the significant peculiarities of the new procedural discipline, as well as having to delve from time to time (if not simultaneously) into extremely technical and diverse matters, they are called upon in the meantime to also carry out the *ordinary workload* of their chambers. This inevitably causes an important extension of procedural time and questions the overall hold of the reform's *judicial economy* goal.

It does not appear reasonable, either, that substantially identical situations (they are the same, only the dimension of enforcement changes) are treated differently—as in front of a different judge—whether they are brought individually or in collective form, thus colliding with the principle of equality set forth under Article 3 of the Italian Constitution.

In addition, with regard to *special rites* such as the *labour* one, there are even stronger doubts. As analysed in Chap. 8, in the *Deliveroo* case, a class action between workers (food-delivery riders) and their employer has already caused concerns. On this occasion, the Tribunal of Milan confirmed the applicability of the class action to labour matters ('Among the individual rights that can be protected, it

---

[51] See *supra*, Chap. 6.

[52] See *supra*, *Part III*.

[53] See *infra*, Figures, at the end of this Part.

does not appear that those connected with labour relations can be excluded').[54] At the same time, however, the Milanese court in several passages of the (brief) decision seems to *improperly raise* the standard required for bringing the collective suit, thereby running the risk of making meritorious actions impracticable in concreto. The latent concern, as argued, is that behind the—questionable—statement of 'particular complexity in the correct identification of the actual injuries suffered', in justification of the claim's rejection, there is a(n understandable) *lack of sensitivity* to labour matters that exacerbates the complexity itself of the issues.

Considering the ordinary handling of such matters by the labour judge, for instance,[55] the jurisdictional dichotomy between cases brought through *individual action*—decided by the labour judge—and cases brought through *collective action* pursuant to the new Title VIII-*bis* c.p.c.—decided by the specialised section on company matters, far less expert and accustomed to them—is somewhat disconcerting, we must stress again.

Such a different treatment of substantially identical situations cannot appear reasonable evermore so in relation to issues for which the legislator has deemed necessary a *specialised judge* for ordinary individual claims. The respect of the *principle of equality* under Article 3 of the Italian Constitution is thereby critically put into question.

Furthermore, it may also conflict, to a certain degree, with the fundamental principle of the *natural judge pre-established by law*, enshrined under Article 25, first paragraph, of the Italian Constitution. As is known, this principle is often quoted in other contexts as one of the guarantees set to ensure the *impartiality* and objectivity of the judges.[56]

As such, it appears closely, if not directly, linked to the right to a *fair trial*, enshrined under Article 111 of the Italian Constitution and, through Article 117, first paragraph, of the same Constitution, under Articles 6 ECHR and 47 CFREU. Such a guarantee, as is well-known, regards also the *appearance* of impartiality.[57] This relationship, which ends up encompassing the principle in question—of the natural judge pre-established by law—under the concept of fair trial, enriches it of new nuances, it seems.

In particular, the well-developed case law of the Strasbourg Court is precious in this regard, by stressing, through its 'practical and effective' approach,[58] that the

[54] See *supra*, Chap. 8.

[55] See *supra*, Chap. 6, also for tax matters and the possibility of collective actions in front of the administrative judge.

[56] Italian Constitutional Court, Judgements No. 502 from 1991, point No. 4.1 of Points of law, Nos. 131 of 1996, point No. 3.2. of Points of law, No. 327 from 1998, No. 419 from 1998, point No. 2 of Points of law, No. 393 from 2002. See also CJEU, Grand Chamber, Judgment of 21 April 2021, *Repubblika v. Il-Prim Ministru*, C-896/19 and CJEU, Judgments of 24 June 2019, *Commission v. Poland*, C-619/18. See Randazzo (2023), p. 92, and Bustos Gisbert (2022), p. 591. See also, foresightedly, Onida (1982), p. 159.

[57] Id. In particular, see Randazzo (2023), p. 93.

[58] See, e.g., ECtHR, *Artico v. Italy*, No. 6694/74, 1980, § 33.

right to a fair trial, as guaranteed by Article 6 ECHR, 'can only be seen to be effective if the observations are actually 'heard', that is *duly considered* by the trial court' and its effect 'is, among others, to place the 'tribunal' under a duty to conduct a *proper examination* of the submissions, arguments and evidence adduced by the parties, without prejudice to its assessment of whether they are relevant'.[59] This is further underscored by the obligation for courts to give *reasoned* decisions.[60] Moreover, the importance of appearances has been ultimately stressed by the Italian Constitutional Court and the CJEU, too, for such purposes.[61]

In light of this, the principle of the natural judge pre-established by law may be seen not just as a mere repetition of the necessary independence of the judge, but also as carrying out other aspects of the fair trial guarantees, hereincluded that of a judge who, even from the outside, *appears* capable of conducting a *proper* examination of the parties' observations and claims.

The criterion of competence at hand, especially in relation to matters which have seen the legislator's choice to attribute the competence for individual cases to other specialised judges (i.e. the labour one), as better-equipped to deal with them, may therefore appear problematic also in respect of Article 25, first paragraph, and Article 117, first paragraph, of the Italian Constitution, the latter in relation to Article 6 ECHR.

It would certainly be interesting, for the future, to examine the filing of collective actions, under Article 840-*bis* and Article 840-*sexiesdecies* of the Code of civil procedure, before these two 'natural' judges, rather than before the section of the tribunal specialised on company matters.

In the meantime, pending jurisprudential developments—perhaps even by raising questions of constitutional legitimacy—, a legislative clarification would be highly beneficial.

11.4.2 Active Standing Rules Hindering Effective Access to Justice

Regarding standing to sue, the 2019 Italian class action regime allows representative actions both from natural and legal persons.

Concerning active standing of *individual subjects*,[62] a distinction must be made between the compensatory class action, per Articles 840-*bis et seq.* c.p.c., and the

[59] Emphasis added. See, e.g., ECtHR, *Perez v. France* [GC], No. 47287/99, 2004, § 8. See also ECtHR, *Kraska v. Switzerland*, No. 13942/88, 1993, § 30; ECtHR, *Van de Hurk v. the Netherlands*, No. 16034/90, 1994, § 59.

[60] See e.g., *H. v. Belgium*, Judgement of 30 November 1987, Series A No. 127-B, § 53. See, e.g., *Sramek v. Austria*, Judgement of 22 October 1984, Series A No. 84, § 42.

[61] See *supra*, fn. 53 and fn. 54.

[62] It should be recalled that both actions can be proposed by non-profit organisations or associations whose statutory objectives include the protection in question. See *supra*, Chap. 6.

collective injunctive action, per Article 840-*sexiesdecies* c.p.c. While the former can be proposed by 'each member of the class' holder of an 'individual subjective right, the latter by 'anyone with an interest' in obtaining an injunction. As already underscored, this norm carries significant repercussions on the objective perimeter of application, since it allows also the enforcement of supra-individual positions through the injunctive instrument.[63]

The absence of homogeneity and individuality (of the enforced positions) requirement, and in general—at least according to some courts[64]—of the admissibility filter, in fact, makes the injunctive remedy significantly more streamlined. To verify it, it does not appear necessary to prove the suffering of a concrete and direct infringement, but rather a mere *risk*, to an interest which *cannot be exclusively* attributed to an individual, but rather to a, or all the, collectivity.[65]

Following the rich doctrinal and jurisprudential interpretative elaboration of Article 100 of the Italian Code of civil procedure—pursuant to which 'to propose or to contradict a claim it is necessary to have an *interest* to it'—, to be read in connection with Article 24 of the Italian Constitution ('Everyone can take legal action to enforce *their* rights and legitimate interests'), it should be intended as a *benefit* for the plaintiff in the event of acceptance of the claim.

Article 24 of the Italian Constitution, in fact, still requires a *personal link* to the claim. It seems, however, in comparison to the stricter requirement for the compensatory class action, that the *injunctive collective remedy* allows for a looser active-standing test in order to encompass the protection of positions which do not pertain solely to the plaintiff, if they can be found to pertain to someone at all. They are, in sum, borrowing an expression from Mauro Cappelletti, 'rights and interests in search of an author',[66] whose justiciability, otherwise, could be harder to prove.

An illustrative example is the diffuse interest to live in a healthy environment, unaffected by climate change. Evidently, everyone would gain a benefit from an order to cease activities harmful to the planet, potentially threatening the whole humankind (hence, the checking of the personal 'interest').[67]

The argument that the global nature of the problem (worldwide concurring activities and consequences) might quash the 'benefit' for single plaintiffs against a single defendant, hence making the claim non-justiciable, has been convincingly dismissed by the Dutch Supreme Court in the well-known *Urgenda* case, citing the

[63] See *supra*, Chap. 6.

[64] Id. See also *supra*, Chap. 7.

[65] Id. See also *supra*, Chap. 4. See also the Italian Council of State, Plenary Assembly, Judgement No. 6 from 2020, recalled therein.

[66] Cappelletti (1976), p. 648, using himself a 'Pirandellian formula'. See also *supra*, Chap. 3 of Part I.

[67] For instance, in its recent decision in *Smith v. Fonterra* in New Zealand from October 2021, the Court of Appeal found that 'every person in New Zealand—indeed, in the world—is (to varying degrees) both responsible for causing the relevant harm, and the victim of that harm'. *Smith v. Fonterra Co-Operative Group Limited et al.*, CA128/2020 [2021] NZCA 552 § 18.

'partial responsibility' doctrine in light of the ECtHR's *principle of effective interpretation*.[68]

Such an individual 'benefit', or position, has indeed a concrete nature, but does not necessarily, amount to an individual subjective position: it goes 'beyond the sphere of individuals to assume a shared and non-exclusive connotation, as the interest of 'all' in relation to a good from whose individual enjoyment no one can be excluded, and whose enjoyment does not exclude that of all others'.[69] Until now, the only way to grant judicial protection to such a concrete individual interests that are not 'wholly or partly exclusive or susceptible to individual appropriation'[70] was to project them into the collective dimension through the means of standing to sue: that is via legal vehicles—associations or other organisations—which synthetised all the concrete fragmented interests of members of the community or category.

The essential innovation of the 2019 Italian reform, instead, is the possibility, until now unconceivable, to enforce such supra-individual positions even for the *individual holders* of the mere fragmented interests, who, in ordinary binary proceedings, would have no entitlement to do so.

---

[68] Supreme Court of the Netherlands, Judgement from 20 December 2019, No. 19/00135. That is: 'Partly in view of the serious consequences of dangerous climate change [...], the defence that a state does not have to take responsibility because other countries do not comply with their partial responsibility, cannot be accepted. Nor can the assertion that a country's own share in global greenhouse gas emissions is very small and that reducing emissions from one's own territory makes little difference on a global scale, be accepted as a defence. Indeed, acceptance of these defences would mean that a country could easily evade its partial responsibility by pointing out other countries or its own small share. If, on the other hand, this defence is ruled out, each country can be effectively called to account for its share of emissions and the chance of all countries actually making their contribution will be greatest, in accordance with the principles laid down in the preamble to the UNFCCC cited above. [...] Also important in this context is that, as has been considered in 4.6 above about the carbon budget, each reduction of greenhouse gas emissions has a positive effect on combating dangerous climate change, as every reduction means that more room remains in the carbon budget. The defence that a duty to reduce greenhouse gas emissions on the part of the individual states does not help because other countries will continue their emissions cannot be accepted for this reason either: no reduction is negligible. [...] Climate change threatens human rights, as follows from what has been considered [...] above. This is also recognised internationally outside the context of the Council of Europe. [...] In order to ensure adequate protection from the threat to those rights resulting from climate change, it should be possible to invoke those rights against individual states, also with regard to the aforementioned partial responsibility. This is in line with the *principle of effective interpretation* [...] that the ECtHR applies when interpreting the ECHR and also with the right to effective legal protection guaranteed by Article 13 ECHR [...] In view of the considerations [...], the Supreme Court finds that Articles 2 and 8 ECHR relating to the risk of climate change should be interpreted in such a way that these provisions oblige the contracting states to do 'their part' to counter that danger. [...] this constitutes an interpretation of the positive obligations laid down in those provisions that corresponds to its substance and purpose [...] This interpretation is in accordance with the standards set out [...] that the ECtHR applies when interpreting the ECHR and that the Supreme Court must also apply when interpreting the ECHR'.

[69] Italian Council of State, Plenary Assembly, Judgement No. 6 from 2020, § 6.1, translated from Italian.

[70] Id.

The obvious effect on the constitutional level is twofold. On the one hand, a possible positive impact in terms of the *effectiveness of access to justice* as there is greater pluralism on the part of the actively legitimised subjects. On the other hand, nonetheless, also considerable uncertainty in terms of *due process* and suitability on the part of the individual to represent and protect positions that are not exclusively his or her own, where his or her fragmented concrete interest could also conflict with that of others. Hence, the importance of the role of the *judge*, once again to be emphasised as a fundamental arbiter for the guarantee of the rules of due process, a process that is no longer individual, since it embraces several subjects and therefore also requires *collective guarantees*, in terms of *participation* (even simply in an indirect and representative way, but still concrete) and *publicity*. This appears even more urgent for an action such as the *collective injunctive* one, in which there is not even the provision of an *adhesion* phase and, according to some tribunals,[71] an *admissibility* one, either.

Its disruptive potential is, in any case, evident. It thus remains to carefully follow case law developments. In fact, should the still-evolving jurisprudence interpret the 'measures suitable to eliminate or reduce the effects of the violations found' (a possibility provided for plaintiffs within injunctive proceedings per Article 840-*sexiesdecies*, para. 7, c.p.c.) as encompassing also those of *economic* nature, the potential of this tool would be even more remarkable.

Furthermore, the rather high penalties for each day of delay in executing the corrective plan, pursuant to Article 614-*bis* c.p.c., examined in the abovementioned *Philips Respironics* case (Chap. 7), should be framed under this perspective, too. Extraordinarily, they are being delivered directly to the class plaintiffs, which have no obligation—in theory—to distribute them among the class (if one, defined, class, for the injunctive remedy, can ever be found). This poses fundamental problems of adequacy of representation and fairness, as—potentially—a single individual holder of a mere concrete fragmented interest reaps all economic benefit from a delayed execution of the injunction related to a diffuse good, not exclusively his or her, but rather shared with several others.

On the other hand, if well-implemented (and regulated), this could open to door to partial forms of fluid recovery, or *cy-près*, distribution, too (see *infra*); especially if their usability were to be rejected for compensatory class suits.[72] The *damages* distribution function of these techniques, nonetheless, would mandate careful *coordination* considerations, given the—questionable—impossibility to bring together the two collective remedies.

Returning to the issue of active standing, in addition to natural persons, both class action models also allow actions from '*organisations* or [...] *no-profit*

[71] See *supra*, Chap. 6.

[72] See *supra*, Chaps. 6 and 9. See Kalajdzic (2021), p. 55: 'the availability of cy-près distributions of damages also obviates the need to seek an order requiring the government to make budget allocations, relief that would likely be denied as not justiciable. Although the difference between the two forms of relief is subtle, if not semantic, a class action judge familiar with the use of cy-près might be amenable to the argument'. See also Reddish et al. (2010).

associations whose statutory objectives include the protection' of the rights or interests prejudiced. However, it is established that 'only organisations and associations registered in a *public list* set at the Ministry of Justice' may propose the action. Article 196-*ter* disp. att. c.p.c. further provides that the 'Ministry of Justice, in agreement with the Minister of Economic Development, after consulting the competent parliamentary committees', by its decree, poses 'the requirements for registration in the list referred to in Article 840-*bis*, para. 2, of the Code, the criteria for suspension and cancellation of the registered organisations and associations, as well as the contribution due for registration and its maintenance'. It should be noted, to this regard, the subsequent (April 12, 2022) publication of said decree, effective from 27 April 2022, thus allowing the proposition of appeals also by no-profit legal persons with statutory objectives coinciding with the protection sought.

Among the most notable *requirements* for registering to the mentioned list, the choice to limit registration only to entities established at least *two years* prior, while understandable for reasons of seriousness and reliability of the claimants, does not seem appropriate at all. It prevents, in fact, the proposition of collective actions through *ad hoc* legal vehicles. Indeed, in concert with the requirement of continuous activity (even with territorial branches), it seems to converge precisely towards the formation of a dangerous *oligopoly* of organisations or associations dedicated to class actions, as already much-stressed above (Chap. 6), thereby quashing with several constitutional principles (i.e., Articles 2, 3, 24, 118 and 117 of the Italian Constitution, the latter in relation to Articles 6, 13 ECHR and 47 CFREU).

It is worth stressing again the *exponential increase* in organisational and economic burdens of litigation in the case of a collective action compared to an individual one. Except for the so-called 'idealistic claimant',[73] few natural persons are incentivised to choose the former route and, even if they wish to, they may not have sufficient resources to proceed.[74] For this reason, it would be particularly valuable to be able to resort in all circumstances—even those of a purely local nature—to flexible legal vehicles created *ad hoc* to bear such burdensome charges.

By maintaining the other requirements and the judge's control at the admissibility stage, their independence and adequacy to represent the class would still be guaranteed. Alternatively, *limiting from the outset* the legal entities authorised to propose an appeal would represent a significant closure in terms of the effectiveness of access to justice, as this would continue to be guaranteed only to the wealthier, or exclusively to a predetermined, and thus more easily influenced, narrow circle.

To prevent the significant and bold innovations proposed by the 2019 Italian legislator from finding space only in theory, or worse, lending themselves to abusive

[73] Cappelletti (1975a), p. 25.

[74] In the words of the ECtHR, *Gorraiz Lizarraga and Others v. Spain*, No. 62543/00, 2004, § 38: 'in modern-day societies, when citizens are confronted with particularly complex administrative decisions, recourse to collective bodies such as associations is one of the accessible means, sometimes the only means, available to them whereby they can defend their particular interests effectively', recently cited in ECtHR, *Verein KlimaSeniorinnen Schweiz and Others v. Switzerland* [GC], No. 53600/20, 2024.

practices, it is therefore desirable, under a constitutional compass, for the Ministry to reconsider opening registration also to recently established organisations or associations, as advised by the positive comparative experience from common law or other European countries, such as, once again, the Netherlands.[75]

The ECtHR itself in the recent, much-debated and landmark, *Verein Klimaseniorinnen*,[76] on climate change matters, has had the opportunity to comment on the issue of standing for 'obvious deficiencies or dysfunctions in government action or democratic processes', which inevitably affect all society. Thereby, while still stressing the need to ensure effective protection of fundamental rights, the Strasbourg Court has highlighted the need to avoid the opposite risk: that of contravening the prohibition of the *actio popularis* by allowing 'broad access to the judicial branch as a means of prompting changes in general policies' and, consequently, risking the disruption of 'national constitutional principles and the separation of powers'.[77] This matter appears particularly relevant in cases concerning the general public, such as climate change, in which 'virtually anybody' within a given jurisdiction could fall under the category of potential victims.[78]

The solution proposed by the ECtHR in relation to standing, however, is different from the one currently provided for Italian class actions. In order to recognise *locus standi* for associations, the Strasbourg Court, in fact, requires that *(i)* they pursue a dedicated purpose in accordance with their *statutory objectives* in the defence of the concerned human rights, *(ii)* they are 'genuinely *qualified and representative* to act on behalf of those individuals who may arguably claim to be subject to specific threats or adverse effects of climate change on their life, health, well-being and quality of life as protected under the Convention'.[79]

The test conducted by the ECtHR, therefore, is a *flexible* one, under a case-by-case approach. There is certainly not a formalistic list of requirements which should be *a priori* verified by the executive, like in the Italian case for class actions. In particular, the more detailed reflections from above[80] on the legitimacy of the two-year previous constitution of no-profit organisations should be recalled. This provision, in fact, appears against the rationale of the legislator, the principle of effective interpretation and that of horizontal subsidiarity, pursuant to Article 118, fourth paragraph, of the Italian Constitution, which, as is known, favours the autonomous

---

[75] Kramer and Tzankova (2021), p. 100: 'The Dutch experience also demonstrates that ad hoc foundations are needed in a mature civil (law) justice system: over time longstanding associations may suffer from agency issues as well and struggle to properly fulfil their role due to constraints of various types. Ad hoc organizations make sure that a proper system of checks and balances with respect to longstanding associations remains in place'. See also Giussani (2019), p. 1574; see also Issacharoff (2012), p. 44.

[76] ECtHR, *Verein KlimaSeniorinnen Schweiz and Others v. Switzerland* [GC], No. 53600/20, 2024.

[77] Id., § 484.

[78] Id., § 485.

[79] Id., § 524.

[80] See *supra*, Chap. 6.

initiative of citizens, also in associated form. This principle, as analysed above, promotes the realisation of activities of general interest by those subjects, *in concrete terms*, best placed to protect, or implement, them.[81]

11.4.3 Distribution, Liquidation and Class Definition

The issues of distribution and liquidation of damages have already been extensively touched above.[82] Reference to such considerations shall therefore be made for detail.

It still seems mandatory to underscore the necessary changes concerning this crucial phase. The new figure of the '*common representative* of the adherents' does not seem like a sufficiently technical nor expert subject. More flexibility should be awarded to the judge in identifying, case by case, the best technical expert—or roster of experts (see the *Brazeau* case, Chap. 9, *supra*)—to assist him, or her, during distribution.

Concurrently, explicit reference to distribution criteria in the provisions from Title VIII-*bis* c.p.c. would be highly beneficial, too. *Lumps sums*, *sub-classes*, different *tracks* and a *unitary common parameter* are valid examples. They are still applicable, but an express mentioning of them would certainly foster their use by the Italian judiciary.[83]

A provision of *fluid recovery* or *cy-près* mechanisms for distribution would be very positive, too, like—regarding the latter—in Section 27.2 of the Canadian Class Proceedings Act from 1992. Direct economic compensation to each member of the class, in fact, may not always be the best solution for the injured class. This has been discussed above, while commenting Judge Weinstein's remarks on the mass personal injury litigation in the US. In cases like *ILVA* or *Philips Respironics*, for instance, the possibility of setting up a foundation in charge of medical monitoring and covering costs for any disease that may arise in the future in any member of the class (e.g., even children not yet born) seems way more preferable.[84]

Currently, these solutions can be reached in Italy only through *settlement* agreements. The *opt-in regime*, however, does not give class plaintiffs much negotiating power in this regard, like it may do in other jurisdictions with opt-out regimes. Hence, the importance of allowing such a type of relief, not directed to individual members of the class, but to collective *ad hoc*-created or specifically selected foundations or organisations, also pursuant to the principle of subsidiarity under Article 118 of the Italian Constitution.[85]

---

[81] Id. See also Chaps. 3 and 4.

[82] See *supra*, Chap. 6.

[83] Id.

[84] See *supra*, Chap. 7.

[85] See *supra*, Chap. 6.

The Canadian Class Proceedings Act from 1992, introduced in relation to the *Brazeau* case, appears like a particularly positive model to follow for future legislative improvements in Italy. For instance, regarding *homogeneity*, the definition of '*common issues*' under the Canadian Class Proceedings Act, as '(a) common but not necessarily identical issues of fact, or (b) common but not necessarily identical issues of law that arise from common but not necessarily identical facts' would indeed solve most of the jurisprudential and doctrinal Italian debate.[86]

Regarding class formation and adhesion, instead, a margin of flexibility for judges in choosing whether to proceed with an *opt-in or opt-out regime* would be beneficial, too, once the action is admitted and the specific circumstances and necessities of the case have been examined, e.g. like in the Belgian model.[87] To this regard, as discussed, also more elasticity in the *evidentiary phase* would be appropriate. This would entail moving from a strictly documental nature, allowing also other types of proof to be presented to the court—i.e., witnesses—so that a more nuanced decision can be reached.[88]

11.5 A Final Lesson. Pluralism and Integration

The final lesson we can draw from the present investigation is that the process of setting up efficient mechanisms for fundamental rights' enforcement is far from complete. The current paths of protection, either political or judicial, are simply not sufficient, in light of the most powerful contemporary social and constitutional changes.

Setting up mechanisms of collective redress may indeed be the answer to re-equilibrate some of the otherwise too unbalanced, elusive and, therefore, irresponsible power dynamics of the new millennium. Class actions indeed have the potential to become valuable vehicles for the pursuit of common values, for bridging profound social and economic gaps and for putting on the discussion table, at the very least, issues that a *democratic* society must deal with, but which the current democratic process does not seem always capable to.[89]

At the same time, however, they all present significant risks of due process guarantees, for defendants and for the class members who are not parties to the proceedings, but merely *represented*. The issue of *adequate* representation should, therefore, be carefully considered. Rather than by legislators when drafting the regulations, it should be assessed by courts when confronted with each dispute, in light of the concrete specificities of the case.

---

[86] See *supra*, Chap. 9.

[87] See Voet (2021), pp. 137 *et seq.*

[88] See e.g. the six continuous days of extensive evidence phase in the *Plata* case, with numerous witnesses, too: *supra*, Chap. 9.

[89] See Angiolini (2012), p. 187, on the relationship between 'democracy', and politics, on the one side, and 'justice', on the other.

Important ramifications in terms of representation and due process concern the element of *funding*. It really is 'the crux of the matter',[90] given the often-unsurmountable costs of litigating group, or even mass, claims.

Without adequate economic backing, it is simply impossible to conduct class litigation. In this regard, it seems useful to recall once again the Italian constitutional jurisprudence on legal aid, in relation to which the Constitutional Court has emphasised how such an institution aims to ensure 'the effectiveness of the right to act and defend oneself in court, which the second paragraph of Article 24 itself of the Constitution expressly qualifies as an inviolable right'[91] through the 'removal, in harmony with Article 3, second paragraph, of the Constitution'[92] of 'the economic difficulties that may oppose the concrete exercise of the right of defence'.[93]

At the same time, the investors' potential conflicts of interest towards the defendant, but also towards the class itself, even simply because of an interest to push for settlement or not, cannot be ignored. This is a further critical aspect of funding. Such third-party investments should be regulated and controlled, to avoid that they fall prey to abuse and to the pursuit of interests alien to those of the class.[94]

At the same time, collective litigation should not be intended either as a black-and-white type of scenario. It aggregates the subjective positions of many, and, as a consequence, it presents interests within the class that may be conflicting. The mentioning of the interests of ILVA's workers and shareholders, in relation to the residents' injured right to health, probably presents a too unbalanced conflict between opposing values.[95] But it does give the idea of the complex and intricated patchwork in which we live, and in which prejudices and harms occur in the contemporary society. Hence, the importance of delivering the most nuanced opinions for the judges, ensuring participation *through* representation and *adequate* representation of *all* the stakeholders involved in the conflict at stake.[96]

This objective may only be achieved, following the essential realisation at the end of this work: through a *pluralism* of sources, operations and actors, all

---

[90] Voet (2016), p. 201.

[91] Translated from Italian, Italian Constitutional Court, Judgments No. 157 from 2021, No. 80 from 2020, No. 178 from 2017, No. 101 from 2012 and No. 139 from 2010; Order No. 458 from 2002; see also the recent Judgement No. 121 from 2024. See also *supra*, Chap. 4 and Randazzo and Maglica (2025).

[92] Id. In particular, see Italian Constitutional Court, Judgment No. 80 from 2020 and the recent Judgement No. 121 from 2024. See also *supra*, Chap. 4.

[93] Translated from Italian, Italian Constitutional Court, Judgment No. 46 from 1957, subsequently cited in Italian Constitutional Court, Judgment No. 149 from 1983; in a similar sense, see Italian Constitutional Court, Judgments No. 35 from 2019, No. 175 from 1996 and No. 127 from 1979; see also the recent Judgement No. 121 from 2024. See also *supra*, Chap. 4.

[94] See Kramer et al. (2025).

[95] See, *supra*, Chap. 7. See also Ucín (2022) and Fuller (1978), pp. 353 *et seq*., whose stressing of the '*polycentric texture*' of political issues is therein recalled.

[96] See Cappelletti (1975b), p. 399, and Cappelletti, (1975a), p. 62.

integrated together in a 'holistic framework, or, as was mentioned above, a 'multi-layered framework of regulation, lawmaking and law application".[97]

The driving force of the CJEU and ECtHR in the *multilevel* system of fundamental rights' protection has been underscored to this regard,[98] through the increasing tendency of seeking support in terms of *authority*—and even (indirect) *democratic legitimacy*—in these apex courts' decisions, as well as in the regulatory background in which they operate.

This serves the process[99] of creating an 'European constitutional space'[100] in which the "community of courts' and the 'dialogue' which takes place between them, marked by the principle of loyal cooperation, promote the full implementation of the principle of the primacy of European law and ensure the smooth functioning of the interdependencies between the different legal systems, national and European'.[101]

As already highlighted, such a system is characterised by a 'concurrence of remedies, designed to ensure the full effectiveness'.[102] In this cooperation, aimed 'to construct increasingly integrated safeguards', ultimately it is 'for the common judge to decide, in relation to the characteristics of the concrete case [...] the most appropriate remedy',[103] under a *bottom-up* approach of fundamental rights' protection[104] tailored on a case-by-case consideration.

This trend also finds assistance in *reports* and *scientific findings*. The complexity and intricacies of most of the current society's 'mass conducts' carry implications that transcend the expertise of a single individual, let alone a single discipline. The consequence is the necessity of *integrating*, once again, courts with technical support; a technical support which should be *flexible*, malleable in relation to the concrete features of each case. Once again, the need for an *active and dynamic* role of the *judge* to ensure such a coordination in the quest for a more effective enforcement of rights.[105]

---

[97] See Voet (2017), p. 138, quoting 'the pivotal work' in Belgium of Van Gerven et al. (2010), pp. 515–23.

[98] See Randazzo (2023).

[99] See von Bogdandy (2022), as well as, in relation to the process, which is ever ongoing, Hviid Jacobsen and Poder (2008), p. 70, commenting Zygmunt Bauman, as cited *supra*, in Chap. 1.

[100] Pitruzzella (2024). See also Randazzo (2023) and Pizzorusso (2002).

[101] Translated from Italian, Italian Constitutional Court, Judgement No. 210 from 2024, point No. 3.2 of the Points of law, referring also to Article 2 TEU (and thus the common values therein enshrined).

[102] Id.

[103] Id., in relation to the matter of so-called '*doppia pregiudizialità*'. Such reflections appear relevant, in any case, also for the present discussion.

[104] Viganò (2023), p. 82.

[105] See again Chayes (1976). In relation to the ECtHR, see also Lemmens (2019). See, furthermore, in particular, Cappelletti (1994), pp. 177 *et seq.*, arguing for an increasing accountability ('*responsiveness*') of judges, not towards political actors (i.e. political parties), but towards *society* itself, based on the argument that the judicial process has an essentially participatory nature and, therefore, is 'potentially democratic'. This could (should) be done, according to Cappelletti, through

Finally, integration should not concern only the paths of judicial enforcement. Class actions are not the procedural *panacea*, as already stressed. They can efficiently address some of the enforcement gaps left by more traditional dualist procedural mechanisms for standardised and mass claims. At the same time, however, other issues will continue to be better addressed by other means of judicial enforcement, *in primis* those of constitutional review. Judicial enforcement, on the other hand, is not the cure to all issues, either.[106] It also raises important questions regarding the respect of the legislator's discretion, a discretion, at times, possibly exercised through inaction.[107]

As a matter of fact, walking the path of judicial enforcement alone does not appear sufficient. The most significant results can be achieved only through a close *coordination* of litigation strategies with political campaigning and legislative involvement, in what has been defined as '*integrated advocacy*'.[108] This entails, to foster more effective social justice, also building alliances with other intermediate bodies (e.g., labour unions, political parties, other social movements),[109] in wider not-strictly and not-merely legal tactics and governance structures. In sum, especially when the focus of the enforcement is beyond a simple economic redress, but rather to tackle deeper structural and systemic inefficiencies, the effort must necessarily be coordinated with *larger political campaigns*.

The involvement of other powers, the legislative and executive one, must be sought to reach more effective and long-lasting results, keeping in mind that the second pillar of constitutionalism, next to the guarantee of fundamental rights, remains always the *separation of powers*.[110]

---

academic and media critiques, but most importantly only if decisions are made adequately *public* and *reasoned*. For this, in specific contexts (e.g., constitutional review), the use of dissenting opinions may be useful: on this matter, see also Calamandrei (1954). Rodotà (1982b), pp. 508–509, using the fortunate expression 'dance on the eggs', and, recently, Zanon (2024). On the 'social' role of judges (and public prosecutors), to be conceived as actors embedded in the social fabric tasked with 'giving voice to the law and strenght to rights', see Rordorf (2020), pp. 126 *et seq.* See also Silvestri (1997), pp. 53 *et seq.*, in regard to the legitimation and limitations that tie the judge to the social community to which they belong.

[106] Angiolini (2012), pp. 202 *et seq.*

[107] Zanon (2021).

[108] See Cummings (2018), p. 152: 'Overall, the new canon campaigns to change law and social practice reveal a pattern of legal mobilization I call *integrated advocacy* in which lawyers: (1) work in collaboration with nonlawyers in coordinated efforts; (2) engage in a range of legal advocacy, inside and outside of court, to pursue movement goals; and (3) deploy legal and nonlegal strategies in pursuit of policy reform and implementation. The *form* of legal mobilization in new canon campaigns thus diverges from the old canon emphasis on lawyer control and elite planning oriented toward rights-based court challenges. Yet the *outcomes* of the new canon campaigns reveal a familiar balancing of positive gains—new laws, short-term upticks in enforcement, public attention, and grassroots mobilization—against long-term enforcement backsliding, countermobilization by opponents in the judicial and political arenas, and internecine movement disputes'.

[109] Id.

[110] Article 16 of the *Déclaration des Droits de l'Homme et du Citoyen*, from 1789: 'Toute société dans laquelle la garantie des droits n'est pas assurée, ni la séparation des pouvoirs déterminée, n'a point de Constitution'.

In conclusion, the final lesson to highlight is, once again, one of pluralism,[111] flexibility and integration. Coincidentally, they are all key ingredients of that very globalisation phenomenon which, with technological advancement, has propelled the constitutional transformations at the basis of the present work.

References

Angiolini V (2012) Diritti umani. Sette lezioni. Giappichelli, Torino
Barile P (1984) Diritti dell'uomo e libertà fondamentali. Il Mulino, Bologna
Bognetti G (1998) Lo stato e i gruppi di interesse negli ordinamenti borghesi. Giuffrè, Milano
Bustos Gisbert R (2022) Judicial Independence in European constitutional law. Eur Const Law Rev 18:591
Calamandrei P (1953) Processo e giustizia. In: Cappelletti M (ed) Calamandrei P (1965) Opere giuridiche, I. Morano, Napoli
Calamandrei P (1954) Processo e democrazia. In: Cappelletti M (ed) Calamandrei P (1965) Opere giuridiche, I. Morano, Napoli
Cappelletti M (1975a) Appunti sulla tutela giurisdizionale di interessi collettivi e diffusi. Giurisprudenza italiana 127:49–63
Cappelletti M (1975b) Formazioni sociali e interessi di gruppo davanti alla giustizia civile. Rivista di diritto processuale:361–402
Cappelletti M (1975c) Governmental and private advocates for the public interest in civil litigation: a comparative study. Mich Law Rev 73(5):793–884
Cappelletti M (1976) Vindicating the public interest through the courts: a comparativist's contribution. Buffalo Law Rev 25(3):643–690
Cappelletti M (ed) (1978) Access to justice. Giuffrè, Milano
Cappelletti M (1993) Alternative dispute resolution processes within the framework of the world-wide access to-justice movement. Mod Law Rev 56(3):282–296
Cappelletti M (1994) Dimensioni della giustizia nella società contemporanea: studi di diritto giudiziario comparato. Il Mulino, Bologna
Chayes A (1976) The role of the judge in public law regulation. Harv Law Rev 89:1281–1316
Cheli E (1996) Il giudice delle leggi. Il Mulino, Bologna
Crisafulli V (1978) La Corte costituzionale tra Magistratura e Parlamento. In: Scritti giuridici in memoria di Piero Calamandrei, IV. Cedam, Padova
Cummings SL (2018) Law and social movements: reimagining the progressive canon. Wis Law Rev:441–502
Elia L (1982) La Corte nel quadro dei poteri costituzionali. In: Barile P, Cheli E, Grassi S (eds) Corte costituzionale e sviluppo della forma di governo in Italia. Il Mulino, Bologna, p 489
Elia L (1992) Le norme sulle formazioni sociali nella Costituzione repubblicana. In: Various Authors (ed) Studi in onore di G. Vignocchi. Mucchi, Modena, pp 545–553
Fioravanti M (1999) Costituzione. Il Mulino, Bologna
Fuller LL (1978) The forms and limits of adjudication. Harv Law Rev 92(2):353–409
Giussani A (2019) La riforma dell'azione di classe. Rivista di diritto processuale 6:1572–1600

[111] On the final lesson of pluralism, see Cappelletti (1975c), p. 883. See also Elia (1992), p. 553, translated from Italian: 'I also hope that Tocqueville's pluralism [...] will help us solve the problems of our democracy by extending and strengthening a strong safety net against the 'decaying effects' of the political class and party system'. On the necessity, or at least appropriateness, of a renewed (judicial) 'pluralism revolution' in the enforcement of rights, we shall refer one last time to the concluding remarks ('Regaining paradigms lost') from Chap. 3.

Hviid Jacobsen M, Poder P (2008) The sociology of Zygmunt Bauman: challenges and critique. Ashgate Publishing, Farnham
Issacharoff S (2012) Class actions and state authority. Loyola Univ Chicago Law J 44:369–390
Kalajdzic J (2021) Climate change class actions in Canada. Supreme Court Law Rev 100(2):31–58
Kramer X, Ahmed M, Dori A, Ucín MC (2025) Sustaining access to justice: new avenues for costs and funding. Hart Publishing, Oxford
Kramer XE, Tzankova IN (2021) From injunction and settlement to action: collective redress and funding in The Netherlands. In: Uzelac A, Voet S (eds) Class actions in Europe. Holy grail or wrong trail? Springer, Cham, pp 97–130
Lemmens K (2019) Criticising the European court of human rights or misunderstanding the dynamics of human rights protection? In: Popelier P, Lambrecht S, Lemmens K (eds) Criticism of the European Court of Human Rights. Shifting the convention system: counter-dynamics at the National and EU level. Intersentia, Cambridge, pp 23–40
Mezzanotte C (1984) Corte costituzionale e legittimazione politica. Tipografia veneziana, Roma
Mezzanotte P (2022) Class action e Costituzione: dimensione metaindividuale dei diritti e ruolo della giurisdizione. Nomos, p 1
Mezzetti L (2007) La giustizia costituzionale: storia, modelli, teoria. In: Mezzetti L, Ferioli E, Belletti M, D'Orlando E (eds) La giustizia costituzionale. Cedam, Padova
Mezzetti L (2010) Legittimazione democratica e tecniche interpretative della Corte Costituzionale italiana. Pensamiento Constitucional 14:70–139
Morrone A (2019) Suprematismo giudiziario. Su sconfinamenti e legittimazione politica della Corte costituzionale. Quaderni costituzionali 2:251–290
Onida V (1982) Giurisdizione e giudici nella giurisprudenza della Corte costituzionale. In: Barile P, Cheli E, Grassi S (eds) Corte costituzionale e sviluppo della forma di governo in Italia. Il Mulino, Bologna, p 159
Pace A (2011) Interrogativi sulla legittimità costituzionale della nuova 'class action'. Rivista di diritto processuale, p 1
Pitruzzella G (2024) La costruzione dello spazio costituzionale europeo nel dialogo tra Corte di giustizia e Corti costituzionali. Quaderni costituzionali 4:795–821
Pizzorusso A (1976) Intervento. In: Le azioni a tutela di interessi collettivi. Atti del convegno di studio. Cedam, Padova
Pizzorusso A (2002) Il patrimonio costituzionale europeo. Il Mulino, Bologna
Randazzo B (2023) Access to justice in a multilevel constitutional system, protecting human rights. Giappichelli, Torino
Randazzo B, Maglica A (2025) La disciplina generale delle class action italiane alla prova delle garanzie costituzionali ed europee. Federalismi.it 5:158–196
Reddish MH, Julian P, Zyontz S (2010) Cy Pres relief and the pathologies of modern class action: a normative and empirical analysis. Florida Law Rev 62(3):620
Rodotà S (1976) Le azioni civilistiche. In: Le azioni a tutela di interessi collettivi. Atti del convegno di studio. Cedam, Padova
Rodotà S (1982a) La Corte, la politica, l'organizzazione sociale. In: Barile P, Cheli E, Grassi S (eds) Corte costituzionale e sviluppo della forma di governo in Italia. Il Mulino, Bologna, pp 489–514
Rodotà S (1982b) La Corte, la politica, l'organizzazione sociale. In: Barile P, Cheli E, Grassi S (eds) Corte costituzionale e sviluppo della forma di governo in Italia. Il Mulino, Bologna, p 515
Rordorf R (2010) L'azione di classe nel novellato art. 140 bis cod. consumo: considerazioni (e qualche interrogativo)., in Il Foro Italiano
Rordorf R (2020) Magistratura, giustizia, società. Cacucci, Bari
Scoditti E (2022) Per una teoria costituzionale dell'interesse legittimo. Il Foro italiano 5:162
Silvestri G (1997) Giustizia e giudici nel sistema costituzionale. Giappichelli, Torino
Taruffo M (2001) Some remarks on group litigation in comparative perspective. Duke J Comp Int Law 11:405–421

Trocker N (1990) Gli interessi diffusi e la loro tutela dinanzi al giudice civile. In: Various Authors (eds) Nuove dimensioni nei diritti di libertà. Scritti in onore di Paolo Barile. Cedam, Padova, pp 193–218

Ucín MC (2022) And what if the courts could strengthen our democracies? Leiden Law Blog. 9 July 2022

Van Gerven W, Lierman L, Deel A (2010) Veertig jaar later, Privaaten publiekrecht in een meergelaagd kader van regelgeving, rechtsvorming en regeltoepassing. Kluwer, Mechelen, pp 515–523

Viganò F (2023) Il rinvio pregiudiziale come strumento di dialogo tra Giudice comune, Corte di giustizia e Corte costituzionale. In: Alberti J, Di Cristofaro G (eds) Il rinvio pregiudiziale come strumento di sviluppo degli ordinamenti. Pisa, Pacini, p 82

Voet S (2016) The crux of the matter: funding and financing collective redress mechanisms. In: Hess B, Bergström M, Storskrubb E, Wahl N, Cramér P (eds) EU civil justice: current issues and future outlook. Hart Publishing, Oxford, p 201

Voet S (2017) Where the wild things are. Reflections on the state and future of European collective redress. In: Keirse A, Loos MBM (eds) Ius Commune Europaeum. Intersentia, Cambridge, p 138

Voet S (2021) Class actions in Belgium: evaluation and the way forward. In: Uzelac A, Voet S (eds) Class actions in Europe. Holy grail or wrong trail?, Springer, Cham

von Bogdandy A (2022) Strukturwandel des öffentlichen Rechts. Entstehung und Demokratisierung der europäischen Gesellschaft. Suhrkamp Verlag, Berlin

Zanon N (2021) I rapporti tra la Corte costituzionale e il legislatore alla luce di alcune recenti tendenze giurisprudenziali. Federalismiit 3:86–98

Zanon N (2024) Le opinioni dissenzienti in Corte costituzionale. Zanichelli, Bologna

Figures

Figure 1: Class Actions Filed in Italy (2021–2024)

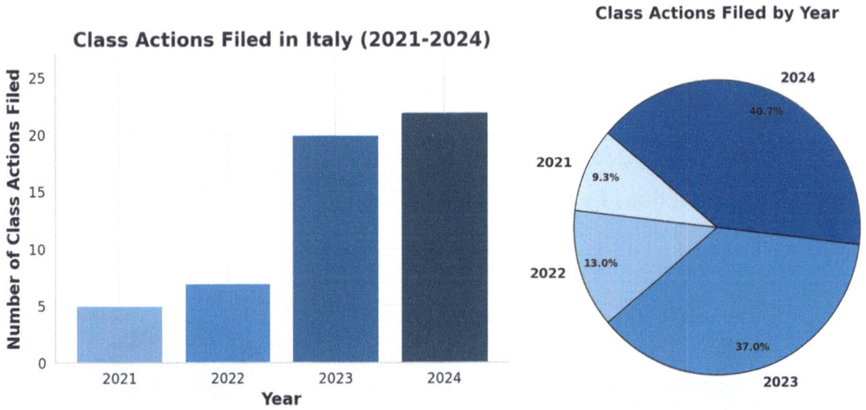

Legend: total number of class actions filed each year in Italy since 19 May 2021, date of the entry into force of the 2019 reform (Articles 840-*bis et seq.* c.p.c.), here-included also those brought under the new consumer-limited discipline from 2023 (Article 140-*ter et seq.* cod. cons.), until 31 January 2025.

A. Maglica, *Collective Dimensions of Access to Justice*, European Union and its Neighbours in a Globalized World 23,
https://doi.org/10.1007/978-3-031-94522-9

Figure 2: Class Actions by Remedies Sought

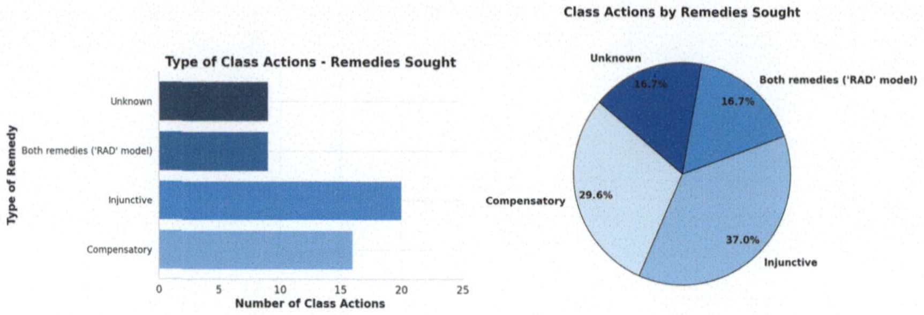

Legend: different types of class actions brought since 19 May 2021, date of the entry into force of the 2019 reform (Articles 840-*bis et seq.* c.p.c.), hereincluded also those brought under the new consumer-limited discipline from 2023 (Article 140-*ter et seq.* cod. cons.), until 31 January 2025. As is known, the latter regime allows joint compensatory and injunctive suits, whereas the former requires the filing of separate actions. Furthermore, in some cases there is no information available on the portal on the type of remedy sought, so as to properly identify them.

Figure 3: Class Actions by Field of Law

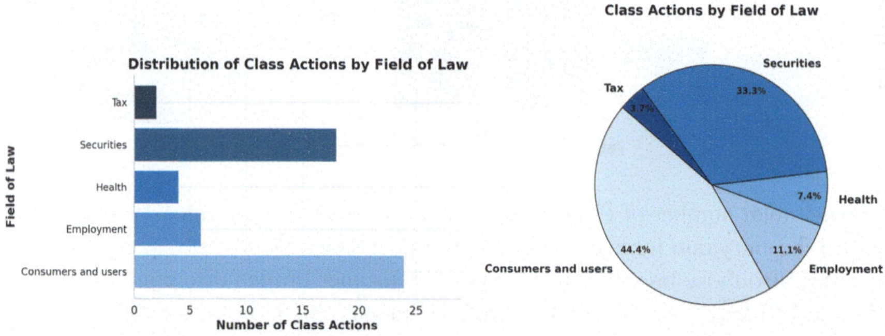

Legend: distribution of class actions brought since 19 May 2021, date of the entry into force of the 2019 reform (Articles 840-*bis et seq.* c.p.c.), hereincluded also those brought under the new consumer-limited discipline from 2023 (Article 140-*ter et seq.* cod. cons.), until 31 January 2025, across the different substantive fields of law. Those brought under the latter regime, as is known, can be both for consumers and users and securities.

Figure 4: Class Actions by Tribunal

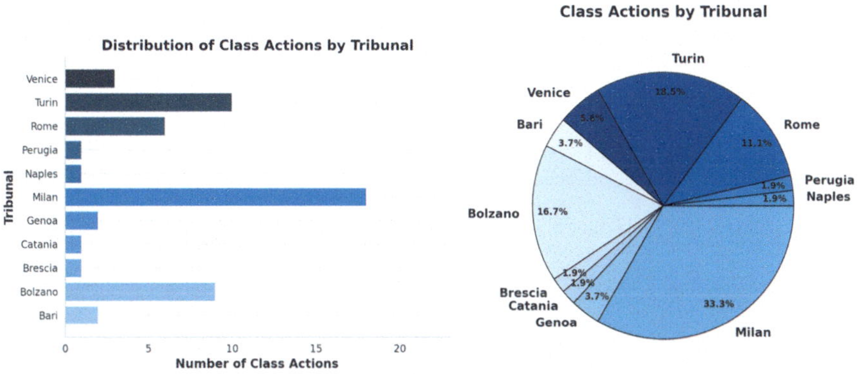

Legend: distribution of class actions brought since 19 May 2021, date of the entry into force of the 2019 reform (Articles 840-*bis et seq.* c.p.c.), hereincluded also those brought under the new consumer-limited discipline from 2023 (Articles 140-*ter et seq.* cod. cons.), until 31 January 2025, across the different Italian Tribunals. As is known, the competent court is the one from where the defendant has its seat.

The manufacturer's authorised representative in the EU is Springer Nature Customer Service Centre GmbH, Europaplatz 3, 69115 Heidelberg, Germany. If you have any concerns regarding our products, please contact ProductSafety@springernature.com

Printed and bound by CPI Group (UK) Ltd, Croydon, CR0 4YY
01/10/2026
02225921-0009